INSIGHT GUIDES

Mediterranean
CRUISES

Discovery
CHANNEL

APA PUBLICATIONS
Part of the Langenscheidt Publishing Group

INSIGHT GUIDE

Mediterranean CRUISES

Editorial

Managing Editors
Tom Le Bas
Lesley Gordon
Editorial Director
Brian Bell

Distribution

UK & Ireland
GeoCenter International Ltd
The Viables Centre, Harrow Way
Basingstoke, Hants RG22 4BJ
Fax: (44) 1256 817988

United States
Langenscheidt Publishers, Inc.
46–35 54th Road, Maspeth, NY 11378
Fax: 1 (718) 784 0640

Canada
Thomas Allen & Son Ltd
390 Steelcase Road East
Markham, Ontario L3R 1G2
Fax: (1) 905 475 6747

Australia
Universal Publishers
1 Waterloo Road
Macquarie Park, NSW 2113
Fax: (61) 2 9888 9074

New Zealand
Hema Maps New Zealand Ltd (HNZ)
Unit D, 24 Ra ORA Drive
East Tamaki, Auckland
Fax: (64) 9 273 6479

Worldwide
Apa Publications GmbH & Co.
Verlag KG (Singapore branch)
38 Joo Koon Road, Singapore 628990
Tel: (65) 6865 1600. Fax: (65) 6861 6438

Printing

Insight Print Services (Pte) Ltd
38 Joo Koon Road, Singapore 628990
Tel: (65) 6865 1600. Fax: (65) 6861 6438

©2004 Apa Publications GmbH & Co.
Verlag KG (Singapore branch)
All Rights Reserved

First Edition 2004

ABOUT THIS BOOK

This guidebook combines the interests and enthusiasms of two of the world's best-known information providers: Insight Guides, whose titles have set the standard for visual travel guides since 1970, and Discovery Channel, the world's premier source of nonfiction television programming.

The editors of Insight Guides provide both practical advice and general understanding about a destination's history, culture and people. Discovery Channel and its popular website, www.discovery.com, help millions of viewers explore their world from the comfort of their own home and encourage them to explore it firsthand.

Insight Guide: Caribbean Cruises is structured to convey an understanding of sea travel by cruise ship as well as to guide readers through the sights and activities on dry land.

◆ The **Features** section, indicated by a yellow bar at the top of each page, covers the cultural history of the Caribbean and cruising tips in a series of informative essays.

◆ The main **Places** section, indicated by a blue bar, is a complete guide to all the shore excursions and sights worth visiting. Places of special interest are coordinated by number with the maps.

◆ The **Travel Tips** listings section, with an orange bar, provides a handy point of reference for information on travel, hotels, shops, restaurants and more.

The contributors

This book was produced by **Tom Le Bas** and **Lesley Gordon**, both Insight

Guides managing editors. Tom Le Bas also wrote the Porto Vecchio (Corsica), Portoferraio (Elba) and Portovenere ports of call. The book's introduction, *The Sea of Dreams*, was written by **Douglas Ward**, the respected author of the cruise industry's "bible", the *Berlitz Guide to Ocean Cruising and Cruise Ships*.

Lisa Gerard-Sharp, a contributor to several Italian titles and also to *Insight Guide Caribbean Cruises*, wrote *The Magic of the Mediterranean*, *Cruising under Sail* and *The Romance of Sail*. Lisa also wrote the Sardinia section and described the ports of Messina and Brindisi.

Tony Peisley, a journalist and cruise specialist, covered many of the ports of call, including Lisbon, Venice, Athens, all of Cyprus, most of France and Corsica, the Bay of Naples ports

and various others including Cádiz, Taormina, Livorno, Kefalloniá, Mykonos and Santorini. He also plotted the history chronology, and wrote *The History of Mediterranean Cruising*.

Insight Guide veteran **Marcus Brooke** wrote about the rich heritage of the region in *Archaeological Treasures*. Project editor of most of Insight Guides' North American titles, **Martha Ellen Zenfell**, wrote the Barcelona, Palma de Mallorca, Genoa, Portofino, Rome, Palermo, Valletta and Tunis ports of call. Artist and writer, **David Whelan**, contributed *Cruising in the Movies*, *The Art of Cruising*, *Cuisine: Cruising à La Carte*, *Cities at Sea*, *Casinos Afloat* and *The Entertainers*.

Maria Harding, a seasoned cruise writer and newspaper journalist, wrote *Spas at Sea*, the *A to Z of Mediterranean Cruising* and *Families at Sea*. In the Places section, she supplied the text on the Canaries, Madeira, all of Morocco, Croatia, Istanbul and Egypt, plus Porto, Gibraltar, Mao, Corfu, Rhodes, Bizerte, Iráklio, Thessaloniki and Kusadasi.

Sue Bryant, editor of *Cruise Traveller* magazine, wrote *Cruise and Stay*, *Cruise Lectures* and *Planning a Shore Excursion*. She also compiled the comprehensive Travel Tips section, and most of the Spanish ports of call plus many of the Greek ports, most of Sicily, the French and Spanish Atlantic ports, much of southern and Aegean Turkey including Bodrum and Marmaris, Syria, Lebanon and the Black Sea ports plus Portimão, Port Vendres, Sète, Toulon, Ciudadella and Ibiza. **Pam Barrett** refined the entire Mediterranean Cruises narrative and wrote the *Places* introduction. The book was indexed by **Liz Cook**, and proofread by **Sylvia Suddes**.

Map Legend

▬ ··	International Boundary
▬ ▬ ▬ ▬	State/Province Boundary
⊖	Border Crossing
▬•▬	National Park/Reserve
▬ ▬ ▬ ▬	Ferry Route
Ⓜ	Metro
✈ ✈	Airport: International/ Regional
🚐	Bus Station
❶	Tourist Information
✉	Post Office
✝ ✝	Church/Ruins
✝	Monastery
☾	Mosque
✡	Synagogue
▰	Castle/Ruins
♠	Mansion/Stately home
∴	Archaeological Site
∩	Cave
⚑	Statue/Monument
★	Place of Interest

The main places of interest in the Places section are coordinated by number with a full-colour map (e.g. ❶), and a symbol at the top of every right-hand page tells you where to find the map.

CONTENTS

Costa Victoria
cruises into Venice.

THE SEA OF DREAMS

Douglas Ward, the world's foremost authority on cruising, charts the sharp growth in Mediterranean voyages

"To dream and dream…" wrote Homer in *The Iliad*, a poem set in the Mediterranean region. Those dreams have remained a potent siren call for travellers through the centuries. When, in 1844, P&O offered the 33-year-old writer William Makepeace Thackeray a voyage to the eastern Mediterranean in return for publicity favours, he jumped at the opportunity, and in the resulting *Notes of a Journey from Cornhill to Cairo* he reported that, when the ship entered the Bay of Gibraltar, the water looked bluer than anything he had ever seen, "except for Miss Smith's eyes".

By the 1920s, cruising to the Mediterranean had become almost commonplace, with sailings from Britain of at least three weeks' duration. In 1961, an important milestone was reached when Epirotiki Lines introduced fly-cruising, taking the bold step of arranging flights, a cruise, and transport to/from the port, all wrapped neatly in a package that could also include overnight hotel accommodation for those wishing to extend their stay. Today more than 50 cruise companies and tour operators offer ocean-going Mediterranean cruises of between three and 30 days, using around 100 vessels. May to October is the standard cruise season, although it can start as early as March and continue as late as November.

Some port authorities, strangled by official bureaucracy, have been slow to respond to the steady growth in cruising, scarcely distinguishing between cruise ships and ferries and assuming that all cruise passengers want the same holiday experience. Some ports (Athens, Barcelona, Cannes/Nice, Portofino, Venice) suffer from congestion. But improvements are on the horizon, and cruising's popularity is set to expand further, with companies wooing not only North Americans and Europeans en masse but also, increasingly, catering to individual nationalities. Some companies target entire families, from grandparents to grandchildren, while others operate child-free ships.

Although no single cruise covers every port, cruise ships do offer a comfortable way of exploring the area's rich mix of cultures, history, traditions, architecture, lifestyles and cuisines. For some, the appeal is mainly the educational experience of sampling unfamiliar cultures. For others, it is the chance to have a safe, crime-free holiday – something that can't always be guaranteed on land. And, for romantics, it is a chance to fulfil their ambition of sailing the Mediterranean's azure waters in the wake of Homer and Thackeray. The cruise industry is, after all, in the business of selling dreams. ❑

Douglas Ward is author of the annual Berlitz "Ocean Cruising and Cruise Ships", which surveys more than 250 cruise ships in detail.

PRECEDING PAGES: the *Grand Princess* at full throttle; the *Star Clipper* epitomises the romance of sailing ships; Cunard Cruises take you to another world.
LEFT: sailing into crystal clear waters in Kefalloniá, Greece.

THE MAGIC OF THE MEDITERRANEAN

*The Mediterranean has long held an appeal for people from northern climes
and a cruise enables you to sample many of its attractions*

The American novelist F. Scott Fitzgerald enthused about the hot sweet south of France, "the soft-pawed night and the ghostly wash of the Mediterranean below" in *Tender is the Night,* a champagne toast to his love affair with the Mediterranean, especially the incandescent glamour of the Cote d'Azur. His dazzling novel is a montage of magical moments rather than a true mirror since, in the 1920s and 1930s, only a select band of North Americans had the means to live out their fantasies. Here, the summer élite revelled in parties in gilded white palaces, gambled in the casinos, and indulged in illicit liaisons. The best-selling writer E. Phillips Oppenheim (1866–1946) slept aboard a yacht which was known as the floating double bed; the women were expected to stay awake at night to deal with the mosquitoes.

Early hedonists

Yet if the Americans invented the summer season on the Mediterranean in the years between the two world wars, the British were the pale winter migrants who preceded them. Even so, the balmy Mediterranean climate wrought its own magic: these were Victorian values on vacation. The French and Italian Rivieras represented what the painter Renoir (who lived near Cannes) called "a hothouse into which fragile people take refuge". In these soporific, lemon-scented surroundings, the British simplified the south but, at the same time, were deeply affected by it.

From the 1850s onwards, the British royal family, the Russian tsars and the German emperors took to the Côte d'Azur in earnest. It was but a short step from winter retreat to royal playground. "Princes, princes, princes. If you like them, you're in the right place," com-

---

PRECEDING PAGES: P&O's *Adonia* in Villefranche.
LEFT: Antibes attracted the smart set in the 1920s.
RIGHT: the Casino at Nice in Edwardian times.

plained French writer Guy de Maupassant of Cannes in 1884. And the party played on: the Noel Coward song, *I Went to a Marvellous Party,* was inspired by his visit to a high-society affair on the Riviera.

Selling a dream

Today, we can all succumb to an idealised image of the Mediterranean good life. The tang of citrus in the air; a terrace overlooking endless olive groves and vineyards; a frescoed church over the next hill, just beyond the Classical ruins; cobbled streets leading to whitewashed walls and a secluded inn studded with hand-painted tiles; a patrician villa with terracotta rooftops owned by an amiably impoverished count; a shady courtyard full of old friends; tables piled high with cool green grapes or oozing purple figs; pastel-coloured yachts bobbing gently in the harbour, just out of sight. Depending on individual taste, the dream may include a flamenco night, a harvest festival, or a muezzin's call to prayer happening off-stage – all familiar Mediterranean mood music. Yet on these shores, Mediterranean nightlife may just mean nursing a brandy on a jasmine-scented terrace, all alone but for the companionable chirruping of cicadas.

Even so, travelling as soft porn for sedentary wage slaves has now become a seductive but ultimately disappointing dream machine. After the first fix of an idyllic Tuscan farmhouse, you begin to long for something a little more exotic: a crumbling palace in Palermo, perhaps; a princely apartment overlooking the Parthenon;

a Moorish villa in the hills of Andalusia; or a rickety *riad* in Marrakesh. The list of unfulfilled desires is endless.

Yet the pleasure, and the advantage, of a cruise is that you don't have to plump for an idealised image of the Mediterranean. Instead, a procession of evocative ports unfurls to suit every mood, exposing a kaleidoscope of cultures as cloying as chocolates. One day may bring gondolas swishing down the Grand Canal in Venice; a new dawn greets glitzy yachts sailing below the Monte Carlo Casino; the week ends with ferry boats chugging along the Bosphorus, past mosques, minarets and waterside mansions.

Multi-cultural Mediterranean

If it's Monday, then it must be Corfu, with a patina of Englishness covering a Greek hybrid character: in Corfu Town, you can appreciate Italianate architecture while drinking Greek coffee in a French-style café before watching English cricket by the Esplanade, all the while pondering the island's Roman, Byzantine and Venetian heritage.

But if it's Sunday, it must be Venice, so you can wallow in wistfulness for a day, dreaming of ghostly Doges. Venice is both a perfect time capsule and a canvas for projecting poetic fantasies; the watery city reflects and intensifies one's moods, aided by changeable light and a capricious climate. With its mythic status and slightly sinister air, Venice was an essential port of call on the Grand Tour, attracting visitors to the notion of slowly crumbling splendour. The spectral city rewarded them with a sense of having come too late to a world too old.

This feeling of impermanence underlines most cruises, leaving a delicious after-taste of nostalgia. Yet, unlike an upbeat Caribbean cruise, a Mediterranean cruise is the place to ponder on ruined civilisations, the patina of age, and the pointlessness of regrets. In case that sounds too gloomy, the cruise swiftly serves up vibrant cities such as Barcelona and Nice, with the taste of every new culture matched by the local cuisine.

Ultimately, it is the heritage of ancient cultures, passions, drama and excess that draws visitors to dip their toes in the Mediterranean. It is essentially a cluster of sun-baked, southern, seafaring cultures that defy the cool rationalism of the northern temperament. Moreover, in terms of sheer diversity, the Mediterranean arguably represents the world's greatest cultural spread of any comparable geographical area. The sea laps the shores of Western Christendom and the Muslim world, Europe, Asia and the Middle East.

The veteran travel-writer Eric Newby lists the daunting number of civilisations that have left their mark here: "Minoans, Egyptians, Greeks, Macedonians, Israelites, Phoenicians, Romans, Etruscans, Carthaginians, Persians, Arabs, Assyrians, Armenians, Jews, crusaders of various nationalities, Byzantines, Genoese, Turks, Venetians, Dutch, English, French, Spaniards, Slovenes, Croats, Barbary pirates and a cast of billions."

Preserving identity

Countries bordering the Mediterranean have weathered invasions and intermingling for over 5,000 years. Scrape the surface of every seemingly unique nation state and you unearth traces of myriad civilisations underneath. This is literally true in destinations as diverse as Athens, Rome, Palermo or Tunis: any new building project inevitably reveals Roman foundations or Classical columns. Yet the miracle is that each country remains obdurately itself. Despite wars and vicissitudes, little has diluted national pride, or even island identity. The Corsicans pride themselves on their divergence from the diversity. This is as true of tiny outposts such as Malta and Gibraltar as it is of countries as significant as Spain, Italy, Greece and Turkey.

In the case of Malta and Gibraltar, the inhabitants simply consider themselves unique. Malta, marooned between Sicily and North Africa, is a beguiling cruise destination, with one of the most spectacular natural harbours in the Mediterranean.

The attractive capital, Valletta, is set in tawny-coloured bastions, with the medieval walled town of Mdina even more appealing. Although studded with prehistoric sites and early Christian catacombs, the island is best

French model while the Sardinians claim that allegiance to Italy is only a small part of their island identity. As for the Greek Islands, the residents of Rhodes, Crete and Corfu delight in their Greek spirit and Classical heritage, but it is a racial pride nurtured by a glorification of their own island history, whether Crusader, Minoan or Venetian.

Despite the intermingling down the centuries, the result is not the proverbial melting pot, a lumpen stew of similar peoples, but models of

LEFT: the smile on the face of the Sphinx.
ABOVE: detail from a 19th-century painting, *View of Naples from Capodimonte.*

known as the former headquarters of the Knights of St John. Founded as a charitable order in Jerusalem in 1099, the Knights soon became Crusaders, battling against the infidel Turks, and were based in Malta from 1524.

The rock at the end of the world

The Straits of Gibraltar once marked the end of the known world to the peoples of the Mediterranean. Westwards lay the Atlantic, with its fearful high rollers and dangerous currents. The settlement, huddled around the base of the Rock, guards the narrow Straits opposite the hazy mountains of Morocco, and is a popular port of call. Known as the gateway to the

Mediterranean, Gibraltar makes its tiny presence felt if approached from the sea, and has as bewildering a history as anywhere in the Mediterranean. Gibraltarians are descendants of the Spaniards, Genoese Jews and Portuguese who remained after the 18th-century Great Siege, when the Spanish failed to capture the Rock. The limestone rock is studded with massive fortifications and siege tunnels, which encompass the remains of a Moorish castle, a reminder that the settlement underwent seven centuries of Moorish domination. Later came the Battle of Trafalgar and, later still, World War II, when Eisenhower masterminded the

between the 11th and 14th centuries to recover the Holy Land from the Muslims. The First Crusade (1095–99) led to the capture of Antioch and Jerusalem but the ensuing massacre of Muslims and Jews provoked rage and retribution from the Arab world. In 1099, the devastating response from the Great Mosque in Baghdad was: "Your brothers in Syria have no home other than the saddles of their camels or the entrails of vultures."

Although the territorial gains from the Crusades were inconclusive, the impact upon Mediterranean societies was substantial. Many of those who followed in the wake of the

1942 North Africa landings here. Granted to Britain by the Treaty of Utrecht in 1713, Gibraltar remains quintessentially Mediterranean: a quaint mix of colonial outpost laced with Andalusian sultriness and British seaside-postcard sauciness.

Wars and their aftermath

War and invasions have helped determine the fate and character of the Mediterranean lands. Leaving aside the wars of antiquity, and the rise and fall of the Greek, Roman, Moorish and Ottoman empires, there have also been wars between civilisations and faiths. The Crusades were wars initiated by European Christendom

pilgrims and Crusaders created commercial links, or even settled on the far-flung shores of the Mediterranean. The great military orders, from the Knights Templar to the Knights of St John, also have their roots in pilgrimages and the Crusades.

Echoes of the Crusades, and the repercussions for Christian–Muslim relations still reverberate today, fanning current world conflicts. In 2001, US President George W. Bush stunned the Islamic world by saying, in reference to American retaliation for the September 11 attacks on New York: "This crusade, this war on terrorism, is going to take a long time." As the Muslim uproar swelled, Bush swiftly apologised, but the damage had already been done. Even the BBC, in its Persian news broadcasts, had translated Bush's remark in the way that the Islamic world understands it, as a war against the Muslim infidels.

Disputes, trade and culture

Some places in the Mediterranean still have troubled parentage or disputed national allegiances: Cyprus is beset by Greek and Turkish claims while the British ownership of the Rock of Gibraltar is fiercely contested by Spain. On a far greater scale, the state of Israel has its right to exist challenged by its Arab neighbours,

cross-fertilisation that marks the region today. The Greeks traded between the colonies of Magna Graecia in southern Italy and North Africa, while the Romans shipped goods from all corners of the empire, from Carthage to Ephesus, Pompeii and Constantinople. The great trading routes out of the Orient, Persia, Arabia and Byzantium all converged on the Levantine ports and were linked to the rest of the Mediterranean.

By the 15th century, the major Mediterranean ports traded in Oriental spices and seasonings, silks, perfumes, pearls and precious stones. Meanwhile, furs and the human cargo of slaves

while the creation of a fully fledged state of Palestine remains a matter of bloody dispute. Given the uncertainty in the region, from the "pacification" of Iraq to terrorism in Turkey, it is hardly surprising that many ships have been repositioned from the Eastern to the Western Mediterranean.

Yet trade, even more than war, has shaped the civilisations of the Mediterranean world. Trade fostered close commercial and cultural links across the seas, spawning the artistic

LEFT: music and poetry were important in daily life in Moorish Spain.
ABOVE: the Doge's Palace in Venice, painted in 1840.

came from the Black Sea; hides and silver were brought from the Balkan hinterland; cotton and sugar from plantations in Egypt and Cyprus; and wax, honey, oil and wine came from Greece, Sicily and Apulia, with the Venetians operating a salt and grain cartel. Such Mediterranean goods were traded for Flemish cloth and English wool.

It was just a short step from commercial exchange to cultural cross-fertilisation. It was in Sicily, not Greece, that the great tragedian Aeschylus lost the tragedy-writing competition to young Sophocles, and here too that Archimedes made seminal discoveries in the fields of geometry, mechanics and hydrostatics.

In Spain, the Moors borrowed the best of Roman engineering skills and allied them to Persian irrigation systems. However, art and architecture represent the finest flowering of cross-cultural pollination. The Normans may have introduced Gothic architecture to southern Europe, but the form was subverted by Moorish models. The Arabs were preceded by the Greeks, Romans and Byzantines who planted their architectural models on Mediterranean shores. As for art, Byzantine goldsmiths, craftsmen and iconographers left shimmering mosaics in basilicas in Constantinople, Venice, Ravenna, Sicily, Greece and the Levant.

The greatest Mediterranean trading cities were the most open to cultural borrowings, as was the case with the Italian city states of Genoa, Pisa, Venice and Amalfi. Their maritime trading empires spanned the Mediterranean, enriching the cultural fabric of the home cities with an eclectic mix of Byzantine, Moorish, Norman and Spanish models. Yet, in the end, much comes back to the Greek contribution and the spread of Hellenistic culture around the Mediterranean world. Ephesus, set in modern-day Turkey, was one of the seven wonders of the ancient world, a Greek city founded in the 4th centuryBC that flourished as the chief port in the Aegean under Roman rule.

Cradle of civilisation

As the cradle of Classical civilisation, Greece has left a huge legacy in the fields of mythology, mathematics, science, architecture, sculpture, philosophy and politics. Greece saw in the dawn of democracy, even if it was hardly majority rule, one-man, still less, one-woman, one-vote. Even so, the ballot box existed, public debate was lively and free, orators were in their element, and enfranchised citizens could invoke banishment on tyrants for the sake of the public good. Athens enjoyed its greatest glory during the Classical period of ancient Greece. The perfect symmetry of the Parthenon, perched on the top of the Acropolis, remains an eternal anchor in the hectic lives of proud Athenians.

During the Hellenistic period, from the death of Alexander the Great in 323BC until the accession of the Roman Emperor Augustus in 27BC, Greek culture colonised the Mediterranean. During this period, Alexandria, in ancient Egypt, was at the heart of the Hellenistic world. Founded by the emperor in 331BC Alexandria was the region's chief port, Egypt's capital for 1,000 years, and a cosmopolitan cultural centre to this day. The port's Pharos lighthouse, one of the wonders of the world, may have disappeared, and the city's ancient treasures scattered around the world, but culturally the city is still drenched in Christian Coptic and Muslim culture.

Greek glories

The Mediterranean is encrusted with place names that evoke the glory of the Greek empire. The Hellespont, lying at the crossroads of Asia and Europe, is linked to Homeric myth and to illustrious naval battles dating from the times of the ancient Greeks. This is where Leander drowned while crossing the straits to meet his lover, Hero. Many centuries later, Lord Byron made the crossing successfully, with or without divine intervention. It was also at the Hellespont that Alexander the Great sacrificed a bull to Poseidon in mid-stream before setting off to Asia in 334BC. As King of Macedonia, Alexander crossed these straits for the campaign against the dominant Persian empire. After a resounding victory, he was greeted as a pharaoh in Egypt, and hailed as a son of Zeus elsewhere.

The forcefulness of Alexander's personality and the sheer scope of his empire left a lasting mark on the peoples he governed. His conquest of eastern and western lands around the Mediterranean also helped elevate him to mythical status, rivalled only by such figures as Julius Caesar and Charlemagne in other eras.

Although now known as the Dardanelles, the Hellespont has greater resonance. On the plains beyond, German archaeologist Heinrich Schliemann laboured to unearth the legendary city of Troy and its hoards of gold and jewellery in the 1870s. Romantics like to add that he was aided by his beautiful Greek wife, Sofia, who bore an uncanny resemblance to Helen of Troy.

Athens, reached via its home port of Piraeus, is home to the Acropolis and, in the foothills, a churches, peeling mansions, toppled Classical columns and the vestiges of pine groves. Athens may be the most mythical of modern cities but painful memories of the Ottoman occupation are ever-present. Presidential guards parade solemnly in their comical pom-pom slippers, with each of the 400 pleats on their kilts symbolising one year of Ottoman occupation of Greece.

The rise of Rome

After Greek decline, Roman civilisation rose to the challenge. Italy was rightly derided as "a geographical expression" by Metternich, the

cluster of time-bleached temples and monuments. The Agora, the hub of urban life, is the site of the well-preserved Temple of Hephaistos and the Stoa of Attalos. The capital city spruced itself up for the Olympic Games in 2004, with an archaeological park, a pedestrianised trail that links all the major Classical sites via paths fringed solely with the herbs and trees that grew in antiquity. The departing view is of the jagged Athenian skyline, with its mix of spiky skyscrapers, squat Byzantine

LEFT: Sofia Schliemann, wife of the German archaeologist, wearing Trojan jewellery.
ABOVE: the Acropolis, Athens, from an 1825 collection.

great statesman, since prior to the 19th century, the only time the peninsula was united was under the Romans. By the 3rd century BC, Rome had subdued the various Italian tribes and was the hub of a great empire stretching from England to North Africa. Yet even before the Romans, the history of northern and southern Italy followed divergent patterns, at least until Italian Unification in 1870. While the north developed a culture based on independent city states, the south, including Sicily, was exposed to a succession of foreign invaders, from the Phoenicians, Greeks, Arabs, Normans and Angevins to the Aragonese, Spanish and Austrians. The ancient Greeks established colonies in Naples and neighbouring Paestum, as well as in Taranto and Sicily. Some of the greatest ruins from antiquity are in Southern Italy, especially in Sicily, led by Agrigento, Segesta and Selinunte. Even so, the Greeks' lessons in democracy often fell on stony ground, especially in Sicily: a democratically calibrated society is laughably unSicilian. Yet the legacy of this cultural melting pot is the Levantine atmosphere of many southern Italian cities, from Puglia to Palermo.

A voyage through time

In the case of Italy, a Mediterranean cruise becomes a voyage back in time. Nowhere represents ghostly splendour better than Venice, a superior theme park for the soul, with its shimmering Grand Canal and Gothic palaces. The uninspiring port of Livorno is the gateway to Tuscany's greatest cities, Renaissance Florence and medieval Siena. Further south lies Civitavecchia, the cruise port commonly used for Rome and excursions to the Vatican and St Peter's, or the ancient Roman sites.

Further south, the port of Naples plunges visitors into the city's roaring street life, reminiscent of an Oriental *souk*, while a typical day trip whisks pleasure-seekers to the chic island of Capri, with the Roman Villa Jovis, built by the decadent and licentious Emperor Tiberius. Visitors with an archaeological bent can choose the Roman ruins of Herculaneum or Pompeii, cities entombed under volcanic ash during the cataclysmic eruption of Vesuvius in AD79.

In Sicily, the disappointing port of Messina is the gateway to a trek up explosive Mount Etna, with the port of Palermo better placed for Moorish Sicily. Sicily may be Italian but the islanders are only Latin by adoption. They look back at Magna Graecia or Moorish Sicily but tend to be jaded with their exotic past. Mostly they sleep-walk their way through history, as if it were a bad play in a forgotten language. This is the legacy of a land whose heyday was 700 years ago, with the inhabitants the products of racial overdose.

Lasting legacies

Much of Mediterranean culture resonates to the chords of cultural one-upmanship between the heavyweight Italian and Greek civilisations, with the heritage of Classical Greece and Magna Graecia balanced against the weight of

the redoubtable Roman empire. As the cradle of civilisation, Greece certainly had a head start. Since then, scholars of antiquity have enjoyed pitting Greek artistic purity, political idealism and intellectual curiosity against Roman rationalism, political pragmatism and all-conquering imperial aspirations.

Not that these civilisations were ever polar opposites: the Roman model, from its Greek-inspired mythology to Hellenistic-inspired architecture, was heavily dependent upon the Greek Classical model. Southern Italy has Greek ruins that often surpass those in Greece. Even the much-lauded Italian Renaissance

looked to the glories of ancient Greece for its inspiration in everything from philosophy and first principles to literature, learning and the arts. This seminal cultural movement was originally both a revival and reinterpretation of Classical values, even if it eventually gained a momentum of its own, particularly in painting, sculpture and architecture.

Yet, just as Greek culture had ramifications beyond its borders, so did the Roman empire. The Mediterranean shores are dotted with Roman remains, from Carthage in Tunisia to Ephesus in Turkey and Baalbek in Lebanon. The legacy of the Roman empire was also the Latin language, as well as a universally accepted calendar and a coherent body of law that still underpins the continental legal system. The other lasting legacy was Christianity and the institution of the papacy, with its power-base in Rome. By way of response, the Greeks can point to democracy and mythology, with one value system shaping modern society and the other propping up Western psychiatry and literature.

The mysterious East

Istanbul owes its origins to both the Greeks and the Romans. Founded by the Greeks in about 676BC as Byzantion, it was renamed Byzantium after the Roman conquest, and then became Constantinople, first the capital of the Eastern Roman Empire, then the centre of the Ottoman empire. At its peak, Constantinople was the commercial hub of the Levant and held sway over the seas. As the Ottoman empire, its reach was unrivalled, with Constantinople cast as the administrative centre of this sprawling eastern Mediterranean world. The Ottoman empire spanned six centuries and came to an end only in 1922, when Turkey was declared a republic. Until the mid-17th century, the empire stretched from the Atlas mountains to the Caucasus, and from the Adriatic to the Persian Gulf. At its greatest, it embraced Syria, Palestine, Iraq, Egypt and North Africa as far west as Algeria. It also reached into Romania, Bulgaria, Hungary, Greece and the Balkan territories of Yugoslavia, not to mention its hold over a cluster of islands in the eastern Mediterranean.

In fact, the empire had naval mastery of the eastern Mediterranean for much of the 17th century, taking Tunis from the Spanish, Fez from the Portuguese, and Crete from the Venetians. However, the emergence of anti-Ottoman coalitions from the late 17th century onwards exposed the empire to inroads from the Habsburgs and Russians, who were more in tune with national sentiment.

Moreover, the prevailing influence of Islam among Muslim Turks was at odds with the Christianity of many of the empire's subjects in the Balkans. As a result, the Ottomans lost Hungary and the Black Sea territories, as well as losing influence over their remaining Christian

subjects. Imperial stagnation and decline spelt the end of the imperial dream.

Yet while the dream lasted, it provided inspiration for *A Thousand and One Nights* fantasies and fuelled the myth of the exoticism of the East. No topic caught the European male imagination more than the tales of bevies of beautiful concubines held in harems purely for the delight of one master, the Sultan. As a secret world of the senses, the harem, and the symbolism of its lovely songbirds imprisoned in a gilded cage, has lost little of its allure. The greatest harem of all was housed in the Grand Seraglio in Constantinople (Istanbul), the

labyrinthine palace to generations of Sultans. In this city within a city were mosques, military courts, treasure-houses, libraries, galleried pavilions and, at its heart, the glorious harem, the mysterious world within a world. Sadly, since the penalty for showing undue interest in the imperial harem was death, only scant accounts remain of life within the walls.

Such was the fear of sullying the harem's purity that even suggestively shaped vegetables were deemed erotic and banned from these cloistered courtyards. The Sultan's secret garden of delights was policed by separate units of white Caucasian and black African eunuchs, supported by bevies of female slaves and

---

LEFT: a group of philosophers depicted in a mosaic from Pompeii.

RIGHT: Algerian women in the 1830s.

administrators. The so-called black eunuchs comprised young Africans who had been castrated by Coptic monks on the Nile and then buried up to their waists in warm manure as a primitive post-operative treatment. The concubines tended to be Armenians, Georgians and Romanians, who were considered more beautiful and vivacious than the native Turkish women. The imperial harem survived until 1909, on the European side of the Bosphorus, but the Sultan's 370 concubines and 127 eunuchs were reduced to a mere four of each when the Sultan Abdul Hamid was forced into exile in Salonika. And so ended the glory days

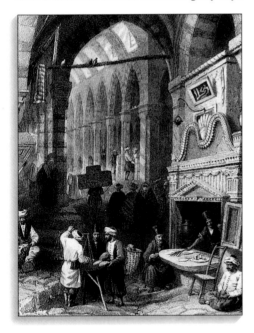

of the last great extant palace sited at the crossroads of Europe and Asia.

Foot in two continents

Today's Turkey, lying partly in Europe and partly in the Middle East, still has a foot in two continents yet is an ancient civilisation in its own right, bounded by Iran, Iraq, Syria, Bulgaria, Greece and the former Soviet Union. The original Sultan's palace, harem and several stunning mosques can still be visited on a day trip to the port of Istanbul. The other highlights are the exotic bazaars, home to carpet-sellers, fez-makers, caviar-dealers, silversmiths and spice-sellers, as well as to the dodgy dealers

Eric Newby decries as "purveyors of shiny black leather jackets of the sort worn by Balkan assassins working outside the Balkans".

African links

As for cruising Egypt, the Lebanon, Morocco, Tunisia and Palestine, these lands have been termed the wilder shores of the Mediterranean, the Levant, the biblical lands. The Egyptians were indeed the first recorded people to sail the Mediterranean, on modified river boats propelled by punt-shaped hulls and single sails. Alexandria might have lost its lustre, but from the port you can visit the pyramids of Giza, one of the surviving wonders of the world. In the Lebanon, Baalbek is among the best preserved Classical ruins in the Middle East, while Byblos is a precious, ancient city.

Along with Tangier in Morocco, Tunis is the most popular port of call in North Africa, with visits to the ruined Phoenician city of Carthage, recolonised by the Romans. Given the indecipherability of the Roman ruins, it makes sense to call in at the superb Bardo Museum in Tunis, which has some of the finest Roman mosaics in the world, salvaged from different North African sites, and ranging from portraits to myths and maritime scenes.

If any Mediterranean country can lay claim to having deep cultural links with Africa and Europe, it is Spain. Early in the 8th century, Spain succumbed to the Moorish conquest, with little resistance from its Celtic-Iberian inhabitants. In its 8th-century heyday, Córdoba was one of the most enlightened and cultured cities in the Mediterranean world. The Moorish golden age came to an abrupt end in 1232, however, when the last dynasty took flight to North Africa. Even so, Toledo, Granada, Seville and Cádiz all flourished in Moorish Spain, but the interplay with Christian culture means that the greatest churches originally began as mosques.

As for palaces, Granada's Alhambra is the apogee of Moorish architecture in Spain. Seville's Holy Week processions, meanwhile, manage to encapsulate the emotional fever pitch of a Mediterranean Christian festival and the Moorish passion beyond. Hooded devotees escort sacred images to the ear-splitting sound of a funeral march. In Cádiz, arguably Europe's oldest continuously inhabited city, the riotous pre-Lenten carnival provides an even clearer link with pagan antiquity.

As a popular cruising destination, Spain's ports of call provide access to Andalusian Seville (via Cádiz), to the Moorish Alhambra in Granada (via Málaga) and to Mallorca, via Palma, the island's capital. Barcelona, closer to the French border, differs from most other Spanish ports of call by being resolutely European in temperament and design. As well as being the capital of Catalunya, Barcelona considers itself on a par with the grandest European cities, and makes for one of the liveliest ports of call. From Europe's most bizarre church (the unfinished Sagrada Família) to streets lined with talented buskers, tapas bars

robust flavours and fresh, wholesome ingredients. Moreover, the delicious combination of local food and drink, including red wine, is linked to longevity, a healthy heart and a low incidence of cancer, the perceived killer diseases of modern Western society. The recipe for health is a diet rich in olives, virgin olive oil, garlic, honey, wine, ripe tomatoes, pasta, rice, fish, citrus fruits and vegetables.

Whether eating out in Barcelona or Beirut, Tunis or Taormina, Athens or Alicante, Corfu or Capri, diners face an array of common foods, albeit served in a bewildering variety of ways. In short, a meal served in an old-time Greek

and designer boutiques, Barcelona exudes exuberance from every street corner.

Mediterranean food

Barcelona is as good a place as any to sample Mediterranean cuisine, preferably while watching twinkling lights shimmering on a wine-dark sea. The Mediterranean diet is rightly celebrated as one of the world's healthiest and most life-giving cuisines. For most Westerners, it represents archetypal comfort food, full of

LEFT: Istanbul's Grand Bazaar during the period of Ottoman rule.
ABOVE: the splendours of the Moorish court in Spain.

taverna, a family-run Italian trattoria or a frenetic Lebanese *mezze* den should still include classic Mediterranean staples. Whether it is bread drizzled with olive oil, grilled sardines served with ripe tomatoes, or tiny squid blistering on a charcoal grill, the dishes are a delight for jaded palettes.

The sweet-toothed tend to be better served the further east they sail into the Mediterranean, with Turkish delight and Lebanese pastries in store at exotic ports of call. In essence, cuisine, as much as the mystique of ruined civilisations, is part of the Mediterranean magic. After all, even the ancient Romans must have marched on their stomachs. ❑

Decisive Dates

1835 Arthur Anderson inserts fake advertisements for "cruises in the Shetland Isles" in his own *Shetland Journal*. He was in the process of co-founding the Peninsular Steam Navigation Company which was soon offering some real cruises to the Mediterranean. By then it had become the Pensinsular and Oriental Steam Navigation Company – or P&O.

1867 Mark Twain reports back on the high cost of the shore excursions on his first cruise – on several ships and lasting nearly a year – through the Mediterranean.

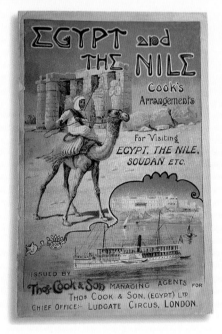

1872 Thomas Cook organises the first "world" cruise. Involving several ships, it went through the Mediterranean and took 220 days to reach Cairo.

1881 The Oceanic Yachting Company buys the *Ceylon* from P&O and she becomes the world's first full-time cruise ship.

1889 Orient Line (later part of P&O) operates its first Mediterranean cruises – on the *Chimborozo* and *Garonne*. They are joined in 1895 by *Lusitania*.

1904 P&O converts a liner *(Rome)* into its first-ever full-time cruise ship, the *Vectis*.

1910 Cunard Line (founded 1840), introduces its first cruise ships. They combine transatlantic crossings with Mediterranean cruises, starting in New York and ending in Southampton in the UK.

1932 British India's *Neuralia* operates the line's first-ever educational cruise to the Mediterranean. These specialist cruises are suspended during World War II and do not resume until 1961.

1949 *Caronia* is built for Cunard as a transatlantic liner but becomes a cruise ship known to her UK passengers as the *Green Goddess*.

1954 Swan Hellenic operates its first cruise (from Venice to the Greek islands). The line's offbeat itineraries with a classical or cultural theme and expert on-board lecturers continues today, although the line has long since been owned by P&O.

1955 Epirotikl Line operates the first Greece-based Greek islands cruises which are booked as fly-cruises by the mainly US and British passengers.

1959 Costa Cruises first cruise, on *Franca C*.

1960 Popular Royal Mail Lines ship, the *Andes*, makes her first cruise.

1961 Sun Line Cruises formed to operate Aegean/Mediterranean cruises.

1965 P&O completes the takeover of Orient Steam Navigation (Orient Line).

Mid-1960s–1977 A series of UK entrepreneurs and tour operators charter ships to operate budget-priced trips or fly-cruises to the Mediterranean. They end either through parent company collapses or the consequences of the 1973 oil crisis.

1974 P&O's *Canberra* begins cruising from Southampton, mainly to the Med. She becomes UK passengers' most popular cruise ship.

1974 Greek-owned Royal Cruise Line takes delivery of *Royal Odyssey* – the first cruise ship deliberately designed for fly-cruising, as her passenger capacity (400 passengers) deliberately matches that of one of the new Boeing jets.

1980 Sea Goddess Cruises is formed by a Norwegian consortium. This is the first five-star-plus line offering luxury yacht-style cruising. Its ships have cruised the Mediterranean ever since.

1982 The UK cruise market hits an all-time low when the government requisitions three cruise ships to help the Falklands War Task Force.

1983 Ocean Cruise Lines is formed by UK entrepreneur Gerry Herrod to operate ships primarily for North American passengers.

1985 Lauro Lines' *Achille Lauro* is hi-jacked by Palestinian terrorists during a Mediterranean cruise and one US passenger is killed. Security standards are upgraded and there have been no successful terrorist attacks on any cruise ship since.

1986 Seabourn Cruise Line is formed to take the luxury cruise concept introduced by *Sea Goddess* a stage further, using three larger ships.

1987 Norwegian Caribbean Lines becomes Norwegian Cruise Line (NCL) as it expands its operations to other regions including the Mediterranean.

1988 P&O buys Sitmar Cruises and merges it with Princess Cruises in the US; Carnival Corporation buys Holland America and Windstar Cruises. All have since introduced Mediterranean cruises.

1989 Greek-owned Chandris Group creates the new, upmarket Celebrity Cruises.

1990s Royal Caribbean Cruise Line (RCCL) becomes Royal Caribbean International (RCI).

1993 Festival Cruises formed by George Poulides. It starts operating Mediterranean cruises in 1994 on converted ferry the *Azur*.

1994 The second-largest UK tour operator, Airtours, sets up a cruise line: Sun Cruises. From 1995, the ships go to the Mediterranean in the summer and their cruises are combined with Airtours' regular package holidays.

1995 Sun Line and Epirotiki merge as Royal Olympic (now Olympia) Cruises. The combined company orders two new ships – *Olympia Explorer* and *Olympia Voyager* – for Mediterranean cruising.
The *Achille Lauro* catches fire and sinks. Her operator acquires two replacements, then becomes Mediterranean Shipping Cruises (MSC), part of Gianluigi Aponte's container shipping company. P&O introduces *Oriana*, the largest ship ever purpose-built for UK cruise passengers. It is followed by another new, larger ship, *Aurora*.

1996 Thomson Cruises is revived but operates ships on charter rather than buying them. Like Airtours, it combines Mediterranean cruises with land holidays in Mallorca. The combination of Airtours and Thomson creates a new market for cruising in the UK with the number of passengers doubling in just three years to more than half a million.

1997 German-owned Aida Cruises is set up to attract younger passengers for informal, budget-priced cruising. Orient Lines, set up by Gerry Herrod in 1993 to replace Ocean Cruise Lines, operates its first Mediterranean cruises on *Marco Polo*. Carnival Corporation and Airtours jointly buy Costa Cruises (Carnival later buys out Airtours share), while Royal Caribbean buys Celebrity Cruises.

1998 Carnival buys Cunard Line and NCL buys Orient Lines although, in 1999, NCL itself is bought by new Asian company, Star Cruises.

1999 Festival Cruises introduces the first of three new ships: *Mistral*. Princess Cruises' *Grand Princess* becomes the largest ship ever to cruise in the Mediterranean.

2000 Spanish tour operator Pullmantour charters its first cruise ship for Mediterranean cruises marketed exclusively in Spain. A record 100,000 UK passengers cruise from Cyprus but troubles in the prime destination, Israel, cause numbers to drop.

2001 Royal Caribbean and P&O Princess (P&OP), the world's second- and third-largest cruise companies, agree to a merger but the largest, Carnival Corporation, makes a counter-bid for P&OP and in 2003 completes a merger with the UK company. Españoles Cruceros (Spanish Cruise Line) is

formed by Spanish travel company Iberojet, ferry line Trasmediterránea and Festival Cruises and begins operating *Bolero* for Spanish passengers.

2002 Island Cruises, a joint venture between Royal Caribbean and First Choice, begins operating *Island Escape* on Mediterranean cruises combined with First Choice package holidays.

2003 P&O launches Ocean Village. Its eponymous ship is based in Palma, Mallorca in summer and its cruises are targeted at younger passengers. P&O switches two ships from Princess Cruises. MSC introduces the first of two new ships, *MSC Lirica*, which will spend summers in the Med. The first 105,000 gross tonnage ship built primarily for European passengers, *Costa Fortuna*, begins cruising.   ❑

LEFT: an early advertisement for a Thomas Cook's tour to Egypt. **RIGHT:** TV presenter Ulrika Jonsson naming the *Ocean Village* in Southampton.

THE HISTORY OF MEDITERRANEAN CRUISING

Mediterranean cruises were for the tough and adventurous when they began in the mid-19th century – a far cry from the comforts of today

The first Mediterranean cruises took place about 160 years ago and it must be said that they were not exactly an overnight success. But what passengers experienced then bore little relation to the relaxed, pampered existence their modern counterparts enjoy on today's high-tech cruise ships, filled to the gunwales with every possible creature comfort.

Those first cruises were the brainchild of Scot Arthur Anderson. To test the water for this concept in 1835, he put fake advertisements for pleasure cruises in his own *Shetland Journal* publication. By 1844, the company he co-founded (P&O) was operating the real thing but to the Mediterranean rather than the North Sea as those original adverts had promised.

Innovation and publicity

To promote these cruises to Malta, the Eastern Mediterranean and – after a side trip up the Nile and Mahmoudieh Canal to Cairo – back to England from Alexandria, the company arranged for William Makepeace Thackeray to sample one in 1846. As "Mr M.A. Titmarsh", he wrote *Notes of a Journey from Cornhill to Grand Cairo*, a journal describing his cruise experience. This is where the first difference between Mediterranean cruising then and now becomes clear, for his cruise was on not one but three ships – *Lady Mary Wood*, *Tagus* and *Iberia* – taken in succession.

Stabilisers were also conspicuous by their absence on these vessels, as Thackeray makes clear: "The sun brought all the sick people out of their berths this morning and the indescribable moans and noises which had been coming from behind the fine painted doors on either side of the cabin happily ceased."

But there were compensations, as Thackeray discovered out on deck at 2am when he saw

"millions of the most brilliant stars shining overhead – the night was so serenely pure that you saw them in magnificent airy perspective." He was less impressed by his experiences ashore on excursions to Jerusalem and Cairo but this seems due to his deep-felt suspicion of all things (and people) foreign. This coloured his view of the cruise but, at that time, any publicity was good publicity.

Mark Twain was another to find the experience more wearying than uplifting and he was also one of the first cruise passengers to complain about the cost of shore excursions – $5 in gold for each one he took while on a $1,250 voyage to the Holy Land in 1867.

Two years later the Suez Canal was opened and, in 1872, Thomas Cook organised what it described as a "world" cruise (the first real world cruise was not until 1922 – on Cunard's *Laconia*) – a 220-day voyage on a succession

LEFT: a graphic 1920s poster depicts the port of Marseilles – the port for cruises to North Africa.
RIGHT: a fashionable cruiser in 1931.

of ships and trains through the Mediterranean to Cairo. Soon, though, cruises became single-ship experiences rather than multi-ship marathons and, as the ships themselves improved in quality, so did the reviews.

Voyages for all

In a 1913 book on steamship companies, G.A. Mitton described P&O's *Mantua*, which cruised the Mediterranean in the autumn, as "a floating hotel... specially fitted for the purpose as people make their home on her for three weeks or more, only landing to see the sights". Although an anonymous critic of the time had insisted that

there were only six occupations for sea travellers: "to eat, drink, sleep, flirt, quarrel or grumble", Mitton had it about right when he pointed out that: "Very many people owe any glimpse they may have had of other countries in the midst of their hemmed-in lives to these sea-trips.

"They vary in price so that those who love luxury can have it but those who care more on earth for getting out of their cages than anything else and have little to spend can also be taken at reasonable prices."

Mantua had taken over from *Vectis*, P&O's first full-time cruise ship. But the Oceanic Yachting Company was the first line to have a full-time cruise ship – the *Ceylon,* in 1881 –

while Orient Line (later to become part of P&O) was the first to operate regular single-ship cruises in the Mediterranean – on *Chimborozo* and *Garonne* in 1889, with the *Lusitania* added in 1895.

Cunard got in on the act in 1911–12 with two new ships – *Laconia* and *Franconia* – designed for cruising (from New York to the Mediterranean) as well as transatlantic line voyaging.

By this time, the typical Mediterranean cruise itineraries were well-established – and were not very different from those offered today.

E.R. Dowell, a P&O Captain, described a 1909 voyage: "A fine passage was experienced to Piraeus – the Dardanelles being passed next morning about breakfast time. An arrival was made at 6.45am and at 9am Messrs Cook's excursion started for a tour of inspection of the many places of interest in Athens and vicinity."

Post-war pleasures

World War I now intervened, with the heavy human casualties on all sides matched by many ship losses. But, as the Roaring Twenties got underway, the demand for post-war pleasures ensured the return of cruising with ships like P&O's *Viceroy of India* offering new levels of luxury with an indoor pool and lavish public rooms including a replica of a baronial hall.

Even the Great Depression of the 1930s failed to stem the demand for cruising, especially to the Mediterranean. For the 175,000 British passengers in 1930, though, it was still as class-ridden as society elsewhere. Ships were at least two-class and sometimes three-class and there were plenty of rules – written and unwritten – for on-board behaviour.

This is clear from a glance at the pages of a guide *All at Sea* produced in 1931 by tailors to the toffs – Moss Bros. This was the first of a series of books promoting different kinds of holiday and – not so subtly – the kind of clothes people needed to buy to fit in with their fellow travellers. For men, the writer advised against tails as "rather absurd at sea" and silk dressing gowns as "not the best thing to walk back to our cabin in after bathing".

Instead, he suggested four pairs of flannels, a soft felt hat and a beret, two bathing suits, a couple of tweed coats, and a dinner jacket "which need not be particularly thin this side of Suez, after which it must be".

He pointed out that one-class ships would

always sell themselves as "first class" and that, on two-class ships, "it is significant how often you see the first-class people drifting aft to get a bit more fun by day and night".

He warned of the dangers of striking up friendships too early in the voyage as "the Regius Professor of history, who was so enthrallingly interesting in Athens becomes a crashing bore homeward bound in the Bay" and of the permanent dangers of being "swindled by native dealers" when going ashore.

But, although the language has taken on new meanings since, he did sum up the enduring appeal of Mediterranean cruising pretty well:

of a week, offers an educational experience.

Troop-carrying shipping company British India saw that as a particular appeal for school-children and so, in the 1930s, began using its ships for occasional cruises carrying groups of children with their teachers.

Once again war intervened but, in the 1960s, BI returned to the concept and designated a series of ships for this kind of educational cruise, until another war, in the Falklands, put a permanent end to it 20 years later.

Swan Hellenic, who ran these cruises, is still going strong. Set up as an offshoot of Swans Travel Bureau, it first chartered a ship for a

"No restaurant in London, no country ball, no festive private dinner can produce that peculiar magnetism of merriment and bonhomie that pervades a well-run ship when she has 'gone gay' in the night watches."

Education and culture

The advantage the Mediterranean offered over other destinations was that nowhere else are so many countries, cultures and histories so closely grouped together that one cruise, even

Mediterranean cruise in 1954. Passengers took the boat train from London Victoria to Venice to join the cruise, which was notable for the presence of four classical scholars who lectured on the places visited and accompanied the shore excursions. This highbrow formula has been retained more or less unchanged ever since although the line is now owned by P&O (and ultimately by the Carnival Corporation).

The cruising market

North Americans dominated the Swan Hellenic passenger lists between 1950 and 1990 (now it is the British) and it was with North American tourists in mind that Greek line Epirotiki started

---

LEFT: boisterous games on the SS *Chusan*.
ABOVE: the famous dancing Tiller Girls rehearsing on the SS *Laconia*, 1925.

the first-ever Aegean Islands cruise programme out of Piraeus, on the *Semiramis* in 1955.

Until quite recently, Mediterranean cruises have been filled almost exclusively by either British or North American passengers. Other Europeans have been slow to appreciate the cruising pleasure literally on their own doorstep. Costa Cruises, now the most popular Mediterranean cruise line for Europeans, operated its first cruises in the region at the late 1950s but for the next 10 years concentrated on line voyages.

The coming of jet aircraft capable of crossing the Atlantic and Pacific oceans spelt the end of

most liner routes, though, and Costa – like other lines, including Cunard – fell back on cruising through necessity rather than commitment.

Although Cunard's *Green Goddess* (the original *Caronia*) was one of the most popular cruise ships of the 1950s and 1960s, she was – like Royal Mail's *Andes* and Union-Castle's *Reina del Mar* – essentially a converted liner making traditional cruises to the Mediterranean from the UK or USA. UK tour operators and other entrepreneurs also made something of a splash with chartering old liners for cheap and cheerful cruises to the Mediterranean. This experiment burgeoned quickly and then ended suddenly with the oil crisis of the mid-1970s.

A bright future

For the first steps towards a brighter future for Mediterranean cruising, it was initially the new rather than established lines or tour operators that made all the running.

While the Scandinavians behind Norwegian Caribbean Lines and Royal Caribbean Cruise Line were effectively inventing modern cruising with low-cost, weekly Caribbean cruises, Greek-owned Royal Cruise Line built a ship *(Golden Odyssey)* in 1974 that was deliberately designed to have the same capacity as the new Boeing jets and exclusively to operate fly-cruises in the Mediterranean.

There have been hiccups along the way, with the *Achille Lauro* hi-jacking in 1985, the first Gulf War and the Balkan conflicts of the 1990s, September 11 and then the 2003 Iraq war all causing cruise lines problems.

But, although there have been short-term falls in passenger numbers from North America, UK travellers have remained loyal to the Mediterranean. Their numbers were boosted when the tour operators returned to cruising in the mid-1990s. This time, they home-ported their ships in the Mediterranean region and flew passengers out to combine their cruises with the operators' existing package holidays on Mallorca and other islands.

Also, over the past 10 years, more Europeans have woken up to the value of taking a Mediterranean cruise. Their newfound enthusiasm has been stimulated by the creation of pan-European lines Festival Cruises and Mediterranean Shipping Cruises, which have joined Costa in filling their ships with passengers from several different European countries (Italy, Germany, France, Spain and the UK).

The ongoing Israeli–Palestinian conflict continues to keep some previously popular Eastern Mediterranean ports (Haifa, Ashdod) off the cruise map and the fast-growing market for short cruises to Israel and Egypt from Cyprus was fated to disappear almost as quickly as it emerged.

But cruise ships – unlike hotels – are moveable feasts so, while some Eastern Mediterranean cruises have been lost, many more Central and Western Mediterranean itineraries have been added to replace them. From 2004, Louis Cruise Line starts a new programme of cruises out of Malta in an attempt to replicate its initial success with Cyprus.

There will also be more ships in the Mediterranean targeting North American passengers. Their numbers had been gradually building until September 11 prompted many to holiday closer to home. But ship numbers increased in 2003 and, despite the Iraq war again limiting US passenger numbers, the cruise lines are convinced of the Mediterranean's enduring appeal to North Americans.

Size and style

It is not just that there are more ships – the vessels are themselves getting larger. Princess Cruises' *Grand Princess* was the first 100,000-ton ship to cruise the Mediterranean (in 1999) and her sister ship, *Golden Princess* has also cruised in the region.

At the end of 2004, Costa's first-ever 100,000-ton ship, the unfortunately named *Costa Fortuna*, became the third and now Royal Caribbean International (RCI) is talking about bringing what is currently the world's largest cruise ship (*Queen Mary 2* is a liner first, cruise ship second), the 137,300-ton *Voyager of the Seas* (or one of her four sister ships) to the Mediterranean in 2005. These ships carry nearly 4,000 passengers and come with their own ice-skating rink and a rock-climbing wall up the funnel.

It will complete the set for the Mediterranean, which already hosts the whole range of cruise ships from the tiny *Sea Dream* (formerly *Sea Goddess*) yacht-style ships and the sail-cruisers of Star Clipper and sail-assisted Windstar ships through the medium-sized tour operator and niche operator vessels up to the other mega-ships of RCI, Princess, Holland America Line, Costa and P&O Cruises.

There is not just a wide choice of size but also of style, with lines reflecting the changes in society that dictate less formality and more flexibility. In Germany, P&O-owned Aida Cruises was set up in 1996 to appeal to younger passengers with more activities on-board and more active shore excursions. This concept has been copied for P&O's new UK Ocean Village.

Another recent trend has been towards ships spending more of the year in the Mediterranean, which is proving to be a genuine year-round destination. Although this development was initially prompted by cruise lines needing to find new uses for the increasing number of ships in their fleets, there is no doubt that there is a benefit for passengers in choosing to cruise the Mediterranean in the off-peak months. In midsummer, the icon destinations (Venice, Rome, Florence) are invariably very hot and increasingly crowded. It can be a far more pleasurable experience to visit in the cooler winter months.

However, massive ongoing investment by ports throughout the Mediterranean is designed to make cruise visitors' experiences more enjoyable at any time of the year.

Passenger facilities are being improved as terminals are being enhanced or newly built. There are even brand new cruise ports, such as Savona in Italy.

This all reflects the growth in cruise passengers worldwide and to the Mediterranean in particular. In 2002, the Mediterranean maintained its position as the most popular cruise destination after the Caribbean, with about 1.2 million of the 11.3 million cruises booked that year.

From the UK, though, the Mediterranean remains the number-one choice. In 2002 it attracted 354,000 (43 percent) of the 824,000 cruisers. Include the Atlantic Islands in the figure, and it was 427,000 (52 percent). ❏

LEFT: Aristotle Onassis on his yacht *Christina* in 1968.
RIGHT: the Duke of Windsor and Mrs Wallis Simpson, later to be his wife, on an Adriatic cruise in 1936.

ARCHAEOLOGICAL TREASURES

Whether you prefer your ruins Classical, Hellenistic or Roman, there are plenty of them to be found around the shores of the Mediterranean

For some, to cruise the Mediterranean is to enter a time capsule and be transported back two, three, even eight millennia. On these voyages of exploration, outstanding and upstanding ruins can be seen, and atmospheric sites, which spawned legends of the ancient world, absorbed. Most of the sites are from the Classical (459BC–323BC), the Hellenistic (323BC–30BC) or the Roman (30BC–AD325) periods: a few are from earlier civilisations.

All Seven Wonders of the World, except for the Hanging Gardens of Babylon, belong to the Mediterranean and its hinterland. The lighthouse of Alexandria; the Colossus of Rhodes; the statue of Zeus at Olympia; the Temple of Artemis at Ephesus in Turkey; south of it, the Mausoleum of Halicarnassus; and the Great pyramids of Giza on the outskirts of Cairo.

Bibliophiles, thespians, plumbers, roués, spa and health-club devotees, physicians, fortune tellers, lovers of cemeteries will all be detained by remarkable remains – libraries, theatres, latrines, brothels, gymnasia and palaestra, *Asklepieions*, oracles, cemeteries – on their voyages around the Mediterranean.

Bible devotees can follow in the footsteps of St Paul: cruise ships call at or near places he visited in Cyprus, Malta, Turkey, Greece and Italy on his four great journeys. Memories of St John can be savoured at Ephesus in Turkey and on the Greek island of Patmos.

As your vessel sails through the waters that bathe the Greek islands, ponder that the Ionian Sea, which in summer is often enveloped in a gauze-like haze, is called after the Greek goddess Io, loved by Zeus, who turned her into a heifer in an attempt to conceal her from his wife, Hera. Sail east into the Aegean, named after tragic King Aegeus of Athens, and all is brilliant bright and pellucid. Not for nothing is the Ionian female while the Aegean is male.

PRECEDING PAGES: detail from the Medinet Halan at Luxor. **LEFT:** divine couple preserved for posterity in Naples Archaeological Museum. **RIGHT:** guarding the pyramids, Cairo.

Delights of Delos and Delphi

The highlight of any archaeology aficionado's Mediterranean cruise must be the uninhabited Greek island of Delos where Apollo and his twin Artemis were born after Zeus had moored this hitherto floating island with chains of adamantine. Leto did not give her son breast

milk: she fed him ambrosia and nectar and, instantaneously, he grew up tall and straight. Those fortunate enough to arrive at Delos when the sea is still and the meltemi blowing gently will know they have arrived in Paradise. After visiting the site, especially the theatre quarter with splendid Roman mosaics and the Lion Terrace, climb 110-metre (368-ft) Mount Cynthus; from here you can see the Cycladic islands, the "wheeling ones", which still appear to spin around the enchanted Delos in their midst.

If Delos is the centre of the Cyclades then Delphi is the hub of the universe, the exact spot being marked by a stone, the *omphalos*. Who will not be thrilled when, after disembarking at

Itea, being driven upwards and upwards through a "sea of olive trees" to arrive at Delphi backed by towering Mount Parnassos? A Homeric hymn tells how, after his birth on Delos, Apollo came to Delphi, became the god Python, and pronounced oracles through the intermediary of a priestess. King Croesus asked whether he would succeed in his conquests. The reply was: "Cross the river Halys and you will destroy a great empire." He did, and destroyed his own empire. The Sacred Way winds upwards past the Temple of Apollo, the treasuries and the theatre to arrive at the best-preserved stadium in Greece. At a lower site,

ranean. Here too, are mysterious vaults and caves, the Tombs of the Kings, dating back to the 3rd century BC. The St Paul pillar is where the saint was allegedly tied and whipped, yet converted the Proconsul to Christianity thus making Cyprus the first Christian-ruled country

The glories of Greece

Back in Greek waters all liners make for Piraeus, the port for Athens, the cradle of European civilisation. Here are myriad archaeological treasures of which the most prominent is the Acropolis. Roman as well as Greek ruins abound in the city, readily reached by Metro.

the Sanctuary of Athena, stands a columned rotunda, Delphi's most beautiful monument.

Kourion and Páfos

Another major sanctuary to Apollo is found on Cyprus at Kourion, one of the most beautiful sites in the Mediterranean, whose crowning glory is its theatre. It can be readily visited from the port of Limassol. A few kilometres west of Kourion is the beach of Petra tou Rominou where Aphrodite is said to have sprung from the foam, a claim that is challenged by the small Ionian island of Kythera.

Further west is Páfos which has some of the most beautiful Roman mosaics in the Mediter-

Still on the mainland are Olympia and Epidauros. Even couch-potatoes will thrill to visit the former (reached from the port of Katolo) where the first Olympics was held in 776 BC. Although little remains of the buildings, the setting is idyllic and the layout of the site permits an understanding of the synthesis of the physical and the spiritual which Greek religion, in its highest form, sought to achieve. Baths, palaestra, a chamber for the dedication of offerings, porticos and colonnades for conversation and congeniality – all are moulded into one unit. Here also is the sanctuary of Zeus.

Nauplion (Návplio) is the landing place for Epidauros, a sanctuary of the healing god

Asclepius. It is the Lourdes of ancient days, where came sick pilgrims who had abandoned all hope of cures. Snakes and mazes played a major part in the healing, especially of the mentally sick. The museum contains tablets that attest to the Asclepius's ability to cure baldness, barrenness, migraine and gout. So renowned was Epidaurus as a healing centre that when in 293BC Rome suffered a serious outbreak of plague the senate sent an embassy requesting the serpent of Asclepius. Today, Epidauros is most famous for its 12,000-seat theatre with perfect acoustics, the best preserved in the Greek world and home of a summer festival.

ogy. It is readily visited from Kusadasi, a favourite port for cruise ships. The Marble Avenue with the Library of Celsus and the Temple of Hadrian trumpet the glories of Imperial Roman. Seated in the 24,000-seat theatre it is easy to imagine the scene when St Paul preached "there are no gods made with hands". This proclamation caused the silversmiths to riot and to expel Paul from the city, because it might diminish the sale of their "silver shrines for Diana" (the Roman name for Artemis).

Some will wish to visit the small chapel (House of the Virgin Mary) that Pope Paul V1 visited and confirmed as the site where St John

As your ship enters the harbour of Rhodes (Ródos) the Colossus would have stood to the right. Nothing remains, but there are three classical sites on the island. To visit Lindos, walk or take a donkey to the summit of the acropolis and be stunned by the vistas.

Turkish treasures

From Rhodes the shimmering coast of Turkey is visible and there lie the extensive ruins of Ephesus, the showpiece of Aegean archaeol-

took his mother after the crucifixion and from where she ascended to heaven. Banished to the island of Pátmos St John is said to have lived and written the *Apocalypse* in the Holy Cave of that name. Beyond the cave, at the summit of the island, which offers magnificent panoramic views, is the fortified monastery of St. John.

Further down the Turkish coast is Antalya from where the remains of four classical cities may be reached. Aspendos has a superbly preserved Roman theatre, but it was at nearby Perge that St Paul preached to the doubting. The remains of the Roman aqueduct at Aspendos are impressive, as are the stadia at Aspendos and Perge. Further inland is Termessos, high up in

LEFT: the Temple of Apollo at Delphi.
ABOVE: a statue at Ephesus.
RIGHT: testing the acoustics at Epidauros.

the cool mountain air, known in antiquity as the "Eagles Nest". Legend has it that an underground tunnel joined the city to Antalya. East of Antalya, on the coast, ancient and modern Side, once the home of Cilician pirates, intertwine. Again the theatre, with superb views from upper tiers, is outstanding.

And so to the Bosphorus and Istanbul where one can breathe the dust of ages but where all that remains from the Greco-Roman period is the Museum of Mosaics and scant remains of the hippodrome. On sailing through the Bosphorus, en route to the Black Sea, contemplate when passing under the second bridge that

it was here in 490BC that Darius, the great Persian king, crossed with his army on a pontoon bridge and defeated the Greeks. Arrive in the Black Sea and sail the waters that Jason and the Argonauts covered in search of the Golden Fleece and gaze on the land that gave us copper and wine. Georgians are believed to have been the first to ferment the grape.

Sicily and southern Italy

Many consider the ruins in Magna Graecia, the ancient name for the south of Italy and Sicily, exceed in beauty those in Greece. Who can fail to be enchanted when sitting in the ancient Roman theatre of Taormina on Sicily, to see snow-covered Mount Etna with smoke issuing from it? Or on viewing the unfinished Doric temple of Segesta standing in chaste solitude atop a lonely hill? Sicily is littered with Greek temples. Those at Selinunte, which borders on the sea, are somewhat distant for a shore excursion. Not so the remains of nine temples, built between the late 6th and late 5th century BC, which grace Agrigento's temple-ridge: the Temple of Concord is the most massive, majestic and best-preserved Doric temple in all Italy. At Piazza Armerina stands a Roman house containing 40 glorious mosaics covering nearly 0.5 hectares (1 acre) of floorspace. (Most cruise lines visit one or more Sicilian ports. Hebridean Islands specialise in Sicilian voyages.)

On passing through the Straits of Messina between Sicily and mainland Italy, beware Scylla and Charybdis, two rocks where the Sirens attempted unsuccessfully to lure Odysseus and his crew to a watery death. Plug your ears with wax and tie the captain to the mast – unless there be musicians playing loudly – or you may not be so fortunate as Odysseus.

It is a short journey from Sorrento on the mainland, where cruise ships occasionally anchor, to Paestum where three golden-stoned Doric temples, three of the oldest and best-preserved in the world, occupy a desolate plateau. Best preserved is Poseidon's with 50 limestone columns all standing. The museum houses the "Tomb of the Diver", a rare naturalistic example of Greek funerary painting symbolising the passage from life to death.

Easily reached from Naples, a popular port for cruise ships, are Herculaneum and Pompeii, both engulfed by eruptions of Mount Vesuvius in AD63 and AD79. At both, a picture of Roman life 2,000 years go can be obtained. Herculaneum, much smaller than Pompeii and more manageable, was an upper-class residential town with few public buildings and in whose villas mosaics and frescoes were found.

Public buildings of interest at Pompeii, a vast site, are the Grand Theatre, the Gladiators' Barracks, the amphitheatre, the forum and the paved way leading to it, the many temples, and three bath houses. Numerous art objects found in villas are generally inferior to those found at Herculaneum. Graffiti can be enjoyed in a wine shop which sold undrinkable slops: "May you, landlord of the devil, die drowned in your piss-wine." On the walls of the brothel graffiti describe customers' opinions on services received. Devotees of erotica may prefer to remain in Naples and to visit the Gabinetto Segreto in the Archaeology Museum.

Rome and Tarquinia

From Civitavecchia, the port for Rome, a number of sites may be visited. Eternal Rome stands ready to offer monumental ruins at every turn – the Colosseum, the Baths of Caracalla, the Forum, Trajan's Market, to name but a quartet. Beyond Rome stands the town of Tivoli with the Villa d'Este, a paradise of fountains and gardens. Close by is the fascinating Villa Adri-

(insulae) often containing shops and workshops rub shoulders with luxurious mansions *(domi)*. In a bath house a cartoon of the Seven Sages of Antiquity depicts Socrates and Thales, each sitting in a homely pose, while couplets (in Latin) spell out the connection between constipation and intellectual life.

Closest to Civitavecchia, only 16 km (10 miles) away, the Etruscan necropolis of Tarquinia is all that remains of what was the capital of Etruri, founded in the 10th century BC but starting to decline about the 4th century BC under the growing influence of Rome. Over 6,000 tombs have been uncovered. Etruscan

ana, an enormous site with fanciful buildings, probably the largest and most sumptuous estate in the Roman Empire.

Also near Rome is Ostia Antica, the port for ancient Rome. The *Piazzale delle Corporazioni* from where 70 companies traded, has mosaic pavements with emblems denoting their trades. The temple in the centre of the square is attributed to Ceres, goddess of corn. The capital dedicated to Jupiter, Juno and Minerva is an impressive raised structure. Blocks of flats

LEFT: stark ruins at Selinunte, in Sicily.
ABOVE: cherubim on the wall of the Casa del Vettii in Pompeii, which was owned by wine merchants.

burial places are grand affairs, often copies of houses, which are filled with goods the deceased might require in the after-life. The interiors are covered with wall paintings, as beautiful as any in the Mediterranean.

North African sites

From Tunis, where cruise ships dock (some dock at La Goulette), it is only a few kilometres to the ruins of Carthage, a name that evokes greatness and tragedy. Founded in 814BC it became the capital of the great Carthaginian Empire from where Hannibal set out with men and elephants to cross the Alps. In 146BC it was destroyed by the Romans and ploughed over.

It rose again and became the principle city of Imperial North Africa and a cradle of early Christian philosophy. Today, the ruins are cut through by roads and invaded by suburban villas. A visit to the Bardo Museum in Tunis, with a collection of mosaics is rewarding.

Glorious honey-coloured ruins, enhanced by their position bordering the sea, may be visited from Tripoli in Libya: to the east is Leptis Magna; to the west Sabratha. At the former, often hailed as the best-preserved Roman site in the entire Mediterranean, are an ornate triumphal arch, an elegant theatre, Hadrian's baths, a colonnaded street, a forum surrounded

by porticos and shops, the Severan basilica and the harbour with quays. Most were created in the days of the Emperor Septimus Severus, born here in AD146. Just as fascinating is Sabratha, well endowed with temples, a majestic theatre, reconstructed so that Mussolini could entertain his Nazi guests, and a 30-seat latrine flushed from adjacent public baths.

Greek islands

Mediterranean shores reveal remains of civilisations that had seen myriad dawns before any of the above were founded. From Iráklio, capital of Crete, a local bus will transport voyagers back three or four millennia to Knossos, capital

of the Minoan civilisation, once inhabited by the Minotaur, by Daedalus and Icarus. Spread over 2 hectares (5 acres) are the remains of the Great Palace, containing a torturous labyrinth of terraces, passages and stairways. Purists object to the heavy reconstruction which Sir Arthur Evans favoured, but the queen's flush toilet is genuine as are the *pithoi* (huge Ali Baba jars). Brilliant frescoes on the walls are copies of originals in the splendid Iráklio museum.

Other Minoan ruins may be seen on the Cycladic island of Santorini. Those at Akrotiri, where the reconstruction is less severe than at Knossos, were revealed after removing tonnes of volcanic ash. A flyover bridge grants a bird's-eye view. On the other side of the island stand the Hellenistic ruins of Ancient Thira.

In Valletta (Malta), take a ride on a local bus to the suburb of Paola to admire Neolithic remains from 3,500BC to 2,500BC. Occupying a small area are four temples made of massive megaliths. A vast hypogeum in which remains of over 7,000 skeletons have been uncovered is one of the most important burial sites in the world. St Paul's Bay is where the saint's craft landed after being blown across the Ionian Sea.

The most ancient Mediterranean ruins lie 50 km (30 miles) north of Beirut, capital of the Lebanon. Byblos, more than 6,000 years old, is one of the world's oldest cities. The ruins, which include Phoenician burial tombs, a Roman theatre and bronze-age temples, may not be spectacular, but span seven civilisations.

The pyramids and other magnificent monuments at Giza on the outskirts of Cairo cannot claim to be Mediterranean but may be visited from cruise ships that berth at Alexandria, where exciting underwater explorations are revealing remains of the city of Cleopatra.

Some liners pass through the Suez Canal to the Red Sea port of Aquaba, from where Petra, the "rose-red city, half as old as time", may be reached. The last part of the journey is a 2-km (1-mile) donkey ride through a roofless tunnel, at the end of which stands the façade of the Treasury of the Pharaohs, chiselled out of living rock. Turn past the treasury to find an entire city carved from rock streaked with white, yellow, ochre and pink, which has been compared to the layers of a Neapolitan ice cream. ❑

LEFT: mosaics in the Bardo Museum, Tunis.
RIGHT: the Temple of Bacchus at Baalbek, Lebanon.

Cruising in the Movies

From the earliest days of the cinema, screenwriters have been tempted by the romance of the floating world, cut off and literally adrift, that a luxury liner offers. A world apart with sumptuous staterooms, elegant dining in formal dress, loquacious cocktail companions and moonlit promenades on deck. Along with the wealthy and the powerful in their natural milieu, sometimes more ordinary mortals are allowed to slip in for us to

identify with, as personified by Leonardo DiCaprio's feisty working-class character in *Titanic* and the Marx Brothers in the classic *A Night at the Opera*.

With the men dressed to impress and the women draped to kill – shooting smouldering glances across magnificent ballrooms, girls leaning back on guard-rails, the wind tugging at their hair and skirts – the cruise liner is a set drenched in romantic possibility. The company is refined and the dramatic potential is limitless. Mysteries, comedies, musicals, war stories and the inevitable disaster movies – every kind of cinematic yarn has found glamour and intrigue on deck since the earliest days of moving pictures.

In 1918, Windsor MacKay, the delightful inno-vator of animation, based *The Sinking of the Lusitania* on the turn-of-the-20th-century maritime catastrophe, and led the way for sea-going drama in the cinema.

Comedy on the high seas

The Marx Brothers' chaotic crush and scramble in a tiny stateroom – from their 1935 *A Night at the Opera* – is considered by many fans to be their all-time best scene. All four brothers cram into a small berth along with a manicurist, an engineer and his assistant, several chambermaids, a girl searching for her Aunt Minnie and some stewards. One-by-one they squeeze in, and when Mrs Claypool (Margaret Dumont) opens the door, they inevitably all spill out onto the floor.

In a similar vein, the classic British *Carry On* comedy series featured Kenneth Williams, Sid James, Liz Frazer and all the usual suspects, let loose on the high seas in *Carry On Cruising* (1962).

The trappings of luxury are often the lure for cruise capers. Cabin attendants in razor-sharp uniforms and cabin suites the size of Mayfair penthouses sprinkle fantasy-dust over the schemes of life and love. In 1953, Jane Russell and Marilyn Monroe played "two little girls from Little Rock", working an Atlantic crossing on their way to Paris in their search for wealthy husbands in *Gentlemen Prefer Blondes*. Russell was billed as the star, and certainly gave Marilyn as good as she got, but Monroe's performance of *Diamonds are a Girl's Best Friend*, "square cut or pear shaped, these rocks don't lose their shape", made off with the scene, the rocks and the movie. Directed by Howard Hawks, this was the second movie version of Anita Loos' captivating book. The first was a silent film released in 1928.

Romance Ahoy

Of all the Hollywood stars to stroll loose-limbed and elegant on deck, Cary Grant probably made more hearts throb than most. He starred alongside Nancy Carroll in the 1933 romantic shipboard drama *Woman Accused*.

Grant took to the high seas again with Deborah Kerr on a cruise from Europe to the US in Leo McCarey's 1953 *An Affair to Remember*. A man and a woman meet on a transatlantic liner. Both being involved with other people, they make a pact to meet up at the top of the Empire State Building six months hence, but the course of true love never runs smoothly. This meeting and its complications were neatly reprised in an homage starring Tom Hanks and Meg Ryan in *Sleepless in Seattle,* released in 1993.

The 1942 classic romantic drama *Now Voyager* starred Bette Davis as Charlotte Vale, a woman struggling with mental torment. She falls in love with a married man during a South American cruise and, in a classic twist, finds happiness caring for his mentally ill daughter. She signals her accommodation with reality in the film's timeless closing line, "Oh, Jerry, don't let's ask for the moon. We have the stars."

Disaster at sea

The Poseidon Adventure was one of the first of the 1970s disaster movies. Among the ship-board complement was Leslie Nielsen, who went on to star in the *Airplane* disaster spoof series. In the climactic sinking, the huge ocean liner is capsized by a giant tidal wave. Much of the film from then on takes place in a startling upside-down setting, the few survivors scrambling up onto the bottom of the sinking hulk.

In 1980 *Raise the Titanic* was even more of a disaster at the box office than it was on screen. Sir Lew Grade, one of the film's backers, said, "It would have been cheaper to lower the Atlantic."

The iconic ocean-liner movie of recent years, naturally, was, *Titanic*, made in 1997. So much has it slipped into the collective subconscious that on a recent cruise on a US-based line, with the Greek admiral of the fleet present, an announcement was made at the formal dinner of a problem with one of the engines. With impeccable timing, the East European string quartet struck up the Celine Dion theme tune, and no one batted an eyelid. Well, practically no one. Actually, a US cruise journalist at the admiral's table almost hyperventilated at the irony.

The story of the *Titanic*'s maiden voyage was more accurately and, for most reviewers, more effectively portrayed in Roy Ward Baker's *A Night to Remember.* Starring Kenneth More and with more than 200 speaking parts, the meticulous 1958 reconstruction featured early film appearances from two 1960s TV cult stars, Honor Blackman of *The Avengers* and David McCallum, later *The Man From Uncle.* The climax of the liner's sinking was filmed in real-time, and is a marvellous example of movie tension.

LEFT: Bette Davies and Paul Henreid in *Now, Voyager.*
RIGHT: Deborah Kerr and Cary Grant in *An Affair to Remember.*

Tension and romance

Juggernaught (1974) starred Richard Harris and David Hemmings as a bomb-disposal team helicoptered out to a cruise liner *(The Britannic)* halfway across the ocean. Directed by Richard Lester and with appearances from Omar Sharif and Roy Kinnear, the pace and the intelligent screenplay of this tense thriller ensure that it easily transcends its 1970s "disaster movie" genre.

Kristin Scott-Thomas and Hugh Grant took the British flag onto the ocean waves again in Roman Polanski's dark and erotic 1992 comedy *Bitter Moon.* Also starring Emmanuelle Seigner and Peter Coyote, the story revolves around Grant's fascina-

tion with Seigner in the charged atmosphere of a cruise, and with Coyote's intimate tales of their history. The claustrophobic atmosphere of the liner adds to the tension, with a denouement that was classic Polanski.

Few screenplays have painted a picture of life on the ocean waves that modern cruise-goers would recognise – the closest representation might be the cult US TV series *The Love Boat,* which also inspired a feature-length movie. The series set out on its voyage in 1976 and continued for a decade. But reality is not really the object, and a shipboard romance, with all its glitter and glamour, remains an attractive vessel for the imagination to cut adrift from the pull of reality. ❑

THE ART OF CRUISING

From what to wear and when to book shore excursions to making the most of a day at sea – a few tips to help you enjoy your cruise

After a full day of travelling to meet the ship and weathering the confusions of embarkation, the sight of land slipping away behind the Mediterranean is a moment of rare pleasure. Particularly so when it is glimpsed over the rim of a champagne or cocktail glass. For cruise virgins, this first sniff of sea air is a treat to savour. For old hands on deck, it is the moment that marks the beginning of another romantic odyssey.

The street sounds, smells and exotic tastes of the coming ports of call beckon, as do parties, shows and dances on board. Cocktail bars, poolside service, midnight buffets under the stars and breakfast served in the cabin are all pleasures to look forward to. And everyday life wafts by, dwindling further into the deep-blue wake astern.

Cruise etiquette

Slipping into the rhythm of seaborne life can take some, mostly agreeable, adjustment. Navigating your way around the ship itself can be confusing at first. Big, modern liners often have up to 12 elevators, serving as many decks. Numerous pools, theatres, shops, bars, cafés and restaurants can be hard to orientate around and take in, never mind which side is port and which is starboard. Manfred, head chef on *Costa Victoria,* says: "The ship is like a town. Well, it *is* a town – a pretty big one, too." And, just like when you arrive in a new town, it can take time to get your bearings.

For the record, when you are facing forward, to the bow of the ship, the left, or port side, is the side on which the ship usually docks. Starboard is thought to be a nautical corruption from *steerboard*, the right-hand side, from which the vessel is steered.

Non-European citizens cruising EU waters are required to surrender their passports on

---

PRECEDING PAGES: learning the art of cruising.
LEFT: sunbeds ready and waiting on the *Costa Victoria.*
RIGHT: smiling Silversea staff.

embarkation, and retrieve them when they want to visit non-EU countries such as Tunisia.

Cruise operators encourage guests to register a credit card at the beginning of a voyage for on-board expenses. Otherwise, a bill will be compiled to be settled on the day of departure, and a surprising number of passengers do settle

at the end of the trip in cash. While on board, whether a credit card is registered or not, everything is paid for using a special card issued by the ship. Some cash is needed at the end of the voyage, though, for tipping the housekeeping, cabin and table staff, so remember to keep some cash in reserve. A rare exception is *Ocean Village*, where gratuities are included in the booking price.

Passengers are invariably photographed in their travelling groups at the point of embarkation. Photographers are on hand from then on to record most of the guests at practically all occasions. Around the pool, at cocktail parties, on the dance floor, the snappers pop up like paparazzi, snatching images to be displayed on the next day's photo boards. The boards are often located near the entrance to the dining rooms, for passing diners to admire or chortle at. These pictures, of course, can be bought – for a not insignificant number of euros.

What to wear

The image of cruising has been comprehensively overhauled since the 1990s. The picture of wealthy movers and shakers fashionably lounging around with cocktails in hand has now given way to honeymoon cruises, party cruises and adventure-themed cruises. The choice of ship and cruise will guide the wardrobe selection when you come to do your packing.

An Ocean Village cruise won't shake the mothballs out of formal wear, but smart-casual dress on a Windstar cruise will be more comfortable if the T-shirts are *really* smart, and the chinos are Versace. The required glamour of formal dining and cocktail parties with the captain feature on fewer and fewer cruises now; more's the pity, according to some.

The lines have been seriously attempting to widen their market appeal, and the demands of tuxes and evening gowns were identified as a barrier. Even smart lines like Celebrity now

MEET THE MAÎTRE D'

The ship's maître d'hôtel, normally a master of diplomacy and tact and an assiduous "meeter and greeter", has usually worked his way up from assistant waiter to wine waiter or captain waiter. He has an unenviable role, particularly at the start of cruises when he is often inundated by requests for changes to seating arrangements.

This challenging job involves daily briefings, in-service training and supervision of the dining staff, from the wine waiter to the fruit-juice maker. If most passengers come back late from an excursion, the dining staff has to allow some leeway for meal times, which eats into their own limited free time.

On some ships, the maître d' liaises with the executive chef and the ship's chandler, who is responsible for provisions, including the selection of fresh seafood and fruit at key ports. The maître d' is also one of the key figures involved in assuring standards of cleanliness. Hygiene on board needs to be stringent since any virus tends to be transmitted through the air-conditioning system. Every night, the restaurant may be sprayed with cyrocide, a powerful disinfectant which kills all bacteria and insects. The dining staff may even be called upon to stay up all night to give the restaurant a total spring clean – then they make a party of it, with a dawn feast.

only refer to formal wear as "optional" and this means that many men won't see the need to wear dinner jackets. Celebrity-line diners do still dress to impress, though, and there are usually a number of "formal nights" to show off those sharp suits and sparklers.

One thing that always goes down well, though, whatever the style of cruise, is some beautifully cut swimwear.

Shore excursions

In most ports of call, exploring independently of an organised excursion can be an adventure, and not too much of a challenge for experi-

do strive to provide a high standard of tour. Groups are usually arranged into speakers of the same language, so the tour guide will only have to use one tongue for historical details and insider tips.

Day excursions can be booked as early as the cruise tickets. The lines are keen to sell excursions, so they often encourage early bookings. It is true that some of the more spectacular excursions will be full by the time the ship docks, but usually there is no need to plan more than a couple of days ahead.

Unfortunately, there is no certain way to know in advance whether a guide is going to

enced travellers. Language isn't a great barrier in towns and resorts where cruise passengers are a major source of trade. Payments are nearly always possible by credit card, and, in Europe the euro makes currency conversion simple. Where the ship docks alongside the coaches booked for excursions, there may also be free shuttle buses provided by the cruise line, and taxi drivers ready to bargain for guided tours.

Excursions are normally a more expensive way to visit an attraction, but most cruise lines

LEFT: anticipating a good meal on a Silversea cruise.
ABOVE AND RIGHT: cruising allows you to be as active or as relaxed as you like.

be good or not. Some ships have a helpful and knowledgeable English-speaker in the purser's office. If so, it is well worth getting to know this vital individual early on for advice about the best sights, attractions and excursions. A great tour guide will make the location vibrant and the day memorable. Knowledgeable and friendly presentation, enthusiasm and the ability to take charge of a large group and make it all look easy, are the key. A less-good guide can make an exotic place seem dull and leaden, with a drone of deadpan facts.

Youseff, a tour guide in Tunis, sees himself as an ambassador for his country. With a background as a teacher in Yorkshire, England, he

Spas at Sea

Mediterranean cruises don't just take you to savour the cuisine in the restaurants of France, Spain, Italy and Turkey; they'll also enable you to do it without piling on the pounds. With a bit of willpower, you can turn your cruise into a stay at a state-of-the-art health spa, with sunshine and sea air thrown in for free.

With roomy, well-equipped gyms, thalassotherapy pools, personal trainers and low-fat/low-salt menu options at all meals, not to mention jogging tracks, swimming pools, and aerobics, pilates and yoga

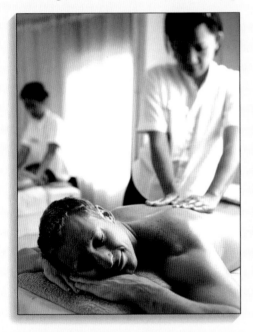

classes, cruise ships make it easy for travellers to stay healthy during a holiday at sea.

It won't necessarily cost you a fortune to go home looking and feeling like a million dollars. While prices for spa treatments like facials, massage and Ionothermie slimming sessions tend to be hefty, there's a lot you can do to get fit without spending a penny. Use of gymnasia and pools is free, as are steam and sauna rooms on most ships (Celebrity Cruises is an exception, since its heat rooms are contained within garden-themed, custom-built health suites equipped with large thalassotherapy pools). Although there are usually charges for specialist classes like yoga, pilates and boxercise classes (though luxury operator

Crystal Cruises offers them free), daily classes in aerobics, aquarobics and body-stretching are free of charge on all ships.

Not surprisingly, the megaships operated by Royal Caribbean, Celebrity Cruises, Norwegian Cruise Line, Princess Cruises, P&O and Costa Cruises have the best-equipped and most varied facilities. They're constantly on the lookout for new treatments with which to tempt passengers; Royal Caribbean has introduced acupuncture, while reiki is offered by Norwegian Cruise Line.

Massages with hot volcanic rocks have become something of a trend since they were introduced by luxury cruise operator Silversea; budget operator Ocean Village offers them in its spa (at more affordable prices). *Ocean Village* was also the first ship to offer the St-Tropez full-body fake tan treatment: it's not cheap and you'll come out looking as if you've wallowed in mud, but shower it off next day and – hey presto – you've got a fabulous tan.

Beware, though, of trendy – and expensive – treatments given a gimmicky new name to justify a higher price. A prime example are Nouveau Yu relaxation capsules. You lie with your body inside them and your head adorned with a special eye mask and headphones, soothed into deep relaxation with warm, scented steam, lights and music. Very nice and worth a try, but many ship spas have now repackaged these as Chakra Rebalancing Capsules and tripled the price – so don't be fooled.

Beware also of spa therapists pushing expensive "aftercare treatments". Some write you out a "prescription" of creams and potions which could end up costing you a small fortune. Don't be embarrassed to ask the price of everything – and always take the list back to your cabin and think about it, or you'll end up with a cupboardful of detox tablets, muscle-easing bath soaks and other stuff you'd be better off buying at your local chemist.

On some ships – notably Princess Cruises and Cunard's *QE2* and *QM2* – you can pre-book spa packages. These range from two-hour treatments to four-day sessions. Again, not cheap, but advance booking might help you stick to a budget.

Also, bear in mind that small cruise ships can be as good for a spa break as the megaships. Royal Olympia Cruises' *Olympia Voyager* is a prime example, with a small but excellent spa and genuine practitioners of Indian Ayurvedic medicine, offering authentic treatments at affordable prices. ❑

LEFT: a passenger enjoys getting pampered during a SeaDream cruise.

explains the cultural nuances of the Arab café, the meanings of the patterns hammered into gates and doors and the etiquette of the souk in a way that brings it all memorably to life. He takes his tours to ancient ruins, museums and the markets, illuminating the atmosphere for his charges each step of the way.

He is the kind of guide who ensures that passengers get the most of their trip. Like him, the best guides work very hard to provide a good tour, and they do appreciate tips. What is more, they are always pleased when passengers let the purser know about an excellent excursion. The purser should appreciate feedback about a bad one, as well.

Practically all organised excursions will schedule in some shopping time at the end of the trip.

Making the most of a day at sea

Ah, what could be finer. If the aim is relaxation, then a day at sea, completely cut off from the world outside, is pure, unalloyed bliss. An instantly enforced retreat, an opportunity to do as little or as much as you like. Enjoy the spa or the gym, flake out by the pool, or just watch the colours of the sea slowly drift from azure to aquamarine. Just knowing that there's nowhere to go, other than here, that there's no way to be in touch with anyone, or for anyone to call you unless you want them to, can be quite liberating.

For vigorous relaxation there are usually indoor and outdoor pools, a hot tub, table tennis and basketball courts and numerous dance classes. The spa may tempt you with plunge pools or saunas, as well as a range of pampering treatments, including massage, aromatherapy and face masks. There are hairdressers and beauticians ready to help with primping and preening.

Swimming pools and sun loungers are always jammed, especially with children: get there before breakfast and conspicuously arrange a towel, novel and beach slippers. Or try one of the indoor or smaller pools, as these are often less crowded. Remember that as the ship moves, the direction of the sun can change, causing confusion on the chaises longues.

There are plenty of distractions on board. Many ships host art auctions, wine-tastings,

RIGHT: the lone lounger proves that it is possible to find peace and quiet on the sundeck.

language classes, yoga groups, lessons in bridge and casino games. Fitness and beauty demonstrations, table tennis, volleyball or basketball tournaments, as well as a range of games and quizzes are arranged daily, and the ship's morning newsletter will keep you abreast of the activities. Many of the larger liners have cinemas, and some of the more up-market cruises offer videos, or video-on-demand in the cabin. Of course, there is also the non-stop party by the pool.

Just taking a map and tracing your route through binoculars can be a very relaxing way to spend quiet time on deck. For many the real pleasure in a "sea day" is to be had from simply

enjoying the ship, the sea, good food and a moonlit stroll on deck.

After dark

If a competitive urge calls from the green baize tables, a trawl around the casino may uncover lady luck, playing blackjack, roulette or the slot machines. There are also daytime classes for prospective gamblers to hone their skills. Bridge is often available for more sedate gaming, and card tables are normally provided away from the casino.

Most evenings will offer some kind of a party, a cocktail evening or a splendid midnight buffet. There are also spectacular shows, of course. Shipboard entertainers are of a high standard these days, recruited, trained, produced and choreographed by specialist agencies ashore, often mounting surprisingly lavish shows. The accent is usually on variety, but the cheap shows full of pink feathers and high-stepping girls are fast giving way to acrobats and tribute bands.

Top tips for passengers

Beauty salon and spa treatments usually get booked up very early in the voyage, so it is worth paying a visit to make appointments as soon as possible after boarding. Days at sea are

obviously the most popular, and become booked up soonest.

Keep in mind that ships are at the mercy of the weather, as well as their technical needs and the influence of outside events. Destinations can be omitted from the itinerary at short notice, so if the highlight of a dream voyage is to visit Pompeii, or the Topkapi in Istanbul, then, to avoid being disappointed, a fly-drive holiday might be more suitable than a cruise.

All the announcements on lines like Costa – whose main clientele are not English speakers – are given in as many as five languages, with English coming last. This is frustrating when it comes to the boat drill and emergency mes-

sages, and when passing on information regarding food, which some of the passengers who heard it first may have demolished before the English announcement has even started.

If you want to dine *à deux*, see the maître d' as early as possible after boarding. You should also do this if you would like to be seated with particular people at dinner. If you leave it to pot luck, then probably you will be at a table with a group, and they are likely to be your dining companions throughout the trip. Remember that there are nearly always two sittings for dinner and, again, your first choice will be the sitting you take for the duration of the cruise. The early sitting is most popular with family groups and older guests. Younger or more sophisticated parties often prefer the second sitting. An exception is Italian and Spanish passengers, where families will go for the second sitting because they are used to eating late.

Be sure to make your smoking preference known early on; more and more lines are declaring non-smoking dining rooms. US-based lines are beginning to extend non-smoking areas even further, although some do have plush, dark, cigar-bars as a way to encourage smokers to continue cruising with them.

Medical facilities and a pharmacy are provided on the ship. They are normally open only from 9am to 5pm, or even shorter hours, and pharmaceuticals and consultations are more expensive than they would be ashore. Out-of-hours cabin visits can be particularly costly. Rest assured, though, that ships' doctors have more than sufficient skills to deal with most medical emergencies.

On the last night, passengers are usually required to pack and leave luggage for collection before dinner. This poses a couple of interesting problems: what to wear for the last night's cocktails and parties, and how to pack it afterwards. Also what to wear for disembarkation. Leaving the ship may not be the key style moment of your voyage, but last night's formal wear is unlikely to strike the perfect chord. A light, hanging suit bag is ideal for this finery (remember not to pack it away in the cupboard), and leave out some casual wear for departure. Elegance preserved to the end. ❏

LEFT: a makeover is good for morale – but you usually need to book it early on days at sea.
RIGHT: poolside service doesn't get much better.

Cuisine: Cruising à la Carte

Over the past decade, cruise passengers' dining expectations have been transformed beyond all recognition. The image of large matrons queuing round the clock at all-you-can-eat buffets has gone the way of cocktail parties thronged with tailcoats, starched wing-tip collars and dickie-bows. Cruise packages are now tailored to well-defined market segments, and every aspect of the trip is designed to reinforce the appropriate

impression. Holidays are now pitched towards the young crowd, first-timers, adventurous outdoor types, family groups and sophisticated seasoned travellers. The menu, service and dining ambience are carefully styled to match the guest groups.

For those new to the cruising experience, the fairly strict meal times may come as a surprise. Except for the very upscale liners, two seatings for dinner and breakfast in the main dining rooms lead to an atmosphere incongruously reminiscent of the British holiday camps of the 1950s and 1960s. Not to mention the quite unceremonious crush outside the huge restaurant doors just before seating. The early sitting provides for a long evening of activities or sleeping, and is popular with families

and older travellers; younger and more sophisticated cruise passengers tend to eat later. Most ships, however, provide copious amounts of food on demand, around the clock.

While the standard of fare still varies from line to line, menus and service now resemble those of comparable hotels and restaurants ashore. On up-market lines such as Celebrity and Crystal, fine dining and silver service will rival some of the more fashionable restaurants in London or New York, with an obligatory string quartet and sweeping staircase, of course.

From the family- or party-oriented operators, although the food may not impress the gourmets, the style and presentation is fresh, modern and relaxed. In fact, on ships like those of the Ocean Village line, formal restaurants are dispensed with entirely in favour of 24-hour buffets and a couple of more intimate, reservations-only bistros.

Celebrity chefs

As with all aspects of cruising, you get what you have paid for in the dining rooms. The consultant or executive chefs for nearly all the cruise lines are well-known or celebrity chefs, and the menus are tailored to appeal to the cruise line's target market. Costa, whose executive chef is the luminary of Lombardy cuisine, Gualtiero Marchesi, provide for their mainly Italian clientele with an emphasis on pasta, red sauces and osso bucco (stew). James Martin (Ready, Steady, Cook) designs the menus for Ocean Village, and Windstar offer California-style nouvelle cuisine, with daily signature dishes from master chefs Joachim Splichal and Jeanne Jones.

The Celebrity cruise line chose Michel Roux, of the celebrated Roux brothers, to design their menus, and he follows this up by sending a sous-chef on regular visits to maintain standards of quality. Back of house, the waiting staff, from their colour-coded side of the galleys, can check the exact presentation of each dish against Polaroid photographs on a bulletin board.

Bright, multi-coloured sugar is spun and woven into dramatic swirls, ribbons, and even human figures, animals and fruit. Ice sculpture, food carving and extravagant decoration often feature heavily.

Regional flavours

Restaurant menus are often compiled to reflect the cuisine of a particular port of call. When in Genoa, there is likely to be the classic pasta Genovese, served with a delicious pesto of basil and garlic with pine nuts. A bouillabaisse might be served in the French Riviera ports, or moussaka in the Aegean.

Special diets can usually be catered for, although vegetarian options are still generally unimpressive, except on American lines. Any dietary preferences should be indicated clearly when you make your booking. For health requirements such as nut-free, gluten-free, low salt or vegan, definitely check that the ship can cater adequately to your needs before confirming the reservation.

Feeding the masses

In spite of the real care and attention that the operators put into menu design and food selection, catering to 1,000 guests at a sitting challenges any chef's skills. The massive bulk of supplies that a ship needs to carry also means that most of the food has to be stored on board for a week or more. On the less costly cruises, vegetables can be served rather soft, fish can be dry and, at the worst, poultry can resemble rubber. The tendency to over-cook comes partly from the priority of food safety. A recent outbreak of stomach virus throughout the P&O *Aurora* is the stuff of nightmares for cruise operators.

Fortunately, all the liners have at least one alternative restaurant. Although dining away from the main restaurants imposes an extra cost, some passengers think it is well worth it, as there are fewer fellow diners, proportionally more chefs and, as a result, better service and a more satisfying meal.

The other opportunity for most lines to really show off their culinary skills is at the midnight buffet. Long lines of tables groan under lavish and extravagant preparations, fantastically decorated and complemented by utterly sinful desserts. To make the most of this feast, it is advisable to skip dinner, or at least, to dine lightly.

Dining ashore

France, Italy, Spain and Turkey all border the Mediterranean, and offer wonderful regional delicacies. Italian cooks in the north specialise in cream, cheese or garlic-based sauces. Polenta, pasta verde, tagliatelle and tortellini are typically northern. Further south, tomato-based *(pomodoro)* sauces are more usual and more olive oil is used in cooking.

France is still internationally known for the finest

chefs and the most ambitious restaurants. Perfectly prepared sauces, delicately dressed salads, succulent meat dishes and irresistible desserts are still close to the French heart. More modest brasseries and cafés can provide welcome delights, too. Just remember that, if the sea is visible from the seat, and especially if the table is outdoors, it's not going to be cheap.

The characteristic Spanish exuberance is easy to detect on a menu. Paella is a massive and hearty rice dish with shellfish or chicken, bursting with flavours of saffron, herbs and garlic. Tapas are a delightful way of presenting small, nibble-sized dishes, and a lovely way to sample the vigorous

flavours of Spanish cooking. They can include calamares (fried squid), the classic Spanish spicy chorizo sausage or bacalao, a traditional salt cod.

Turkish cuisine is prized, particularly for slow-cooked lamb, for pickles and strong garlic flavours, offset with the typical Middle Eastern tongue-lashingly sweet sweets.

The countries of the Mediterranean have long been some of the world's finer larders for fresh fish, fruit and vegetables, olive oil and wine – and most of these ingredients are believed to promote health, too. Add to that a couple of thousand years' worth of practice in perfecting recipes, and there are plenty of feasts in store for passengers in ships' dining rooms. ❏

LEFT: a colourful selection of fruit usually features on a restaurant buffet. **RIGHT:** the perfect way to round off a good meal on a Cunard cruise.

CITIES AT SEA

A cruise ship is like a floating city, but one where everything is designed
for the pleasure and comfort of its temporary citizens

Imagine a typical day at sea. After an early session in the ship's gym or the spa, and a leisurely breakfast, a pleasant morning could be spent between the shops and cafés, perhaps meeting up with friends for coffee, or just soaking the sun's rays on deck. Lunch might be followed by a Spanish class, or relaxing by the pool. In the evening, perhaps cocktails at sunset as an aperitif before dinner, then maybe a film or a show, before taking a leisurely stroll in the moonlight.

Anticipating the wonderful shore excursions and ports of call that a voyage promises, it's easy to overlook the fact that most of the holiday is spent in the floating resort itself. The ship provides the hotel, restaurants, shopping centre and entertainment complex for most of the trip; the excursions and sights ashore are really sideshows.

Modern cruise liners are small but complete glittering cities afloat. They have hospital facilities, places of worship, spaces for most kinds of socialising and sport, including huge pools and outdoor hot tubs and, of course, numerous restaurants, bars and cafés. Everything a town could offer, in other words, but with clean air and no traffic.

Keeping a sea-borne resort running takes a huge international crew working long shifts, including hotel, entertainment and restaurant staff, as well as cleaners and maintenance workers. Wooden or marble floors are kept polished, carpets are vacuumed, paint is cleaned and refreshed and glass is shined constantly. This is one area that shows the differences between the liners, and that is on matters of cost. Luxury lines keep their vessels shiny and ship-shape without passengers ever being aware of anyone scrubbing, mopping or buffing. In contrast, a recent passenger on a low-budget cruise spoke of carpets being re-layed around her as she walked.

LEFT: lavish decor on a P&O cruise liner.
RIGHT: keeping a close eye on events
on board a Cunard liner.

Meanwhile, a full nautical and engine crew scurry in a sailorly fashion to navigate, maintain the course and heading, and keep the mighty turbines turning. The complement of sailors, from the captain down to the most junior naval ratings, is usually about 10–15 percent of the ship's staff.

Aside from the small and exclusive vessels like *Windstar,* which measure about 130 metres (440 ft), modern Mediterranean cruisers run from 240 metres (800 ft) to 270 metres (900 ft), and feed and play host to up to 2,000 passengers at a time.

Supply and demand

This massive floating party consumes a mountain of supplies every week. The *Costa Victoria,* for example, uses 15,850 lightbulbs and carries 32,000 drinking glasses. She generates 75,000 kilowatts of electricity, and burns 550 tons of fuel every week afloat. In that week, the guests and crew drink 2,500 bottles of wine and 8,000 bottles of beer, and eat 2,700 kg (6,000 lb) of boiled potatoes and 725 kg (1,600 lb) of baked potatoes, along with 1,360 kg (3,000 lb) of tomatoes and 1,360 kg (3,000 lb) of lettuce.

Eighty-eight chefs, from six nationalities, dice and cook the vegetables to accompany 1,360 kg (3,000 lb) of beef, and 1,800 kg (4,000 lb) of fish. This huge amount of stock is moved around the ship's cavernous larders and cold rooms with the aid of two fork-lift trucks.

Bakers knead dough, roll pastry and attend to hot ovens 24 hours a day. With regular and predictable menu routines, the ship's butcher is able to dress and prepare cuts of meat a week ahead of use, storing them in massive, walk-in freezers. Menus are designed to repeat weekly on some lines, but only monthly on the more up-market ships, and very often with a celebrity chef as consultant.

Although the menus are predictable, the moods and appetites of the guests are not – a variable that must be taken into consideration. The *Costa Victoria*'s head chef, Manfred, says, "One week we had 1,650 guests, and they ate much more than the 1,900 the next week." The reason was that the average age was lower on the earlier cruise. As Manfred pointed out, in general, younger people eat more.

ON-BOARD SHOPPING

On a Mediterranean cruise there will be many opportunities to shop for souvenirs and local specialities in each port of call, but shopping on the ship during days at sea can provide an altogether different experience. Bear in mind that the shops on board are a little like the shops of luxury hotels: they're convenient but don't always offer the best value for money. However, the duty-free shops on board sell everything from day to day necessities such as shampoo and toothpaste, bottled water and alcoholic drinks to designer watches and souvenirs carrying the cruise line's logo. Here, too, you can buy an extra bikini for a beach excursion you've just booked or shorts and T-shirts to wear while working out in the gym. It stands to reason that the larger the ship the wider the choice of shops and variety of goods on sale. Celebrity's Millennium-class ships have promenades packed with classy gift shops. Princess Cruises prides itself on boutique-style shops that are stocked with designer jewellery and clothing as well as shower gel and shaving cream. It's your choice to indulge in nothing more than a little window shopping while strolling through the ship's shopping mall or treat yourself to designer goodies. Even better, you can probably snap up a bargain or two, as some ships have sales in their shops during the last few days of the cruise.

Trade winds

Like any large community, a liner is also a fair-sized trading entity. Relationships are maintained with specific shops and merchants in the ports of call, and goods bought from traders on a ship's approved list are guaranteed by the cruise line. This provides some value-for-money reassurance, as gifts purchased in yesterday's port-of-call would otherwise be difficult to return or to complain about.

Relations with food and beverage suppliers are important, too. Since the ship calls at a different port every day or two, the larder chefs and buyers are able to insist on very high stan-

growing, and the lines are having to compete for the best employees. Incentives, from training to stock options, are used, and considerable thought is given to career development opportunities, all to encourage staff loyalty. Tours of duty are long – six or seven months on with few or no rest days, then six weeks off for most of the ship's complement – four months on and three to four months off for senior officers.

A list of crew passports would cover all five continents and up to 40 countries, but some nationalities tend to dominate in certain areas. Asians, particularly Indonesians and Filipinos form most of the hotel staff complement. Enter-

dards in both quality and value for money; otherwise they can easily sail their considerable custom elsewhere.

The crew

Crews on the new-style megaships can be up to 1,000 strong, and are drawn from all over the globe. Staff retention is an increasing preoccupation for the lines, and 75–80 percent staff turnover is common. With more and ever-bigger ships, the demand for staff and crew is

LEFT: Norwegian Cruise Line, like most of its competitors, offers a variety of exercise classes.
ABOVE: there are lots of opportunities for indulgence.

tainers are mostly American, Australian or European, but on Celebrity ships there is a high proportion of South African front-of-house crew and Eastern European musicians. On most ships, English is the *lingua franca* for the crew.

Working conditions are demanding. Whenever crew members come into contact with guests, they are obliged to act as ambassadors for the line. They have to be polite, friendly and helpful and, alas, not all passengers make that easy. Senior staff in regular contact with passengers can require fluency in up to five languages, and their associated cultural nuances. On a Mediterranean voyage, passengers are likely to speak Italian, German, Spanish and

Casinos Afloat

The excitement of the turn of a playing card or the drop of a silver ball into a spinning wheel can give a frisson to an evening's on-board entertainment. Cruise lines are only too pleased to spread out the green baize and change cash into chips, to part sea-going gamblers from their cash. The ship's only ATM machine is often helpfully located in the casino, to ensure minimum space between impulse and action. Croupiers dealing blackjack, American roulette and Caribbean stud poker, as well as the ever-popular twinkling and

chiming slot machines, stand ready to welcome eager players after a leisurely dinner.

For North Americans in particular, the casino used to be a major reason for choosing a cruise. As gaming has become more widespread in the US, this is less the case, but the tables are still an attraction, even though the odds offered are usually less good than those ashore.

A key to happy recreational gambling is first to set a firm budget, then to consider every bet to be an expense. A professional gambler once said, "A big difference between me and a tourist player is, when they win, they think they're playing with the house's money. I think: whatever is on my side of the table belongs to me."

Blackjack

The object of blackjack is to draw cards to make a total closer to 21 than the dealer, but without going over 21 ("busting"). Two cards are dealt face up to each player. The dealer's first card is also face up. Each player chooses to "stand" (take no more cards) or "hit" (take more cards, one at a time). An ace is valued as 1 or 11, whichever is best, and all picture cards count as 10. An ace and a card valued at 10 (a 10 or a picture) is blackjack, and pays out 3 to 2. Otherwise, a player closer to 21 than the dealer wins the amount of their stake.

American roulette

The payout for a single number in roulette is 35 to 1. That makes it an enticing flutter, but the odds are 38–1 against winning (36 numbers, plus 0 and 00). Much safer plays are around the outside of the table, the "dozens" (first 12, second 12, third 12 or one of the three "columns"), which pay out 2 to 1. Otherwise, 1 to 1 payouts are offered by "red or black", "odd or even" or "first" or "last 18."

Caribbean stud poker

This simplified variation of five-card stud is played against the dealer, and the game is swift and exciting. Five cards are dealt face down to each player, and the dealer's last card is dealt face up. A player who thinks their hand will beat the dealer's makes a wager and reveals their hand in the "showdown". The dealer's hand requires at least an ace/king combination, otherwise the player wins automatically. If the dealer's hand does qualify, then it is revealed in the showdown. Whoever has the highest ranked five-card poker hand wins the game.

Craps

If the ship's casino has a craps table, it is usually the liveliest in the room. The game moves rapidly, and the table looks bewildering, but the rules are fairly simple. Bets are placed both for and against the dice thrower. "Right" bets are for the thrower succeeding, and "wrong" bets are against. At the first roll, a throw of 2, 3 or 12 is known as craps. This is a win for bets on the "don't pass line" or wrong bets. The numbers 7 or 11 are automatic winners for "pass line" or right bets. Any other number rolled establishes the shooter's "point", and a series commences. The object then is to roll the point again before hitting a 7. ❑

LEFT: when you try your luck on the wheel, you should remember that, in the long run, the house always wins.

French as well as English. Tireless patience is also required to deal with the distinctive etiquette and manners of the differing nationalities: generally speaking, the British expect children to be seen and not heard, the Italians can't see or hear enough of them. German passengers often have a voracious appetite for history, especially facts and figures. The British want to go to the museums, the Spanish and Italians want to shop. French voyagers mainly want to eat, drink and bake in the sun.

Long hours and little time off can be wearing, and considerable attention is given to the crew's recreational facilities. The larger, newer ships

"Inappropriate" relations with guests are still technically punishable by instant dismissal, although it tends to happen only for the most flagrant infractions.

Smaller lines often take the view that staff drinking should be confined to shore visits, and so don't provide staff bars. Quarters for many workers are small. Junior ranks often have to share a two-person inside cabin, but the captain and hotel director are usually provided with spacious suites, often up at the bridge level, and with the best views by far.

Most of the front-of-house work involves social contact with the passengers. Giovani, an

provide games and sports areas as well as television rooms and messes with free or discounted food – all part of the effort to run a happy ship, and to help keep staff on the line for longer.

Some lines, particularly those sailing the larger ships, provide the crew with their own bars for recreation, since access to public areas is limited to the more senior ranks. This is partly to prevent the popular lounges from being swamped with crew, but also to help discourage fraternisation with the passengers.

ABOVE: a skilled bartender ensures that the cocktails contain just the right amount of everything.

avuncular maître d' says, "When I'm at home, my wife says, 'What's the matter, you don't talk, you don't want to see anyone.' It's true. When I'm off the ship, I don't want to do anything but be at home and rest." The head chef on the same liner takes a more positive approach to the rigours of the cruising life, saying, "Sleep? Waste of time."

Nevertheless, the length of time away from home is a strain for many crew members. On shore days, it's easy to find the best deals on international phone calls; just follow the swift trickle of waiters and ratings. Follow them as they leave the call office and you will probably end up at one of the better-value local bars.

Hotel staff

With up to 1,000 staff on board, an overwhelming majority – two-thirds usually – are in the hotel division. This includes the cleaners, cabin attendants and housekeeping maids who make up the rooms every morning, as well as the chefs, waiters and the maîtres d'. Until recently, the hotel division was predominantly Western European, but land-based hotels have improved their wages, making them attractive to some employees. Eastern European nationals have taken some of the places, but the Far East and developing nations now supply the overwhelming majority of hotel division workers.

senior staff. The captain's spirits have to be kept up, after all." Over the admiral's shoulder at that moment could be seen a long table with the captain at the centre, all the guests staring off into space and the captain himself pushing peas around his plate. Although there is certainly truth in what the admiral said, the guests are also just as likely to be frequent travellers and those occupying large suites, seated at the table as a reward for good custom.

Home thoughts

Although it is a taxing life aboard for the crew, during periods of shore leave many find them-

The captain

Captains can be gregarious and delighted to take part in the holiday entertainment, or they can be professional and reserved. "Captains vary," says one hotel director. "This one, he doesn't like to socialise much. The previous captain had cocktail parties all the time, he had passengers dining at his table every night. But it's the captain's choice." On a recent Celebrity cruise, a journalist asked the line's distinguished admiral, Angelos Argyropoulos, over dinner, "How do people get invited to the captain's table?" The admiral said, "People who are likely to be stimulating company, a mixture of interesting guests, will be suggested by the

selves yearning to return to sea. The continuous travelling from port to port becomes addictive, even though a surprising number confess to sea-sickness. After a fairly mild passage along the Ligurian coast, Emy Capurro, an English- speaking liaison officer for Costa said, "I do get a little sea-sick, but in front of the passengers, I have to hide it." Quite how she managed to do so she didn't say, but it is clearly something one can learn to cope with. Her calm disposition certainly betrayed no sign of distress and, when talking about shore leave, she echoes the words of many cruise workers, "The first time I stepped back on the boat, I felt I'd come home." ❑

The Entertainers

Working the boards at sea holds a special appeal for entertainers. Many singers, musicians, comics, magicians and dancers enjoy the long contracts, and regularly sign on for more. Those who don't take to it usually only complete their minimum commitment. Artists are recruited and the shows are produced by specialist agents and production companies ashore.

Auditions are held and the players rehearse, often in Miami or Las Vegas where the shows are custom-built for the cruise line or ship. What they produce are surprisingly impressive samplers of Broadway and London West End shows like *Chicago*, *Cats* and *Mama Mia*. On most lines now, the quality of dance and musicianship is very high. The cheesy old high-kicking shows, featuring big teeth and long legs, are drifting into cruising history. Passengers now are treated to well-crafted choreography and musical arrangements.

Mediterranean cruises tend to feature a wider musical repertoire than their Caribbean and North American sisters. Soft jazz, show tunes, pop, reggae and Calypso are the mainstays, but European routes often feature classical concerts and recitals, too. On most lines, these tend to be mainly piano recitals. An unfortunate consequence of modern technology is that with the widespread use of the synthesiser, only the more up-market cruises are employing violinists or cellists, so the string quartet accompanying dinner or playing in a quiet bar is becoming a rarity. Celebrity is one of the few lines to retain string musicians.

Like all the ship's complement, entertainers work a seven-day week, although dancers and comics can have a fair amount of free time between shows. Musicians have an extra long working day, as they are often called on to entertain the crew after hours, in their own bar below decks. The day doesn't start with the first performance, either. There are instruments and equipment to be moved from the showroom to the poolside, then on to the dance room, and there are the rehearsals, too. Material and arrangements must be frequently refreshed, new charts may have to be learned for a visiting headline singer, and

there are often new members to be worked in. If that sounds like a gruelling working schedule, keep in mind that musicians are an unusual breed of workers; they almost all love doing what they do.

The dance troupe usually have the most free time. The shows are almost always in the evenings, and apart from occasional rehearsals and costume fittings, there isn't too much work for them to do. The dancers are sometimes called on to add social glamour to cocktail parties. On a recent Costa cruise, the four American dancers aboard were asked to mingle with guests at a Fourth of July party. The dancers were poised, faultlessly charming and impeccably dressed. The passengers were

casual, relaxed, and a bit baffled by the attention they received from the gorgeous performers.

There are hazards to the job, though. As well as the massive physical strains that all dancers have to withstand, shipboard hoofers have a moving stage to watch. An Australian dancer on a Costa ship who strained a ligament in her calf, was off the stage for eight weeks. She was transferred to working as an "animator", one of the social hosts who help enliven parties and poolside jollities. The unexpected bonus was that she was then in synch with her boyfriend, himself an animator. Up to then, she said, "By 11 o'clock, he had been socialising all day, and was ready to sleep. But I was coming off the show, bursting with energy." ❏

LEFT: on-board entertainment with a nautical theme – dancers add glamour to the cruises.
RIGHT: a banjo player taking his job seriously on a *Regal Princess* cruise.

Planning a Shore Excursion

With a full-day's shore excursion costing around $100 (£60), passengers can be forgiven for wondering exactly what they're getting. Shore excursions are a vital source of income to cruise lines and passengers are encouraged to book them from the minute they book their cruise, or certainly on boarding the ship. Every day there are lectures about the next day's port, often with a heavy sell to take yet more excursions.

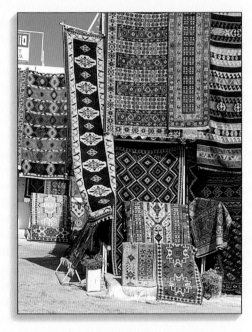

So are these trips worth the investment? In the Caribbean, the spiritual home of cruising, the run-of-the-mill coach excursion has evolved into a dazzling array of adventures, with kayaking, scuba diving, river rafting and jeep safaris now the accepted way of discovering the islands. The Mediterranean, however, seems to be firmly entrenched in the coach tour, mainly because there is no other practical way to ferry large groups of people to the many popular cultural attractions.

Coach tours serve a purpose in providing an overview of a destination, or access to hard-to-reach places. But on a port-intensive European cruise, with a city a day, endless coach tours can be exhausting and end in information overload. So

pace yourself; alternate a heavy sightseeing day with a relaxing one – a long lunch and a wander round a market. If there are alternative tours – kayaking, cycling, sailing – try to include one.

Do-it-yourself cities

Europe lends itself very well to do-it-yourself shore excursions, particularly in cities like Barcelona, Palma and Cannes, where ships dock close to enticing shops, restaurants and intriguing old city centres. With a decent guidebook, a map and a rudimentary knowledge of the destination, it's often more fun to walk around a small area, visit a couple of museums and soak up local life than try and fit the whole city into one afternoon.

Barcelona, for example, has an easy-to-use metro system and many of the highlights, like the Gothic Quarter, the Picasso museum and the contemporary art museum are close together. The Gaudí buildings are a short metro ride from the central boulevard, Las Ramblas. There are tapas bars along the Ramblas in which to collapse for a cold beer en route to the ship after a walking tour.

In St-Tropez, smaller ships drop anchor just outside the glamorous marina, from where it's a short walk to winding alleyways full of expensive, hippy-chic shops. Along the coast in Monaco, a brand new cruise pier means ships can dock rather than use their tenders (a time-consuming and sometimes choppy experience) and passengers can walk round three sides of the marina to Casino Square. Local restaurants, museums and galleries are all keen to encourage cruise business and offer big discounts to cruise passengers in summer.

A spontaneous, independent trip can be fun. In the Aeolian Islands, off the coast of Sicily, look out for inflatable motorboats for hire to whiz away from the overcrowded beaches to the secluded bays. Pack a picnic, mask and snorkel and some sunblock and take a driving licence for ID. Mopeds are also a good way to explore these small islands for anyone confident enough to negotiate Italian roads.

In the Bay of Naples, numerous excursions are on offer, depending where you dock. If it's Sorrento, you can walk the lovely old streets unguided. If you want to see Capri, use public hydrofoils and get there for half the price of an organised tour. Ambitious travellers can even get to Pompeii by train from most points around the bay.

Dubrovnik, too, is easy to explore independently – simply climb up onto the massive walls and walk the perimeter of the city, the terracotta-tiled roofs on one side and sparkling blue Adriatic on the other. Istanbul, if you've been before and seen the Topkapi Palace/Agía Sophia/Blue Mosque combination, is a rewarding and relatively compact city to walk. Take a ferry across the Bosphorus to the less-visited Asian side of the city, or a day cruise to one of the fishing villages near the Black Sea. Visit the spice market, or have a long, lazy lunch on the waterfront. Venice, too, once the basics have been covered, is the kind of place where a sense of atmosphere can only ever be gained by getting lost in the narrow alleys and beautiful squares.

The rules for independent exploration are simple: take a decent map, as the cruise lines usually provide basic photocopies only; don't be too ambitious; and remember that it is your responsibility to get back to the ship on time.

Excursions worth taking

There are some places in Europe where it does pay to take a shore excursion. Kusadasi, for example, on the Turkish coast, is the gateway to the antiquities at Ephesus. Ephesus is a long, hot trek from the port and a well-informed guide will bring it to life for a tour group. Likewise Rome; ships dock at Civitavecchia, a 50-minute road trip away. There is little point in hiring a car unless you really know what you're doing; parking and traffic in Rome are a nightmare. For a first-time visitor, there is so much to see in the city that a guided tour is the best way of getting an overview of important sights such as the Vatican City and the excellent shopping, before making the inevitable plans to return for a longer visit.

Florence, too, is something of a trek from the port at Livorno, but with some lines charging around $80 (£50) just for the transfer it may pay to get together with a handful of other passengers to hire a taxi and a guide through the ship's purser.

In Egypt, ships dock at Port Said and whirlwind tours take in the Egyptian Museum in Cairo and the Pyramids, dodging traffic and jumping queues; only the brave would attempt this journey alone.

Some cruise lines include all their shore excursions in the price. Anyone with a strong interest in culture, or perhaps travelling solo, might consider booking with one of these.

Hebridean Island Cruises is particularly good. The cruises are expensive but the shore excursions are top quality, often with lunch included, or an

---

LEFT: carpets for sale at the Didyma temple site in Turkey. **RIGHT:** playing statues at the Scolastica Baths, Ephesus, named after a wealthy Roman resident.

exclusive tour. One cruise, for example, includes a private visit to Villa Ephrussi de Rothschild on Cap Ferrat in France. Hebridean customers also get a private visit to the UNESCO site of old Ravenna, near Venice, and a beach landing at Nora in southern Sardinia, next to an ancient Roman city.

Swan Hellenic, too, includes shore excursions in every port, with extra trips available at a supplement. As an example, on a round trip to Greece from Venice, guests can see Venice, Delphi, Corinth, Mycenae, the Acropolis, Delos, Rhodes, Knossos and Olympia without paying a penny extra.

Upmarket cruise line Silversea charges for its excursions but throws in the occasional "experi-

ence" on selected cruises. "Experiences" have included a champagne gala at the opera in Odessa, a complimentary three-night extension to Luxor and Cairo from Safaga, and classical music and champagne at Ephesus, in Turkey,

Some cruise lines are moving away from the standard coach trip. Ocean Village, a P&O spin-off aimed at young, adventurous types, offers one-day cookery courses in Italy, camel treks in Tunisia and adventure sports in Mallorca. The ship also carries a fleet of mountain bikes, which are available at a charge for guided cycling tours. Hebridean Spirit has a fleet of bikes, available at no cost. So does SeaDream Yacht Club, a line that offers an informal cruising style in a five-star setting. ❑

CRUISE AND STAY

Cruise-and-stay holidays combine different kinds of experiences and allow you to take a closer look at the culture and character of the area you visit

Combining a cruise with a land-based vacation – known in cruise jargon as "cruise and stay" – makes particular sense in the Mediterranean and the rest of Europe. Pack in a couple of weeks' intensive sightseeing on the cruise and spend a week chilling out on a beach to recover. Or pick a cruise that meanders around glamorous beach resorts and snorkelling spots and add on a week's cultural touring at the end. The main thing to remember is that you will probably need two separate wardrobes – deck shoes, jacket and tie for the cruise and beachwear or walking boots for the stay.

Most cruise lines offer cruise-and-stay options, with varying levels of quality and expertise. Sometimes it pays to book the hotel or land package through a cruise line and sometimes it doesn't, so shop around. Internal travel in Europe is easy these days, with a highly sophisticated network of fast trains and a proliferation of low-cost airlines.

Where the cruise-and-stay holiday operates depends on the way a cruise is packaged. For the British, German and Scandinavian markets, a lot of European fly-cruises operate as inclusive tours, using charter flights, and the length of stay before or after the cruise has to fit in with the tour operator's flying schedule. These tend to be inflexible and an extension to a cruise will often be sold as a week in an hotel.

In the UK, large tour operators like Thomson Holidays and Airtours, which operate regular round-trip cruises out of some of the Mediterranean's principal ports, offer a wide selection of hotels in Mallorca, Corfu, Cyprus and the Canaries. Passengers travel by charter flight from a variety of UK departure points and buy hotel and cruise combinations of seven or 14 nights. P&O's Ocean Village also has a big cruise-and-stay programme in Mallorca, the home base of its ship during the summer.

Choosing the best deal

Anybody buying a cruise-only deal, or flying on a scheduled service, is free to choose the length of their vacation. There are numerous ports around the Mediterranean from which cruises start, many of which make great areas in which to stay on after they finish.

In Spain, Barcelona, Málaga and Palma de Mallorca are the main turnaround ports; all make good extensions to a cruise. Nice and Cannes are the big starting points for cruises in southern France, while in Italy, ships depart from Genoa, Civitavecchia (Rome), Naples or Venice. Athens is the main turnaround port for Greece, while Black Sea and Eastern Mediterranean cruises may depart from Istanbul, although recent security problems mean the cruise industry is likely to take a knock. Lisbon is a popular starting point for Western Mediterranean cruises and those that head south west to the Canary Islands, and makes a great contrast to the island beach destinations.

LEFT: souvenirs in Valldemossa, Mallorca, an island that is a popular cruise-and-stay destination.
RIGHT: time spent in a hotel before or after a cruise offers a chance to get to know a country.

In June, July and August a lot of cruises also depart from the UK ports of Dover, Southampton and Harwich, all within easy reach of London. Many of these head northeast towards the Baltic but some cruise lines, including Fred Olsen and P&O Cruises, sail all the way to the Mediterranean from Southampton.

Travellers from outside Europe may prefer to extend their cruise close to the city into which they fly. For example, fly into Athens and spend a few days visiting the sights, add on a cruise from the port of Piraeus, perhaps taking in the Aegean, or part of the Turkish coast. After the cruise, take an internal flight to

one of the other Greek islands – Crete, maybe – and enjoy a week on the beach, or stay on the Greek mainland and hire a car.

Rome is another popular gateway, with several cruise lines basing themselves at the port of Civitavecchia, 50 minutes' drive from the city. Strangely, cruises from Civitavecchia don't always include sightseeing in Rome, as the ship is only at the port on embarkation and disembarkation days. So add on a few days in the city before joining a cruise sailing south to Sicily and Malta, or north along the Italian coastline to France. On return to Rome, hire a car and drive north to Tuscany and Umbria for a vacation inland, returning to Rome for the flight home.

Barcelona is the gateway to Catalunya and the Costa Brava to the north. Cruises from here usually visit the Spanish coastal ports – Tarragona, Valencia, Almería and Málaga – and the Balearic Islands. Alternatively, they head east along the French Riviera. An extension to a cruise out of Barcelona could include a beach resort on the Costa Brava, or the Costa Dorada to the south of the city; a touring holiday inland as far north as the Pyrenees and Andorra; or a visit to Madrid by train. Be warned that Madrid is almost unbearably hot in August.

Keen golfers might want to choose a cruise starting in Málaga on the Costa del Sol, and stay on for a week afterwards, playing some of the world's finest courses. There are more than 50 to choose from and even a specialist golf cruise could not do them justice. Lisbon, too, is a good port combining a cruise with a resort, either on the pretty Estoril coast just half an hour from the city or, for serious golfers, four hours' drive south to the Atlantic Algarve coast.

Istanbul is another city that cannot be done in a day. For cruises departing here, add on two or three days before the voyage to explore the mosques and markets, and the fabulous Topkapi Palace, which itself takes at least a morning. Likewise for Venice, although August, peak Mediterranean cruise season, is not an especially good month, as the city is packed with tourists and the canals are less than fragrant.

If your cruise starts in the south of France, consider a touring vacation in Provence, or driving up through the Alps to Switzerland as a contrast to the cruise, or simply chill out on a beach somewhere. Bear in mind that all France goes on vacation for a month in August and everywhere is crowded, including the roads.

Organised tours

Sometimes, cruise lines organise their own pre- and post-cruise tours, although this is less prevalent in Europe than in, say, Alaska or South America. Some people prefer an organised tour, in which case Princess Cruises is particularly strong. The company organises a range of escorted land tours; for example, Vienna, Budapest and Prague, before joining a cruise in Copenhagen for a Baltic Capitals cruise, or the slightly incongruous combination of six nights in the Swiss Alps followed by Scandinavia and Russia. The London–Paris–Provence combination is a pleasing one, as travel is by train and the tour heads gradually south before joining one of Princess's ships and sailing from Barcelona to Venice.

Royal Caribbean has a similar offering, with cruise tours visiting Madrid, Seville and Barcelona before joining a Mediterranean cruise; or London and Paris with a northern Europe/Baltic voyage. The tours are a good way of travelling without any nasty monetary surprises, as transport, accommodation, several meals and entrance fees are all included. Sister line Celebrity Cruises has a similar tour, with extensions to Madrid, Toledo and Barcelona before or after Barcelona cruises, and to Lake

combine a land-based vacation with a short cruise in the middle or at either end. Cruises are priced by the day with flights and hotels charged separately. Silversea has special rates in top hotels, with chains like Ritz-Carlton, Inter-Continental and Four Seasons.

Swan Hellenic, which specialises in cultural cruises, moves at a slower pace than some of the one-city-a-day offerings. So while it's not exactly the cruise-and-stay concept, a Moroccan cruise might offer the option of an overnight stay away from the ship in Marrakech, while Lisbon, Málaga, Naples and Venice are just some of the ports in which the company's lux-

Como, Milan and the Italian Alps at either end of a cruise from Venice.

Personalised and specialist tours

Silversea, which caters to the top end of the market, allows passengers to construct their own cruise with its Personalised Voyages programme. Provided there are five consecutive nights on board, guests can break the journey and spend some time ashore before rejoining the ship for some more cruising – or simply

LEFT: Spain is a good cruise-and-stay destination for keen golfers.
ABOVE: a choice of transport awaits passengers.

urious *Minerva II* overnights, giving guests a chance to enjoy evenings ashore.

Orient Lines sells itself as a "destination specialist", which is perfect for anyone wanting in-depth tours. A couple of nights in a hotel are usually included in the price. For example, a cruise from Rome might include two nights in the city prior to departure. Optional city stays at special rates are offered in Athens, Barcelona, Copenhagen and Lisbon and the occasional link-up with the Venice-Simplon Orient-Express train is arranged, taking the train from London to Venice and boarding Orient Line's *Marco Polo* there. Cruising does not come much more decadent than this. ❑

A TO Z OF MEDITERRANEAN CRUISING

Cruising offers lots of alternatives, so to make sure you get the ship that's right for you, it's worth doing some homework before you go

Stretching more than 3,200 km (2,000 miles), from the Straits of Gibraltar in the west across to the Black Sea in the north, the Suez Canal to the south and the shores of Israel, Lebanon and Syria in the east, the Mediterranean is one of the largest and most diverse cruise regions in the world. So what, exactly, is so special about it?

The Cradle of Civilisation, as it is often called, encompasses more than 20 different countries and myriad islands, borders three continents, contains four seas – the Tyrrhenian, Adriatic, Ionian and Aegean – and presents visitors with a rich melting pot of cultures.

Its turbulent history spans more than 5,000 years. It has some of the world's most spectacular archaeological sites and is a repository of the world's finest art and architecture. It serves all that up with a splash of style, a large dash of sunshine, and the spice of varied and delicious cuisine. It is hardly surprising, then, that the Mediterranean is the number-one cruise destination, as far as the British are concerned.

New options

The launch in 2002 of a new budget line, Island Cruises – a joint venture between the Royal Caribbean and First Choice companies – was partly responsible for a 5.5 percent increase in Mediterranean fly/cruise bookings in that year. The new line joined Thomson Cruises and Airtours Sun Cruises in offering seven-day Western Mediterranean runs out of Palma de Mallorca.

In April 2003, P&O's new budget line, Ocean Village, began operating Mallorca-based cruises and cruise-and-stay combinations, a popular development that boosted Mediterranean bookings considerably during its first year of operation.

LEFT: deck games are traditional on Mediterranean cruises and Cunard believes in tradition.
RIGHT: floodlit swimming on an NCL ship.

UK port-to-Mediterranean cruise bookings have also been rising year on year since the millennium. In fact, despite the difficult travel climate, only one sector of Mediterranean cruising has felt a chill; bookings for short cruises from Cyprus to the Eastern Mediterranean have halved in the early years of the 21st century as a result of political unrest in the region.

Such is the Mediterranean's overall popularity that European-based lines Costa Cruises and Festival Cruises have been testing the waters with year-round cruises, giving travellers the opportunity to visit the region's great archaeological sites out of season, when the crowds have gone home and the climate is mild.

Whichever time of year you choose to visit, the Mediterranean is a region just made for cruising. No other type of vacation can quite capture its enormous diversity, taking you effortlessly from one great civilisation to another and showing you some of the world's most magnificent scenery as you go along.

The advent of the single European currency, for all the controversy it has engendered, has made life easier for Mediterranean cruise passengers from the UK and North America, who no longer have to change sterling or dollars into as many different currencies as there are ports on their cruise.

Where can I go?

The range of Mediterranean cruise itineraries is vast; you could find yourself savouring tapas in Cádiz, visiting the awesome Alhambra while Naples is the gateway to the ruined cities of Pompeii and Herculaneum, buried by a volcanic eruption in AD79. Italy-based Mediterranean itineraries allow you to intersperse all this sightseeing with some gentle relaxation in dazzlingly pretty Italian Riviera resorts like Amalfi, Sorrento and Portofino.

Or you could head further east on a cruise to Turkey, the great meeting point of Asian and European cultures, which is home to the ancient cities of Ephesus and Troy, and to the World War I battlefields of Gallipoli (these sites can be visited on trips from the ports of Kusadasi and Canakkale).

Palace in Granada on a trip from Málaga, taking in Gaudí's magnificent buildings in Barcelona, or soaking up the sun and enjoying the great beaches and nightlife in the Balearic Islands of Mallorca, Menorca and Ibiza.

The fabulous volcanic scenery of the Canary Islands and the colourful *souks* of North Africa feature on some Mediterranean itineraries, while others will wrap you in the sophistication of chic French Riviera ports like Cannes, Villefranche, Nice, Monte Carlo and St-Tropez.

You can marvel at the exquisite buildings and canals of Venice and take in the matchless treasures of Florence and Rome via the Italian ports of Livorno and Civitavecchia, respectively;

Other Mediterranean cruises will take you off to explore the ancient sites and sunny, whitewashed towns of mainland Greece and the Greek Islands, where Athens, Corfu (Kérkyra), Rhodes, Crete (Kríti), Santoríni, Zákynthos, Katákolo (for Olympia), Mýkonos, Vólos, Delos, Gýthio (for Sparta) and Návplio (for Epidaurus, Corinth and Mycenae) are all popular ports of call.

Then there's Valletta, the bustling capital of Malta; Sicily, where ships dock in the colourful capital, Palermo, or visit the sophisticated resort of Taormina, close to dramatic Mount Etna. Stylish Sardinia and beautiful, rugged Corsica are also on many itineraries.

And if you've "done" the main Mediterranean cruise ports, you could try a cruise via Istanbul and the Dardanelles to the Black Sea, a region that combines brilliant sunshine with a strong draught of Eastern exoticism.

Black Sea itineraries generally include calls at a couple of Mediterranean hotspots and a two-day stay in Istanbul, a wonderful city endowed with one of the world's most spectacular skylines and home to the famous Blue Mosque, Topkapi Palace and the colourful Grand Bazaar.

Ships then proceed through the Bosphorus to Black Sea ports like Odessa and Yalta in the Nest Castle, which perches precariously on a clifftop. Varna is a pretty Bulgarian beach resort with 2nd-century Roman baths and a stunning cathedral, while neighbouring Nessebur, a UNESCO World Heritage Site, is a delightful medieval town of cobbled streets, timber-framed houses and numerous beautiful old churches. Some cruises will also call at Batumi, where you'll find the world's second-largest Botanical Gardens

Joining a Mediterranean cruise

British holidaymakers taking a Mediterranean cruise have two options – fly out to join their

Ukraine and Varna or Nessebur in Bulgaria. Odessa – a faded but still magnificent city of pastel-tinted houses and grand Parisian architecture – is home to the famous Potemkin Steps and a beautiful circular Opera House. This is the place for culture lovers, as ships' excursions often include a night at the ballet.

Yalta is the site of the Levadia Palace, the former summer residence of Tsar Alexander II; here you can explore the Romanov apartments and enjoy dizzying views from the Swallow's

LEFT: coming into harbour on a SeaDream ship…
ABOVE: …and having fun with high-powered toys in its wake.

ship at a port such as Palma, Piraeus (Athens) or Genoa, or join a UK-based ship for a round-trip sailing from Dover or Southampton. There are pros and cons to both methods.

Fly/cruising means passengers get straight to the sun – but face all the hassle of an airport to do so. And they have to go easy on snapping up bargains on their travels, or there could be baggage excess charges to pay on the flight home. UK-based cruises are less trouble for British passengers in that they can simply drive, or take a train or coach to the port. They can also shop to their heart's content, secure in the knowledge that they can stash the loot in their cabin and just load it into the car when they get back.

Families at Sea

There was a time when the rule on cruise ships was that children were to be seen but not heard. Nowadays, you won't see much of them, either – but only because they'll be too busy off enjoying themselves in on-board children's clubs. The massive shipbuilding programme that has transformed the face of cruising includes the provision of outstanding children's facilities on modern ships. Not only do youngsters get their own mealtimes, menus, pools, play areas and age-related activity programmes, they can also – on

some Mediterranean ships – spend an afternoon zapping Jurassic Park velociraptors, zooming around a racetrack, or exploring beneath the waves in a virtual-reality simulator.

From 2005 – when Royal Caribbean brings its giant Voyager-class ships to the Med for the first time – they can go rock climbing, roller blading and ice-skating too – without even leaving the ship. But before you get the youngsters all excited, check out which ships offer the best family facilities.

The big ships

The 70,000 ton-plus mega-ships operated by P&O Cruises, Princess Cruises, Royal Caribbean, Celebrity Cruises, Holland America Line, Norwe-gian Cruise Line and Costa Cruises are top of the tree at catering for families. Children get acres of space and superb facilities, ranging from computer rooms to teen discos, mini-theatres and virtual-reality arcades. Fully supervised programmes include everything from T-shirt painting, treasure hunts and talent contests to water polo and arts and craft lessons. Many ships now offer a children's drinks card, which can be bought at the beginning of the voyage and entitles youngsters to limitless soft drinks for the duration of the cruise.

The budget ships

Lower-priced ships run by tour operators Thomson (Thomson Cruises), Airtours (Sun Cruises) and First Choice (Island Cruises) have been a hit with British families because they're cosy and affordable. They also offer a range of cruise-and-stay combinations, so families can combine a week's cruise with a week at a Spanish seaside hotel, for example.

Generally these companies use older ships, so facilities are less glitzy and activity programmes don't run all day, but there are playrooms and reasonable facilities for keeping youngsters entertained. An exception is P&O's new, budget-priced *Ocean Village*, which provides the most up-to-date facilities for children and teenagers in the budget sector, including day-long, activity programmes and a free-until-midnight nursery.

Do remember to check:

● exactly what children's facilities are available on the ship you've chosen and that they're open and available when you want to travel;

● minimum ages for using children's clubs – some won't accept kids in nappies; others insist on having a parent in attendance for toddlers;

● the duration of daytime children's club activities;

● staff qualifications and security arrangements at the play centre;

● what the situation is if you want to leave children on board and go ashore – most ships insist that very young children are not left, as they may become distressed;

● the cost of babysitting (some ships offer this free until midnight; others charge by the hour);

● what's on children's menus and when meals are available;

● availability of family cabins, cots, pushchairs and special-offer prices for children. ❑

LEFT: children's on-board activities, like this one on a Cunard liner, get more and more sophisticated.

On the other hand, they should be prepared for a couple of days of British weather at the start and end of their cruise (not such a problem in summer, but worth considering in the spring and autumn months). They'll also be crossing the unpredictable Bay of Biscay, which can cut up rough – so it can be a good idea to pack seasickness tablets just in case.

Getting around ashore

This guidebook is designed to equip you with enough information to get around Mediterranean ports of call under your own steam, so you won't find taking a ship's shore excursion

get back to the ship before it sails. Should there be a delay, ships will wait for tour buses to return, but not for individual passengers.

The downside is that you'll be travelling en masse along well-worn tourist trails – fine if you just want a quick and hassle-free look at the main sights, but frustrating if your preference is for going off-track and getting under the skin of a destination.

In fairness, cruise lines have done much of late to expand shore excursion options beyond the usual coach tours. For example, Ocean Village offers biking, hiking, roller skating and even abseiling ashore. And, while excursions

is your only option for seeing the sights. The advantage of shore excursions *(see page 68)* is that the price generally includes entrance to sites and attractions, and knowledgeable guides who will take you smoothly around major areas of interest, obviating the need to make your own arrangements.

Most will also allow some free time to explore and shop on your own, while full-day tours usually include lunch at a good restaurant where the quality of food is guaranteed. Taking a shore excursion also ensures that you'll

ABOVE: the MSC *Lirica* has reliable, friendly children's club staff, who give parents the chance to relax.

can be costly, the budget lines (Thomson, Airtours, Sun Cruises, Island Cruises and Ocean Village) have largely managed to keep the price at an affordable level.

Not so the mega-ships, where shore excursions are getting increasingly expensive. A day trip from Livorno to Florence and Pisa can cost as much as £250 ($400) per person at current rates – excessively hefty, even with a decent lunch included – while a simple return coach transfer from Civitavecchia to Rome can set you back more than £100 ($160) a head.

This is partly down to protectionism among European guide and ground handling organisations, which are particularly powerful in Italy and charge pretty much what they like; but it's also attributable to the vast increase in cruise capacity created by the huge number of new cruise ships – 91 new ships were launched in the 1990s and a further 51 entered service between the beginning of 2000 and the end of 2003. Increased capacity means more competition and therefore pressure to bag bookings by slashing up-front cruise prices.

In some ways, the customer benefits, because the initial price is lower, but cruise lines with repayments to make on new ships must make up the lost revenue somehow, and many do it by hiking up the cost of shore excursions, as

well as other optional extras like alcoholic drinks, health-spa treatments and on-board speciality restaurants.

That said, it's up to you to decide how much or how little you spend. All food in ships' main dining rooms is still included in the cruise price, as is access to state-of-the art gymnasia, children's clubs and swimming pools, and most ships also allow passengers free use of steam and sauna facilities. As for excursions, it's a good idea to gather information in advance on the ports you will visit, so you can make an informed choice about which places you could see independently and which would be worth the cost of an excursion.

Cruising options

Nearly all the major cruise lines have ships in the Mediterranean in the summer months, so you can choose from a wide variety of ships, from budget to luxury class, from sailing ships to cultural cruises.

If you would like to combine a cruise with some time ashore, the Med is one of the top destinations for cruise-and-stay holidays, with add-on options ranging from city breaks in European cities to bucket-and-spade stays on the Balearic Islands.

Even outside the main summer season, the Mediterranean has pulling power; great cities like Venice, Florence and Rome and archaeological sites like Ephesus, Pompeii and Egypt's Valley of the Kings are seen at their best in the spring and autumn months when they are less crowded and the weather is cooler, which can be an advantage when you are sightseeing rather than lying on a beach.

(For contact details of all Mediterranean cruise operators see Travel Tips, page 339.)

Choosing a ship

Cruise ships used to be divided into three categories – budget, premium and luxury, but the shipbuilding boom of the 1990s and early 2000s created a new category – the so-called contemporary ships. This means new vessels which, though charging budget-level fares, offer more modern and varied facilities than traditional budget-class ships.

To make life even more confusing, some cruise lines have varied fleets, made up of ships of different categories. For example, the budget-price sector includes some modern ships, like Ocean Village's *Island Escape*, and though prices are low, it's worth considering ships in this sector as cheap certainly doesn't equate to cheap-and-nasty.

The premium sector includes not only modern ships but also smaller sailing vessels and older but well-presented ships offering cultural cruises with experts on board to give passengers a real insight into the Mediterranean through on-board lectures and tours ashore.

To find a Mediterranean cruise that's right for you, ask yourself a few basic questions about what you want and need from a holiday, then check out the different categories of cruise ship to find one that suits you. Points to take into consideration are:

● Are you travelling alone, as a family, or as a couple?

● What is your budget? Include not only the cruise price but also the amount of money you can afford to spend on board.

● Do you enjoy the sophistication of dressing for dinner or prefer a more casual, informal atmosphere?

● Do you see a Med cruise as a good way to find out about the region's history, art and architecture, flora and fauna? Or is your plan simply to have a break, soak up some sun and enjoy a few nice lunches and shopping ashore?

● On board, would you prefer an intimate ship where you can find your favourite watering hole and stick to it? Or would you rather take your pick of various bars and restaurants?

● Do you enjoy an active, sporty holiday?

● Do you hate the thought of travelling with a lot of other people?

● Do you want to combine a cruise around different destinations with a stay ashore?

Budget ships

Operators include Thomson Cruises, Airtours Sun Cruises, Louis Cruise Lines, Island Cruises, Ocean Village, Mediterranean Shipping Cruises, Royal Olympia Cruises and Festival Cruises. The last three lines offer a mix of older budget and new contemporary ships

In this category, you can expect (by and large) older, smaller ships with fewer modern facilities. They will all have a good choice of lounges and bars but gymnasia and spa facilities will be less swish than on modern ships, as will children's clubs.

Budget ships are good for those who like their ships cosy, intimate and fairly traditional. In some cases, cabins on older ships will have better proportions than the pre-built boxes used on contemporary ships.

However, they are disappointing if you like a variety of restaurants and are bored by the old-fashioned, "fishnet and feathers"-style evening entertainment. There are exceptions, though – Ocean Village, although budget priced, is out to attract younger, first-time cruisers by offering them good children's facilities and up-to-date entertainment, including tribute bands and

LEFT: cruise passengers trying not to over-exert themselves.

RIGHT: the *Grand Princess* lives up to her name.

stand-up comics. It also offers fairly swish facilities, including two alternative restaurants; while Island Cruises has a spice market-style buffet food court and an à la carte restaurant on board the *Island Escape*.

These vessels are excellent for those who prefer smaller ships and like a quiet environment (although Island Cruises and Ocean Village, aimed at a younger clientele, can get a bit more raucous). Europhiles who enjoy practising foreign languages will enjoy Mediterranean Shipping Cruises and Royal Olympic, while nervous first-time cruisers will feel more at home with the wide range of Mediterranean

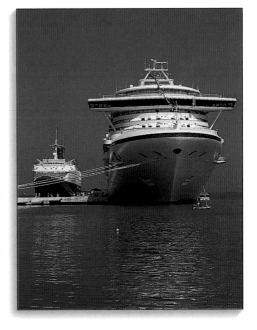

cruise-and-stay options that are available from the tour operator-owned cruise lines.

Contemporary ships

Operators include Carnival Cruise Lines, Norwegian Cruise Line, Royal Caribbean International and Costa Cruises

In this category, you can expect massive, new, ultra-modern ships with room for up to 3,500 passengers. Facilities will include an array of bars and lounges (often themed); multiple pools, dining rooms and speciality restaurants; state-of-the-art spas and gymnasia; and well-equipped children's centres offering supervised all-day activities.

Ships in this category are good for those who like a lively environment and plenty of choice about everything, from where to eat and drink to what activities they can participate in. On board Royal Caribbean's massive, 137,000-ton Voyager Class ships, for example, you can try your hand at rock climbing, roller blading, and even ice skating, as well as all the usual on-board activities.

Contemporary ships are not for you, however, if you hate queues. With a large number of passengers aboard, embarking and disembarking the ship and even grabbing a bite at the buffet inevitably involve quite a long wait.

Travellers on a tight budget will find the price of on-board drinks, spa treatments and shore excursions pretty hefty.

If you're not put off by these factors, these ships are excellent for families, as facilities for children and teenagers are excellent. Teenagers in particular will love the virtual-reality video arcades and teen clubs. Contemporary ships are an excellent choice for people who really want a resort that floats.

Premium ships

Operators include Swan Hellenic, Celebrity Cruises, Holland America Line (HAL), P&O Cruises, Princess Cruises, Fred Olsen Cruise Lines, Orient Lines, Cunard Line, Voyages of Discovery and sailing ship operators Windstar Cruises and Star Clippers.

On Holland America, Celebrity, P&O and Princess lines you should expect similar facilities to those of contemporary ships, but the difference is that there are fewer people using them. You'll also get better-quality food – not only in service-charged speciality restaurants but also in the free-to-use main dining rooms.

Other premium lines, such as Fred Olsen, Voyages of Discovery, Cunard and Swan Hellenic, feature smaller and/or older ships but the facilities are always well-maintained, the food is good and there will be an optional programme of lectures on board.

These ships are good for those who enjoy "floating resort" cruising but like an added dash of style. Travellers who like to expand their minds will enjoy Orient Line's *Marco Polo*, Cunard Line's *QE2* and Swan Hellenic's *Minerva II*, which have knowledgeable lecturers providing a real insight into the ports visited. Windstar and Star Clippers ships, on the other hand, appeal to those who love boats and watersports and want to visit smaller, off-beat ports that are inaccessible to larger ships.

However, ships in this category are disappointing if you don't do your homework, as they vary greatly and not all premium ships are the last word in modernity (Fred Olsen and Orient Line ships, though classy, are older vessels), while some premium ships (for example, those belonging to Celebrity and HAL) are not much different from the contemporary vessels offered by their parent companies, Royal Caribbean and Carnival.

Despite the above caveats, these ships are, on the whole, excellent for travellers who want a bit of style at a reasonably affordable price.

Luxury ships

Operators include Silversea Cruises, Seabourn Cruises, Crystal Cruises. SeaDream Yacht Club and Radisson Seven Seas Cruises

You can expect quite a lot on these ships. Spacious, elegant, all-suite accommodation (except on luxury big-ship operator Crystal Cruises, which offers standard cabins alongside grand suites).

Food and service standards will be high, dining rooms are run like chic restaurants ashore, and excellent in-suite service will usually include the option of having lunch and dinner dishes served course by course in your suite while you relax and watch a video.

They are very good for those who hate feeling they are part of a crowd. These ships, as a rule, are very exclusive – although they have been somewhat less so in recent years, after the post September 11 travel slump and the Iraq War sent cruise fares tumbling.

This category of ship would, however, be disappointing if you like the wide variety of facilities available on the bigger ships (Crystal is your best choice if this is the case). They are excellent for well-heeled travellers who relish luxury and exclusivity – or ordinary mortals

Ratio (PSR) is a good indicator of how roomy the vessel is or how crowded it may feel – and it's easy to work it out.

To find a ship's PSR, simply divide its tonnage (i.e., its size) by the number of passengers it can carry. For a true picture, go on maximum occupancy, where every berth is full, rather than double occupancy, when only every lower berth is occupied, as this gives an idea of how spacious it will feel when three-, four- and five-berth cabins are also full.

For example, luxury operator Silversea Cruises' 28,258-ton *Silver Shadow* carries a maximum of 400 passengers, giving it a roomy

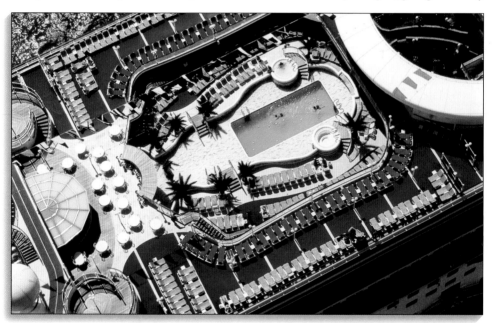

prepared to push the boat out for a once-in-a-lifetime special treat.

Will I feel confined on board?

Are you worried that life on board will send you stir crazy? It is a consideration, but frankly, its unlikely, given the frequency of port calls on Mediterranean-based cruises.

But if you're anxious about feeling hemmed-in, don't think that your only option is to choose a gigantic ship. A cruise ship's Passenger Space

LEFT: Kusadasi fishing boats dwarfed by Holland America's MS *Rotterdam*.
ABOVE: aerial view of a Princess line deck and pool.

PSR of 70.6, while Royal Olympia Cruises' budget-class *Triton*, at 14,155 tons, has a PSR of only 14.9 when it crams in its full passenger capacity of 945.

Getting more information

The Passenger Shipping Association in London (tel: 020-7436 2449) is a prime source of information about all types of cruising, and its website (www.discover-cruises.co.uk) is well worth a look. Some of the luxury cruise lines have set up their own website, www.exclusive-collection. co.uk. If you are a first-time cruise passenger, there is plenty of information available to help you make the right decision. ❏

Cruise Lectures

I t is rather cruelly said of cruise ship entertainers that they're either on the way up or on the way down. Celebrity speakers on cruise ships, however, are different. Guest speakers from the worlds of the arts, academia, the diplomatic services, television, radio and haute cuisine are only too happy to spend a couple of weeks a year in a decent suite at sea, free of charge, in return for a few gigs on board.

Big-name speakers are a great draw. Silversea snagged Ted Koppel, ABC *Nightline* anchor, while

P&O Cruises, which attracts a mainly British audience, runs classical music cruises hosted by popular BBC radio personalities Richard Baker and Henry Kelly. There is also a regular Sixties cruise on which bands like The Fortunes and Herman's Hermits are brought out of semi-retirement.

Veteran BBC weather presenter Bill Giles, meanwhile, accompanies a cruise around the Canary Islands talking about that favourite British subject, meteorology. Cunard Line, on its European and transatlantic sailings, offers a mix of stars of screen and stage. Veteran actor Sir John Mills has been a regular for years, drawing huge audiences, while British darts compere Jim Bowen can be found in QE2's Golden Lion pub, hosting raucous quiz nights.

Cultural choices

By their nature, cruises in the Mediterranean focus on culture, so expect to find historians, archaeologists, Grecophiles, retired diplomats, religious experts, or military and Middle East specialists delivering the entertainment on board. If this sounds a little high-brow, cruise lines also employ vulcanologists, marine biologists, wine experts, celebrity chefs who produce Mediterranean-themed menus, astronomers and gardeners to enhance the Mediterranean cruise experience.

Some cruise lines wheel out the guest speakers for the occasional lecture, while on others, they are an integral part of the cruise. Swan Hellenic, which markets its trips as "Discovery Cruises" and attracts a more intellectual type of passenger than most, has four or five top-notch speakers on each departure, covering all angles of the cruise from natural history to religion, cuisine, wine, weather and history. Orient Lines sells itself as a "destination specialist" and, like Swan Hellenic, calls at some unusual ports, with excellent speakers to accompany most cruises, many of them repeat guests. Hebridean Island Cruises, too, employs expert speakers to bring the destinations to life from its ship, *Hebridean Spirit*. Guests may, for example, find themselves moored off the coast of the volcanic island of Stromboli by night while the expert delivers a talk on volcanoes as Stromboli obligingly spits boiling lava in to the night sky.

Voyages of Discovery, another line which appeals mainly to Brits of a certain age, is a good lower-budget option for those who cannot stretch to Swan Hellenic, Orient Lines or Hebridean Island. Guest speakers accompany every cruise, with recent luminaries including Sir Bernard Ingham, former press secretary to Margaret Thatcher, and Sir Arnold Wolfham, the astronomer royal to the British royal family.

Fred Olsen cruises, meanwhile, carry experts on bridge, ballroom dancing, gardening and garden history, golf, watercolour painting and music, on their various cruises. Passengers learn practical skills as well as hearing the lectures. On the music cruise, for example, a choir, formed from the passengers, gives a performance at the end of the voyage. Appealing to a multi-national and multi-lingual audience is difficult and the more exclusive cruise lines try to bring on big names who will have international as well as intellectual appeal.

Seabourn, for example, has had Tony award winner and writer Alan Arkin, comedienne and actress Dixie Carter, celebrity chef Rick Moonen and *Jeopardy* host Alex Trebek on board as part of its Dress Circle programme.

Radisson Seven Seas calls its themed voyages "Spotlight Cruises" and again, aims to please both British and US guests. "Antiques Boatshow", for example, is a tour of the Baltic with the BBC TV *Antiques Roadshow* team, who provide tips on antique hunting, antique-themed tours of the Baltic capitals and, at the end of the cruise, a re-creation of the television programme to reveal which guest has scored the best bargain ashore. Radisson also runs music cruises with celebrities and, for example, a Beatles tribute band, throwing parties on deck and concerts in the ship's theatre.

Self-improvement

The latest big thing in cruising is self-improvement. Much of the entertainment on board now is geared towards learning a new skill, not just refining one's bridge or ballroom-dancing skills. With the launch of the new *QM2*, Cunard has moved upmarket in its lecture themes, with a partnership with the University of Oxford, which will supply authors, historians, artists and scientists as part of Cunard ConneXions, a "cultural enrichment" programme on sailings from Southampton. Guests will be able to take courses on a variety of topics as varied as British and American Music and Culture of the 1960s, Shakespeare in Film, Modern Art from the Tate to the Met and the Internet Explosion.

Crystal Cruises has introduced a "Creative Learning Institute" on its newest ship, *Crystal Serenity*, where entire cruises will be dedicated to self-improvement. A film festival, hosted by big-name producers, writers and editors, is planned; while Berlitz will provide language instruction in French and Spanish. Guests can even learn the piano, taught by experts from Yamaha. Crystal has also recruited experts from the Society of Wine Educators, Tai Chi Cultural Center, Barnes&Noble.com and interior-design school Parsons School of Design to bring new life to cruising. Whatever happened to lazing around the pool?

...and decadence

Some lines stick to a more decadent theme. Silversea, one of the most deluxe cruise lines of all, offers culinary cruises in conjunction with Relais et Châteaux, with which it has a partnership. Guests

enjoy a week of cookery demonstrations rounded off by a lavish gala dinner, prepared by the guest chef for that particular cruise. Wine cruises are hosted, too, by wine retailers, growers and makers. In Europe, these are combined with vineyard and cellar tours and, of course, tastings. Crystal Cruises runs a series of Wine and Food Festival sailings, with big-name chefs including Wolfgang Puck (who has designed some of Crystal's menus) on board, or a crack team of Italian chefs who will provide special regional cuisine for Prego, the Italian restaurant on all three of Crystal's ships.

Radisson is the only cruise line with an official link to Le Cordon Bleu and there is a Cordon-Bleu

restaurant, Latitudes, on *Seven Seas Mariner* and *Seven Seas Voyager*, its two top-rated ships. Every year, there are master-classes in Le Cordon Bleu Classe Culinaire des Croisieres, run by visiting Le Cordon Bleu chefs, where guests learn how to prepare dishes served in the cruise line's own Cordon Bleu restaurants. Upon graduation, guests receive a chef's apron and a certificate of participation.

Better still, Radisson operates the occasional theme cruise featuring those three great European specialities, music, wine and food, accompanied by a pleasing combination of classical musicians, wine growers and celebrity chefs. The cruise ends in Venice, a fitting finale to the whole, well-rounded European experience. ❑

LEFT: Ted Koppel, America's ABC TV news anchor, is a popular celebrity speaker.

RIGHT: top chefs can show you how to do it.

CRUISING UNDER SAIL

A growing number of operators are offering all the romance of the great days of sailing, but with 21st-century comforts thrown in

Long before there were jets, there was a jet set, but their methods of transport, if they can be called anything so mundane, were yachts, on which high society from both sides of the Atlantic met and mingled. This is still true of the Mediterranean in summer, even if highlife and lowlife are often flirting aboard the same yacht. The Caribbean winter set billows into a Mediterranean summer, unfurling the sails of celebrity super-yachts. The world may be their oyster, but nothing surpasses Côte d'Azur chic in summer. Nor is there any point floating around in the Atlantic when the yachtie in-crowd is paddling in the Mediterranean. Cruises mostly favour "the milk run" on the high seas of cool, the star-studded route from Monte Carlo to Cannes and St-Tropez, which sweeps onto the Costa Smeralda in Sardinia. Minnows follow in the wake of the sleek super-yachts owned by the Italian fashion mafia, Armani, Prada and Valentino, or by princely sailors such as King Juan Carlos of Spain or the Crown Prince of Denmark.

An air of elitism

At the stretch-limousine end of the market, yachts come complete with peaked-cap servility, champagne and canapés, the lifestyle befitting a shipping tycoon. If snobbery is a feature of cruising, it is an art form on the finest-crewed yachts, which thrive on their air of élitism. The yacht belonging to the late Aristotle Onassis can now be chartered by clients who only feel at home with a deck-side heli-pad or state rooms hung with Old Masters.

Few are allowed to forget that European royalty, emperors, sheikhs and heads of state have sampled cruises on this legendary vessel. Even if the bar stools are no longer covered in whales' foreskins, the opulent yacht dazzles with special effects, including a pool that converts into a dance floor. You can now swim in the pool in which Onassis wooed Maria Callas,

entertained Winston Churchill, joked with John Wayne and sang along with Frank Sinatra.

Even so, the romance of the sea is best sought on an historic tall ship, or on a replica sailing ship, rather than on a glamorous crewed yacht. Fortunately, a raft of vintage vessels still evokes a bygone era.

Vintage vessels

Foremost among them is *Sea Cloud*, both the largest private yacht ever built and the most historic sailing ship in commission. Now maintained as a sleek cruise ship, this glamorous art-deco barquentine is a tribute to the opulent taste of its owners, publisher Edward Hutton and his wife, Marjorie Merriweather Post, the US cereal heiress. The carefree couple took delivery of the yacht in 1931, and spent four years sailing the world. In the Galápagos Islands they even picked up a tortoise, which became *Sea Cloud*'s lucky mascot. The yacht's sumptuous 1930s décor echoes the design of suites in the Carlton or Waldorf Astoria, considered the last

---

LEFT: the freedom of the seas on the *Star Clipper*.
RIGHT: a passenger enjoys being part of the action.

word in luxury. The three-masted yacht is still home to many of the original antiques and oil paintings, and preserves its appeal in parquet floors, burnished brass and teak decks.

Yet while the master suite is a picture of masculine mahogany and nautical wood-panelling, Marjorie's distinctly decadent suite was inspired by Versailles, with a flouncy French canopied bed and lashings of gilt, Louis Philippe chairs, Carrara marble fireplaces and ornate Venetian mirrors. Today, the vintage vessel plies the Mediterranean for part of the year, so romance is not dead.

The romance of sail also lives on in *Sea Cloud II*, a gleaming white, three-masted tall ship, the companion to *Sea Cloud*. Even though it is a contemporary sailing ship, the style harks back to the 1930s, when its sister-ship was built. The art deco retro style and the grandeur of 2,970 sq metres (32,000 sq ft) of sail rekindle the effortless glamour of the era.

Yet there is another class of sailing ship that seeks to recall the time of tall ships. The swashbuckling days may have gone but, down by the docks, the sailors on the tall ships still do a nice line in nautical nostalgia. Replica clippers, such as the *Stad Amsterdam*, can be chartered by wealthy modern adventurers, but more acces-

MEDITERRANEAN MOMENTS

As far as fashion in sailing is concerned, the Mediterranean holds the trump cards. The 2004 Athens Olympics has seen a revival of interest in cruising in tall ships around the Greek Isles. The Olympic flame returns to its spiritual home and Athens solves the accommodation crisis by housing guests in cruise ships moored in Piraeus harbour.

The spotlight falls on the Mediterranean again, as the great cruising port of Genoa assumed the mantle of European Capital of Culture in the same year. Given its ancient seafaring traditions, Genoa is rightly presenting itself as the capital of the sea, with a restored waterfront, maritime fortress and superb aquarium. The award-winning regeneration of the Porto Antico, the Old Port, has moved the city's centre of gravity back to the sea, confirmed by the Museum of the Sea and the creation of exhibition and concert centres nearby.

For yachties, the climax must be the 2007 America's Cup, with fair winds bringing this legendary regatta back to Europe. As well as delighting the Spanish yachting fraternity, the event invests Mediterranean waters with all the glamour and thrills of the world's greatest offshore race. The regatta is destined for Valencia, which beat a rival bid from Naples, and will make seductive southern Spain a showcase for Mediterranean sailing.

sible are the sailing vessels in the tall ships tradition. Operated by such individualistic cruise lines as Star Clippers and Windstar, these graceful ships sashay into small ports with the wind filling their galleon-like sails.

Set against the soft Mediterranean light, these square-rigged windjammers readily conjure up an era of cutlasses, buccaneers and buried treasure, exotic cargoes and distant ports of call. These latter-day tall ships, often four-masted barquentines, even make voyages similar to those of several centuries ago, following the spice routes between the Mediterranean and the Middle East.

it aims to offer a genuine sea-going experience, with the ship operating under sail for about 70 percent of the voyage. The fleet's *raison d'être* is to recreate the romance of sailing, but softened by creature comforts.

The routes vary every year, in response to demand, but generally cover either the western Mediterranean, focusing on France and Italy, or the eastern shores, focusing on the Greek Isles and Turkey. Forthcoming cruises feature France and Italy, with one route covering the Côte d'Azur, Corsica, Monte Carlo and Portofino and another covering Cannes, St-Tropez and the Costa Smeralda in Sardinia.

Pride of the fleet

The pride of Star Clippers' fleet, the graceful five-masted *Royal Clipper*, claims to be the largest true fully rigged sailing ship afloat today, with a full complement of 42 sails. Modelled on the German windjammer *Preussen*, which was sunk in 1907, this spectacular square-rigger has her hull painted in the traditional chequerboard pattern of merchant sailing ships.

Wind-power may be backed by a state-of-the-art navigation system, but unlike its rivals,

This is the proverbial milk run, the classic route for the glitterati, who, like swallows, swoop off to the Côte d'Azur in summer, migrating to the Caribbean in winter. Alternative sailings visit Rome, Sicily and Malta or Venice, Dubrovnik, Taormina, Sorrento and Rome.

Cruise veterans praise the freedom of being able to fling off your shoes and feel the warm teak deck underfoot. These ships almost wear a badge of honour as the "anti-cruise cruise line" catering to those who wish to shun regimentation and indulge in feeling piratical. Instead of the blandness of a floating resort, there is the intimacy of a private yacht, all burnished brass and gleaming mahogany rails. Instead of over-

---

LEFT: it's easy to get used to a little bit of luxury.
ABOVE: a view from a clipper's rigging.

crowded excursions, expect remote ruins, underwater wrecks and time spent pottering around small ports. Few miss the congested cruise ports the sardonic clipper captains intolerantly dismiss as "stinkpots". And who can resist dinner on deck under the stars instead of the queue-jumping and tray-wrangling in the buffets that can be part of mealtimes aboard typical cruise ships.

All hands on deck

Seasoned clipper-hands never lose the sense of wonderment they feel when looking up at a sky crammed with sails and rigging. On Star Clip-

per ships, passengers can scuttle up the rigging to the crow's nest or nestle in the nets either side of the bowsprit. From the eyrie of these huge hammocks suspended above the sea are inspiring views of lofty sails, a starlit sky or daunting bow waves. Instead of official entertainment, there is an un-chatty parrot, story-telling with the Captain, or solitary midnight swimming. Socialites content themselves with turning up at glamorous ports at cocktail hour.

But even in choppy weather, nothing beats standing on the upper deck at night, under full sail, with a strong wind at your back, and succumbing to the pleasure of seeing the waves under a starlit sky. On a recent cruise to Athens, crowds gathered on deck to watch an awesome thunderstorm over Piraeus that would have entertained the gods.

Wind down with Windstar

Compared with Star Clippers, there is little swashbuckling about sophisticated Windstar. No one swabs the decks or hoists the sails on these slickly computerised, diesel-sail ships; the majestic sails unfurl at the touch of a button. This award-winning fleet operates four sailing yachts that combine the elegance of traditional clipper design with super-yacht engineering. On board, these luxurious ships exude a private yacht-like atmosphere, creating camaraderie and even lasting friendships among shipmates. Windstar also prides itself on offering casual elegance, style and luxury with a laid-back attitude. Forget Broadway revues, mindless gambling and the lectures on investments offered by mass-market cruises; most passengers seem to enjoy the simple life at sea, undercut by a spirit of adventure.

Windstar cruises tend to cover a greater variety of ports than their rivals, and fine-tune their routes every season. A typical cruise includes a world-class city, such as Venice or Istanbul, as well as a clutch of smaller ports chosen for their Mediterranean mood or glamour, whether it is St-Tropez or Santorini, Monte Carlo or Mykonos, Portofino or Capri. Yet whether the eastern or western Mediterranean beckons, passengers have their fill of blue-domed churches and bell towers, picturesque ruins, lemon groves, gnarled olive trees, white-washed houses, palatial ceilings studded with marble mosaics, and bustling bazaars selling hand-made ceramics and rugs.

Sea days encourage relaxation for passengers "ruin-ed out" by ancient civilisations. Windstar often combines the Greek Isles and Turkey's Turquoise Coast, with two of the lines' sailing ships moored side by side at the port of Bodrum. The day opens with a cruise on a traditional Turkish sailboat and sunbathing in a quiet cove, followed by a barbecue back on *Wind Spirit*, with a belly-dancing display on deck, under the stars. Then *Wind Spirit* slips silently from her moorings, maybe with a pod of curious dolphins at her bow, and glides steadily into the seas towards Santorini. The salty mist clears, and overhead the comput-

ideally suited to all sailing boats. Even if the name does no justice to the sea's intense palette of colours, the Turquoise Coast is the place to sail, taking in boisterous Bodrum and Hellenic Ephesus. Bodrum, a sailing mecca since the days of Anthony and Cleopatra, was relaunched by Istanbul bohemians in the 1950s. These romantics sailed the yet-to-be-christened Turquoise Coast in traditional Turkish boats and Bodrum soon became the Turkish St-Tropez. As the capital of the Turquoise Coast, it still makes a sensible cruising base.

Gulets are traditional wooden Turkish boats, hand-built, twin-masted and around 20 metres

erised sails open, billow and snap as the city lights are soon enveloped by the darkness. It is at moments like this that the captain poses the philosophical question: "Do you understand our motto at Windstar Cruises, that we are 180 degrees from the ordinary?"

The Turquoise Coast

Turkey's Turquoise Coast, which dares drift into the distinctly Greek Aegean, represents one of the most sybaritic routes in the region, and is

(60 ft) in length. Although fully equipped with sails, *gulets* can also be motorised, and may be booked as one-day adventures from the cruise line. Even so, a chartered *gulet*, manned by a small crew, is the best way to explore the coast, with its ancient ruins on the hillsides and coves framed by olive and pine groves down below.

The wide variety of bays allows for a different anchorage every night, always in secluded spots. The voyage may take in Cleopatra's private beach and the eternal fires of Mount Olympus by way of pirates' lairs, Roman amphitheatres and ancient Lycian ruins. Unlike on larger boats, the crew all help out, with the skipper lending a hand to produce a "light"

LEFT: sailing into a calm bay, with no other ships in sight, is a magical experience.
ABOVE: taking it easy, at anchor in the bay.

lunch of Turkish *mezze*: smoky aubergine rata-touille, grilled sea bream and spicy meats. Sweet pastries, over-ripe peaches and water-melon put an end to thoughts of further dutiful ruin-visiting, as does the aniseed-flavoured *raki*, the spirit of choice in these parts.

This is one of the most sensuous cruising experiences: a swim as soon as the sun comes up, followed by a breakfast of bitter Turkish coffee, honey, yoghurt and feta cheese; morn-ings spent skirting sandy inlets and jetties too shallow for mooring; afternoons spending time with weather-beaten peasants and hedonistic Turkish sailors; headlands encrusted with ruins;

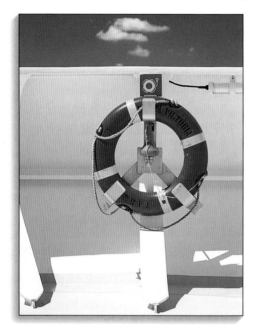

slopes covered in tamarisk and thyme, wild mint and mimosa; Dionysian evenings ending with a swim from the shore back to the boat to fetch another bottle of red wine or *raki*.

Given the azure-coloured seas, warm winds and beguiling scenery, the Mediterranean is a magnet for sailors who wish to charter their own boat. The Mediterranean promises safe adventuring back in time to the cradle of civil-isation, from the Straits of Gibraltar in the west, which the ancients deemed to be the end of the known world, through Spain, where the Moor-ish influence prevails, to the glories of Rome. Voyage a little further afield to reach Greece, Turkey and even the pyramids.

Not that lengthy voyages are needed to appreciate the coast: day-passages tend to be more enjoyable, such is the enticing nature of the coastal landscape and small ports. The Mediterranean is studded with chic marinas, unspoilt bays and lovely islands with secure anchorages. Most people who sail these seas do so in 11–14-metre (35–45-ft) boats, which offer acceptable stability and enough space to survive without throwing your shipmate over-board. To keep mooring costs to the minimum, select a boat that is just under 10, 12 or 15 metres (33, 40, 50 ft) long, since these are the markers used to set mooring fees in most marinas. Rather than a lightweight, semi-racing boat, the best sailing rig for cruising the Mediterranean is the modern junk rig. This comes into its own in southern waters: where other boats pull their sails down and rely on their engines, this one just sails sweetly on.

Yet if romance is more a question of cutlasses and casks of rum, salty yarns and sea shanties, then only a tall ship will do. What is called for is a four-masted barquentine with a buccaneer-ing spirit, a traditional windjammer that sails the Mediterranean with would-be pirates.

A timeless quality

The timeless quality of tall ships triumphs, with the ocean's moods conducive to solitude and pri-vate thoughts. Tall ships are at one with the wind, sky, and romance of the sea. At full sail, the *Royal Clipper* is a rousing sight, gliding silently by on the horizon of a ghostly early morning mist. As the world's largest true fully rigged sail-ing ship, this is the closest most people will come to the romance of cruising under sail.

Robin Knox-Johnston, the round-the-world-yachtsman, sailed on the maiden voyage of a similar ship, the *Stavros Niarchos*, which aimed to test the British tall ship to its limits. He, too, succumbed to the timeless quality of tall ships. After a violent squall, "the noise of the sea was accompanied by the wind singing in the rig-ging, and then the moon came out to outline the rig against the sky and its scudding clouds. It was magical for us all; everything we had read about square rig was actually happening, just as it had 100 years ago, towards the end of the great age of sail".   ❑

LEFT: safety aboard – it's comforting to know everything's taken care of.

The Romance of Sail

The romantic era of sailing ships swept in with the tea trade, when clippers brought scented teas from the China, cotton and sugar from the Caribbean and, later, cargoes of gold from California and Australia. Fast clippers shipped gin, cheese, cloth and even gold-prospectors, and came back laden with sugar, coffee, tobacco and rum from the East and West Indies.

In a sense, the story begins and ends with the *Cutty Sark*, which is the only tea clipper to survive intact from the golden age of sail. The clipper became a legend when it out-raced a steamship in 1894. Similar tea clippers plied the seas until the 1870s, when the shipping of tea became unprofitable because of competition from India, with steamers using the Suez Canal, but sailing ships forced to follow the longer Cape of Good Hope route. Even so, the great square-riggers were still used to ship merino wool and, later, grain from the New World to Europe, a real race since the first ship home could command the highest prices.

In the end, the steam age spelt the end of the age of sail, and the clippers seemed destined for the scrapyard by 1914. The war struck at the merchant navy of all nations: clipper crews discovered they were a sitting target in calm weather while their rigging could be easily crippled by gunfire from enemy ships. Yet even if the age of chivalry was dead, there was still a place for eccentricity at sea. One U-Boat captain regularly regaled enemy captains with salty tales, superb cigars and fine wines, while apologising profusely for sinking their ships.

Racing enthusiasm

Tall ships still make voyages similar to those of several centuries ago, including tracing the spice routes between the Mediterranean and the Middle East. The only difference is that today the voyages tend to be regattas to commemorate such events as the 500th anniversary of Columbus discovering America. Fortunately, the passion provoked by these ships and the public's enthusiasm for the golden age of sail means that certain races survive. In particular, the Tall Ships races are a highlight of the sailing calendar, with the friendly competition taking place in different parts of Europe every year. Run by the International Sail Training Association, the races have turned into

celebrations of the sea, with festivals in each host port. There is clear historical continuity as many participating ships have transported cargo in their time. The Danish ketch, *Jens Krogh*, built as a 19th-century merchant and fishing vessel, is one of the oldest ships in commission, while the Russian square-rigger *Sedov*, the largest sail-training ship in the world, was part of the last great grain race to Australia in 1939, just before World War II began.

Kruzenshtern, the other great Russian relic, has bold black and white sides designed to imitate gunports and so deter pirates. The looming bulk of the Russian ships is a throwback to the era of Soviet dominance when Janka Bielak, a Polish

Auschwitz survivor, persuaded the Russians to come into the race at the height of the Cold War: their participation helped challenge the view of the Russians as faceless militarists. At full sail, the *Kruzenshtern* is a rousing sight, gliding silently by on the horizon of a ghostly early morning mist.

Sheba Oman, the largest wooden sail-training ship in commission today, also presents a dramatic spectacle, with the Omani naval crew dressed in flowing robes, mirroring the unfurled sails. The topsails of this exotic barquentine are emblazoned with the bold red symbols of Oman, a dagger and crossed swords, combining majesty and might. The days of cutlasses, buccaneers and buried treasure may have gone, but the tall ships sail on. ❑

RIGHT: learning the ropes on a tall ship.

PLACES

The Mediterranean is much larger than it looks on most maps and offers a huge variety of ports and shore excursions. This section sets out the choices

Mediterranean cruises cover an extremely wide area and a great variety of destinations, from the Catalan capital, Barcelona, to the Black Sea port of Yalta, from chic Riviera harbours to crusader castles in Syria, not to mention the western Atlantic ports used by ships heading from the UK to the Mediterranean. You could take a cruise each summer for many years before you ran out of new places to go. The advantage of a cruise is that it allows you to get a flavour of a country and its culture and decide whether you would like to explore further on a more extended holiday.

Once you have decided on the kind of ship on which you wish to travel and the broad itinerary that best suits your taste, time and budget, the next step is to look in more detail at the destinations you will be visiting. The following chapters are arranged not strictly by country, but broadly according to itineraries organised by the major cruise lines. Within each chapter, a selection of ports are included, some of which are home ports, or feature on most itineraries that visit a particular area, others that may be ports of call only for small ships or those on specialised, in-depth cruises.

Your time ashore will, necessarily, be limited – in most major ports ships arrive in the early morning and leave in the early evening, so it helps to know what to look out for while you are on land. In order to help you get the most from your visit, we give details of how to get from the dock to the town centre and the places of most interest for sightseeing and shopping. Because many cruise passengers will want to visit places beyond the immediate vicinity, we mention those of most interest and indicate whether they can be reached by public transport or whether a hire car is necessary. All the cruise lines run well-advertised shore excursions, of course, and the most important ones are mentioned here, along with advice on the practicality or otherwise of making these same trips independently.

Some ports, of course, are visited chiefly because they give easy access to towns or sites of great beauty or historical or architectural interest, in which case those destinations receive more attention in this book than the ports of call themselves. Remember, though, that unexpected changes of schedule can occur, due to bad weather or other causes, and a much-anticipated destination may be missed out. Barring that eventuality, all you have to do is choose your itinerary and let your floating hotel take you to the places you've dreamed about. ❑

PRECEDING PAGES: blue seas, white domes, and a ship to take you there; the Assos Acropolis at Behramkale; sailing into the Bosphorus.
LEFT: Venice is a highlight of any Mediterranean cruise.

WESTERN APPROACHES

*A cruise from the UK to the Mediterranean involves stopping off
at some attractive Atlantic ports, ranging from Oporto to
the Canary Islands, Gibraltar and North Africa*

Map
on page
104

The first part of this chapter details Atlantic cruise destinations in France, Spain and northern Portugal that are visited by ships that cruise all the way to the Mediterranean from northern Europe. The second section covers those more southerly destinations that are often thought of as vaguely "Mediterranean" but are in fact on the other side of the Straits of Gibraltar – ports in southern Portugal, Morocco, the Canaries and Madeira.

CRUISING SOUTH FROM GREAT BRITAIN

Any cruise ship sailing from the UK, or perhaps Amsterdam, to the Mediterranean will have to cross the Bay of Biscay, a long and notoriously rough stretch of water between the northwestern tip of France and the north coast of Spain. Many break the journey by calling at some of the following ports en route.

Honfleur, on the Seine estuary in northern France, is an attractive, historic town, notable for its slate- and timber-fronted houses and old fishing harbour. Further along the coast, **Caen**, one-time base of William the Conqueror, provides access to the D-Day beaches, the Bayeux tapestry and Calvados country.

Smaller ships can sail up the Loire to **Nantes**, which has a Gothic cathedral, a medieval castle, and access to the chateaux of the Loire valley. Further south, even fairly large ships can slip up the broad, muddy Gironde, its banks lined with vineyards, to **Bordeaux**, for visits to the chateaux of Medoc and St Emilion.

In the southwestern corner of France, **Bayonne**, **St Jean de Luz** and **Biarritz** all take cruise ships, offering excursions to the Basque country, the Pyrenees and the long, sandy beaches of the region.

San Sebastián (Donostia), on the north coast of Spain, the former summer residence of the Spanish royal court, was razed to the ground in 1813 during the Peninsular War. One of the highlights is the Plaza de la Constitución, built on the ruins, with overhanging balconies numbered to correspond with the former bullring. **Santander** is famous for its cathedral, Roman ruins and palaeolithic caves. Excursions run from here to Bilbao and the spectacular Guggenheim Museum.

La Coruña (A Coruña) is the principal town of Galicia, Spain's greenest region, in the far northwest. The Spanish Armada set sail from here in 1588 and the town has plenty of historical interest. Most cruise passengers take a day trip to the medieval pilgrimage town of Santiago de Compostela. **Vigo**, an alternative gateway to Santiago, is a pretty town with a deep, fjord-like harbour where English and Dutch forces defeated the French and Spanish in 1702. The surrounding countryside is pleasant, too, and ships aimed at a younger market may offer mountain biking, hiking and adventure sports as an alternative excursion.

LEFT: Quinto do Palheiro gardens near Funchal, Madeira.
BELOW: Bilbao's Guggenheim Museum.

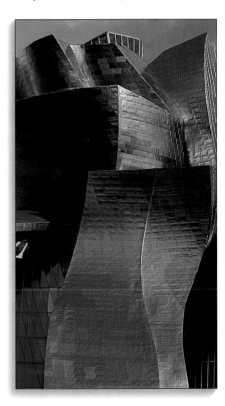

PORTO

Set at the mouth of the Douro River in the heart of wine-growing country, Porto has been a thriving port and commercial centre for more than 3,000 years, and there is an air of elegance about its imposing squares, broad avenues and fine 18th-century merchants' mansions.

The three bridges that span the deep river gorge are famous landmarks, the most notable being the two-tier Donna Maria Pia road bridge, which was designed by Gustave Eiffel.

TYPICAL EXCURSIONS, PORTO

● **City Tour** (usually includes a trip across the Maria Pia bridge to a port tasting at one of the city's wine lodges).

● **Quinta da Aveleda Green Wine Tour** travels north to the wine region of Aveleda, famous for its *vinho verde*.

Arrival and around the dock

As you arrive in port, look out for *barcos rabelos*, traditional flat-bottomed boats which brought port wine down from the Douro Valley to Ribeira's wine lodges. They are pretty much museum pieces now, but it's delightful to see a vital part of the city's history re-enacted.

Money-changing facilities, toilets and metered taxis are available at the main port, on the south side of the Douro. Further along the seafront is **Leixoes**, Porto's seaside resort, which has an artificial harbour created in the 19th century to relieve congestion from the crowded quays along the Douro. The Dom Luis I bridge is the most direct link from the port to **Ribeira**, the oldest district and home to Porto's famous port cellars. You can get a bus, or walk across.

Shopping

Shoes and leather goods, silver and gold filigree jewellery, embroidery, lace and ceramics are all good buys; Rua das Flores is lined with silversmiths, while some of the best leatherware shops are on Rua 31 de Janeiro. Look out for crafts made of cork (Portugal produces half the world's cork supplies) which – along with the obligatory bottle of port – make welcome presents.

BELOW:
the rooftops of
Porto's old quarter.

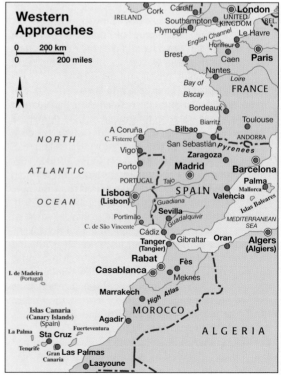

Eating For lunch ashore, you'll find plenty of restaurants and cafés in this area of the city; local specialities include *caldo verde* (green soup made with potatoes, sliced sausage and kale) and *pasteis de bacalhau* (saltcod fishcakes).

Seeing the sights Medieval **Ribeira**, on the river's north bank, is more scenic than the modern city of Porto; it's a fascinating district, well worth exploring, particularly around the 12th-century **Sé** (Cathedral) in Terreiro del Sé, which is a good place to start a sightseeing tour. (From the northern end of Dom Luis bridge, continue along Av. de V. Peres, then turn left.) Inside is a beautiful 14th-century cloister decorated with traditional Portuguese glazed tiles, a 16th-century chapel and a magnificent silver altar which dates from the 17th century. At the front of the cathedral is a high stone balcony offering fabulous views of the city, the river and the surrounding narrow streets, pastel-tinted houses, craft shops and market stalls.

More riches are to be found at the **Palácio do Bisbo**, the former Archbishop's Palace in the cathedral square. Now a museum, it contains fine silver and pewter work and a collection of European and Oriental ceramics. Head north along Av. Dom A. Henriques, then left along Rua dos Clérigos and you'll spot the soaring 74-metre (244-ft) tower of the 18th-century **Igreja dos Clérigos**. This oval-shaped, baroque church is magnificent and well worth a visit.

Feast your eyes on fine art and architecture at the **Nacional Museu Soares dos Reis** (open Wed–Sun and Tues am; fee), which lies to the west of the tower near Rua de Restauraçao. Once the residence of Portugal's royal family, it houses paintings dating from the 16th century and works by the 19th-century sculptor Antonio Soares dos Reis.

A selection of ports laid out for tasting.

BELOW: one of the *barcos rabelos*, Porto's wine boats.

Map on page 104

Bacchus, the god of wine, depicted in azulejos (painted tiles) in Lisbon's Museu Nacional do Azulejo.

Do make time to visit one of Porto's wine lodges in the Ribeira district before returning to your ship. You'll be warmly welcomed, given a brief history of port wine – which was discovered when locals mixed brandy with Douro wine to preserve it for shipment – and invited to taste the products.

LISBON

Although it was put well and truly on the world map when 15th-century marine explorers like Vasco da Gama used it as a base for their expeditions to Africa and India, Lisbon now lacks the immediately recognisable icons of most other European capitals. It is, though, one of the most rewarding to visit.

For a start, as well as having its own relaxed charm and fewer crowds than most capitals (there are only 700,000 residents), it is easy for strangers to find their way around – which is just as well, as Portuguese is not the easiest language to decipher and not a great deal of English is spoken except in the hotels and larger restaurants. Navigating the city is easy because there is a clearly defined centre (Baixa) within easy reach of the two districts which visitors usually want to see (Bairro Alto and Alfama) and there is good, cheap public transport (including the famous trams) and plenty of relatively inexpensive taxis.

Partly as a result of its 1974 return to democracy after decades under a dictatorship which restricted free speech, there is now a great deal of political graffiti sprayed around, but there has been a lot of recent restoration of historic buildings, some of which were originally damaged in the major earthquake of 1755. Much of the Chiado commercial district has also been rebuilt, following a devastating fire in 1988.

Nightlife in Lisbon is not the most exciting, although *fado*, its traditional music, has an authentic, melancholy appeal and many devotees. But ships are usually gone by nightfall and visitors concentrate on the many things there are to see and enjoy by day.

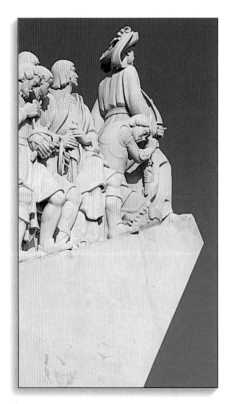

The city is also within easy range of the sophisticated coastal and gambling resorts of Cascais and Estoril with the historic hill-top village of Sintra – Byron's "Eden" – not much further away.

Usually a port of call on cruises between the UK and the Atlantic Islands, on Mediterranean or longer cruises to West Africa and beyond, Lisbon is also occasionally used as a home port. Ships normally arrive early in the morning and depart late afternoon/early evening.

Arrival and around the dock Although occasional early-morning mists sometimes obscure the views, it is always an interesting 15-km (10-mile) journey along the Tagus (Tejo) River, past the Belem Tower and the distinctive Monument to the Discoveries with its statue of Henry the Navigator jutting out into the river. Then, after passing below Europe's longest suspension bridge, your ship docks at the main port (Doca de Alcântara) about 5 km (3 miles) from the centre of the city.

There are plans to create a docking stage and terminal exclusively for cruise ships much nearer the centre but at present cruise lines usually organise (for a fee) a shuttle bus to ferry passengers to and from

Praça do Comercio (20 minutes each way) on the edge of the city centre. The passenger terminal, which is used by ferry and cruise ships, has a café, tax-free shop, gift shop, telephones, a post office and tourist information desk but there is no reason to linger around the port. As well as tour buses and shuttle buses, there are sure to be taxis waiting.

Shopping Portugal remains a traditional Catholic country, so on Sundays and saints' days, most shops are shut. On other days, some stores close for two or three hours at lunchtime, but most stay open. It is still one of the cheapest European countries in which to shop. Look out for laceware and rugs, pottery and ceramics, straw bags and bottles of port wine, sherry or *vinho verde*.

Shuttle buses drop passengers off at Praça do Comercio, near the main shopping district: **Baixa**. There are also some interesting boutiques in the old town, **Alfama**. To the north, near the Castelo de São Jorge, is an "artists' village" where local painters sell their work.

Eating The Bairro Alto is the most popular place to eat out. If you want to experience the real pleasures of eating in the city, go to the typical little local restaurants called *tascas*. There is also a lively collection of restaurants on the waterfront, in the **Doca de Santo Amaro**. Fish and seafood are among the specialities; they include *arroz de marisco,* a delicious rice dish, and a splendid stew, *caldeirada de peixe*, but there are plenty of meat dishes as well.

Seeing the sights Take the shuttle into the city from where there are bus and tram services from Praça do Comércio that run throughout the city. (The

---

Maps on pages 104 & 107

TYPICAL EXCURSIONS, LISBON

● **City tour** (normally half-day).

● The beach resorts of **Cascais** and **Estoril**, and the historic village of **Sintra** (full-day).

● The medieval castle town of **Obidos** (normally half-day).

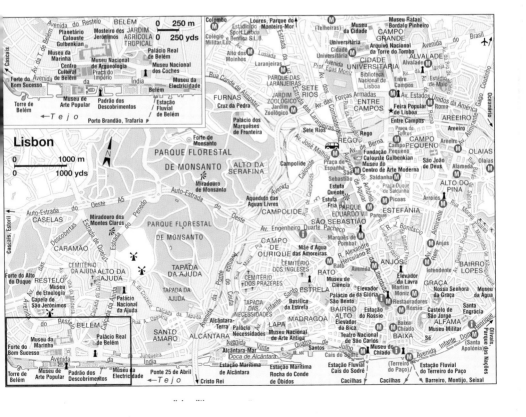

*Lisbon's trams are a
tourist attraction as
well as a good means
of transport.*

main tourist office is in the Welcome Centre on this square.) For around 2–3 euro, a daily travel card, available at kiosks and tobacconists, covers all journeys, including those on the metro. Travelling on the old wooden trams is a wonderful experience. Service No. 15, from the centre to Belém and No. 28, to Alfama, are the most picturesque routes.

Lisbon is one of the smallest European capitals, but there is a great deal to see and do. You will probably see most on one of the shore excursions but if you prefer to travel independently and are happy to walk or take the occasional bus, the city centre, where most points of interest are to be found, is divided into three manageable districts – Baixa, Bairro Alto and Alfama. **Baixa** is a predominantly 18th–19th-century district with a rectangular grid system, created after the 1755 earthquake levelled the old city. It stretches across the flat area flanked by the steep hills of Alfama to the east and Bairro Alto to the west, extending from Praça do Comércio, a large pedestrianised square bordered by pink arcaded buildings, through a triumphal arch over Rua Augusta and past a dozen blocks of shops, banks, cafés and restaurants up to Praça do Rossio.

The colourful **Alfama** district is reached by heading to the right along the north side of Praça do Comércio, turning up Rua da Madalena and then taking any of the roads uphill to the right. These lead to the city **Sé** (cathedral; open Tues–Sun) and into the heart of Alfama, with its narrow cobblestone streets, medieval and Moorish-influenced buildings, wrought-iron balconies with flowers trailing or washing flapping on lines, and its mix of small shops and bars. Across the northern corner of Alfama is the **Castelo de São Jorge** (open daily), the city's original Moorish fortress – well worth a visit and with wonderful views across the city.

On the other, western, side of Baixa is **Bairro Alto**, another historic district with narrow streets, which is now a wealthy residential district. It can be reached on foot or by tram. The 100-year-old lift (Elevador de Santa Justa) near **Praça do Rossio** no longer gives access, as it once did, but you can ride up and down in the ornate carriage of this wonderful iron structure, just for fun.

Other major sights you may want to visit include the **Fundação Gulbenkian** (open Tues–Sun; fee), which has an extraordinary art collection (it's to the north of Lisbon, reached by metro or taxi); the wonderful Manueline **Mosteiro dos Jerónimos** (open Tues–Sun; admission charge to cloisters) at Belém; and the **Padrão dos Descobrimentos** (Monument of the Discoveries), also at Belém. Along the riverside you will also find the National Coach Museum, the Maritime Museum and the Planetarium. If you have time, the stunning architecture and the Oceanarium at the **Parque das Nações**, created for Lisbon's **Expo '98**, at the eastern end of the waterfront, is worth a visit.

Further afield To the northwest of Praça do Rossio is the main railway station, Estação do Rossio (a striking Moorish-influenced edifice), from which there are trains to **Sintra**, a World Heritage site with a Moorish castle, palaces and cobbled streets. The journey takes about 45 minutes by rail, but check carefully on frequency and return times of trains to ensure you are back in time for your sailing. Trains to **Estoril** (about 20 km/12 miles) and **Cascais** (about 24 km/15 miles) run regularly from the Cais do Sodré station, which is on the waterfront, closer to the dock. This is a frequent service (journey times about 20–30 minutes) because it is used by commuters. Estoril has a popular casino and Cascais is still an active fishing village.

Map on page 107

TIP

Walking is the best way to see the city, but there is a good transport system of trams, both the old-style and the new *eléctricos*, buses, taxis and lifts *(elevadors)*. Avoid the inevitable traffic jams by using the efficient Metro.

BELOW: Bairro Alto and Castelo de São Jorge.

PORTIMAO

Portimão is a medieval city in Portugal's Algarve, on the estuary of the Arade River, with the river to the east and the vast, sandy expanse of Praia da Rocha, one of the area's most famous beaches, to the south. While most visitors come for the golf, the sand and the sun, the town is still a commercial port and the most important sardine canning centre on the Algarve. It's also well known for deep-sea sport fishing and, along the estuary, bird watching.

Around the dock Ships have to sail into the river mouth to dock. You'll see the massive sandstone cliffs and wind-sculpted rock formations of the Algarve beaches as you approach, as well as the modern development strung out along the shoreline. Look out for the sand-coloured ruins of 16th-century Fortaleza de Santa Catarina on Praia da Rocha. Only small ships can dock in the port – others use tenders to ferry passengers ashore. Most cruise lines run shuttles to the town centre and to the beach, 3.5 km (5 miles) from the centre.

Seeing the sights The best thing to do in Portimão is to wander around the **old centre**, which is relatively unspoilt, with two-storey houses with wrought-iron balconies and ornate stonework around the windows and doors. Look out for the colourful tiles *(azulejos)* ; you can buy these in several shops along with other ceramic items, some of it fussily ornate.

For lunch, head to the outdoor fish restaurants around the harbour and try the freshly grilled sardines with a cool *vinho verde*. The main **shopping streets** are Rua Comerciale and Rua Vasco da Gama, where you'll find hand-knitted sweaters, and local hand-painted porcelain and pottery. There's a big fish, fruit and vegetable market open daily (except Sunday) till 2pm and a massive travelling market on the first Monday of every month.

Further afield Twitchers will enjoy excellent birdwatching on the estuary of the Arade and the Alvor, a second river to the west of Portimão, flowing through low, pine-clad hills. Alternatively, cross the river bridge to Ferragudo, 5 km (3 miles) to the east, with a long, sandy beach and lots of waterfront restaurants. In the centre are the ruins of the Castelo de São João, which was constructed to defend Portimão from English, Spanish, and Dutch raids.

THE CANARIES

This archipelago of volcanic islands were called "the Happy Islands" by the Romans because of their sunny, temperate climate. There are seven main islands – Gran Canaria, Fuerteventura, Lanzarote, Tenerife, La Palma, La Gomera and El Hierro, divided into two main provinces. The province of Santa Cruz de Tenerife encompasses the eastern islands and has as its capital the port of Santa Cruz de Tenerife, while Las Palmas de Gran Canaria is capital of the western province.

Do try to eat ashore on the Canaries, as fish, fruits and vegetables are top-quality and recipes – a blend of Spanish, African and South American influences –

are memorable. *Papas arrugadas,* potatoes boiled in their skins and served with *mojo rojo,* a sauce of oil, garlic, peppers and paprika, are delicious. Fresh Atlantic fish, grilled and served with *mojo verde* – a coriander and parsley version of the famous sauce – is also excellent, as is *flor de Guia,* the cheese made in Gran Canaria. For dessert, you can feast on locally grown bananas and on *morcillas dulces,* made with grapes, raisins and almonds. Recommended local wines are Malvasía from Lanzarote and the red wines of El Hierro, La Palma, and Taraconte on Tenerife.

As regards **shopping,** the Canaries retain important tax privileges, even though they are now part of the EU, and are a good place to stock up on low-cost alcohol, cigarettes and perfumes. Locally-produced ceramics, basketwork, embroidery, leather goods and earthenware make good mementos or presents.

The Canary Islands are popular winter-sun destinations for UK cruise operators (particularly Canaries specialist Fred Olsen Cruise Lines) offering sailings from Dover or Southampton, and on these the islands are ports of call rather than home ports. However, Tenerife and Gran Canaria also feature as home ports for some repositioning cruises and fly-cruises.

Maps on pages 104 & 111

The Canary Islands are great for children and have a number of huge water parks.

TENERIFE

Tenerife is the largest of the Canary Islands and, scenically, one of the most dramatic places in the world. Dominated by 3,718-metre (12,198-ft) Pico del Teide, this fertile island offers visitors a variety of scenery from beaches to pinewoods, lush banana plantations, spectacular verdant valleys and striking volcanic scenery in the Parque Nacional de las Cañadas del Teide, where you can take a cable car *(teleférico)* up to the rim of the crater.

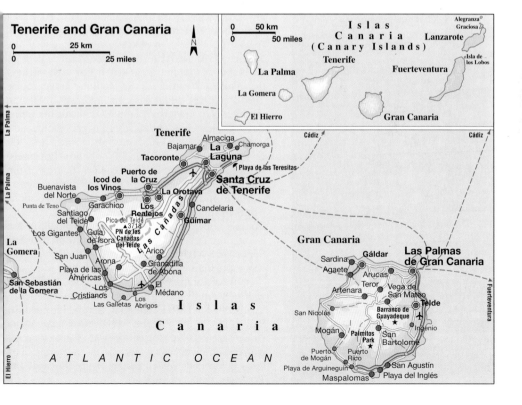

TYPICAL
EXCURSIONS,
TENERIFE
● **Las Cañadas
National Park and
Mount Teide**.
● **La Laguna**.
Tenerife's cultural and
religious centre,
usually combined with
a trip to **Esperanza
Forest** and the
Guimar pyramids.
● **Puerto de la Cruz**
and the **Risco Bello**
aquatic garden.
● **Loro Parque** on the
outskirts of Puerto de
la Cruz *(see main text)*.

BELOW: gnarled
rocks in El Teide
National Park.

Arrival and around the dock

As your ship approaches Santa Cruz, Tenerife's capital and the port for all cruise ships, look out for the towering peak of Mount Teide. Santa Cruz started life as a small fishing village but is now a sophisticated city with top-class bars and restaurants, interesting shops, fine architecture and well-stocked museums.

Getting to it all on foot, though, can be a long haul, depending on which part of the U-shaped harbour your ship has docked in. If you're lucky enough to dock at the bottom of the "U", no problem – just go through the port gates and you'll find the boulevard which runs to the city centre (and taxis right outside).

However, if your ship docks out on one of the port's long quays – no unusual occurence, as Tenerife attracts a lot of cruise ships – you'll face a 15-minute walk just to reach the port gates (though shuttle buses are sometimes laid on). Portaloos are erected on the quay at busy times, but there are no toilets in the terminal, so make sure you've been before you leave the ship.

Outside the port gates you'll find the café-lined town-centre boulevard and, just off it, two or three streets selling bargain-priced electrical goods and CDs – Tenerife's speciality. Also on the waterfront is the Plaza de España, a good place to start exploring, as most of the city's sights and shops are in the streets leading inland from this square.

Shopping

Embroidery and lace-making are traditional island crafts. You probably won't get as far as the Casa de los Balcones in La Orotava, where you can watch it being made, but the centre has 11 branches, some in Santa Cruz. Island craft speciality shops include Artenerife beside the port in Puerto de la Cruz and Artesanas El Sol in Calle Nicolás Estavánez, Santa Cruz. Cigars, hand-rolled from locally grown tobacco, are a good buy. Local wines, hard to find abroad, make good souvenirs, as does Tenerife honey *(miel)*.

Seeing the sights

As you face Plaza de España, the main bus station is to your left. Off to the right is the **Museo Municipal de Bellas Artes** (open Tues–Sun; free), which has some impressive pictures. Up Calle San Francisco is the **Museo Militar** (open Tues–Sat am), which houses El Tigre, the cannon whose shot shattered Admiral Nelson's arm in 1797. To the south of town is the 16th-century **Iglesia de Nuestra Señora de la Concepción** (church of the Immaculate Conception), the town's most important historical building. Nearby, the **Museo de la Naturaleza y el Hombre** (open Tues–Sun; fee) has exhibits illustrating the lives and death rituals of the islands' earliest inhabitants; **Mercado de Nuestro Señora de Africa**, a colourful fruit, flower and vegetable market, is also worth visiting.

On the main highway near the port stands the elegant new **Auditoria**, which is home to the Tenerife Symphony Orchestra. Behind it, beyond the **Castillo San Juan**, is the **Parque Marítimo César Manrique** (open daily; fee), an area of seawater pools, with trees, flowers and waterfalls. To the northeast of town is the long golden sweep of the **Playa de las Teresitas**, the city beach.

Map on page 111

Buses go directly from Santa Cruz bus station (check return times carefully) to the lovely seaside resort of **Puerto de la Cruz**, around 45 minutes' drive away. The main square is the **Plaza del Charco de los Camarones** at the heart of the historic district, surrounded by attractive buildings. To the east lies **Lago Martiánez** (open daily 9am–5pm; admission fee), an attractive lido with seawater lagoons, fountains and palm-fringed sands, a pleasant alternative to the black-sand beaches.

A 5-minute taxi ride to the west of town is **Loro Parque** (open daily 9am–6pm; admission fee), a vast theme park with aquaria, dolphin pools, sea lions, an underwater tunnel and a bat cave. You can get a free train ride there from the Avenida de Venezuela (to the east of Plaza del Charco in Puerto de la Cruz); yellow tourist trains run every 20 minutes.

If it's your first time in Tenerife, though, you really shouldn't miss a visit to **Parque Nacional de las Cañadas del Teide**, surrounding volcanic El Teide, the highest mountain in Spain (3,718 metres/12,198 ft). You can get close to the summit by the Teleférico (cable car), 8 km (5 miles) south of the park entrance and visitor centre. The park is covered with the lunar landscapes of lava fields and full of extraordinary gnarled rock formations, most impressive of which are **Los Roques de García**. This is one place you would be well advised to visit by a ship's tour, as it's very difficult to reach by bus and expensive by taxi.

GRAN CANARIA

Gran Canaria is the third-largest island in the Canaries, but its capital, Las Palmas, is the islands' largest city, a buzzing, lively place, with an enormous port. In the south of the island is the huge resort of Playa del Inglés, with stunning beaches, and the dunes of Maspalomas. Inland, you'll fine old towns like Arucas (the island's banana capital) and historic Teror, while the island's volcanic interior is a landscape of mountains and gorges.

Arrival and around the dock
Las Palmas' Santa Catalina terminal is a major hub for intra-island ferry services and cruise ships, so there is always plenty of activity as you arrive. City buses and those for other part of the island leave from a bus station right in front of the terminal, where you'll also find plenty of taxis, but there is an interesting area of Las Palmas to explore just 5–10 minutes' walk away.

Shopping
Beside the port you'll see **El Muelle**, a shiny commercial centre that houses large stores and small boutiques. There are lots of shopping opportunities in the narrow streets on the other side of nearby **Parque Santa Catalina**, a palm-dotted square full of outdoor cafés. Here you can take advantage of Las Palmas' tax exemptions when buying watches, jewellery and electrical goods. Look carefully though – some things are no cheaper than you would get at home. For good-quality island crafts, go to the **Federación para el Desarrollo de la Artesanía Canaria** (FEDAC) in Calle Domingo J.

TYPICAL EXCURSIONS, GRAN CANARIA

● **Arucas** and **Teror** (see main text).

● **Palmitos Park** visits an ornithological park a few miles inland from Maspalomas.

● **Ingenio** and **Barranco de Guayadeque** – the old sugar capital and a lush ravine.

BELOW: refreshment kiosk in Parque San Telmo, Las Palmas.

Navarro, in the Triana district, where the pedestrianised shopping street of Calle Mayor de Triana has a wide variety of shops.

Eating The best eating areas are along Playa de las Canteras and Vegueta *(see below)*. The former specialises in seafood, the latter has places serving typical island dishes. The Triana district also has some excellent, smart venues.

Farming is hard work in the dry terrain, but the volcanic soil is fairly fertile.

Seeing the sights To get to the attractive district of Triana, take a bus from Plaza de Santa Catalina to **Parque San Telmo**, and walk south along Calle Mayor de Triana. Cross a major highway and you reach **Vegueta**, the oldest part of the city, where Spanish forces first set up camp in 1478. A district of narrow, pretty streets, it centres on **Plaza de Sant Ana**, home of the **Catedral de Santa Ana** (open Mon–Sat, Sat am only; fee includes the museum) and the adjoining **Museo Diocesano de Arte Sacro**. Close by is the lovely 15th-century **Casa de Colón** (open daily, weekends am only; fee). Columbus is said to have stayed here, before setting off on his 1492 voyage, but there is no evidence to support this. Now an atmospheric museum with a pretty courtyard, it recreates the Age of Discovery with exhibits of navigational instruments, charts and weapons. Not far away, the **Museo Canario** (open daily, weekends am only; fee) holds the Canary Islands' most important collection of pre-Hispanic objects, including a room full of Cro-Magnon skulls and mummies.

To the north of the city (get a bus or taxi back past Parque Santa Catalina) is **Playa de las Canteras**, a 3-km (2-mile) stretch of sand, with shallow waters, lots of restaurants, and a good, local atmosphere, as it is frequented mostly by Las Palmas people and visiting Spaniards from the mainland.

Further afield If you prefer to explore independently of the shore excursions offered by the cruise line, buses run regularly from the port-side terminal (or another in Parque San Telmo) to most parts of the island – but leave plenty of time to get back. Or gang together in a group of four or more and negotiate a private tour by taxi; given sufficient numbers, this can work out a lot cheaper than the ships' excursions, but do double-check timings and establish a set rate in advance.

Playa del Inglés in the south (journey time about 50 minutes) is crammed with high-rise hotels, fast-food joints and amusements of all kinds; it is not to everyone's taste, but the beaches are wonderful. The resort adjoins the glorious **Maspalomas** sand dunes, now a nature reserve. The next major resort is **Puerto Rico** to the west. It is lively and family-oriented and has the best watersports facilities on the island. A little further on is the pretty harbour of Puerto de Mogán, with streets built over a series of little canals.

Teror, 22 km (14 miles) inland from Las Palmas and served by frequent buses, is a country town famous for the intricately carved wooden balconies of its splendid houses (one of which can be visited), and the **Basílica de Nuestra Señora del Pino** (open daily; free) which commemorates a vision of the Virgin Mary in the branches of a pine tree, seen by shepherds in 1481. The landscape through which you travel to get there is simply lovely.

The bus or taxi ride to **Arucas**, the island's banana capital, west of Las Palmas, ascends into the mountains. The old part of town has winding cobbled streets, and is overshadowed by the huge, neo-Gothic lava-stone church of **San Juan Bautista**. Both towns can be visited on an excursion, as can the lush gorge of **Barranco de Guayadeque**, where there are inhabited cave dwellings.

Map on page 111

BELOW: there are still lots of small working fishing ports in the Canaries.

LANZAROTE

TYPICAL EXCURSIONS, LANZAROTE

● **The Fire Mountains** travels to Timanfaya National Park *(see main text)*; often includes a wine tasting.

● **Jameos el Agua and the north** explores the former capital, Teguise, then on to the volcanic Jameos del Agua cave.

Lanzarote has one of the most attractive climates in the world, and is worth exploring for its spectacular moon-like volcanic landscape (cataclysmic eruptions in the 1730s and the 1820s smothered the island in lava, creating its weird, other-worldly terrain). The island has 300 volcanoes and has been designated a world biosphere reserve by UNESCO. Beach lovers can soak up the sun and enjoy the colourful volcanic sand beaches (red, white or black); or you can visit some of the buildings and monuments created by the Canary Islands' most famous artist and architect, César Manrique.

Arrival and around the dock   Arrecife is Lanzarote's main port, and cruise ships berth among the cargo docks at Muelle de los Marmoles; a small terminal nearby serves both cruise ship and ferry passengers with toilets, telephones and taxis, and shuttle services operate into the town centre, a 30-minute walk away. There are plans to redesign Muelle de los Marmoles exclusively for cruise calls, moving freight operations to other docks.

Seeing the sights   Arrecife's centre is compact and has shops and restaurants centred around the waterfront avenues Generalísimo Franco and León y Castillo. There is also a decent beach but, while pleasant enough, the town doesn't justify a long stay, although you might want to visit the **Castillo de San José,** a few kilometres north of the centre, a well-preserved fortress that houses a small but impressive **Museo de Arte Contemporáneo**. If you want to see more of the island and are not taking one of the ship's excursions, go inland to the bus station in Via Medular, or get a cab at the rank near the port.

BELOW: Lanzarote transport.

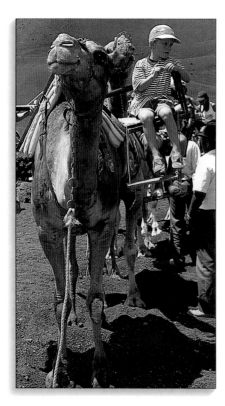

At **Tahiche**, 12 km (7 miles) away, visit the **Fundación César Manrique** (open Mon–Sat; fee), dedicated to the artist. It's based in his house, built on the lava fields and has subterranean chambers created by air bubbles in the lava flow. Manrique's influence can also be seen in the **Jardín de Cactus** (open daily; fee) at **Guatiza**, about 9 km (5 miles) north of Tahiche, where there are more than 1,500 varieties of cacti. Another 10 km (6 miles) will get you to the Manrique-designed volcanic caves of **Jameos del Agua** (open daily; fee). There is a saltwater lagoon inhabited by tiny blind albino crabs, unique to the island, and ethereal mood music accompanies your descent into the cave. You need to be fairly fit, though, as the approach involves walking up 150 steps. The spectacular **Cueva de los Verdes** is part of the complex.

Whatever else you do, try to visit the **Parque Nacional de Timanfaya** (open daily; fee), which encompasses the area known as Montañas de Fuego (Mountains of Fire) with their fantastical shapes created by solidified volcanic lava. This is an active volcanic area, and a guide will demonstrate this by pouring water down a tube into the earth, whereupon a geyser of hot water erupts. The point is also made in the nearby restaurant, where meat is grilled on heat rising directly from the ground. Just outside the park, at Echadero de los Camellos, you can take a camel ride up the volcanic slopes.

A ship's tour is definitely your best bet for visiting the park. You can go by taxi but you may face a long wait to get in, as precedence is given to tour buses.

Map on page 111

FUERTEVENTURA

Fuerteventura lies about 100 km (60 miles) from the African coast, which gives it a virtually rainless climate and a correspondingly arid landscape. Vast dunes of Saharan sand and inactive volcanoes dot the landscape and make it well worth exploring. Fuerteventura was conquered for the Spanish in the 15th century by Juan de Béthencourt, a Frenchman whose name is commemorated in the small town of Betancuria.

Arrival and around the dock Fuerteventura's Puerto del Rosario is less frequented by cruise ships than the other islands and its port facilities are fairly basic, though you shouldn't have trouble getting a taxi. The town centre surrounds the port, so the main areas of interest are within easy walking distance.

Seeing the sights The port itself has little of interest, but ships usually offer a Betancuria tour (you can go independently by bus, but they only run twice daily, and the trip takes around an hour). **Betancuria**, once the island capital, is a lovely old town. You can visit the 17th-century church, **Iglesia de Santa María**, and a good restaurant almost opposite. If you prefer the beach, the best local one is Playa Blanca, about 3 km (2 miles) south of Puerto de Rosario. If time permits, **Caleta de Fustes**, about 10 km (6 miles) south, has an attractive beach and marina or there's **Corralejo beach**, a 40-minute bus ride north.

TYPICAL
EXCURSIONS,
FUERTEVENTURA
● **Island tour** visits Betancuria and the lace-making town of Lajares *(see main text)*.
● **Beach transfer** to one of the Corralejo beaches in the National Park.

BELOW: parrots at La Lajita park in Fuerteventura.

LA PALMA

TYPICAL
EXCURSIONS,
LA PALMA

● **North of the island tour** includes Mirador de San Bartolomé and the Los Tilos evergreen forest, a protected reserve.

● **South of the island tour** visits the sanctuary of Las Nieves, the Caldera de Taburiente *(see main text)* and the Teneguía volcano.

Known as "the fair isle" for its magnificent landscape and rare flora and fauna, La Palma is famed for the remarkable clarity of its skies, which has led to an astrophysical observatory being built at Roque de los Muchachos. The island has one of the world's most impressive volcanic craters, Caldera de Taburiente, 1,500 metres (1,640 yds) deep and with a diameter of 10 km (6 miles), which is crammed with rare animal and plant life. La Palma's volcanoes are still active; the last eruption was in 1971, and beneath the cloak of lava, ash and basalt, archaeologists have found evidence of human habitation dating back to prehistoric times.

Arrival and around the dock La Palma's port, Santa Cruz, is one of the prettiest towns and harbours in the archipelago, and refreshingly uncommercialised. From the harbour gates to the main town is an easy 5-minute walk along Avenida Marítima, a delightful promenade lined with traditional whitewashed, red-roofed houses with intricately carved and brightly painted balconies, known as the **Casas de los Balcones**. Most areas of interest lie just off this main promenade.

Seeing the sights The Plaza de España, in the oldest and most beautiful quarter, has a **16th-century town hall**, the most important Renaissance building in the Canary Islands, and a magnificent *mudéjar*-style church, the **Iglesia de San Salvador**. Left of the square you can enjoy the colour and bustle of the covered market (a good place to try local delicacies), while further along the waterfront is the Plaza de San Francisco, where you'll find another lovely church whose cloister houses the **Museo Insular** (open Mon–Fri; fee). The

BELOW: Botanical Gardens, Madeira.

Centro de Artesania, also on this plaza, offers an opportunity to admire and buy local handicrafts. At the end of Calle Perez Brito is **El Barco de la Virgen**, a life-size replica of Columbus's ship, the *Santa María*, housing the **Museo Naval** (same hours as above).

The best way to get around the island is to take a tour. Most ships offer one to the volcanic **Parque Nacional de la Caldera de Taburiente** to enjoy the strange volcanic landscape and wonderful views. There is a black sand beach and a resort a short taxi ride from the capital at Los Cancajos, but exploring Santa Cruz and enjoying a lazy lunch is an excellent way to spend your time.

MADEIRA (FUNCHAL)

Known as the Garden Island because of the richly-varied plant life which thrives in its sub-tropical climate, Madeira has long been a popular destination – for British holidaymakers in particular. Never too hot in the summer, nor too cold in the winter, it retains a genteel appeal. Occasional attempts to attract younger visitors have failed because what makes the island so special has nothing to do with nightlife or beach parties and everything to do with scenery, shopping and sightseeing. Inland, there are some spectacular views from high points; along the coast there may be no beaches but there are a series of picturesque fishing villages which have inspired artists to travel many miles to paint them.

Madeira is either visited on an Atlantic Islands itinerary (Canaries plus Madeira), en route from the UK to the Mediterranean or, occasionally, on a transatlantic itinerary to/from the Caribbean, but the stay is always for a full day. Usually, ships leave in the early evening but at Easter, Christmas and on a few other special occasions, spectacular fireworks displays are staged above Funchal

Maps on pages 111 & 119

TYPICAL EXCURSIONS, MADEIRA

● Full-day **island tour**.

● Half-hour **helicopter flightseeing tour**.

● Trips to the **island's highest points**: Pico dos Barcelos; Eira do Serrado and the highest sea cliff in Europe – Cabo Girao.

● Half-day tour to **Botanical Gardens** and **Monte**, with a toboggan ride back *(see main text)*.

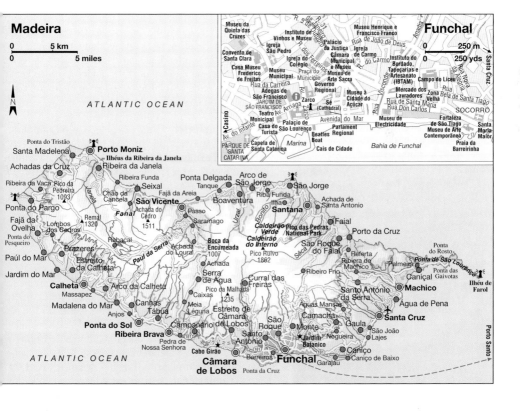

The famous Funchal toboggans.

late in the evening and ships will stay on for these. Occasionally, a ship will dock at the neighbouring island of Porto Santo, which has the beaches Madeira lacks, but not much else to see or do.

Arrival and around the dock The approach to the harbour at Funchal, which lies at the heart of a half moon-shaped bay, is pretty rather than spectacular. As the dock area is right by the city centre, there is an excellent view of the town and the wooded hills above. From the dock, turn right and – depending on how far along the quay the ship is docked – it is only a 10- to 15-minute walk either past a yacht marina lined with seafood restaurants on Avenida do Mar or past the tourist information centre on the parallel Avenida Arriaga, into the centre of Funchal. Along the coast to the left are most of the main hotels including Reid's, which has become a visitor attraction in its own right. There are buses or reasonably priced taxis running along the coast road.

Shopping At one time, it was common to see UK-bound cruise ships leaving Madeira with their holds full of island-made wicker furniture. The furniture is not quite so fashionable now but Madeira remains an excellent shopping port. As well as wicker, there is good embroidered lacework and tapestries and, of course, Madeira wine. Worth a visit, too, are the flower markets in Funchal.

Seeing the sights About half the island's quarter-million population lives in **Funchal**, making it one of Portugal's largest cities, but it has more the feel of a country market town. It is certainly walkable, with most of the more interesting buildings and shops in and around the main square, the **Praça do Município** – where there is a 17th-century church and an 18th-century palace (now the Town Hall – Câmara Municipal). Nearby, the Quinta das Cruzes is an **art museum** with attractive gardens that are open to the public. Further inland, the narrow cobblestone streets become steeper and are only for determined walkers. A short taxi ride will take you to the splendid **Jardím Botânico** on Camiho do Meiro.

Further afield Hiring a car is a good option in Madeira as they are inexpensive and it is a relatively easy island to navigate. But although there is little traffic and the island is small – less than 777 sq. km (300 sq. miles) – journeys can take longer than expected. As you drive up into the hills, the weather can change rapidly, with mist and rain reducing visibility, and there are also some narrow clifftop roads to negotiate, which can be slow-going if you get stuck behind a tour bus. Allow enough time, though, and it does give you freedom to stop at the many view points and interesting villages, and to sample one of the *levadas* – the scenic walks along the traditional irrigation system which draw many enthusiastic hikers to the island for longer stays. Buses are really only an option for short journeys, perhaps west of Funchal to **Câmara de Lobos** – the place which Churchill made famous with his paintings, and a good place for lunch – or northeast of the city to **Camacha**, the heart of the wickerwork industry.

The most popular excursion on the island used to be the **toboggan ride** down from Monte into Funchal, but opinions are now divided on this. It is certainly an experience, but the sledges can leave bruises where you'd rather not have them and there have been stories of visitors being stopped halfway down by sledge pullers and asked for more money – so much so that many cruise lines no longer include the ride in their tours for fear of being blamed for any bad experiences.

Maps on pages 104 & 119

CASABLANCA

Situated on the Atlantic coast of North Africa, Casablanca has been a port since the 5th century BC, but it really came to prominence when the modern city was created under French rule (1912–56); it was modelled on Marseille, with broad boulevards and an easy-to-follow layout, all streets radiating off the main Place des Nations Unies which lies within walking distance of the port. The French flavour is still strong enough to give present-day Casablanca a distinctly European air, and make it the most Westernised of North Africa's cities. It is now Morocco's commercial centre and its largest city.

Casablanca is also a key gateway to the Imperial Cities of Rabat and Marrakech *(see following page)*. Most ships call at Casablanca on sailings out to the Canary Islands and though it is rarely a home port, vessels spend a full day there to cater for shore excursions.

Arrival and around the dock Watch out for a sight of the spectacular Hassan II mosque *(see below)* as you approach Casablanca's 1930s-built port. From the dock, where you will find places to change money, the city centre is only about 250 metres/yds away so it's easily reachable on foot. There is also a railway station just 50 metres/yds from the port although, for places outside the city, you are best advised to take an organised tour or negotiate with one of the taxis waiting at the dockside.

Shopping Casablanca's Central Market lies just inland from the port off the Royale Avenue Pasteur (head left along the boulevard Moulay Abderrahmane and turn right). This is mainly a food market, spilling over with fresh produce, but it is also well worth visiting for the setting, in a beautiful Moorish courtyard. Look out for local mosaic ware, carpets and exquisitely worked leather items. There is also a daily antiques market on Boulevard Mohammed Ben, which runs in front of the port.

Seeing the sights The massive cream and turquoise-coloured **Hassan II mosque**, which overlooks the sea and lies at the end of Mohammed Ben Boulevard, deserves a closer look; its prayer hall can hold 25,000 people and has a sliding roof so that devout Muslims can worship in the open air; its soaring minarets are among the tallest in the world.

Just back from the waterfront is the **old medina**, or Moroccan quarter, which has some lovely examples of grand Moorish architecture. Further away from the seafront is the **new medina** – a facsimile built by the French – and this is a good place to hunt for rugs,

TYPICAL EXCURSIONS, CASABLANCA
● Full-day tour to **Marrakech**.
● Full-day tour to **Rabat**.
● Half-day **city tour** of Casablanca.

BELOW: dressed to impress in Casablanca.

The beautiful ablutions basin in the Hassan II mosque.

copperware and local crafts. Also worth seeing is the striking **Cathedrale du Sacre Coeur** which, although built in the 1930s, is elaborately neo-Gothic, complete with gargoyles, and has some fabulous mosaic-style stained-glass windows.

If you'd rather spend the day at the beach, take a taxi (be sure to negotiate the fare in advance) to **Mohammedia**, a popular resort roughly 30 km (18 miles) north of Casablanca, which has a marina, good beaches and even a golf course and casino.

Further afield Many visitors use Casablanca as a port for getting to the exotic desert city of **Marrakech**, the 11th-century "Pink City", which lies at the foot of the Atlas mountains and encapsulates all the exoticism of Morocco within its ancient reddish-brown walls. The chance to explore its winding alleys, hidden gardens and bustling bazaars should not be missed. Most tours will include the 12th-century Menara Gardens, which have wonderful mountain views, and the 800-year-old minaret of the Koutobia Mosque, which dominates the Marrakech skyline. Lunch, a visit to unforgettable Djemaa el-Fna square – with its musicians, acrobats and snake charmers – and a chance to browse in the bazaars will also be included.

Tours are also offered to **Rabat**, the modern capital of Morocco. These visit the Mohammed V Mausoleum, a prime example of Moorish architecture, and the Grand Mosque, which lies next door and has a famous unfinished minaret, the Hassan Tower, which has stood for eight centuries. The atmospheric Kasbah of the Oudayas and the magnificent archways of the King's Palace also feature on many tour itineraries.

BELOW:
Casablanca's old medina.

AGADIR

Map
on page
104

Agadir is Morocco's largest, most cosmopolitan resort, having been rebuilt after a devastating earthquake in 1960. Despite the consequent lack of historical sights, it's a pleasant place to spend a sunny day, with a magnificent beach, good restaurants, golf courses, a colourful souk and a pretty park – the Vallée des Oiseaux – which provides a pleasant walk from the beach into town. Agadir is used as a gateway to Marrakech, and ships usually stay a full day to allow time for excursions.

Arrival and around the dock The cruise terminal lies at the northwest tip of Agadir's main attraction, its 8-km (5-mile) long, crescent-shaped **beach**, which is kept very clean and largely free of touts. The central stretch is the best, a five-minute taxi ride or 15–20 minutes' walk along the coast road; here you'll find cordoned-off areas with sunbeds and umbrellas available for hire. The town and the souk lie behind the central area of the beach and it is probably best to take a taxi. They are lined up at the port, but agree the fare in advance or make sure the driver switches his meter on; most journeys around the town should cost less than 15 dirhams (£1/$2), though drivers may impose a supplement for pick-ups at the port. Beware of invitations to visit "my cousin's shop".

Shopping For local atmosphere and a good choice of handicrafts, head for the **souk**, a walled area on Rue Chair al Hamra Mohammed Ben Brahim where you can find local pottery, copperware and brassware. Other good buys are cedarwood carvings, chunky silver jewellery and the soft leather slippers known as *babouches*.

TYPICAL
EXCURSIONS,
AGADIR
● Full-day trips to
Marrakech (one and
a half hours' drive).
● Half-day tour to
Taroudant, one of
Morocco's oldest
cities.
● Agadir **city tour**.

BELOW: lemons and
olives play an
important role in
Moroccan cooking.

Seeing the sights Ships' city tours take you around the modern city and up to the ruins of the **old Kasbah**, something you could do by taxi if you wanted. Or you could walk into town, visiting en route the **Valle des Oiseaux**, a pleasant park with aviaries and a miniature railway. But Agadir is really about relaxation and enjoyment, rather than sightseeing; soak up some sun and enjoy a stately camel ride along the beach, then head for a good restaurant and a lazy lunch. There are some excellent places right on the waterfront, Rue de la Plage, offering everything from fish, kebabs and couscous to pasta, pizzas and omelettes – ideal for families with mixed tastes. Just back from the seafront, on Boulevard du 20 Août, you'll find pretty courtyard restaurants complete with greenery, fountains and cane chairs; this is also a good street to head for if you want to sample traditional Moroccan food. *Harira* (a thick vegetable soup) and *pastilla* (chicken or pigeon meat, lemon-flavoured eggs and almonds wrapped in filo pastry and dusted with sugar and cinnamon) are recommended. For excellent fresh fish, try one of the restaurants on Boulevard Hassan II.

You could work off lunch with a round of golf at the **Agadir Dunes Golf Club** or the **Golf Du Soleil Resort**, which has a spectacular Moorish clubhouse (10–15 minutes by taxi).

Further afield Most ships offer tours to **Marrakech** *(see page 122)* and **Taroudant**, an historic settlement dating from the 11th century and the chief market town of the Sous Valley, which is full of Berber stallholders; you can take a horse-and-trap ride around the 18th-century city walls. Both places could be visited independently by hire car, or by taxi if you negotiate a good price, but it is far better to go on an organised excursion, to ensure that you are back in time for the ship's departure.

TANGIER

Home to many nationalities and a crucible of different cultures and religions, Tangier is a wonderfully exotic city perched on the northwestern tip of Africa. Morocco's oldest continually populated city, its history dates back to 1000BC when it was founded by the Berbers. From 1932, Tangier was a tax-free zone and a playground for the wealthy, and although it was unified with Morocco in 1956, it still retains a cosmopolitan air and a blend of different cultures. It offers a true flavour of old Maghreb Africa, with its hidden courtyard gardens, grand mosques and churches and bustling kasbah. In a prime position overlooking the Straits of Gibraltar, Tangier is a port of call in its own right, rather than a gateway to other Moroccan cities. This means some ships stay for less than a full day.

Arrival and around the dock There is nothing spectacular about your arrival into port but the cruise ship dock (by the passenger terminal) is just 800 metres/yds from the city centre. Even so, there is a bus shuttle service into town and there are always plenty of taxis waiting. Money-changing facilities are available, but credit cards are widely accepted throughout the city.

TYPICAL
EXCURSIONS,
TANGIER
● Half-day **city tour**, centring on the medina (old town). Some tours include a drive along the coast to **Cape Spartel** lighthouse.
● Tetouan – a gracious town in a fruit-growing valley.

BELOW: brassware for sale in Tangier's old market.

Shopping The Kasbah – set at the highest point of the medina – is a hive of activity; here you can see local craftsmen practise the traditional arts of carpet weaving, leather working and pottery making, and you can buy the finished products – after a good haggle over a glass of mint tea. Look out for beautifully painted pots with complex, mosaic-like designs, and jewel-bright carpets.

Map on page 104

Seeing the sights Tangier's **medina** (near the harbour) is fascinating. It was originally built by the Romans and its grand mosque stands on the foundations of a temple to Neptune, god of the sea, while Petit Socco Square covers what used to be the forum. The **Grand Socco** (otherwise known as Place du 9 Avril 1947) is the heart of the medina and crammed with traders from the mountain villages. The Kasbah has, in its time, been home to Roman governors, Byzantine nobles, Arab princes and Portuguese crusaders – as well as the British, who demolished the ancient medieval fortress when they left Tangier in 1685. The fortress was rebuilt by Sultan Moulay Ishmael in the 17th century.

For a drink – or lunch – with a view, go to the **Hotel Continental**, a vast, white, 19th-century building on the edge of the medina, overlooking the harbour. Restaurants in the medina serve Moroccan specialities like *Samal Mahshi be Roz* – fish stuffed with rice and almonds, and served in a tamarind sauce.

Walking it off, don't miss a visit to the Kasbah's **Dar el Makhzen**, a fine example of Moroccan architecture, built in the 17th century as a home for the sultans and their harems. Nowadays it's an art museum. Another lovely building – also now an art museum – is the **former American Embassy**, which lies off Rue du Portugal near the Grand Socco. The elaborate fretwork surrounding its main gate is remarkable.

BELOW:
the lighthouse
at Cape Spartel.

Further afield If you've time, grab a taxi to the **Grottoes of Hercules**, which lie roughly 10 km (6 miles) to the west of the city and – according to legend – are the caves where Hercules recuperated from his 12 labours. Ships' tours go to **Tetouan**, a delightful 16th-century town overlooking the lush Oued Martel valley; and to century-old **Cape Spartel lighthouse**, at the confluence of the Atlantic and Mediterraean. You can hire a car and visit them independently, but excursions are the best way to make sure you are back in port in time.

TYPICAL
EXCURSIONS,
CADIZ

● A half-day **city tour**
(usually walking) of
Cádiz.

● A full-day tour of
Seville.

● A full- or half-day
tour to **Jerez de la
Frontera**, including
visits to sherry
bodegas.

CÁDIZ

Cádiz was founded as an outpost of the Phoenician trading empire; the Romans transformed it into Europe's gateway to Carthaginian Africa, the Muslims conquered it in the 8th century and the Christians regained it in 1263. With the opening up of the New World in the late 15th century, Cádiz entered its Golden Age. Since then, it has grown and prospered, although it is not as well known as its neighbour, Seville. It has some excellent beaches, but is strangely underrated and tends to attract more Spanish than foreign visitors. However, its compact old town, impressive cathedral and other historic buildings have a similar appeal to those of Seville, if on a smaller scale.The other reason for Cádiz's growing popularity as a cruise port is that it is close to Jerez de la Frontera, the centre of Spain's sherry-making industry.

Cádiz is the main cruise gateway to Seville, as only the smallest cruise ships (usually 5-star luxury vessels) are able to transit the Guadalquivir River and dock near Seville's city centre. Because most first-time visitors want to spend most, if not all, of the day in Seville, ships tend to arrive at Cádiz in the early morning and leave in the evening.

BELOW: a cruise
liner in Cádiz waits
for returning
passengers.

Arrival and around the dock Cádiz appears almost out of nowhere with only sea and empty coastline on either side of it. It is now a busy commercial port and naval base, which makes few concessions to passengers. There is no cruise terminal so, from the ship (usually docked at Reina Sofía pier), head left and it is a 5-minute walk to the port gate. This gate is opposite an information kiosk (good for maps, car hire and souvenirs) and is easy to miss. Don't – the next exit is a dusty 2 km (1 mile) along the quay. Almost immediately across the busy Avenida del Puerto is the main square, Plaza de San Juan de Dios, with a **tourist information office**, and the shopping area.

Shopping Joining the European Union and then the single currency ensured that the days of bargain-shopping in Spain have long gone. But there are still some interesting buys – leather goods and shoes, along with ceramics, represent good value because of the quality of their design and finish.

Cádiz has plenty of shops, some of the most interesting tucked away in the narrow side streets, while Seville has the range of stores and goods expected of a major international city. There are also street markets, including several selling only flowers, in both cities.

Seeing the sights The only point of booking a tour of Cádiz is to have the benefit of the information you will get from a guide. Otherwise, starting from Plaza de San Juan de Dios, it is easy to find your own way around a city which is compressed into a small isthmus. To the right behind the square is the 18th-century **New Cathedral** (La Nueva; open Tues–Sat am; fee). The view from the top is worth the long climb up its internal staircase.

Maps on pages 104 & 136

BELOW: the imposing New Cathedral.

Seville has some wonderful, authentic tapas bars.

BELOW: graceful arches in the Reales Alcazares.
RIGHT: La Giralda, the gilded tower.

Bear right again from the cathedral and you are in the old town, its narrow streets lined with tall **Moorish-style houses** with flower-decked balconies mixed in among some small shops. These lanes are too narrow for any traffic apart from a few noisy scooters.

There is a modest local museum, the **Museo Histórico Municipal** and the more ambitious **Museo Provincial** (open Tues pm–Sun am), with works by Zurbaran and Murillo. and a church, Santa Catalina, where Murillo fell from scaffolding before finishing his painting of *St Catherine's Mystic Marriage*. But the real pleasure of Cádiz is in just wandering about, stopping for the occasional drink or tapas at one of the many bars along the way.

Further afield   There are taxis (or car hire) to Seville or Jerez as an alternative to the ship's excursions. Taxis congregate where you disembark the ship. As ever, rates should be negotiated in advance but it is more difficult than in some ports to find drivers who speak good English. There are trains from Cádiz Cortadura station approximately every hour to Seville (journey time 1 hour 40 minutes), all of which stop at Jerez (journey time 40 minutes) on the way.

Seville, which is 120 km (75 miles) from Cádiz, is a large sprawling city which records Spain's hottest temperatures in midsummer, so don't expect to cover too much ground on foot if visiting in July or August, but it is a beautiful place for just soaking up the atmosphere. Start at the **Cathedral** (open daily; fee) and **La Giralda**, the great, gilded tower beside it, before visiting the **Reales Alcazares** (open Tues–Sun; fee), built in 1366 in *mudéjar* style (a mixture of Muslim and Christian influences). The palace and the gardens are magnificent. Both stand on the edge of the **Barrio de Santa Cruz**, the former Jewish

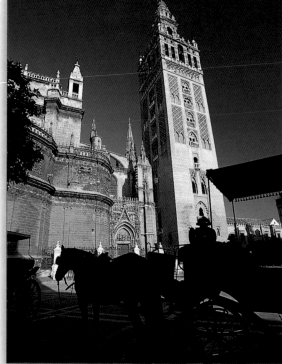

Map on page 136

quarter, where the narrow streets and squares of whitewashed houses and enticing restaurants are festooned with trailing bougainvillaea. If walking becomes too much, take a ride in one of the horse-drawn carriages that line the Plaza Virgen de los Reyes right next to the cathedral.

Jerez is only 38 km (22 miles) from Cádiz and, as well as the sherry *bodegas*, there is a bull-fighting museum, flamenco centre, equestrian school and clock museum. Check with the tourist information office at the port or when you arrive in Jerez for details of tours to all of these places.

GIBRALTAR

The British seized Gibraltar from Spain in 1704 and, despite the Great Siege of 1779–83, when the Spanish tried to retake it, it has remained in British hands ever since – a subject of great contention with the Spanish government. It is a popular port of call with cruise passengers because it offers bargain shopping and is compact enough to provide a wide range of experiences in a short period of time. Because it is so easily explorable, ships are not bound to spend a full day here. Bear in mind that customs regulations forbid cruise passengers visiting Gibraltar from going over the border into Spain.

Arrival and around the dock Gibraltar's main centre lies an easy 2-km (1-mile) walk up a straight road from the port. At the terminal you'll find toilets, telephones and money-changing desks (the currency is the Gibraltar pound – note that this is not legal tender in the UK). Shuttle services into town are usually offered from the port and there are plenty of metered taxis available for those who want to tour on their own.

TYPICAL
EXCURSIONS,
GIBRALTAR
● **Rock Tour** – short trips taking in the main sights, notably Europa Point, St Michael's Cave and the Apes' Den.
● **Dolphin Watching** aboard a boat with an underwater viewing cabin and hydrophonic sound equipment.

BELOW: when the apes leave, legend says, Gibraltar will fall.

SAILING THE STRAITS

Ships entering the Mediterranean from the Bay of Biscay, or from a transatlantic voyage, will pass through the choppy Straits of Gibraltar, the narrow channel that separates Europe from Africa, the Atlantic from the Mediterranean. Try to be on deck as the ship enters the Straits, not least because the turbulent water is the feeding ground for schools of dolphins and sperm whales.

As you enter the Strait (just 13 km/8 miles wide), from the Atlantic, the massive, limestone Rock of Gibraltar is on the port (left) side. The Romans believed this to be one of the two Pillars of Hercules, the second of which, Jebel Musa, is visible to starboard, in Morocco. The Strait is the only point at which water from the Atlantic can enter the Mediterranean basin. The depth and narrowness of the channel and the speed at which water flows through it means violent winds can often blow up unexpectedly.

Flocks of migratory birds pass over the Straits. From March to May and August to October, honey buzzards, black kites, storks, griffon vultures, short-toed eagles, ospreys, buzzards and sparrowhawks can all be spotted. Look out, too, for the massive water catchment slopes on the eastern side of the Rock, which used to catch rainwater that was stored in giant reservoirs inside the rock.

Shopping As you walk into the centre from the port you'll discover a large open-air courtyard mall crammed with shops and restaurants. Gibraltar's Main Street and its adjoining lanes and byways also offer plenty of shops, pubs and cafés – electrical goods are available here at bargain prices, but check that they are compatible with UK voltage. The tax-free haven of Gibraltar is widely regarded as one of the best shopping centres in the western Mediterranean and it's a good place to stock up on glassware, china, leather goods, alcohol, cigarettes and perfume. Also look out for silk and cashmere garments.

Seeing the sights After shopping you can enjoy a bit of peace at the **Alameda Gardens**, a gorgeous riot of flowering hibiscus, roses, mimosa and oleander. Don't miss a visit to **St Michael's Cave** (open daily; fee), an imposing natural phenomenon with an upper hall linked by subterranean passages to a lower cave which leads on to other chambers, 82 metres (250 ft) below the surface, with an underground lake. The upper hall is frequently used as an auditorium for concerts. The cave's stalagmites and stalactites make an impressive backdrop for twice-daily *son et lumière* performances.

The walled **Moorish Castle**, which is believed to date from the 8th century, is another sight that must be seen, not least for its Tower of Homage – which has survived 14 sieges – and the 48-km (30-mile) stretch of Great Siege tunnels, the **Upper Galleries** (tower and galleries open daily; fee), dug by the British when the rock was surrounded by Spanish and French forces in 1779. Inside the fortified walls of the castle you can see a daily Changing of the Guard ceremony. The castle complex is also well known for the wide variety of friendly – and mostly very English – pubs within it.

BELOW:
the powerful bulk
of Gibraltar.

See more Moorish relics at the **Gibraltar Museum** (open Mon–Sat; fee), built over a 14th-century Moorish bath house, which tells the Rock's story from prehistoric times, focusing particularly on the Battle of Trafalgar (1805). Admiral Nelson's ship, the *Victory*, carrying his body, preserved in brandy, stopped at the Rock for repairs en route to England. Many of the Trafalgar dead are buried on Gibraltar, although the **Trafalgar Cemetery** was, in fact, operational from 1708 to 1835 and was used for the burial of English seamen who died from wounds at three naval battles besides Trafalgar.

The Barbary apes – the only apes still living wild in Europe – are a joy to behold; there are about 160 of them, some living in the **Apes' Den** (open daily; fee). According to tradition, Britain will lose Gibraltar only when the apes go. During World War II, when numbers were diminishing, the army built the den in order to encourage the apes and bolster morale. Other apes live in the area surrounding the Great Siege tunnels, where you'll spot whole families and can watch mothers supervising the juveniles' play. Look out for black-furred babies but do not approach them – and beware if you see an ape pouting at you, as this is a warning to keep your distance.

A cable car runs from the Grand Parade up to the Rock Restaurant with magnificent views across Algeciras Bay and the Strait to Morocco's Rif Mountains. Halfway up, it drops visitors off to see the apes. At the top station, multi-lingual tapes can be hired to give you an overview of Gibraltar's history.

Gibraltar has more than 300 days of sunshine a year and there are several beaches on which you can make the most of it. Eastern Beach is the largest, but by far the prettiest is Catalan Bay, which has fishing boats and good seafood restaurants where you can have a pleasant lunch. ❑

Map on page 136

Red pillar boxes make British visitors feel at home.

BELOW: a sparkling view from the top of the Rock.

Military
Heritage
Centre
↓ Entrance

SPAIN

A cruise allows you to experience the many different faces of Spain, from the sultry south to sophisticated Barcelona and the individual atmosphere of the Balearic Islands

Map on page 136

T he ports of Mediterranean Spain are visited by almost all cruise lines operating in the western Mediterranean. They vary from the cosmopolitan city of Barcelona, often used as a home port, to smaller, less-visited places such as Palamós and Tarragona. Visitors will be struck by the different cultural influences: Barcelona looks to northern Europe, while more southerly ports, from Alicante to Málaga, betray Spain's strong, early links with North Africa. Some ports are primarily used as transit points for accessing inland sites of particular interest; Motril, for example, is the gateway to the Moorish treasures of Granada. Others are destinations in themselves: Valencia, surrounded by rice fields, is a much underrated city. The Balearic Islands, also on cruise lines' itineraries, have an atmosphere all their own, from Catalan-influenced Palma de Mallorca, to Maó, Menorca's capital, which has not shaken off all remnants of its past under British rule. For Cádiz and other Atlantic ports, see the previous chapter.

PRECEDING PAGES: sandy beaches attract many visitors to Spain. **LEFT:** the Alhambra, Granada. **BELOW:** smart Puerto Banus.

MARBELLA

Marbella has been the most prominent resort of the Costa del Sol since the 1970s, attracting celebrities and royalty to its smart marinas, flashy bars and sumptuous hotels. The port is visited mainly by small yacht ships like those of Windstar Cruises, as a day trip, and tenders are used to ferry passengers ashore. Other small ships, like the Sea Dream yachts, call at neighbouring Puerto Banus, where they moor just outside the main marina basin.

Arrival and around the dock The main impression when approaching the Costa del Sol is the scale of development, with pastel-coloured swathes cut into the sun-baked hillsides as yet another villa-and-golf combination goes up. Marbella itself, though, is a pleasant town with whitewashed houses at the centre around the Plaza de los Naranjos (Orange Tree Square). It's easy to walk here from the dock.

Seeing the sights People-watching and shopping are the main activities here. Sit in one of the cafés around Plaza de los Naranjos, wander the narrow streets browsing designer shops, visit the 17th-century church of **Santa María de la Encarnación** or the somewhat obscure museums, including the **Bonsai Tree Museum** and the **Museo del Grabado**, displaying contemporary art.

Further afield There are excursions to the *pueblos blancos* (white villages) and to Granada and Sevilla. You could do them alone, but the shore trips make it easier. Beaches on the Costa del Sol are busy, but nothing special. There's a water park a short bus or

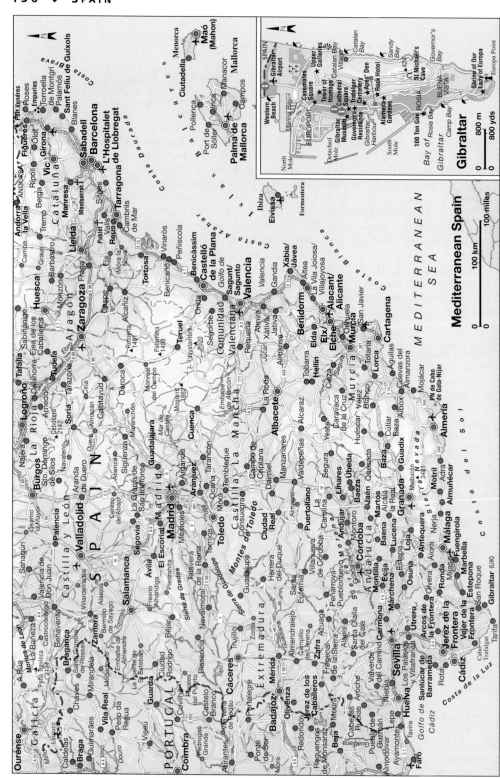

Mediterranean Spain

Gibraltar

taxi ride along the coast at Benalmadena, and numerous golf courses within easy reach – book in advance, especially in spring and autumn, and arrange to be met by a taxi at the port.

Map on page 136

MÁLAGA

Málaga is the principal city on the Costa del Sol, situated midway between Gibraltar, at the western end, and Almería, at the eastern limit. It has the main airport and is a busy port and a thriving commercial centre, quite different in character from the mass of holiday resorts either side of its boundaries. Most cruise lines visiting the western Mediterranean call at Málaga. Some lines will overnight here, giving passengers a chance to fit in more than one excursion.

Arrival and around the dock   Like many Andalusian coastal towns, Málaga is overlooked by a ruined, hilltop fortress, dating back to the 9th century. Gibralfaro fortress can be seen from the sea, perched high on its hill. Just below it is the 11th-century Alcazaba, another fine relic from the Moorish occupation. Two or three ships often berth at once in the Port of Málaga, which is spacious but somewhat lacking in passenger facilities. It's a 15 to 20-minute walk from the quayside to the city centre around Plaza de la Constitución and Calle Puerta de Mar, where there are plenty of bars, boutiques and department stores.

Seeing the sights   The park by the port is grimy and somewhat depressing. Instead, head for the lovely gardens around the **Alcazaba**, which also houses the local archaeological museum. Climb the steep path on the eastern side to the castle (or take a taxi) for views of the coast. Back in the centre, among streets of elegant, late 19th-century buildings, the **Cathedral**, on Calle Molina de Lários, dates from the 16th century and is built on the site of a former mosque in a mixture of Gothic, baroque and Renaissance styles. The **Museo Picasso** (open Tues–Sun; fee) opened in 2003 and houses one of the world's most valuable collections of the artist's work.

Further afield   Most cruise passengers use Málaga as a base from which to explore Andalucía. It is easy to hire a car and take off into the hills, although attempting to do **Granada** in a day is ambitious; there will be long queues to get into the Alhambra, so it's better to travel with a pre-booked coach party. **Ronda**, **Mijas**, **Marbella**, **Puerto Banus** and, if you're really ambitious and have a good 12 hours, the beautiful **Alpujarras** hills, are all accessible by hire car. Most of these places are also offered as ships' excursions.

MOTRIL

Motril is used principally as an alternative to Málaga as a gateway to the Alhambra in Granada and receives several large ships a year. The town is not like some of the more glamorous ports along the Costa del Sol and has no major attractions; it's better known as a commercial and fishing port and a shopping centre. Cruise ships usually call here for a full day.

TYPICAL EXCURSIONS, MARBELLA and MALAGA

● **Granada**. Alhambra, Generalife Gardens and the old city.
● **Ronda**. Spectacular town on a deep ravine.
● **Mijas**. The closest of the *pueblos blancos*.
● **Las Alpujarras**. Hills and villages.
● **Seville**. A long drive *(see page 128)*.

BELOW: the new Picasso Museum in the Buenavista Palace.

TYPICAL
EXCURSIONS,
MOTRIL and
ALMERIA

● **Granada**. The
beautiful Alhambra
palace, the Generalife
Gardens and lovely old
town. A tour will
ensure you get a
pre-booked ticket.
● **Mini Hollywood**
(from Almería). The
desert film set where
numerous Spaghetti
Westerns were filmed,
including *Once Upon a
Time in the West* and
A Fistful of Dollars.

Arrival and around the dock

Arrival and around the dock The eastern side of the Costa del Sol is characterised by vast fruit groves of sugar cane, oranges, lemons, custard apples, avocados, mangos and bananas, sprawling either side of the town. In the background are the snowy mountains of the Sierra Nevada. Motril itself is a busy commercial port and all most people see of it is the quayside as they board their bus for Granada. The old town centre is slightly inland, the other side of the busy highway which runs the length of the coast.

Seeing the sights There's a reasonably attractive town centre, with a baroque, 17th-century **Ayuntamiento** (town hall), the **Casa de las Palmas**, a 16th-century sugar mill with a small museum, and the **Parque de las Américas** is worth a short stroll for its lush vegetation, and to see the baroque shrine of Nuestra Señora de la Cabeza, built on the site of a former Moorish palace. Motril has two beaches, Playa Poniente and Playa Granada.

Further afield With a full day and a hire car you could drive into the **Sierra Nevada** mountains and go hiking in the foothills, the fabulous **Alpujarras**, with tiny, white villages, sheer slopes and rushing streams. There are some great local restaurants for lunch, too; mountain ham and trout are specialities. The Alpujarras trip is often offered as a ship's excursion.

ALMERIA

Several cruise lines use Almería as a day stop for visits to Granada, although it merits a day in its own right, with its Moorish architecture and desert landscape, once used as the setting for many a Spaghetti Western.

BELOW: a view of
the Alhambra.

Arrival and around the dock   The approach to Almería is stunning. The town lies surrounded by semi-desert at the foot of a range of mountains, its coastline alternating between long, sandy beaches and steep cliffs. The city has a North African flavour, with dazzling white Moorish-style houses, a ruined Alcazaba (fortress) and the crumbling Castillo de San Cristóbal, overlooking the harbour. Ships dock in the main harbour, right by the city centre.

Seeing the sights   There's lots to see in the old centre, with pleasant, shady squares, narrow, winding alleys, *Mudéjar*-style architecture and the pretty **Plaza Vieja**, a 17th-century arcaded square on which sits the pink-and-cream Ayuntamiento (town hall). The fortified cathedral, with four towers, was used as a safe haven from Berber pirate attacks on the city in the Middle Ages. If you climb up to the splendid **Alcazaba**, built in the 10th–11th centuries, be warned that there are some 200 steps. The Torre del Homenaje, at its highest point, dates from the 15th century. There's plenty of shopping within walking distance of the centre, too.

Further afield   If you hire a car you could visit Nijar, a village known for its rugs and pottery; the whitewashed Moorish village of **Mojacar**; or take in the stunning coastal scenery in the **Capo de Gata** nature reserve.

CARTAGENA

The ancient port of Cartagena lies on the coast of Murcia province, its great indented bay guarded by rocky promontories, each topped by a fort. It is one of Spain's busiest commercial ports and a naval base.

Map on page 136

TYPICAL EXCURSIONS, CARTAGENA
● The most popular excursion is a countryside and coastal tour that includes the nearby religious sanctuary of **Fuensanta** *(see main text).*

BELOW: Almería city has a Moorish character.

A little girl dresses up for a local festival, of which there are a great many in Spain.

Arrival and around the dock As you approach, look out for the old fortresses on the arid hilltops that flank the harbour, and for the naval ships patrolling the area. Cruise ships moor directly on the Alfonso XII quay in front of the city, the second largest in the region, and it's easy to walk into town. The area surrounding the Alfonso XII quay is undergoing improvements, with a new marina and shopping mall planned, as well as a new cruise terminal. A new National Museum of Underwater Archaeology will have gardens with bars and restaurants in pavilions evoking the architectural style of the early 20th century. The city centre is about five minutes' walk from the dock.

Seeing the sights Cartagena takes its name from the Carthaginians, whose leader, Hasdrubal, founded it in 221BC. Around the centre you can see the carefully preserved remains of old **city walls**, a castle constructed probably in Carthaginian times and a church that was formerly a 13th-century cathedral. The city used to be the Romans' principal settlement in their Iberian stronghold. It also bears Moorish influences from the centuries of Moorish rule in the area.

Further afield Cartagena is the gateway to the relatively undiscovered region of **Murcia**, with its pretty Costa Cálida (Warm Coast), huge inland lagoon (Mar Menor), ancient towns, mountains, fishing villages and world-class golf at **La Manga**, and the religious sanctuary of **Fuensanta**. All are best visited on a half-day shore excursion – striking out alone is not really feasible.

BELOW: Alicante's gaily paved promenade.

ALICANTE

Alicante is a busy, appealing city on the Costa Blanca, with strong historical links to North Africa. As the cruise ship approaches, the skyline is dominated by the massive hulk of the 16th-century Castillo de Santa Bárbara, from which there are sweeping views of the city and bay.

Arrival and around the dock The vast fortress, clinging to a huge, craggy rock, Monte Benacantil, is an impressive introduction to the city. The tangle of streets that make up the old town sprawls over the hillside beneath the castle, while the seafront is lined with modern buildings, bars, restaurants and smart yacht marinas. Ships dock right in front of the city, within easy walking distance of the main sites of interest.

Shoppers don't have to look very far – there are two shopping centres on the seafront, the Levant Quay and a mall and cinema complex at the western end. More enticing, however, is the old city and the broad promenade, Esplanada de España, lined with palm trees and paved with an enormous tri-coloured marble mosaic. Tourist trains and a tram run along here to the nearby beaches, although Alicante itself has a fine beach, Postiguet, within comfortable walking distance of the port.

Seeing the sights You can hike up a twisting path to the **Castillo de Santa Bárbara** (open daily; admission fee), 166 metres (545ft) above sea level,

Map on page 136

or take a taxi. The fortress dates from Moorish times but the site has been occupied since the Bronze Age. The **old quarter** below has a strong North African influence, with steep, stepped streets and whitewashed houses with hidden courtyards containing intricate mosaics. There's also a museum of modern art, and an excellent **Museo Arqueológico** (open Tues–Sun; fee). In the heat of the day, Alicante's a sleepy place, but by night the streets are packed.

Further afield If you hire a car you can visit **Elche** (also called Elx, as Alicante is gradually changing to Catalan names), a World Heritage Site about 30 km (18 miles) south on the motorway. It has a lovely garden, the **Huerta del Cura**, and is surrounded by Europe's most impressive palm forest. In August a mystery play is performed in the splendid **Basílica de Santa María**. Elche can also be visited on a cruise-line excursion.

VALENCIA

One of Spain's most interesting and underrated cities, Valencia is vibrant, exciting, stylish and unspoilt by tourism. It's easy to explore independently.

Arrival and around the dock Valencia is where paella was invented and the city is surrounded by rice-growing paddy fields, watered by an irrigation system laid down by the Romans. The busy port is some 4 km (2½ miles) from the city centre and the approach is not especially interesting, but the city itself is beautiful and the whole seafront has recently been renovated. Some cruise lines run shuttle buses from the port to the Plaza del Ayuntamiento in the centre; otherwise, there are plenty of taxis and they will cost about €6 one way. Most ships spend a whole day here, but even with a half-day call you can see most of the main places of interest.

Seeing the sights Most of the attractions are around the Plaza del Ayuntamiento, the central square where the town hall is located. The **Catedral** – a mixture of Romanesque, Gothic and baroque and allegedly the home of the Holy Grail – is further north, between Plaza de la Reina and Plaza de la Virgen. Its unfinished bell tower, called the **Miguelete** (open daily; fee) offers far-reaching views. The ancient **Barrio del Carmen** area, west of the cathedral, is good for shopping, atmospheric bars and restaurants.

The city's museums are well worth a visit. The **Museo de Bellas Artes** (open Tues–Sun; fee) on the north bank of the Turia River houses works by El Greco, Goya and Velázquez. The **Ciudad de las Artes y Ciencias** (City of Arts and Sciences Museum; open daily; fee) is a huge complex with interactive displays, an aquarium, a planetarium and an OMNIMAX cinema; while the Museo de Las Fallas contains floats and memorabilia from the city's renowned annual festival, Las Fallas, a wild event in March involving huge bonfires, spectacular fireworks and carnival parades; the festival celebrates the medieval tradition of carpenters building huge bonfires of wood shavings.

TYPICAL EXCURSIONS, ALICANTE

● **Guadalest**. An old Muslim settlement, within the walls of a ruined castle, reached through an idyllic landscape of orange and avocado groves (half-day tour).

● **Valencia and Cartagena**. Both are offered as day trips *(see main text for details of both)*.

BELOW: the Plaza del Ayuntamiento, Valencia.

TYPICAL EXCURSIONS, VALENCIA

● **Sagunto**. Some lines offer a trip to this historic town, once besieged by Hannibal, which has impressive Roman remains *(see main text).*

Shopping Valencia has great shops. For clothing, jewellery, perfume and leather, look around Plaza del Ayuntamiento. For antiques, traditional clothing and basketware, the shops in Barrio del Carmen are better.

Eating Everyone who visits Valencia should sample its paella. Almost everywhere sells it. A good one will contain chicken on the bone, large prawns, squid, clams, red peppers and lashings of saffron. Some restaurants do a vegetarian version. Also look out for *fideua*, a similar dish made with noodles, rice and black squid ink. Along the **Playa de las Arenas** you'll find a string of good restaurants (it's on the tram route, or take a taxi).

Further afield If you've seen the city before, or fancy a trip into the countryside, you could hire a car and drive through the beautiful Turia River valley. At **Chelva** are the remains of a Roman aqueduct, but it's about 50 km (30 miles). Closer (about 20 km/12 miles up the coast) is **Sagunto**, sacked by Hannibal in 219BC, where a Roman theatre in the hillside has been renovated, and there is an ancient castle to visit (ships' tours also visit Sagunto).

TARRAGONA

The ancient Roman city of Tarragona is a popular stop on the Catalan coast, with the sandy beaches of the Costa Dorada (Daurada in Catalan) extending for miles to the north towards Barcelona. This stretch of coast is known for its calm water and amazing quality of light. Outside the city, sandy beaches and small resorts back onto carob trees, vineyards, hazel and almond groves (beautiful when in blossom in early spring) and gnarled olive trees.

BELOW: the splendid door of Tarragona's cathedral.

Map on page 136

Arrival and around the dock As the ship approaches port, look out for the "Mediterranean Balcony", a steep cliff on which part of the town is built. The busy commercial port is huge, with several different quays. The inner basin is directly in front of the old city but cruise ships usually moor further away from the centre and shuttle buses are used to ferry passengers into town.

Seeing the sights There's plenty going on around the inner marina basin, with shops and restaurants open until late at night, but most people come here for the Roman antiquities, dating back to the 3rd century BC, when Tarragona was in its heyday. You can follow the **Passeig Arqueològic**, a walking tours of the ancient city; it is long and fairly arduous, with lots of steps and cobble-stones, but it's worth it to see the spectacular **amphitheatre** (near the beach) and the **Museu d'Arqueologia**, which houses an important collection of Roman artefacts. You'll also see the **old city walls** and a two-tiered **Roman aqueduct**. The part-Romanesque **Catedral**, which was begun in the 12th century, is famous for its Gothic façade and the intricately carved figures on either side of the main door.

Further afield The impressive **Monestir de Poblet** (open daily; fee) was founded after the reconquest of Catalunya from the Muslims. It is still inhabited by monks but can be visited (some cruise lines offer excursions). If you prefer the beach, **Salou** is one of the nearest resorts, with lovely golden sands, and the **Port Aventura** theme park (open daily in summer; fee) which may interest anyone travelling with children (and some who aren't). Salou can be reached by train and the theme park has its own railway station.

TYPICAL EXCURSIONS, TARRAGONA
● **Archaeological Walk** – 5-hour tour of the main sights.
● **Poblet**. There are sometimes trips to the ancient monastery *(see main text)*.

BELOW: there's always street entertainment on Barcelona's La Rambla.

BARCELONA

BELOW: one of
Barcelona's classy
design shops.

Established around 230BC, probably by the Carthaginians, Barcelona was developed as a port by the Romans. The old city, known as the Barri Gòtic (Gothic Quarter), has buildings dating from the 13th–15th centuries, but with some Roman ruins still visible. Christopher Columbus' triumphant return in 1493 from the first voyage to the New World was to Barcelona. He is commemorated entering the city on horseback in pictures and engravings, and there is a monument to him in front of the harbour *(see page 147)*.

Barcelona was the capital of Catalunya long before the emergence of a unified Spain, and today it is a bilingual metropolis. The Catalans are fiercely proud of their language, which could not be published or taught under Franco's dictatorship, and Catalan (Catalá) has prominence on all signs and most menus. However, because so many people come from other parts of Spain, especially the south, to work in the city, Spanish (Castillian) is spoken just about everywhere. Because of this influx, Catalunya is the source of many styles of flamenco (not traditionally Catalan music), now being rediscovered and revitalised by new generations of guitarists, singers and dancers.

Visual art has also flourished here in the Mediterranean sun. Picasso, Miró and Tàpies all lived in Barcelona, and are represented in significant museums dedicated to their work. No one made more of the city in their image than the architect Antoni Gaudí, though. His joyous, playful style weaves across the city, and his basilica, La Sagrada Familia, begun in 1882 and still under construction, is an incomparable marvel, and an essential part of a visitor's itinerary.

This is a vivacious and cosmopolitan bar town, a shoppers' paradise, a living museum of architecture and a city of gorgeous parks. A first visit for just a day

can't be more than an introduction, but the city isn't overwhelmingly large and it is easily accessible, so treat it like tapas and pick just a few of Barcelona's many specialities to taste.

Map on page 146

Arrival and around the dock The first view of Barcelona from the sea is the green mount of Montjuïc, topped with a castle and pine trees. The cranes of the harbour appear below, and the waving masts in the marina behind the modern shopping complex. Then the city comes into view – an attractive sprawl, predominately in sandy yellow and white, with the coast stretching away beyond. From the very first sight, it becomes obvious that Barcelona is a relaxed city, in an elegantly chaotic way. Ships dock at the south end of town. Most cruise lines lay on shuttle buses to the city, usually stopping near the Sector Naval. Black-and-yellow taxis line up to take passengers into town or to out-of-town sites. By cab or by shuttle bus, the foot of La Rambla is a 10-minute drive from the quay, around sweeping roads through working docks. At the terminal there are souvenirs for sale, a duty-free shop and a wine and spirits stall, but the goods and prices are easy to beat in town.

A green tree creature is not an unusual sight in Barcelona

Ships berth close enough to the town that, if you aren't tied to an excursion, you might linger over breakfast and disembark at a leisurely hour. Most of the major sights of Barcelona are close enough together that a few bus, taxi or metro rides can make a go-it-alone itinerary a relaxed affair (you can get inexpensive multiple-journey tickets – *tarjeta multi-viaje* – valid for bus and metro). If you are planning on a beach day instead, though, the sands can get crowded early on, so it might be better to get coffee and croissants at the first sitting on board, then make for the beaches.

BELOW: the Olympic Port.

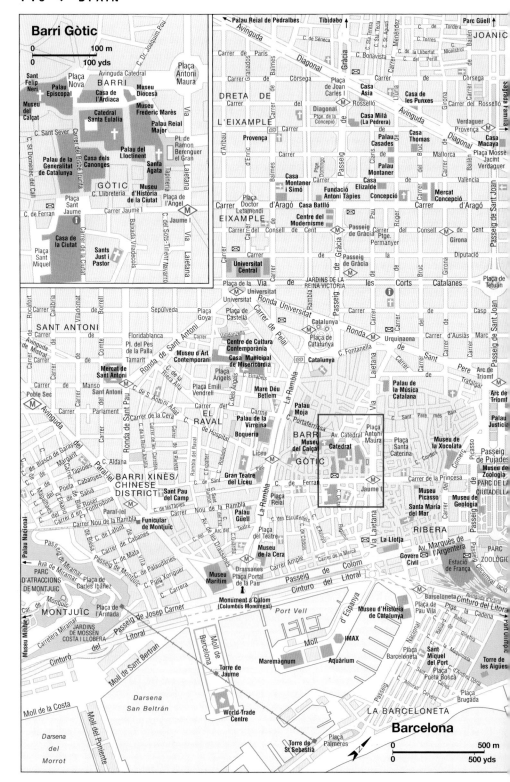

Barcelona

Shopping Barcelona has some of the best shopping in Europe, and prices remain low by comparison. Market stalls – especially those in La Boqueria (see page 148) – proffer exciting foods, leather goods, ceramics and souvenirs. The Mercat de les Encants, a flea market, is highly recommended on Monday, Wednesday, Friday and Saturday (Plaça de les Glòries metro stop). Fashion, jewellery and gifts are presented in an elegant and appropriately expensive setting along the Passeig de Gràcia. For a one-stop shopping trip, the huge department store El Corte Inglés has foods, wines, perfume and clothing all under one roof in the Plaça de Catalunya. Nearby are major fashion chains like Gap, and the Spanish chain store Zara is particularly good value here. Shoppers with an afternoon cruise departure need to be alert to siesta hours. This is true throughout the Mediterranean, but the shopping here is so good and the long lunch hours go on till about 5pm, so it could be easy to miss the boat, so to speak. However, some of the major stores adopt northern European hours and stay open all day.

All dressed up for the fiesta – Barcelona has lots and they're all good fun.

Eating Barcelona is a gourmet's delight. As well as a wealth of seafood, there's an emphasis on robust, regional cooking. The city also attracts chefs from other parts of Spain, especially Galicia and the Basque country. The Passeig de Gràcia area has some upmarket places, the Barri Gòtic some very typical ones, and the Port Olímpic some good choices among more average ones. And there are tapas bars everywhere. Two local institutions are the Set Portes, near the waterfront and Francia station, and Los Caracoles, in the Barri Gòtic.

BELOW:
the Plaça Reial
is always busy.

Seeing the sights The **Monument a Colom** (Columbus Monument) at Portal de la Pau, has a lift (fee) that elevates visitors to a spectacular view of the city and harbour. The statue of Columbus stands high on an ornate column. It's a perfect introduction to Barcelona as it is right by the harbour and the enclosed viewing gallery provides an enjoyable orientation. The windows carry diagrams annotating major features of the view.

By the modern marina, over the gracefully arched swing-bridge known as **La Rambla de Mar**, is the **Port Vell**, on which you'll find the Maremàgnum shopping complex with souvenir and fashion shops, numerous restaurants, a cinema, indoor street-theatre, music and clowns. Like the whole marina, it teems with people; yachties scuttling around on boats, women carrying shopping, tattooed sailors, office workers out for a stroll, teenagers hanging out, or cruise passengers and other tourists. Beside it is the huge **L'Aquàrium** (open daily; fee).

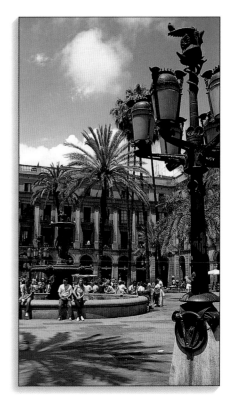

Tiny cable-cars of the *teleferic* network take you over the harbour from Barceloneta to the World Trade Center on the Moll de Barcelona, and then to the foot of Montjuïc hill. The ride over the water is inexpensive and guaranteed to be exhilarating.

Facing the marina, the port end of **La Rambla** has pavement cafés on one side and tattoo parlours, peep shows and sex shops on the other. In the evening this area can get quite rowdy. The centre of the tree-lined Rambla is a paved area, with cafés, street performers,

*The sinuous façade
of Gaudí's Casa
Batlló*

pavement artists and market stalls selling everything from postcards to parakeets. From early in the morning to very late at night, this strip is a non-stop show. The shops and cafés become more upmarket the further you go up La Rambla.

Off La Rambla, about a third of the way up and to the right, is **Plaça Reial**, an arcaded square with palm trees, a fountain, and art nouveau street lamps designed by the ubiquitous Gaudí. Twinned with the Piazza Garibaldi in Mexico in 1998, the square has a range of bars and restaurants, from no-frills backpacker haunts and super-cool flamenco clubs to the stylish and popular Quinze Nits and Taxidermista restaurants. Keep an eye on your belongings while in the square – it has a bad reputation for opportunistic thieving

Further up La Rambla, past an intriguing umbrella shop and off to the left is **La Boqueria** covered market, officially known as **Mercat Sant Josep**. This is primarily a food market, but there are clothes, luggage and leather stalls, too. Under the cool span of the iron canopy, a fantastic array of fresh food, nuts and cured meats are invitingly displayed. Stalls offer *jamon*, fresh fish on rafts of ice, olive oils and delicious *pan de datil* (wrapped date cake). Inviting snack counters serve meats, sandwiches, paella, coffee and beers, often under posters of allegiance to a football team or political issue.

The **Gothic Quarter** (Barri Gòtic) covers the area bounded by the ancient Roman walls – some of which are still preserved – and lies roughly between Avinguda de la Catedral and Carrer dels Escudellers, and between Carrer Avinyó and Via Laietana. Behind the Cathedral are a warren of narrow streets linked to squares. Cafés and bars are plentiful, and one or two fine restaurants are to be found here too. **La Seu** (cathedral; Plaça de la Seu; open daily; free) was begun in the 13th century, and has a façade added in the 19th century. There are high

Map on page 146

Gothic arches and a blend of medieval and Renaissance styles. The cathedral precincts also encompass three medieval palaces: **Cases dels Canonges**, the **Pia Almoina**, a recently restored Gothic treasure, and the 15th-century **Casa de l'Ardiaca** (Archdeacon's Residence).

In the Plaça de Ramón Berenguer are Roman walls, a 40-meter (120-ft) bell tower and a bronze equestrian statue of Ramon Berenguer III. Plaça de Sant Just is perhaps the best evocation of old Barcelona, a proper neighbourhood square with local shops, a church, a Gothic fountain and the 13th-century Palau Moixó.

Gaudí The architectural gaieties of *modernista* architect Antoni Gaudí weave throughout the city (*modernism* is the Catalan version of art nouveau). In street lamps as well as unmistakable edifices, his joyous and unpredictable curves are everywhere. The **Palau Güell** (Carrer Nou de la Rambla; open Mon–Fri, guided tours; fee) is the house he designed for his patron, Count Güell. The **Parc Güell** (open daily; fee), with sinuous, organic fantasies of steps, mosaics and gardens also contains the Casa-Museu Gaudí, where he lived for the last 20 year of his life. It lies to the northeast of the city and it's best to take a taxi.

The pale, softly waved walls of **La Pedrera** (Passeig de Gràcia; open daily; fee) are only the dressing for this extraordinary apartment building, officially called Casa Milà. Inside are curved windows and courtyards, graceful staircases and a sinuous, vaulted basements. Part of the exhibition in the lofts demonstrates how Gaudí used gravity to model structures with wires and weights, with a skeletal model of the Sagrada Familia upside down. The roof of La Pedrera is a treat, with undulating arches, fantastic chimneys and ventilators of glass and pottery shards, and a fabulous view over the city.

TIP

Continue northeast along the waterfront and you'll come to Platja Barceloneta, the city beaches, and the Port Olímpic, in front of the "village" built for the 1992 Olympics.

LEFT: La Sagrada Familia.
RIGHT: sculpture at the Fundació Miró.

Pablo Picasso – his museum is one of the most visited sites in Barcelona.

But his masterpiece is unarguably the extraordinary, unfinished temple, **La Sagrada Familia** (Metro Sagrada Familia; open daily; fee). Gaudí worked on this project for over 40 years, until his death, and it is still, very gradually, being completed by contemporary artists and architects.

Museums There are more than 100 museums and art galleries in Barcelona, with themes as varied as chocolate in the **Museu de la Xocolata** (Antiguo Convent de Sant Agustín; open daily; fee); erotica at the **Museu de l´Erotica** (La Rambla; open Tues–Sun; fee); and perfume in the **Museu del Perfum** (Passeig de Gràcia; open Mon–Sat; fee). The **Museu Militar** (Castell de Montjuïc; open Tues–Sun; fee) presents an extensive collection of military effects and model castles in the fort, spectacularly sited at the top of Montjuïc. The **Museu Marítim** (La Rambla; open daily; fee), housed in the splendid, Gothic royal shipyards, contains fascinating exhibits on naval history. The **Museu d'Història de la Ciutat** (Plaça del Rei; open Tues–Sun; fee) in the Barri Gòtic takes you underground to the city's Roman foundations, and up into the former royal palace buildings. The **Museu d'Història de Catalyuna** (Moll de La Barceloneta; open Tues–Sun; fee) is a bright, modern museum that concentrates, as the name suggests, on Catalan history.

The **Fundació Joan Miró** (Parc de Montjuïc; open Tues–Sun; fee) opened in 1974, purpose-designed by architect Josep Lluís Sert, a close friend of Miró. Worth visiting just for the view and the luscious setting in parkland, the gentle shapes and luminous colours of Miró's work come to life here. Among the 10,000 works of this Catalan artist are paintings, graphics and sculpture. Highlights include sculptures on the roof and a fountain of flowing mercury.

BELOW: the Dalí Museum in Figueres, the town where he was born.

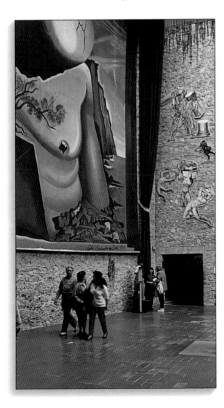

The **Museu Picasso** (Carrer Moncada; open Tues–Sun; fee) is unmissable. Picasso had a great attachment to Barcelona, where he grew up, and while he did not want his work exhibited here during Franco's regime, he relented towards the end of that period and, in 1970, donated over 2,000 of his works, including paintings, sculptures, engravings and drawings, some dating from his childhood. The museum is housed in a series of adjoining medieval palaces.

Sailing away from the dancers, bars, shops and museums of Barcelona is nearly always followed by the promise of a return visit.

Further afield The mountain range and monastery of **Montserrat** (often offered as a ship's excursion) can be reached independently by train from the Plaça d'Espanya (1-hour journey). The highest peak in the range is 1,235 metres (4,050 ft), the views are amazing, and the monastery, housing La Moreneta (Black Virgin) is an important place of pilgrimage. A famous boys' choir sings here twice a day. There are plenty of facilities up here for the constant stream of visitors.

The sophisticated resort of **Sitges** can be reached by road if you hire a car or by a 40-minute train journey from **Sants** station, if you ensure you get a direct train. This pretty place has three good little museums, a baroque parish church, two lovely beaches and a handful of excellent restaurants.

PALAMOS

Palamós is a quiet, somewhat isolated fishing port on the Costa Brava, used principally for access to the Salvador Dalí Museum in Figueres.

Arrival and around the dock Ships dock on a long pier next to the deep-water harbour, crowded with fishing boats. The arrival of a cruise ship is a big event in Palamós and locals will often turn out to greet the ship and have a good look, particularly if it's one of the beautiful sailing ships of Star Clippers.

Seeing the sights Palamós itself is pleasant, and pretty much off the beaten track, apart from a growing business in summer homes for British ex-pats. Tuesday is market day and there's an evening fish market, too. The town centre has several fish restaurants and bars. However, most visitors to Palamós visit the spectacular Salvador Dalí Museum in **Figueres**, a couple of hours away by coach, with several of Dalí's more prominent pieces on display. The friendly market town of Figueres is pleasant to wander around after visiting the museum.

THE BALEARIC ISLANDS

The Balearic Islands, lying off the northeast coast of Spain, form one of the Spanish autonomous provinces. Historically part of Catalunya, they have their own versions of the Catalan language, and the people are fiercely proud of their island identity. Although sometimes associated with the tackier kind of package holidays, the Balearics are beautiful islands with many peaceful corners and historic towns and, in Mallorca, some rugged mountain scenery.

Maps on pages 136 & 146

TYPICAL EXCURSIONS, PALAMOS

● **Salvador Dalí Museum** in Figueres (half-day tour).

● **Medieval Girona** (full-day).

● Roman remains and mosaics at **Empuries** (half-day tour).

● **Tours of the area**, including the ancient villages of Ullastret, Peratallada and Pals (half- or full-day tour).

BELOW: an Ibiza woman not on her way to a disco.

IBIZA AND FORMENTERA

**TYPICAL
EXCURSIONS,
IBIZA**
● **Formentera**. Full-
day trip to the
neighbouring island
(see main text).
● **Boat trips** and
diving trips to the
Medes Isles (half-day).

Despite its reputation as club capital of Europe, Ibiza is a beautiful, mainly peaceful island with a fascinating history and lots to see. An increasing number of ships calls here in summer; if possible, pick one which spends the evening or at least departs after dark, as Dalt Vila (the old town overlooking the port) is stunning at night when it's all floodlit.

Arrival and around the dock It's worth being on deck for the arrival in Ibiza. If you sail close to Formentera, the sleepy island off Ibiza's southeast coast, look at the incredible hue of turquoise in the water.

Closer to Ibiza itself, the capital, Eivissa, as it is now known in Eivissenc (the local dialect of Catalan), sprawls around the port and up the hill behind it, where the massive ramparts of Dalt Vila (High Town) are in amazing condition. The old town itself clings to the hilltop and is packed with historical interest. The row of crumbling old houses on the narrow spit which juts out into the harbour is Sa Penya, the former fishermen's district. Much of the rest of what you can see is reclaimed land, but this is the original thing.

Ships dock right up against the Passeig Marítim. Walk from here towards Dalt Vila and you're in the heart of the action. The area of Sa Marina, around the base of the rock, is packed with open-air bars and restaurants (none of them cheap), market stalls and hippy-chic boutiques. After sunset, the area is packed with revellers parading the streets before heading to the nightclubs.

Seeing the sights Climb up the steep, narrow streets to Dalt Vila and another world unfolds: one of whitewashed houses, cobbled alleys and old

BELOW:
Ibiza's nightlife is
not for the timid.

ladies knitting in shady doorways. The massive city walls date from the 16th century. Inside the walls are the squat **Catedral de Santa Maria de las Neus** and the beautifully laid-out **Museu Arqueològic de Dalt Vila** (open Tues–Sun; fee), with relics from prehistory and the Phoenician and Punic occupation of the island. There's also a solid-looking castle and a small **Museu d'Arte Contemporani** (open summer: Tues–Sun; fee).

Maps on pages 136 & 156

The rest of Ibiza is easy to explore independently as it's so compact and has a good bus network from the Passeig Marítim, but you will need to hire a car or scooter for the more out-of-the-way places. Motorboats run shuttle services from Eivissa to various bays and resorts; on Wednesday, there will be regular boats towards Es Canar in the north, where there's a big hippie market, purely for tourists but colourful nonetheless.

The beauty of Ibiza is the walking (Sa Talaiassa in the south is a two-hour trail from Sant Josep, with breathtaking views from the top) and the tiny, hidden bays around the southwest coast. Sant Antoni and Platja d'en Bossa, the main resorts, are packed in summer. For a bare-all beach, try Ses Salines in the far south. It's a nudist beach with a couple of glamorous *chiringuitas* (beach bars).

Bright window boxes contrast with the whitewashed walls in Ibizan towns.

Further afield Some cruise lines offer excursions to **Formentera**, although you may as well do this independently. The hydrofoil (from near where the cruise ships dock) takes 30 minutes. Hire a bicycle at the dock on Formentera and take off. The island is as sleepy as they come but you'll see salt pans, fish hanging out in the sun to dry, megalithic remains and very old stone walls and ancient windmills. At the opposite end of the dumbbell-shaped island is **Faro de la Mola**, a lonely lighthouse featured in Jules Verne's novel, *Journey Round the Solar System*. You have to be pretty fit to cycle this far – the round trip is 40 km (25 miles). The island's bus service is unreliable but cars can be rented at the port.

BELOW: Palma's Palau de l'Almudaina is as imposing as the cathedral.

PALMA DE MALLORCA

Mallorca's distinctive history dates back to Bronze Age civilisations. Over the millennia, visitors, invaders and conquerors have all left their marks on the island; there are architectural relics and remains from the Phoenicians and Carthaginians, the Arabs, Greeks and Romans, all suffering repeated attacks by the Vandals. Since then the 13th-century Catalan conquerors and more recently, tourists have brought their own contributions to the island's culture.

The city of Palma is sprawling and busy, but most of the highlights are concentrated in a relatively small area, in and around the old town. Most cruise ships visit Palma for a full day, and many stay as late as midnight, so you can enjoy the restaurant and bar life.

Arrival and around the dock A strip of land appears on the horizon about three hours before the ship actually reaches Palma. It grows larger and closer until the grey craggy cliffs tumble into the sea and the golden sands come into view, splashed with white spray. Closer to the coast, dinghies with furling sails and sleek fishing boats cut between the ports and bays of the dramatic coast.

As the ship slows to turn into the harbour, the bulk of the **Castell de Bellver** commands the bay from the nearest hill to the west, and the Gothic slabs of the **cathedral** buttresses stand out from the east of town, dominating the bay from all sides. **The terminal** is airy and modern, a two-storey building with a duty-free shop (city maps and camera film available) at the rear. Passengers disembark at the upper level, and either take coaches from the ground floor for excursions, or take the covered walkway for about 10 minutes to the bus terminus, where taxis also await. Boats can be rented from here, too.

Shopping Head for **Porto Pi Centro**, an easy walk from the bus terminus, a sweep of retail-drome housing some famous stores, including Zara, Mango and Disney. **Avinguda Jaume III**, in the city centre, is the major shopping street, lined with chic leather and clothing shops as well as department stores, including a huge branch of Spain's biggest, El Corte Inglés. Also on this street is an outlet of the quirky, and currently fashionable, shoe company, **Camper**, which is based in Inca, in the centre of the island; and of **Perlas Majorica**, manufacturers of Mallorcan cultured (artificial) pearls.

Seeing the sights A taxi ride into the centre takes about 10 minutes. Taxis are fairly expensive, but plentiful. Travelling along the quayside the well-preserved city walls stand proud, topped by the occasional windmill. The road is lined with bars designed to appeal to boating and cruising visitors.

At the far side of the bay is **La Seu** (cathedral; open Mon–Sat; fee for museum and treasury). Begun in 1230 but not completed until four centuries later, it has flying buttresses in Catalan-Gothic style and a much-later wrought

BELOW: save your legs by taking a cart ride in Palma.

iron altar canopy (*baldachino*), by Gaudí. The lovely **Palau de l'Almudaina** (open Mon–Fri and Sat am; fee) stands to the west of the cathedral. In the **Parc de la Mar** below, the cathedral is mirrored in a lake, and in the nearby **S'Hort del Rei**, a lovely Arabic-style garden, there are fountains and pools, flowers, shrubs and trees.

Map
on page
156

From behind the cathedral, sightseeing tours are offered in carriages drawn by tired-looking horses. On the corner of Carrer Palau Reial the handsome **Palau March Museu** (open Mon–Sat; fee) exhibits excellent modern sculpture on its palm-lined terrace, and paintings in the interior. An elegant café serves particularly good coffee. Along arcaded Carrer Palau Reial, past some smart cafés, you reach the impressive Ajuntament (town hall) in the Plaça del Cort, in the centre of which stands an ancient, gnarled olive tree. Off to the right, in a large, airy, square with outdoor cafés and bars, is the fine 14th-century church of **Santa Eulàlia**. To the other side of the **Plaça de Cort**, elegant art nouveau buildings house designer, antique and technology shops.

On the far side of the cathedral, cobbled streets too narrow for cars form the old **medieval quarter**. It's best visited outside the hot hours of siesta, as it can be quite airless. These attractive alleyways are fascinating; large doorways in heavy, ochre-coloured walls give tantalising glimpses into shady courtyards, usually with ferns and palm trees, and stone staircases leading to upper levels. Apartments, art galleries and a few small museums are housed inside these intriguing entrances. Museums include the **Museu de Mallorca** (Carrer Portella; open Tues–Sun; fee), an excellent history museum; and the **Casa Museu Torrents Lladó** (open Tues–Sat am; fee), the beautifully furnished home and studio of the 20th-century Catalan painter.

An elegant coffee house, once the favourite haunt of Joan Miró.

BELOW: flowers for sale in La Rambla.

The 10th-century **Banys Arabs** (Arab baths) close by are a delight. The serene courtyard with a well, towering palms, flowers and ferns, along with a few tables and chairs and a soft-drinks machine, are perfect for a picnic. To the side of the courtyard, the baths themselves are entered through a keyhole-shaped Arabic arch. The brick beehive dome of the baths is supported by a ring of columns. This is the only complete Moorish building remaining on the island.

Cruising out of Palma at night, the festive lights of the city twinkle behind the ship for longer than the cocktails usually last.

Flying the flag in a rocky bay.

Further afield

One of the nicest trips is to the pretty hilltop town of **Valldemossa**, on the north coast, with a former monstery and palace, and the secluded clifftop home of Austrian Archduke Ludwig Salvator nearby at Son Marroig, where there are sometimes sunset concerts. In order to attend the concerts you should do this on a ship's tour, but it is possible to hire a car and go it alone, and include the nearby village of **Deià**, once home to Robert Graves.

MAO (MAHON)

Maó, the island capital, has one of the best harbours in the Mediterranean – which is why it was seized by the British in 1708, during the War of the Spanish Succession. They shifted the capital from Ciutadella to Maó, and kept the island for nearly a century, apart from two periods when they were forced to relinquish it for short periods. In 1802 Menorca reverted to Spanish rule.

Not far from town are some fine relics of Menorca's Bronze Age inhabitants including *navetas* (boat-shaped buildings used as ossuaries), and the later *taulas* (T-shaped structures made from two massive blocks of stone) and *talayotic* towers. Ships usually spend a whole day here to allow time for full-day tours around the island.

Arrival and around the dock
Be sure to be up on deck for the approach to Maó, as the white houses clinging to its rocky coastline make a dazzling sight and the old town rising sheer above the harbour is impressive. The cruise dock area lies very close to the old town, which is reached via broad white steps amd a curving road (Ses Voltes) leading up from the waterfront. There is no passenger terminal at present but there are plans for one to be completed by 2005–6.

Shopping
Maó is a good place for ceramics, for the island's Pou Nou brand of casual cotton clothes and the colourful, comfortable Menorcan sandals called *abarcas*. All can be found along the harbourside, as can the **Destileria Xoriguer**, which distils and sells the island's gin, but they can be bought all over the city and in Ciutadella. Shops mostly observe Spanish siesta hours.

Seeing the sights
Maó's main sights are easily seen on foot in an hour or so. At the top of Ses Voltes, in the busy **Plaça d'Espanya**, looms the Església del Carmen. A lively food, clothes and souvenir market is held daily in the adjoining cloister, the **Claustre del Carme**, where there is also a subterranean supermarket and a café with a sunny terrace offering fantastic views over the harbour. To the other side of Ses Voltes, in the **Plaça de Sa Constitució** stands the **Església de Santa Maria**, which dates from the 13th century but was completely rebuilt in the 18th. It's worth a visit for the Catalan-Gothic interior, and its organ, one of the world's largest and most beautiful. Another imposing building in the square, the **Ajuntament** (town hall), was built on the site of a medieval fortress, of which very little survives.

Parròquia de Sant Francesc d'Assís (open daily; free) lies a short walk away. Completed in 1792, after many years' work, it was the church of a Franciscan monastery, of which only the cloister remains; this houses the extensive collections of the **Museu de Menorca** (open summer: Tues–Sat; winter: Tues–Fri; fee). Exhibits range from *talayotic* finds to Greek and Roman amphorae, Islamic tiles and Spanish and British ceramics. Close by, the 15th-century **Port de Sant Roc** is Maó's only surviving medieval town gate.

Maps on pages 136 & 156

TYPICAL EXCURSIONS, MAO

● **Menorca tour.** Includes the Naveta des Tudons and Ciutadella *(see main text)*; the fishing village of Fornells, and a drive to the highest peak, Monte Toro.

● **Half-day tour.** Usually includes Binibeca Vell, an architect-designed village in the south.

BELOW: Maó's Town Hall (Ajuntament).

TYPICAL
EXCURSIONS,
CIUTADELLA
● **Beach trips** to Cala
Blanca and Cala en
Bosc, to the south
(full-day).
● **Naveta des Tudons**
(see main text),
together with other
prehistoric sites: Son
Catlar and Torre
Trencada (half-day).
● **Horse riding**,
dinghy sailing and
jeep safaris (half-day).

Frankly, that's about it as far as sightseeing goes, but its enjoyable to stroll about admiring the fine Georgian houses, which are a legacy of British rule, and absorbing the atmosphere before settling down for lunch. The harbourside is lined with restaurants, many specialising in fish and seafood, others serving traditional dishes like *caracoles con allioli* – snails in garlic mayonnaise – or *lechona* (roast suckling pig).

Further afield If you hire a car, it won't take you long to reach **Fornells**, an idyllic fishing village on the north coast (also offered as part of a ship's tour), where you can wander along the waterfront, visit a clifftop tower and have a splendid lunch in one of the many renowned fish restaurants.

CIUTADELLA

Ciutadella is quite different from Maó, Menorca's main cruise port. While the former is all elegant Georgian architecture, Ciutadella, which means Little City, is distinguished by honey-coloured palaces, narrow streets and beautiful squares. Most ships spend a day or part of a day here and passengers are tendered in, as large ships cannot fit along the canal-like entrance to the harbour.

Arrival and around the dock As the ship draws near the long, narrow inlet to the harbour, you will see elegant summer homes on one side and the 16th-century Castell de Sant Nicolau standing guard on the other, before the sand-coloured walls of the city rise above the port.

The best way to explore the town is on foot. Taxis are hard to come by from the tender landing point and it's a steepish slope up from **El Port**, so anyone with

BELOW: shiny
specimens in a
vintage car rally.

walking difficulties may want to consider an excursion or a hire car. At the top of the slope is the **Plaça d'es Born**, the main square, a former parade ground now lined with cafés and market stalls. The neo-classical **Palau Salort** (open Mon–Sat; fee) and Renaissance-style Palau de Torresaura face the crenellated former town hall. From the square, an attractive pedestrian thoroughfare bisects the old town, passes the solid-looking **Catedral de Santa Maria**, and runs to **Ses Voltes**, an attractive arcaded square from where a little shopping street continues eastwards. Here you'll be able to buy the local sandals *(abarcas)* and good-quality, island-made casual clothes. In one of the narrow side streets stands the **Convent i Església del Socors**, which houses the **Museu Diocesà** (open May–Oct: Tues–Sat; fee); in another, you'll find the busy fruit, vegetable, meat and fish market (open mornings).

The harbourside (El Port) is lined end-to-end with restaurants, and is the place to eat while you watch the sun go down in the evening, or the yachts bobbing in the water at lunchtime.

Further afield If you hire a car there's lots to see. For **beaches**, go south. Try Cala Blanca, just a few kilometres away, or Cala d'en Bosc, where there's a good marina. A bit further afield, go to **Cala Santa Galdana**; apart from the beaches, watersports and other facilities in this busy little resort, you can walk through pinewoods to quieter beaches close by. On the main road towards Maó, just outside Ciutadella, is the **Naveta des Tudons**, a Bronze Age burial chamber, believed to be the oldest roofed building in Europe. Torre Trencada and Torrellafuda are two other prehistoric sites just off the road. Cruise lines offer excursions to most of these places.   ❑

Horsemanship is a major part of Menorcan festivals.

BELOW: Ciutadella harbour – lovely by day or night.

FRANCE AND CORSICA

From the bustle of Marseille and the sleek glamour of Cannes and Nice, to the pretty hilltop Riviera towns and the rugged beauty of Corsica, this is a part of the Med for those who like variety

Map on page 167

A cruise-line itinerary that takes in the ports of southern France and Corsica will whisk you into the edgy, exciting atmosphere of Marseille, the sophistication and heady Mediterranean scents of cities like Cannes and Nice, the unreal fun of St-Tropez with its celebrity connections, and the anomaly that is the independent protectorate of Monaco. There are quieter places too: the fishing villages of Port Vendres and Sète, used as gateways to the walled city of Carcassone; and pretty Villefranche, which inspired Jean Cocteau. And there are several ports of call on the island of Corsica, which, though wild and rugged and seemingly a different world from the Riviera ports, is still essentially very French in character. For Bordeaux and other Atlantic ports, *see page 103*.

PORT VENDRES

Port Vendres is a pretty fishing village just 15 km (10 miles) from the Spanish border. Like Sète, it is used by cruise lines as a gateway to medieval Carcassone, 120 km (75 miles) inland. Its big advantage is that it is only 2 km (1 mile) from the lovely Catalan village of Collioure, inspiration for Matisse and Picasso, among others, and a great place to spend a day.

Arrival and around the dock The biggest attraction of the harbour, which is also used as a cargo port, is the fish auction, held between 4.30 and 6pm every day except Sunday. Port Vendres itself has little to see, although there are plenty of bars and cafés around the fishing harbour, all close to the port.

Seeing the sights Buses and taxis run to **Collioure**, or you can walk the 2 km (1 mile) to the hilltop village. There's a 13th-century castle and a tangle of old streets to explore, packed with art galleries, souvenir shops, restaurants and expensive boutiques. It's easy to see how the cobalt sea, bottle green pines and ochre houses inspired Matisse when he worked here in 1905. Alternatively, you could hike along Cap Béar to the beach at **Plage des Elmes**.

Further afield All cruise lines run excursions to **Carcassone**, the best-known walled town in France, with 52 towers, two concentric surrounding walls and 3 km (2 miles) of ramparts. The old religious buildings, scene of many battles, are well preserved. The town has become something of a tourist trap, with dozens of souvenir shops and themed restaurants, and it can get very crowded, but it does have a fairytale aspect. **Perpignan** is also accessible: an ancient and interesting town with a cathedral, a 13th-century palace and an atmosphere more Spanish than French.

PRECEDING PAGES: shutting out the midday heat. **LEFT:** St-Tropez market. **BELOW:** a cruise ship almost dwarfs Marseille Cathedral.

SÈTE

**TYPICAL
EXCURSIONS,
PORT VENDRES
and SÈTE**
● **Aigues-Mortes**
(half-day tour).
● **Montpellier** (half-
day tour).
● **Carcassone** (full-
day tour; *see main
text for all three
towns*).
● **Wine tasting** and
gastronomic lunches.

Cruise ships use the port of Sète, a fishing village in medieval times, as a gateway to the big attractions of Montpellier and Carcassone, two of the best-preserved medieval towns of southwest France.

Arrival and around the dock Cruise ships dock at the Gare Maritime, from where you can walk to the town centre, which is criss-crossed by canals and waterways, lined with pastel coloured, terraced houses and seafood restaurants. Although most people take off on excursions, the town does have a pleasant buzz on summer days and it's not difficult to while away a few hours sitting by one of the canals.

Seeing the sights The upper part of Sète sprawls over the slopes of Mont St-Clair, which overlooks the vast Bassin de Thau, breeding ground of mussels and oysters. If you're feeling energetic, climb up from the harbour to the *cimetière marin*, the sailors' cemetery, where poet Paul Valéry (1871–1945) is buried. The Musée Paul Valéry, opposite the cemetery, has a room dedicated to his work. Further up the hill are impressive views of the coast.

Further afield Trains run regularly to **Montpellier**, 28 km (17 miles) inland, although you would have to take a taxi from the dock to the SNCF station on Quai Maréchal-Joffre. This ancient university town has a beautiful old centre, which is just as easily explored alone as with a guide. **Carcassone** is an hour and a half's drive away, although traffic can be heavy and parking difficult in peak season; you would be better off taking a tour *(also see page 163)*. The medieval fortified town of **Aigues-Mortes**, once an embarkation point for the Crusaders, offers beautiful panoramas of the Camargue.

BELOW: Marseille's
Vieux Port.

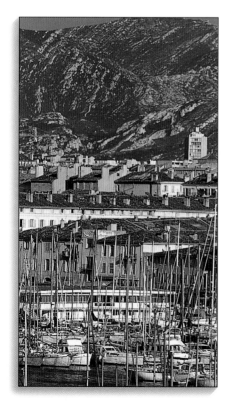

MARSEILLE

Founded as Massalia in the 6th century BC by Greeks from Phocaea, Marseille has been a significant Mediterranean port ever since. As well as being a premier port for southern Europe and Africa, it was the place where Louis XIV moored his huge fleet. During the revolution, Marseille gave France her national anthem, *La Marseillaise*.

Yet, like many working ports, it suffers from a bad reputation. Although it is still often referred to as "the crime capital of the Mediterranean", investment and a more rigorous civic attitude have helped clean up the city's act, at least in daylight. Many of the older buildings have been scrubbed and renovated, and the Hôtel de Ville is chocolate-box pretty. The marina is thick with craft both large and small, bobbing primly on the water below the hungry seagulls.

Arrival and around the dock Sunlight glistens on the deep blue water and rich brown hills of the French Riviera. The city sprawls off to the right – modern high-rises under brown and white hills and, through the tangle of dockside cranes, the first view of Marseille gives a taste of its rough glamour.

Map on page 167

Cruise ships normally dock in Marseille for a full day. In the terminus, about 15–20 minutes' drive from the harbour front, there is a bar, and shops offering a variety of French goods *(see below)*. Shuttle buses are frequent from the dock to the Vieux Port (Old Port). There is a taxi rank up here, too, although their fares are quite high.

Shopping Scents and aftershaves, good-quality bath oils, linens, T-shirts, striped sailor shirts, paté de fois gras and wine can all be bought in the terminus shops, and natural fruit juices, fabrics and lovely, if expensive ranges of olive oil-based skin-care products on a row of stalls outside. There are French fashions to be found around Cours Julien at the top of Le Canebière, but Marseille is mostly known to shoppers for the folkloric arts and crafts of Provence, ranging from soaps to wooden nativity figures *(santons)*. In France, of course, food and wines are always worth shopping for.

Eating The area around the Vieux Port is the place to go, and while you're here you really should try the local dish – *bouillabaisse*, a rich, fish stew. Marseille compares with Paris or Cannes for the unholy shock that the price of a coffee at a pavement café will unleash, but lunch with a view of the harbour is worth paying a little extra for.

Seeing the sights For visitors, Marseille life centres around the **Vieux Port**. A blue and white, open-sided **Petit Train de Vieux** leaves every 20 minutes from the Quai du Port, close to where the shuttle-buses drop passengers off. Trains take sightseers on two different routes; a one-hour tour to the cathedral,

TYPICAL EXCURSIONS, MARSEILLE

● **Panoramic Marseille** and shopping (half-day).
● **Tour of Marseille** (half-day).
● **Avignon and Marseille** (full-day).
● **Aix-en-Provence** (full-day).
● **Avignon & Les Baux** (full-day tour; for Avignon and Aix, *see main text*).

BELOW: street life near the harbour.

The imposing bulk of Marseille's Cathédrale de la Major.

or a 40-minute tour of the old town, known as the Panier Quarter. Ferries to Château d'If, Îles du Frioul *(see next page)*, and charter boats depart from the harbour, too.

The **Hôtel de Ville** (1653) looks onto the harbour, facing across the bay towards the cathedral. Flags of the tricoleur hang at the front above the ornate ironwork and huge windows. Still a working municipal building, it throngs with typically well-dressed French officials.

The main boulevard from the old port is **La Canebière**, Marseille's main street. The lovely turn-of-the-20th-century carousel immediately sets a distinctly French tone. On the right of the street, is the bright and modern **tourist information office**. A Carte Privilèges bought here is very good value, giving a day's entry to many of the museums. Among the cafés and perfume shops on La Canebière are the **Maritime Museum** (open daily; fee), and the fashion museum, the **Musée de la Mode** (open Mon–Fri; fee). Dwarf palm trees nestle among towering street lamps along the wide, busy boulevard. Off La Canebière, a right turn leads into Rue Longues des Capucins, where there is a bustling Arab street market selling spicy foods, tacky toys and trinkets.

A taxi or metro ride (Metro Cinq-Avenues) takes you to the relaxing gardens of the **Palais Longchamp** (Avenue Longchamp) in the Place Bernex, a semi-circular colonnade looking out over fountains in formal grounds. The Palais was built in 1838 as the water-tower for the city. The building also houses the **Musée de Beaux-Arts** as well as the **Natural History Musée d'Historie Naturalle** (both open Tues–Sun; fee).

Looking like a ramshackle ancient village, **Le Panier** gives an impression of old Marseille. Beginning just behind the Hôtel de Ville are the steep streets and

BELOW:
some secluded bays can be visited only by boat.

steps up the hill, past tree-shaded restaurants, modern fountains and three- to five-storey buildings with balconies and handsome shutters.

In Place de la Major stands the **Cathédrale de la Major** and high on the hill above the bay, the **Basilique-de-Notre-Dame-de-la-Garde** is worth visiting, not least for the fantastic view from its distinctive tower, which is an attractive local landmark. Bus No. 60 goes from Cours Ballard, or you can take a metro to Joliette.

Map
below

Further afield A short ferry ride from the port takes you out to **Château d'If**, a castle on a small island which was the setting for Alexandre Dumas' novel *The Count of Monte Cristo*. The same ferry also goes on to the **Îles du Frioul**, an archipelago of craggy islands with rocky beaches and crystal blue lagoons, heavenly for swimming. For hardy hikers there are also magnificent views of the bay and the sea. If you are making this trip without an organised excursion, keep an eye on the wind. When the *mistral* becomes strong, the ferry can be delayed, and could jeopardise getting back to the cruise ship in time for departure, so check with the ferry operator before setting out.

Cruise lines run tours to **Aix-en-Provence** and **Avignon**, but both can be visited independently by bus (the bus station is in Place Victor Hugo to the northeast of town) and are well worth a trip. Aix is known for a beautiful central boulevard, the Cours Mirabeau, elegant 18th-century fountains and a number of cosmopolitan restaurants. The medieval walled city of Avignon is a gem, with the famous bridge (the Pont d'Avignon), the Palais des Papes, built when the papacy was based here in the 14th century, and a lively central square, the Place de l'Horloge.

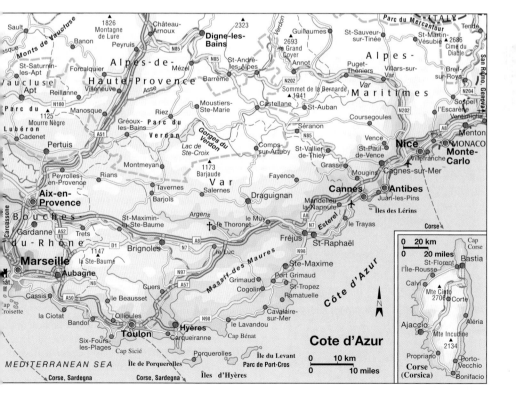

Lavender fields look as lovely as they smell.

TOULON

Toulon has been the principal naval base of France for three centuries and despite a fair amount of urban sprawl, retains a sense of traditional charm in the narrow old streets between the Vieux Port and the town centre. The city itself is overlooked by old forts, notably the imposing mass of Mont Faron. Offshore to the east are the Îles d'Hyeres, a popular national park, while in the hinterland are the mountains and vineyards of the Var.

Arrival and around the dock You'll see the old city sprawling out before you, backed by Mont Faron. Those interested in naval history may want to be on deck to look out for French warships around the docks.

The old town is located directly behind the port, just along the busy seafront from the passenger terminal. The main street is the broad Boulevard de Strasbourg. Vieux Toulon, the most interesting part of the town, lies between this street and the harbour. If your ship docks in the morning, head straight for Le Marche, the dazzlingly colourful flower, fruit and vegetable market (open daily till 2.30pm) on Cours Lafayette, which runs perpendicular to the sea.

Seeing the sights Things to see along the cobbled streets of the old city include the Romanesque **Cathédrale Ste-Marie-Majeure** and the **Musée de la Marine** (open Wed–Mon; fee). In a handsome building on Place Monsenergue, the museum is packed with ships' artefacts and figureheads. The **Musée d'Art de Toulon** (open daily pm; free) contains Provençal and Italian art.

For a panoramic view, take the funicular *(téléferique)* from Boulevard l'Amiral Vence near the Hôtel La Tour Blanche up Mont Faron. As well as the views of the port and the sea, there's an interesting museum, the **Mémorial du Débarquement en Provence** (open Tues–Sun, limited hours; fee) documenting the Allied landings in Provence in 1944.

Further afield Some cruise lines run shuttles to the beaches; Plage du Mourillon, one of the better ones, is 2 km (1¼ miles) east of the heart of town. Excursions include tours of the **Provençal countryside**, speckled with medieval hilltop villages, and visits to the dramatic **Gorges du Verdon**. **St-Tropez**, **Nice**, **Cannes**, **Antibes** and **Monaco** lie from one to two hours east along the coast. The coast road itself is a lovely, scenic drive; outside high season, it's worth hiring a car just to drive around, find a decent spot for lunch and relax on the beach.

BELOW: St-Tropez harbour in the evening light.

ST-TROPEZ

It is hard to imagine now, but in Roman times St-Tropez was a place of Christian pilgrimage. Much later, the patronage of writers like Guy de Maupassant (1850–93) and artists like Paul Signac and Henri Matisse (in the first half of the 20th century) began to make this once-sleepy fishing village a fashionable place to visit. And after the literati came the glitterati with Roger Vadim making *And God Created Woman* in 1956 and turning both Brigitte Bardot and St-Tropez into movie stars. It is now a magnet for the

Map on page 167

rich and famous – Bardot, Elton John and Mick Jagger have all owned villas here – and those who like to watch, mix and mingle with them.

St-Tropez – like Cannes – is particularly favoured by the smaller, luxury, five-star ships which tend to stay late into the evening to allow passengers to enjoy the lively nightlife.

Arrival and around the dock The small dock area is designed for private yachts, not cruise ships, so cruise visitors are tendered in either to the Vieux Port or Nouveau Port (old and new ports) but, as these are just 150 metres/yds apart, there is little chance of confusion. From the new port, you walk straight past the old one into the town. There are no terminals but there is a tourist information centre near each landing stage (the main one is on Quai Jean Jaurès, by the old port).

On all sides of the ports is a host of cafés, restaurants and shops which sell mainly nautical items to the yachties who can walk into the shops straight off their floating gin palaces – which all add to the colour of the harbour area.

There are taxis along Quai Jean Jaurès but, unless you want to go out of the resort, they are not necessary as St-Tropez starts right there and it is much easier and quicker to walk around it.

Shopping There are designer labels in abundance but, as far as local produce is concerned, look out for handicraft items – from trinkets to carpets – made in Cogolin, a village near Grimaud. These appear in shops and the Tuesday and Saturday markets in the linked squares, Place des Lices and Place Carnot. The main shopping street – Rue François Sibilli – links the old port and the squares.

TYPICAL EXCURSIONS, ST-TROPEZ

● The hillside villages of **Ramatuelle and Gassin**, and a historic village, **Grimaud**.

● **Port Grimaud**, a modern resort built around a series of canals and lagoons.

● The 12th-century **Cistercian Abbey at Thoronet**, and wine-tasting (all usually half-day tours).

BELOW: Pampelonne beach near St-Tropez.

Seeing the sights One of the most popular attractions, the **Musée de l'Annonciade** (open Wed–Mon; fee), a 16th-century chapel-turned-museum of art, features original works by Signac, Bonnard, Dufy and their contemporaries. It is located between the ports on Place Grammont, Quai Gabriel Peri. From Quai Jean Jaurès by the old port, turn sharp left and there is long narrow promontory lined with cafés and restaurants with superb views of the Gulf of St-Tropez. Alternatively, head directly inland and you are in the old town – a maelstrom of designer boutiques, cafés and restaurants cheek by jowl along every crowded street and alleyway.

In July and August, there are organised walking tours from the main tourist office but it is really easier to do it yourself. The town church, the Église de St-Tropez, is right in the centre but the main icon is the 16th-century **Citadelle**, an imposing fort on a hill overlooking the old town. This is walkable from the dock and, although some effort is required to reach the top of the ramparts, the view across St-Tropez and its bay is spectacular. There is a maritime museum, **Musée Naval** (open Wed–Mon; fee) in the dungeon.

There is a public beach (Graniers) just below the citadelle and by the fishing harbour (Port des Pecheurs) but the better (private) beaches like Tahiti Plage are past the headland, at least 3 km (2 miles) away on an 8-km (5-mile) stretch of sand called Pampelonne. To reach them, either take a taxi (expensive) or one of the frequent beach shuttle mini-buses (from Place des Lices on Boulevard Vasserpt, a 10 to 15-minute walk to the right of the old port). But, especially in midsummer, expect a frustrating start to the journey in the seemingly permanent traffic jams on the roads out of the resort. There are fees to use the beaches, on which topless and – on a couple of them – bottomless sunbathing is the norm.

BELOW:
perfume for sale
in a Menton store.

Map on page 167

Taxis are an alternative – although not necessarily a cheaper one – to the shore excursions visiting nearby **Ramatuelle** and **Gassin**, pretty hilltop villages surrounded by vineyards and windmills. **Port Grimaud** (10 km/6 miles), is a picturesque little town built in the 1960s over a series of waterways; while Grimaud itself is a medieval town with a ruined château. A little further afield (16 km/12 miles) is the historic Roman city of **Fréjus**, with a Roman arena and a 12th-century cathedral.

CANNES

That old cliché about a sleepy fishing village transformed into a major tourist resort rings true for Cannes. Discovered by the British in the 1830s, the place now bears little resemblance to its former modest self and is arguably the grandest of all the French Riviera resorts. It is swisher than Nice, more glamorous than Villefranche and – thanks to the media circus of its annual film festival – perhaps even more famous than St-Tropez.

Although it is no place for quiet strolls and relaxed contemplation, for glamour and glitz it is hard to beat. Set in the Bay of Cannes, it is a convenient gateway to the Côte d'Azur with excellent transport links to other Riviera resorts.

Cannes is occasionally used as a home port by lines with smaller ships – luxury five-star or sail-cruisers. Home-porting ships will depart early evening but visiting ships often stay until late evening to allow passengers to enjoy the renowned Riviera nightlife.

Arrival and around the dock A few smaller cruise ships can dock at Cannes but most have to anchor off and tender passengers into a small quay which also handles local ferries. It is an attractive scene in on the tenders, as the quay is at the far corner of a busy square with colourful market stalls stretching in front of a line of open-air cafés and restaurants.

The small terminal has seating and check-in desks for embarking passengers as well as telephones, cash ATMs and an adjacent tourist information centre. A new, larger, two-tier terminal with a greater range of passenger facilities is being built and should be completed in time for summer 2005.

Turn left outside the terminal and immediately left again and you are in the market square, which has a bus terminal at the far end. The railway station is a five-minute walk in the other direction (behind the Palais des Festivals and Boulevard de la Croisette).

Shopping As well as perfume from nearby Grasse, look out for uniquely designed glassware from the glassworks at Biot, a village 12 km (7 miles) away. Otherwise, there are numerous stores and boutiques showcasing the latest designer label fashions.

Seeing the sights Cannes is easily explored on foot. Just west of the Vieux Port is the oldest part of town, **Le Suquet**, an area of narrow streets full of interesting shops and cafés, with a medieval church, Notre-Dame de l'Espérance, and a 12th-century castle, which houses the **Musée de la Castre** (open

TYPICAL EXCURSIONS, CANNES
● **Monaco**, medieval Eze (half-day).
● **Nice** and medieval **St Paul-de-Vence** (half-day).
● Full day go-as-you-please tour to **Nice** and **Monaco**.
● Half-day to **St-Tropez, Nice, Monte Carlo, Eze, St Paul-de-Vence** or **Grasse** *(see main text).*

BELOW: music is an essential part of local fêtes.

Enjoying lunch in the sun outside Cannes' Carlton Hotel.

Wed–Mon; fee) with interesting ethnographic and archaeological collections. But the major draw is in the opposite direction: the palm tree-lined **Boulevard de la Croisette** which stretches eastwards from the Palais des Festivals (venue for the Cannes Film Festival in May) opposite the terminal, and along the seafront to the other end of the bay. This is where the action is: the swish hotels, smart casinos, stylish boutiques, discreet art galleries and marinas packed with lavishly fitted yachts. Lunch at any of the many cafés and restaurants is an expensive business but it is worth pausing for a drink just to watch the beautiful people that Cannes continues to attract.

For a different view of Cannes, head for the Observatory of Super-Cannes, a suburb just north of the railway station. This has lifts up to viewing platforms overlooking Cannes and the coastline.

Further afield Most of the places on the organised tours are easily reached by bus and/or train. Buses run regularly from Place Bernard Cornut Gentille, just beside the terminal, to **Nice** (including an airport stop, which is crucial if you are travelling independently and need to connect between flights and the ship). There are also buses from the terminal to **Villefranche** and **Monaco** *(see pages 175 and 176)* and to **Grasse**, the perfume capital. The latter is a pretty inland town where you can visit the Musée International de la Parfumerie and the Fragonard Parfumerie, both of which run tours and show how scents are made. You can also, of course, buy perfume, and visit the house where the painter Jean-Honoré Fragonard was born in 1732, and which is dedicated to his work.

By rail, you can also reach the Riviera resorts of **Juan-Les-Pins**, **Antibes**, **Nice** and **Villefranche** in an hour, with Monte Carlo just over an hour away.

BELOW: the seafront at Nice is always thronged with people.

NICE AND VILLEFRANCHE

Nice and Villefranche are just 5 km (3 miles) apart but, while Nice is a major resort with many grand and modern hotels, wide avenues full of department stores, large squares, historic churches and several major museums *(see page 175)*, Villefranche remains a small, relatively uncrowded town with plenty of Gallic charm but no major historical attractions. For cruise visitors, though, either place is a genuine attraction in its own right as well as being convenient bases from which to explore other parts of the Riviera.

The two ports are so close together that not only are the shore excursions identical from both but ships will sometimes substitute Nice for Villefranche if sea conditions rule out tendering passengers ashore, which is why the two ports have been grouped together here. Ships can dock at Nice but, despite the proximity of an international airport, it is only rarely used as a home port. For both, though, a full-day stay is the norm, with the occasional ship extending its time in Nice until about 11pm.

Arrival and around the dock It is well worth being up on deck as your ship approaches Nice to capture a first glimpse of the palm tree-fringed Promenade des Anglais which stretches along the beach of the Baie des Anges. Arguably, the approach to – or, even better, the sunset departure from – Villefranche is even more impressive. The steeply terraced streets of this pretty, centuries-old fishing village set against a densely wooded backdrop create a delightfully timeless picture.

At Nice, the port area (Lympia) is at the eastern end of the bay. Currently, cruise ships dock in a small basin where all the ferries also embark. There are

Maps
on pages
167 & 173

TYPICAL
EXCURSIONS,
NICE

● Full-day tour along the Lower, Middle and Grande Corniches to **Monaco** and the medieval village of **Eze** *(see main text).*

● Full-day tour of **Nice, Cannes** and medieval **St Paul-de-Vence** *(see main text).*

● Full-day go-as-you-please tour to **Nice** and **Monaco**.

● Half-day tours to **Nice, Monte Carlo, Eze, St Paul-de-Vence** or **Grasse**.

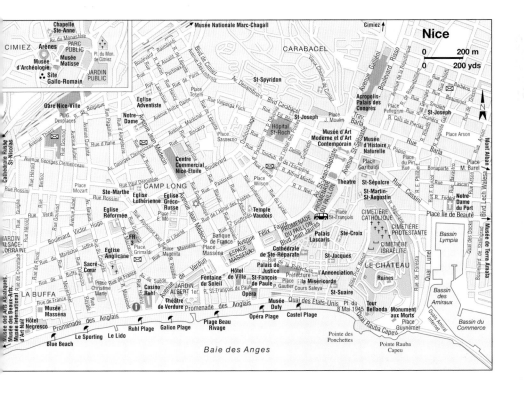

Nice

plans for a new cruise ship-only dock area with a purpose-built terminal. When that is completed, more ships will home-port in Nice but, for the time being, there are few facilities in the dock area (although there are bars and bistros nearby). It is, however, only a short walk to the most interesting part of Nice – the old town (Vieux Nice) – and not much further to the lengthy Promenades des Anglais, lined with splendid *belle époque* mansions and hotels, and overlooking a series of 13 fee-charging beaches. Between the port and the old town, there is also a worthwhile detour up 400 steps to the beautiful gardens of **Le Château**.

Tenders bring you into a small jetty at the western end of Villefranche. As all sea traffic – including small ferries and pleasure boats to the nearby Riviera ports – use this jetty, the tenders often have to wait 5–10 minutes to dock.

There is a new, small passenger terminal that has a useful tourist information desk, with details of local attractions, bus and train timetables. Next door is a ferry booking office and there are several public telephones, too.

The centre of Villefranche is just behind the terminal, across the road and up a series of steps. Alternatively, turn right to walk along the seafront to a long, narrow beach which curls around the eastern end of the bay. Up the steps at the bend of the bay takes you, via a pretty 10-minute walk, to the exclusive neighbouring resort of Beaulieu-sur-Mer.

Shopping There are few bargains and even less scope for haggling anywhere along the French Riviera but there is an excellent range of quality stores and goods in Nice, Around avenue Jean Médecin, which has a range of international stores and a US-style mall; and there are some unusual crafts and jewellery in smaller places such as St-Paul-de-Vence. Around the Cours Saleya (*see below*) there are some interesting old shops selling good-quality olive oil and oil-based soaps and other products. But the major attraction is perfume – there is one perfume factory in Eze and numerous others in the perfume capital, Grasse.

Eating In order to appreciate the true Niçoise atmosphere, the best places to eat are in Vieux Nice, especially around the busy Cours Saleya. You can choose among upmarket fish restaurants and down-to-earth places selling *socca*, the local version of pizza, and, of course, *salade niçoise*.

Seeing the sights – Nice From a ship docked in Nice, it is a pleasant 20-minute walk westwards, around the Quai Rauba Capeu, along Quai des États-Unis and past Nice's original main promenade (Les Ponchettes) to the entrance (under a walkway with illustrations of how Nice looked in past centuries) to **Vieux Nice**. The mixture of colourfully painted houses, narrow streets, cafés and restaurants makes it the most attractive part of the city, and the most walkable. Worth a visit are the 17th-century **Cathédrale Ste-Réparate**, the 18th-century baroque **Chapelle de la Miséricorde**, and the splendid **Palais Lascaris**.

One of the greatest attractions, though, is the huge and colourful fish, flower and vegetable market on

BELOW: the flamboyant Negresco Hotel is a Nice landmark.

Cours Saleya (behind Les Ponchettes) held every morning except Monday, when there is an antiques market.

If you have time, include the **Musée d'Art Contemptorain**, the **Musée Nationale Marc Chagall** and the **Musée Matisse** on your itinerary (all open Wed–Mon; fee). The first is easily walkable, northeast along Rue Jean Jaures; there are buses to the others, but they're best reached by taxi if time is limited.

Further afield It is cheap and relatively easy to reach the other Riviera resorts and villages by train, bus or taxi, if you prefer to go independently instead of taking a ship's excursion. Nice Ville is the main station (on Rue de Chateauneuf, a 20-minute walk from the seafront via Avenue Jean Médecin and Place Massena). There is a tourist information centre right outside on the left. Buses start their journeys from a terminal in Rue Jean Jaurès and most stop in Place Massena as well.

St-Paul-de-Vence is an idyllic medieval hill village, but it is mainly visited for the **Fondation Maeght** (open daily; fee), a museum just outside town (up a short steep hill) displaying works by Chagall, Miró, Braque and others in a lovely setting. **Eze**, just east of Nice, is perched high above the sea, crowned with the remains of a castle. It is dramatic and pretty but somewhat overrun with visitors in the summer.

Seeing the sights – Villefranche Despite the fact that so many ships call here, it is a quiet, relaxed place to visit. This is partly because so many passengers take a tour or travel independently to the neighbouring Riviera resorts, but also because the area between the seafront road and the upper road (part of the Lower Corniche), is just a succession of narrow pedestrianised streets, steps and alleyways with shuttered houses painted in pastel shades. Here, and along the seafront, are many cafés, restaurants and *patisseries*. It is pleasant to spend at least half the day here, just watching the world go by. The main place to visit is the **Chapelle de St-Pierre**, a tiny fishermen's chapel, its interior decorated by Jean Cocteau (1889–1963), who loved Villefranche.

Getting to Nice and Monaco from Villefranche

Nice and Monaco are both easily reached by bus, train or taxi from Villefranche. There are taxis outside the terminal. The main bus stop is about 20 minutes' uphill walk on Avenue Albert I (Lower Corniche) but there is a less-frequent mini-bus service (to Nice only) opposite the terminal – check times with the tourist information desk. The most convenient service, though, is by train. The station is less than 10 minutes' walk from the terminal, at the top of some steps just opposite where the beach begins – look out for a French railways (SNCF) sign on the wall as the steps are partially obscured from the promenade. Frequency varies according to the time of day but there are usually two or three trains an hour with Nice just seven minutes away, Cannes 25 minutes and Monaco, less than 20 minutes in the other direction, and the fares are very reasonable.

Maps on pages 167 & 173

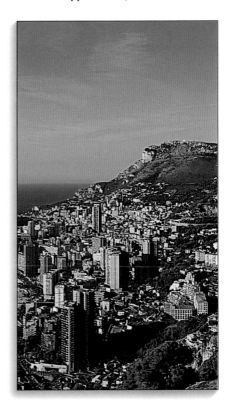

Modern sculpture in Place Massena, in the centre of Nice.

BELOW: looking down on Monaco.

MONTE-CARLO

For a place less than 5 sq. km (2 sq. miles) in size, Monte Carlo attracts a lot of attention, but no one could say it does not live up to the exciting image it has created for itself – even if it seems somewhat unreal. It really is glitz and glamour all the way, starting with a harbour where some of most lavishly appointed yachts have never seen the open sea, their owners preferring to tie-up permanently at one of the world's most fashionable addresses.

A resident of Monaco's Musée Océanographique.

On the three land sides of the harbour are Monaco's three main districts: Monaco Ville, La Condamine, and Monte-Carlo. Walking (which not many do) or being driven around the steep, winding, narrow streets that link these districts, it is hard to imagine drivers negotiating the same bends at 160 kmh (100 mph) plus, when the Grand Prix circus comes to town every year.

But it is easy to see why the Monte Carlo race is the most glamorous sporting event of them all. It's not just the yachts but the swish hotels, smart apartments, fashionable stores and boutiques and, of course, the Grand Casino – Europe's first when opened in 1856 – which create the buzz. Many of the street names also remind you of the mixture of history and Hollywood that has been part of the Grimaldi family, who still rule the Principality. In 1297, François Grimaldi captured the fortress at Monaco and his family bought the surrounding area from Genoa 11 years later. The current Prince (Ranier III) has ruled Monaco since 1949, but made his biggest mark on the world stage by marrying film star Grace Kelly in 1955, who died in a car crash on the Corniche in 1982.

BELOW: prickly succulents in the Jardin Exotique.

Still independent (although a French protectorate), Monaco continues to thrive on a mixture of manufacturing, financial services, tourism and gambling revenues. For cruise visitors, it is also a good base for exploring the French Riviera.

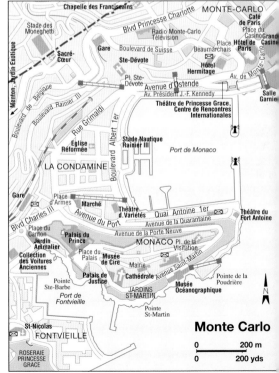

Monte Carlo

| 0 | 200 m |
| 0 | 200 yds |

Monte Carlo usually features as a port of call although a major redevelopment of the cruise port begun in 2003 could see more ships home-porting here in the future. As with all the French Riviera ports, with which Monte Carlo shares a deserved reputation for a lively nightlife, ships tend to arrive in the morning and leave late in the evening.

Arrival and around the dock The largest ships still have to anchor off the port but a lot more are able to dock alongside now there is a new floating dock on the ocean side of the inner harbour. This was completed in 2003, replacing the previously designated cruise berth on the Monte Carlo side of the harbour at which only the smaller ships could dock.

Eventually, there will be a full-service cruise terminal by the new dock, along with a range of other tourist facilities (cafés, bars, etc.) but at present there are just telephones and ATMs. However, the dock is just a five-minute walk from La Condamine, the business, commercial and residential area overlooking the harbour. At ground level (along Boulevard Albert I) there are plenty of cafés, bars and restaurants from where you can admire the yachts in the harbour.

Shopping There are some interesting arty-crafty shops in the narrow lanes of Monaco Ville, and the predominant souvenir is Grimaldi memorabilia – royal flags, coats of arms, etc. But real shoppers go for the latest designer-label fashions and accessories. The main stores are in Monte Carlo (Boulevard des Moulins, Avenue des Beaux-Arts and Avenue Princess Grace) but there is also a range of stores and boutiques in La Condamine (Rue Grimaldi and Rue Caroline). Should you be interested, Princess Stephanie has her own swimwear label.

Map on page 176

TYPICAL EXCURSIONS, MONTE CARLO

● Full-day to **Nice and Cannes** or **Cannes and Grasse**.

● Half-day scenic **French Riviera drive**.

● Half-day to **Eze and Cap Ferrat**.

● Half-day **Monaco Highlights** or shorter walking or tram tours.

● Half-day to **St Paul-de-Vence** or **Antibes**.

BELOW: the *Wind Surf* in Monte-Carlo.

TYPICAL EXCURSIONS, AJACCIO

- Half-day tour to the **Prunella Gorges** and **Lake Tolla**.
- Full-day tour to the **Calanches de Piana, Cargese, Pinto, Filitosa** and the **Spelunca Gorges**.
- Shorter, tours include visits to **Cupulatta**, home to many species of turtles, and the coastal nature reserve of **Scandola**.

BELOW: Napoleon's bedroom, Ajaccio.

Seeing the sights From the new dock, the old town, Monaco Ville, sits up on the hill to the left, while the new town of Monte Carlo is up on the headland to the right (via La Condamine). Either is walkable from the ship with a lift at the east end of Rampe Major (from Quai Antoine) a welcome alternative to negotiating the steep hill to Monaco Ville.

Highlights of Monaco Ville are the elaborate Changing of the Guard (daily 11.55am) at the Palais du Prince; the tomb of Princess Grace in the Byzantine-style Cathédrale St-Nicolas; and several museums, of which the pick is the **Musée Océanographique** (open daily; fee), with aquariums filled with rare marine life and exploration equipment used by Jacques Cousteau, a former director of the museum. A tourist train starts and finishes tours of Monaco Ville from outside this museum.

The highlight of Monte Carlo is the famous **Grand Casino** (one of several casinos in Monaco), which operates a dress code and requires an entrance fee to the gaming rooms and for players to show passports. Along with the connected Opera House, it stands in Place du Casino on the headland looking back at the harbour.

Lifts and escalators to the upper levels of La Condamine are a shortcut to the station (Boulevard Ranier III) and to the **Jardin Exotique** (open daily; fee) which has a colourful collection of sub-tropical plants. To reach the garden, go left along Ranier III from the station and cross Boulevard de Belgique.

There are frequent trains to Eze, Villefranche, Nice, Antibes, Juan-les-Pins and Cannes (1 hour 15 minutes for the latter), which are alternatives to the organised tours and considerably cheaper than taxis. About 12 minutes by train in the opposite direction is pretty little **Menton**, the last town before the Italian border. Best known for the **Jardin Botanique Exotique** and other tropical gardens, and for the little **Musée Jean Cocteau** (open Wed–Mon; fee) on the Bastion du Port, Menton also has a lively market, good restaurants and steep, narrow streets to explore.

CORSICA

Corsica has been described as the "Scented Isle" because of the fragrance of its maquis – the low-level layer of evergreen herbs, plants and flowers among its sometimes densely wooded interior – but Corsica's appeal really lies in its majestic scenery, with spectacular mountains in the interior, some superb coastline. Many of the old port towns, notably Bonifacio and Calvi, are extremely picturesque. The independently-minded people have fought many battles over the centuries, and the island retains a strong sense of identity to this day. Napoleonic souvenirs mixed in among some attractive local handicrafts and ceramics plus a variety of coral jewellery are the main items of interest for shoppers. The jewellery is attractive if – like most purchases on the island – expensive.

AJACCIO

With the lesser-know Bastia, Ajaccio is the most important city in the "Scented Isle" of Corsica. There is some dramatic scenery inland, while the city itself is a fascinating mixture of old and new and happily

basks in its strong Napoleonic connections – the great man was born here. Ships usually stay a full day, although shorter stays are sometimes scheduled.

Arrival and around the dock The port is towards the northern end of the Bay of Ajaccio and, although there is much modern building in the city, the citadel overlooking it creates an impressive historical impression as you approach port. Most ships dock rather than tender passengers ashore, and there are plans to extend the pier to cater for bigger ships and persuade some lines to home-port here, from 2005. There is a new convention centre, the Millenari, which doubles as a passenger terminal and has exchange facilities and phones.

Seeing the sights Most excursions start with a tour around Ajaccio itself but this is easily accomplished independently. The main **market place** (selling handicrafts as well as food) is within sight of the pier. The **Old Town**, which sits below the citadel and within which are Maison Napoleon (no public access) and the cathedral where he was baptised, is just a short walk from there. The main shopping street – Cours Napoleon – borders the old town. In the newer part of the city, there are wide, tree-lined boulevards, parks and squares, and numerous statues of Napoleon, notably in the main square (General de Gaulle).

There are beaches within the city limits (the best is down the steps from Boulevard Lantivy), boat trips to the pretty **Îles Sanguinaire** just offshore in the bay, and plenty of taxis to take you further inland – albeit at a high price. There is also a railway station, from where there are regular scenic, if slow-moving, services to Corte, the original island capital.

Further afield Most of the interesting places in the vicinity are best visited on ships' excursions. They include a trip through the maquis-covered mountains to the **Prunella Gorges** and **Lake Tolla**. Another goes through the red granite mountains, granted UNESCO Heritage Site status, to the **Calanches de Piana**, the villages of Cargese, Pinto and Filitosa, with its legion of granite warriors, and the Spelunca Gorges.

CALVI

Very much a resort town now, Calvi is an attractive destination in its own right as well as being close enough for excursions to some of Corsica's best-known or most historic attractions.

Arrival and around the dock Like Ajaccio and Bonifacio, the first impression when approaching this Corsican port is the imposing presence of a huge citadel overlooking the town. Quai Landry is attractively landscaped and has many cafés overlooking the waterfront but it lies on a busy road, behind which lies the centre of the resort's vibrant nightlife. Ships have to anchor off and tender into the port area. Stays are either a full or half day.

Seeing the sights Within Calvi, there are two levels: the new town down by the port and an older quarter up towards the citadel. These are best explored

Maps on pages 167 & 176

TYPICAL EXCURSIONS, CALVI

● Full- or half-day tours of the **northern and central** part of the island.

● Full- or half-day trips to **Ajaccio** (see main text).

BELOW: the citadel overlooks Calvi marina.

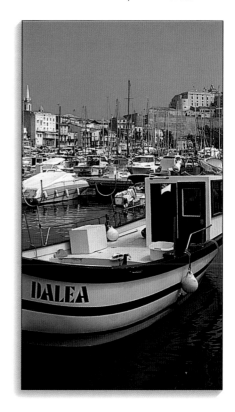

There is no shortage of statues of Napoleon in Ajaccio. This one is in Place Foch.

BELOW: welcome shade in the heat of the day.
RIGHT: eating out in St-Florent.

on foot, with the **Cathédrale St-Jean Baptiste** and the **Oratoire St-Antoine** the most impressive buildings along the way to the huge 15th-century **Citadelle**. To explore outside Calvi independently, there are (costly) taxis, locally booked coach excursions, or a train service either inland or, notably, to the lively resort of L'Île Rousse further up the west coast.

BASTIA AND ST-FLORENT

Bastia, the original capital of the island before the French replaced it with Ajaccio when they took control of Corsica, lies at the northern end of the east coast and remains an industrial, commercial and residential hub rather than a resort. St-Florent, a tiny harbour town at the northern tip of Corsica, has, in recent years, become a popular resort, with tourist development now beginning to stretch across the narrow Cap Corse to Bastia.

Arrival and around the dock First impressions on arriving in Bastia are of a sprawling and not particularly attractive city but right behind the new harbour is the attractive main square (St-Nicolas) with numerous outdoor café terraces. The harbour area of St-Florent, which is used by many private yachts, is lined with cafés, restaurants and shops.

Seeing the sights The Vieux Port of Bastia, easily walkable from the new harbour (via Place St-Nicolas), is the most attractive and interesting part of town, and is overlooked by an impressive citadel. The lengthy distances down the coast, or inland to the most interesting destinations, usually make the shore excursions, touring the northern half of the island, the most cost-effective option.

St-Florent, although short of decent beaches, is an attractive, atmospheric cruise port with shady squares, narrow cobbled alleys and a lively café society. It is easily walkable and there are taxis to take visitors to Bastia or further afield. A tour of the **Nebbio vineyard region** is best done on an organised excursion.

Map on page 167

PORTO VECCHIO

An old Genoese port in the south east of Corsica, Porto Vecchio is an attractive place somewhat off the beaten track in southeastern Corsica. The town dates from 1539 when the Genoese built fortifications – most of which remain today – to repel attacks from pirates and invaders from northern Africa.

Arrival and around the dock Porto Vecchio is at the end of the long eponymous gulf, framed by typically Corsican craggy hills covered in fragrant *maquis* scrub. If you wish to walk, the dock is a 10-minute stroll from the marina – past the commercial dock area – from where it is a further 5–10 minutes uphill to the old town. There are some cafés by the marina and you can arrange taxis from here if you miss those meeting your ship.

The tourist office is in the main square (Place de la République) by the 14th-century **Jean-Baptiste church**. The 16th-century **Porte Genoise** functioned as the town's only entrance, and the sturdy fortifications command expansive views across the harbour and surrounding countryside.

Further afield Most people who come to Porto Vecchio will visit **Bonifacio**, 28 km (16 miles) away, either on a guided tour, a shuttle bus organised by the cruise company, or by taxi. There is only one public bus per day, taking 30 min-

TYPICAL EXCURSIONS, BASTIA, ST-FLORENT and PORTO VECCHIO
- Half- and full-day tours of **northern Corsica**, from Bastia.
- Half-day tour from St-Florent to **Nebbio region** of vineyards, mountains, valleys.
- Half-day tour of **Bonifacio** from Porto Vecchio.
- Half-day trip to the mountains at **Bavella**.

BELOW: Bonifacio's 13th-century citadel.

Map on page 167

BELOW: Bonifacio's Haute Ville is built into the rock face.
RIGHT: Bonifacio, strongly fortified.

utes. Taxis cost around €40–45 one way. You can also take this bus to Figari via Sartene, Propriano (1 hr 45 mins), Olmeto and Ajaccio (3 hr 30 mins).

Excursions also travel to **Bavella**, high in the mountains. The white-sand beach at **Palombaggia** is one of the best in southern Corsica. If you don't take a pre-booked tour, the only realistic way to reach these places is by taxi or hire car.

BONIFACIO

On the southern tip of the island, Bonifacio is the ideal gateway to Corsica. The harbour affords excellent views of the towering cliffs that surround it but the town, while full of historic interest, is far from twee or picturesque: just like the rest of Corsica, in fact. Although they occasionally may be shorter, cruise-ship stays are usually a full day. Most ships have to anchor off and tender passengers in, even though it is the smaller cruise ships (particularly sail-cruisers) that opt for Bonifacio as their Corsican port of call.

Arrival and around the dock This is one of the most impressive arrivals in Mediterranean cruising. Turning from the sea into the Goulet de Bonifacio, the sheltered inlet, it is easy to imagine the days when the port was a pirate stronghold. Surrounded by white chalk cliffs and overlooked by the medieval citadel, even the compact Bonifacio townhouses are designed fortress-style to withstand sieges. Now, of course, the only invasion is by passengers from visiting cruise ships and the only pirates own the smart cafés, restaurants and souvenir shops that line the quayside and charge French Riviera prices.

The town centre (or the lower level of it) is right behind the quay so there is no need for shuttle-buses or taxis unless you want to go out of town. A recent addition to the harbour front is a small but smart terminal which passengers pass through from where the ships or tenders dock.

Shopping The ubiquitous souvenir is a bust of Napoleon, or his likeness on some piece of pottery or, even tackier, a tea-towel. Far better buys are the carved olive wood or cork bowls, which can be used for salad. Look out, too, for the attractive coral jewellery, although this does come at a fairly high price.

Seeing the sights There is no need to take an organised tour of Bonifacio itself, although a boat trip around the inlet does offer the best views of the ancient houses perched precariously on the cliffside and is the only way of exploring the cave of **Sdragonato** which has a hole in its ceiling that is bizarrely shaped just like the island of Corsica.

It is, though, a steep walk up the rock face, via the rough-hewn 15th-century "King of Aragon's Staircase", or a much longer walk by road up to the imposing 13th-century **Citadelle** and **Haute Ville**. Taxis are an option here but are generally too expensive for longer trips away from Bonifacio.

Further afield A hire car is advisable if you want to explore, but driving is tricky because of the narrow, winding roads. Public transport is infrequent. ❑

ITALY FROM GENOA TO THE BAY OF NAPLES

Map on page 188

Italy's Ligurian and Tyrrhenian coasts are central to Mediterranean cruising, taking in the underrated city of Genoa, the sparkling Riviera, the glories of Rome and the magical Amalfi coast

The western coast of Italy was once controlled by Genoa, a powerful mercantile and banking city which, in its 14th-century golden age, had ports and colonies stretching as far as the Black Sea. Today, these places are visited by cruise ships mainly to offer access to the glories of Florence, Siena and Rome – although Genoa and Naples are vibrant cities in their own right, and the ports on the stunning Amalfi coast attract smaller ships. Sailing west from Naples, the natural firework display that is Stromboli is a highlight on the way to Sardinia, which combines rugged beauty with cosmopolitan chic. Other Italian and Adriatic ports are covered in subsequent chapters.

SAVONA

Allied with Carthage against the Romans, Savona has been a significant harbour town since the 3rd century BC. Local art and architecture survive from the Middle Ages. Savona is known for figurative blue and white pottery, and glassware from nearby Altare. Local wines include Rossese di Dolceacqua, an attractive northern Italian red, and the white wines Pigato and Vermentino. Savona is a home port for some lines, and ships usually make a full day's stay.

Around the dock There is a long, single-storey terminal building with a large reception and embarkation area. There is also a small independent café in the port. It's a 20-minute walk into town, or there are frequent taxis.

Seeing the sights The **Municipal Art Gallery** in the 16th-century Palazzo Gavotti (Piazza Chabrol) features works by Picasso, Miró, Magritte, Man Ray and De Chirico. Savona's historic centre is near the port, and has palaces and churches from the 14th to 19th centuries. The church of **San Pietro** is a fine example of baroque architecture. To the south of town are beachfront cafés and restaurants.

GENOA

The great port of Genoa (Genova) is often bypassed by tourists eager to get to Florence or Pisa. Yet this vibrant, colourful city, Italy's largest Mediterrenean port, has a tremendous amount to offer. Designated the European City of Culture for 2004, Genoa still retains the feel of a gritty working port and its maritime heritage is reflected in the magnificently restored waterfront at the Old Port (Porto Antico), featuring the Museum of the Sea, world-class concert

PRECEDING PAGES: pretty little Portofino. **LEFT:** Neptune at Genoa's Old Port. **BELOW:** Palazzo Ducale, Genoa.

Map on page 188

and exhibitions centres and an excellent aquarium. Away from the harbour, this is not a city that lays out its treasures in wide easy boulevards. Only by exploring the narrow, twisting and sometimes very steep streets of the old quarter, between the prettily eccentric *trompe l'oeil* and lovely, but discreet little shops, do Genoa's secrets gradually begin to emerge.

Genoa is a centre of trade and banking, with a merchant history stretching back to the 5th century. The prosperous trading port flourished under Roman rule, and became a free commune in the 10th century. Providing supplies for the crusaders brought tremendous wealth and a small empire, with possessions from Spain to the Crimea. Christopher Columbus lived here for part of his childhood, and the house that his father leased has been reconstructed on the original site. Genoa was in the world's headlines in 2000 when the G8 summit drew massive crowds of protesters.

There is also a wide range of shopping opportunities. Via Orefici is a centre of goldsmiths, and many of Italy's top designers are represented in the streets radiating from the magnificent Piazza Ferrari. The Mercato Orientale at the edge of the historic centre is reckoned to be one of Europe's best markets. *Trenette* and *trofie* are the two local pasta specialities, both of which are delicious when served with the local pesto.

Genoa is a home port for some lines, and so is usually a full day's stay. For other lines it is available as an excursion from Savona.

TYPICAL EXCURSIONS, GENOA

● **Genoa**. City tour (3 hours).

● **Genoa**. Aquarium (3 hours; *see main text*).

● **Portofino**. Half-day tour to this picturesque little resort *(see main text)*.

Arrival and around the dock

Genoa crowds attractively around the hills above its harbour. This is a large and busy working port, and cruise ships dock in the industrial port area, from where it is a rather uninspiring 20-minute walk (turn right when you exit the docks and simply follow the main road) to the old port with its tourist information office, aquarium and other attractions. There are two neighbouring cruise terminals; the Stazzione Maritima at Ponte dei Mille – a large two-level building which was completely restored and upgraded for the G8 summit in 2001 – and the terminal at Ponte Andrea Doria, a 1930s building which is being refurbished. A new terminal and extra cruise-ship berth is being built at the Ponte Parodi, which is the closest to Genoa's historic old town. This will not be complete until 2007.

Stazione Principe, from where trains depart for Santa Margherita (close to Portofino), is within easy reach of both terminals. To enter the old part of the city from the dock area, you need to get across the main Strada Sopraelevata highway and look for Via di Prè – an interesting, long narrow street that runs parallel with the main road. This leads to the Via del Campo and on into the old town.

BELOW: opulent detail in Chiesa Santa Maria.

Seeing the sights

The main tourist information office is by the aquarium at the old port. The small kiosk is well supplied with travel information, and the helpful staff speak good English.

For the **Acquario** (aquarium; open daily; fee), crowds and queues can be huge, so it's worth knowing that tickets can be bought in advance for use later in the day. The shelled or scaly occupants include angel fish, seals, turtles, giant Japanese crabs, luminous gold medusas, alligators, crocodiles, rays and coral; in fact it's hard to think of a water dweller that isn't represented.

Two bottleneck dolphins have a huge tank to play in, and a whole wing is given to shore and shallow-water dwellers like rays, lizards and turtles. One of the last tanks has irrepressible, stripy Humboldt penguins diving, swimming or just waddling and peering beakily. In front of the aquarium is the **pirate galleon** *Neptune* (open daily 10am–1pm; fee). This elaborate and ornate replica of a Caribbean brigand starred in the 1986 Roman Polanski film *Pirates*. The *Neptune* has a 5-metre (15-ft) figurehead of the sea-god himself.

Turning inland from the harbour with its modern attractions, Genoa's ancient secrets begin to unfold in the lively street market of the **Piazza Banchi**. A *trompe l'oeil* church – the **Chiesa di San Pietro della Porta** – was built in the 16th century above the commercial buildings in the square, and was recently renovated as a pastel extravaganza. Also here is the impressive **Loggia dei Mercanti**; built in the 18th century, this massive, marble-floored hall once housed the stock exchange and now frequently hosts exhibitions.

The narrow alleyways of the historic centre twist and wind off from the piazza. Tucked away in the Piazza della Santa Maria Magdalene is a radiant jewel of a church, the **Chiesa Santa Maria Magdalene**. It is vastly opulent, from the frescoes depicting the life of Christ on every vaulted offertory, to the Wedgwood-blue organ loft.

BELOW: one of San Lorenzo's imposing stone lions.

A rare, wide-open space, the **Piazza Ferrari** is the hub of the city. The fashionable shopping streets Via XX Settembre, Via Roma and Via XXV Aprile converge with Via Dante here. The centrepiece is a large fountain which

Map
on page
188

provides welcome cooling water on a hot afternoon. The **Palazzo Ducale** borders the northwest side of the square. The interior has a large white vaulted room and an airy columned courtyard.

Along Via Tommasso on the Piazza San Lorenzo is the 13th-century black and white marble **Duomo** (cathedral; open Mon–Sat; fee), also known as San Lorenzo. With shallow Gothic arches, and steps flanked by docile-looking reclining lions, this is an outstanding Pisan-style building and campanile. The dome was designed by Alessi.

On **Via Dante** on the right from Piazza Ferrari, and in the shadow of the old city gate, is a reconstruction of the young Columbus's home, **Casa di Columbo**. A copy of the lease from the monastery to Columbus's father, dated 18 January 1455, is displayed in front of the house.

For shopping, Louis Vuitton, Baccarat and Ferragamo have stores in **Via Roma**. Small antique and carpet shops and an Illy café nestle in **Via XXV Aprile**, popular with the expensively-dressed at lunchtime. Through the ivy-draped arch of the Galleria Garibaldi tunnel, **Via Garibaldi** is just one of the streets lined with 16th-century mansions and *palazzos* built with the wealth that came from Genoa's maritime power.

For a panoramic overview of Genoa, the port and the Mediterranean, a **cable car** runs from the Piazza dell'Annunziata up to the ancient fortifications.

The ornately decorated Palazzo San Giorgio in Genoa.

Further afield Most cruise lines will operate excursions from Genoa to the picturesque town of **Portofino**, but it is possible to get there on your own – either by train or bus; there are frequent trains from Stazione Principe to Santa Margherita (for Portofino) – the faster ones do the journey in 30 or 40 minutes.

BELOW: ancient Genoa, viewed from offshore.

Other possibilities include the genteel Riviera resort of **San Remo**, the beautiful **Cinque Terre region** south of La Spezia and even Pisa and Florence, but these are a little too distant for most cruise passengers (although transport links from Genoa are good).

PORTOFINO & SANTA MARGHERITA

Portofino (meaning Port of Dolphins) has been a magnet for the beautiful people since the 19th century. It's easy to see why; the port is a gorgeous, tiny natural harbour, tumbling eastwards through a steep, wooded bay. Fish dart and sparkle in the clear, deep green waters under the Ligurian Riviera sun. It is linked to Santa Margherita by a picturesque coast road which winds around the promontory. Buses depart every 20 minutes – buy tickets from newspaper vendors, not on the bus.

Neither Portofino nor Santa Margherita have docks for liners, so a tender service ferries passengers to shore. Sunbathing and sightseeing are the main attractions, but in Portofino there are extremely upmarket stores selling clothes and jewellery.

Arrival and around the dock If you are tendered into harbour around breakfast time, you will see, on gleaming yachts nearest the town, tanned guests being served with buck's fizz, scrambled eggs, croissants and coffee. Further out in the harbour, the poorer seafarers have to serve, and sometimes even prepare, their own. In spring the air is fragrant with apricot, almond and peach blossom, while scooters and cicadas provide the soundtrack. Clustered around the cobblestones of the marina are restaurants, bars and cafés catering to the movie stars and ocean-borne gentry. Surprisingly, the coffee is not the most expensive in the Mediterranean, and is served in tastefully matched china, on immaculate linen. The shopping area is just a couple of streets clustered around the harbour, where Cartier, Missoni and Hermès stores are frequented by bronzed folk with perfect hair.

Seeing the sights The **Hotel Splendido** presides majestically over the cove. Formerly a Benedictine monastery, the building was remodelled at the turn of the 20th century into what is now one of the world's most desirable hotels.

On the east side of the bay is a steep but lovely sculpture park, where large stone turtles climb up the wooded steps. It's ideal for a cool interlude, but the opening hours are as unpredictable and whimsical as the collection. Further above the harbour, a beautiful walk leads through shady woods with glorious glimpses of the bays on either side, to the **Santuario di San Giorgio**. The walk winds down along the cypress-combed promontory to the point where a bar has thoughtfully been provided next to an elegant, silver-domed white lighthouse.

Boats run regularly, frequently and inexpensively between Portofino, Santa Margherita and the **Abbazia di San Fruttuoso**. The mouth of the bay of San Fruttuoso is the location of an underwater statue

TYPICAL
EXCURSIONS,
PORTOFINO
● Genoa. Half-day
city tour.
● Genoa. Half-day
visit to the aquarium.

BELOW:
even the dogs are
elegant in Portofino.

of Christ. Taken to Genoa for restoration and the replacement of one hand, the statue was returned as part of the celebrations for Genoa, as the 2004 European City of Culture.

In front of the Abbazia is a small, lovely and very popular beach with two bars, beach chairs and umbrellas for hire. Boats offer fishing trips and excursions from the harbour. In the Abbazia itself are exhibits of exquisite amber, pottery from the 13th to the 15th century, and historic masonry from the monastery, all with helpful annotations, almost all in Italian. The cloisters give lovely views of the bay.

Santa Margherita was once a quiet little fishing village. Now it's a prim and pretty little town of harbour-front bars, cafés and restaurants. There are sandy beaches, rare on the promontory, at which changing cabins, loungers and parasols are for hire from the beach bars.

Narrow streets lead away from the harbour, packed with excellent delicatessens and a few designer clothes shops, mostly with yachty themes. The American bar of the Master restaurant is a good place to refresh yourself and people-watch, and excellent risotto and pizzas are to be had from the outdoor tables at Da Alfredo on the Piazza Martin della Libertá.

Fresh fruit for sale in Portofino market.

PORTOVENERE

A visit to Portovenere is a highlight of any cruise. Perched at the end of a long, thin promontory, its cheerfully coloured tall buildings crowd against the steep slopes, with the cliffs of the Cinque Terre plunging into the aquamarine sea all around – a magical setting which is only enhanced when arriving by ship.

BELOW: opportunities for shopping and sailing in Portofino.

Arrival and around the dock Cruise ships cannot dock in Portovenere so those going ashore are tendered in. The waterfront has the usual collection of tourist shops, attractive pavement cafés and fish restaurants. The tourist office "Pro Loco" is set at the back of small Piazza Bastreri to the right of the waterfront.

Seeing the sights Most people head up to the Gothic marble- and granite-striped church of **San Pietro**, superbly situated at the far end of the promontory. From the terrace, a popular setting for open-air concerts, there are tremendous views towards the precipitous forested hills of Cinque Terre and Lerici. A staircase leads up to **Grotta Arpaia**, known as Byron's Grotto. This stretch of coast will forever be linked to the fateful musings of the English Romantic poets. Lord Byron, a strong swimmer then living in a villa in neighbouring La Spezia, loved the wildness of the waters around Portovenere. However, in 1822 his friend Shelley was drowned while attempting to sail from Livorno to Lerici, where he had a small house.

Narrow winding backstreets and flights of steps lead steeply up to the Romanesque parish church of **San Lorenzo**, which has Gothic and Renaissance additions. Directly above is the **Castle** (open daily am and pm but closed noon–2pm; fee); in medieval times Portovenere was a fortified outpost of the Republic of Genoa, but the Genoese structure was largely dismantled in 1453, and the present castle is baroque. Via G. Capellini, lined with old houses with decorated facades and old-fashioned shops, leads back down to Piazza Bastreri.

Further Afield There are two buses every hour to/from **La Spezia** (journey time 30 minutes; buses depart from outside the Grand Hotel on the northern side

TYPICAL
EXCURSIONS,
PORTOVENERE

● **Pisa** (full day).

● **Florence** (full day) –
sometimes combined
with **Pisa**.

● The **Cinque Terre**.

BELOW: San Pietro commands the entrance to the harbour at Portovenere.

of the harbour), Italy's largest naval port and an attractive enough place to wander around for an afternoon. Of more interest is the scenery of the **Cinque Terre** – it is possible to strike out on foot from Portovenere (the tourist office has details and maps of marked footpaths running through the region). Boat trips from Portovenere are popular along the Cinque Terre coast. Further afield, but easy to reach by train or bus from La Spezia, are Pisa, Florence and – in the other direction – Genoa. From Portovenere there are boat trips to the Isola Palmaria, colonised by Benedictine monks in medieval times.

LIVORNO

Founded in the 16th century by the Grand Dukes of Tuscany – the Medici Family – **Livorno** has been a key Italian port ever since (Leghorn, the anglicised version of the port's name, has thankfully fallen out of fashion). An elegant city of baroque and Renaissance villas until the first half of the 20th century, Livorno was repeatedly and disastrously bombed during World War II. Rebuilt, the modern city had become somewhat rundown by the 1990s, but is now showing signs of greater prosperity – some of it brought about by the increasing number of cruise ships calling here. It is Italy's third-largest seaport and, as well as an on-going restoration of the town, there are firm plans for a new cruise terminal complex, with hotels and a convention centre.

For most cruise visitors, Livorno is simply the gateway to **Florence** (Firenze; Uffizi Gallery, Il Duomo, Ponte Vecchia), **Pisa** (Leaning Tower) and the Tuscan towns of **Lucca** and **Siena** and their surrounding countryside. Most cruise ships arrive in the early morning and leave early or late evening to allow enough time for excursions into Florence. Only very occasionally do cruises start or finish here.

Arrival and around the dock

This is not one of the most exciting arrivals in Mediterranean cruising, with the ship docking in the heart of a busy commercial port that is no more scenic close up than it looks from the ship as it approaches. Ships dock either at the cruise terminal or around the corner in the cargo area of the port. Turn left outside the terminal and it is a short walk (about 200 metres/yds) past the security check-point out to the main road.

Next to the check-point is a tourist information kiosk where, along with town maps, you can get information on the bus services which stop right outside. There is a ticket machine by the bus stop although it only takes euro coins. All buses go to Livorno's main square (Plaza Grande), 5 minutes' drive away.

You can also walk into town by turning right out of the port onto an overpass. It takes about 10 minutes to reach the main shopping street, Via Grande, on the left, which leads into Plaza Grande.

However, if your ship docks in the cargo area, your only option for reaching the centre – aside from a long (45-minute), dusty and pretty uninspiring walk – will be the shuttle provided by the cruise line, either free or for about €4 each way. This drops off and picks up just off Plaza Grande. Whichever part of the port your ship deposits you in, you will not want to linger long in the immediate vicinity.

Map on page 188

TYPICAL EXCURSIONS, LIVORNO

● **Florence**. Full-day tour *(see main text)*.
● **Pisa**. Half-day tour.
● **Pisa** and **Florence** as full-day tour.
● **Scenic drives in Tuscany**. Half-day tour, some with visits to vineyards for winetasting, others to the walled, garden city of **Lucca**, where Puccini was born.

BELOW: San Miniato, on a hill above Florence.

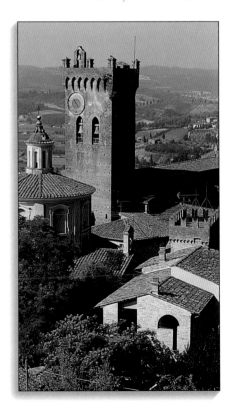

The famous Leaning Tower of Pisa, stabilised since 2001.

BELOW: the Ponte Vecchio spans the River Arno.

Shopping For women, shoes, clothes and jewellery are the draw. For men, sharp suits, leather and suede jackets are popular. There are some classy shops in Livorno (Via Grande) and also in Pisa but the best, inevitably, are in Florence. At the gold and silver jewellery shops and stalls on the Ponte Vecchia over the Arno River in Livorno, you may get some joy from haggling but don't expect discounts in the stores found in the main shopping streets like Via Tornabuoni, which runs from the Arno to Piazza Antinori.

Seeing the sights Although the port area is instantly forgettable, a stroll around the town centre can be rewarding. There are some pretty bars and cafés along the river inlets from the Ligurian Sea and the historic, crumbling **Fortezza Vecchia** (north of Plaza Grande) is worth a visit. There are fragments of many periods of Livorno's history here, from Roman remains in the dungeons to a Romanesque tower and 14th-century walls. The restored Fortezza Nuova, meanwhile, is now a conference and festival centre. Between the two forts is the canal area of **Venezia** – seedy, but with an intriguing atmosphere.

Getting to Pisa and Florence A ticket bought at the bus stop machine outside the cruise terminal will also cover the 15-minute journey from Plaza Grande to the railway station on bus No. 1, as long as you catch that bus within an hour of buying the ticket. There is a train to Pisa every 15 minutes or so (except in the middle of the day when it drops to every 30 minutes); the journey takes about 20 minutes and the fare is very reasonable. There is also a direct shuttle bus (bookable in advance on some ships) from the port to the railway station, but it only runs seven times a day.

Maps on pages 188 & 197

The reason for taking this tortuous route to Pisa is not just to save on the price of the excursion or a taxi fare – the fact is that taxi drivers are unwilling to take cruise visitors the short distance to Pisa unless you agree to a longer tour of the city or beyond. It is the same story at Pisa station, where you need to catch another bus (from Stand A – tickets from the station newspaper stand) to the Campo dei Miracoli (Field of Miracles) for the Leaning Tower, the Duomo and the Baptistery. By the afternoon, though, taxi drivers will be happy to take you back to the ship, either from Pisa or Livorno.

There are trains to Florence from both Pisa and Livorno stations. Frequency is between one and two trains an hour in each direction, from both. Journey times are between 75 and 90 minutes from Pisa and 90 minutes and 2 hours from Livorno. If there are two or more of you, though, it is still worth considering the morning taxi tour option in preference to the ship's excursions to any of the main attractions – Florence, Pisa, Lucca or Siena.

With a round trip taxi fare to Florence costing €220–260 (2004 rates), for example, it will usually work out cheaper for three or four people than buying excursion tickets, although you must agree a price in advance and, if possible, choose a driver with good English and awareness of when the ship departs.

However, if you choose to take an excursion, most lines now offer a choice of fully escorted, half-day escorted, or completely go-as-you-please tours to the major galleries, museums and designer-label stores. Some cruise lines are now even operating shuttle services to/from Florence (for which you pay).

Once in Florence you will want to walk around – in fact, most of the city is pedestrianised. But it is not a huge city and the Arno River running through does make it easy to keep your bearings.

Michelangelo's David.

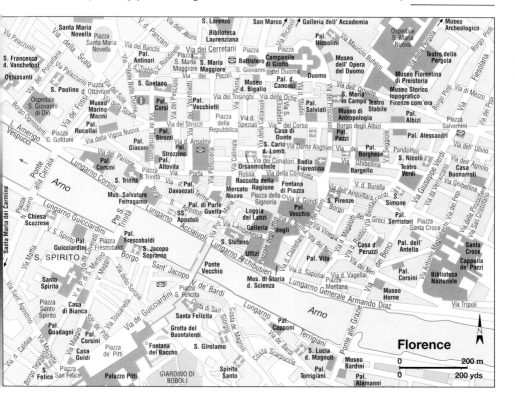

There are usually long queues for the Uffizi Gallery so you may have to trade off a visit there for seeing some of the other sights. And there are so many of them: the Duomo, the Baptistery, a host of elegant squares and splendid palaces (especially the Palazzo Medici-Riccardi). If you are in the Uffizi area and have time, try Alfredo's, the surprisingly modestly priced restaurant with a balcony overlooking the Arno and the Ponte Vecchio, cross the bridge from the Uffizi side, turn left and the restaurant entrance is 50 metres/yds along on the left).

PORTOFERRAIO AND ELBA

As every schoolboy knows, Elba was the island of exile for Napoleon Bonaparte from which he soon escaped – only to lose the Battle of Waterloo and be re-exiled, this time more successfully in the South Atlantic. There are plenty of reminders of the great man on the island, which nowadays prospers through its burgeoning tourist industry.

Arrival and around the dock Approaching Portoferraio it is easy to see why Nelson called this the safest harbour in the world – overlooked as it is by the seemingly impregnable bulk of the Medici and Stella forts and the Torre del Martello. Cruise ships dock right in the town, a couple of minutes walk from the attractive old harbour.

Seeing the sights With such a favoured location, it is not surprising that Portoferraio can trace its origins way back into antiquity – according to Greek mythology it was one of the ports of call for the Argonauts, and the Romans and Etruscans both settled here, when it was known as Fabricia. However, the port really came of age in the mid-16th century, when the Medicis made it their main base for defending their domains against troublesome Saracen pirates.

At the dock, the Molo del Gallo, you're right below the fortifications of the old part of the town. Turn right as you disembark and walk round the corner to the old harbour, then uphill to **Fort Stella** (open daily; fee) or simply head straight uphill from the dock to reach the **Medici fort**. At the far side of Fort Stella from the harbour is Napoleon's residence, the **Villa dei Mulini** (open daily; fee). Most of its charm lies in the period furnishings and Italianate gardens.

The old harbour is lined with cafés and shops, with the main shopping streets around Piazza Cavour reached through the distinctive Porta a Mare archway at the centre of the harbour.

Further Afield Elba is small, so if you have a full day you can reach pretty much anywhere by taxi. Buses depart from just round the corner from the port (turn left) in the new part of town to **San Martino** (Napoleon's summer residence; open daily; fee) every hour, only 6 km (4 miles) away. The villa here is compact, but has the most exquisite views down to Portoferraio. Napoleon's Nile campaigns of 1798–99 are recalled in the Egyptian-style frescoes in the house. There is a fine garden shaded by evergreen oaks and terraced vineyards.

The spectacular drive westward from Portoferraio to **Marciana Marina** passes a number of popular beaches, including Le Ghiaie, noted for its multicoloured pebbles, and La Biodola, considered the chicest beach on Elba. From Marciana, a cable car lurches over crags and chasms to the summit of **Monte Capanne**.

Maps on pages 188 & 200

CIVITAVECCHIA (ROME)

Civitavecchia was commissioned as a port in 106BC by the Emperor Trajan, because it was in the ideal geographical position to serve the city of Rome. It continues to do so today and is one of Italy's best equipped ports. Civitavecchia is the start or finish point of many cruises, but those ships passing through will normally spend a full day here to allow passengers to visit Rome, some 80 km (50 miles) to the southeast.

Rome (Roma) itself is a highlight of any Mediterranean cruise and a walk in the Eternal City is a stroll through the history of Western civilisation. Ancient ruins, magnificent churches and works of Renaissance art combine with the energy and colour of modern Italy to make this one of the world's most fascinating and enjoyable cities. Its incredible history has seen it become the epicentre of one of the largest and most powerful empires the world has ever seen; the home of the Catholic Church and, as such, a place of pilgrimage for millions; one of the major centres of the world-changing 15th-century Renaissance; and the capital of the Italian nation state. A single day is never enough to properly explore Rome, but having said this, even a short visit is immensely rewarding.

Arrival and around the docks   As the ship turns into dock, Civitavecchia doesn't appear promising. Apart from the castellated bastions of

TYPICAL EXCURSIONS, CIVITAVECCHIA

● **Rome**. All excursions, not surprisingly, lead to Rome, and all take a full day. Cruise lines all offer a mainstream city tour. Most lines also offer **themed tours** – concentrating, for example, on the Vatican, or ancient Roman ruins.

BELOW: the Colosseum in all its glory.

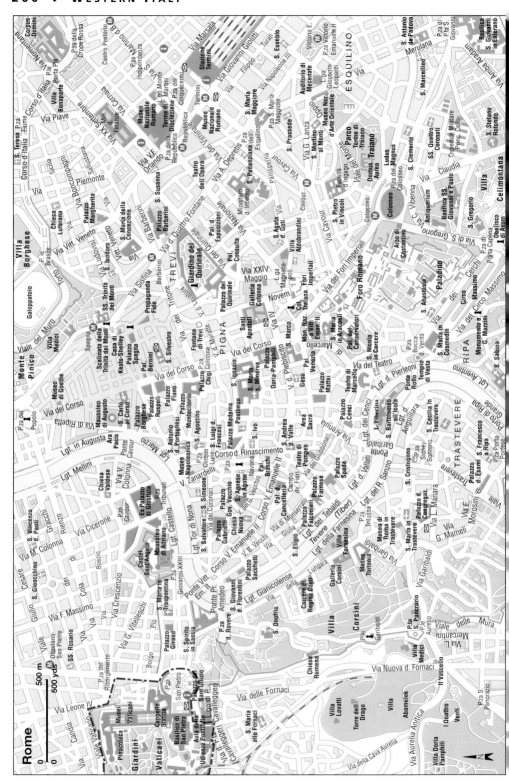

Rome

a medieval dominating the harbour, the most striking impression is of cranes and other industrial port accoutrements. In fact, this belies a pleasant town with attractive colonnaded villas surrounded by greenery.

Shuttle buses and taxis wait on the narrow quayside by the long, low terminal building to make the short journey into town. There is an attractive, tree-lined harbour and the medieval fortress, **Forte Michelangelo**, is open to the public. The town is well known for shoe-shopping, and it is a pleasant day out for anyone who doesn't want to go to Rome. Beyond the railway station are fish restaurants set right over the water and a number of small beaches. These are not great for swimming, though, because of the proximity to huge ships in the port.

Getting to Rome Organised cruise-line excursions to Rome are always available, but assuming you have enough time in port, it's quite easy to travel independently by train. The journey is fast, 50–75 minutes depending on the train, and cheap, the price also varying with the type of train. Tickets can be bought on the train at no extra charge. At the Civitavecchia railway station, the red-tiled roof, the excellent coffee, the flowers and faded charm common to most Italian stations are in evidence. Chianti, Prosecco and other Italian wines and beers are on sale in the shop for a fraction of the on-board prices.

In the morning there are two trains to Rome every hour. Times vary, but the Italian railway, Trenitalia, has a good website for timetables. The English language version is at www.trenitalia.com/home/en. For the Vatican, get off at San Pietro station if possible, otherwise stay on until Termini, the main terminus for Rome. Validate your return ticket by punching it in one of the machines on the platform.

Shopping in Rome If going it alone, plan your trip accordingly and be aware of the siesta hours, when nearly all shops and some museums and galleries are closed – normally 1–4pm, although this can vary seasonally. Nearly all shops are closed on Sunday, which, unfortunately for shoppers, is a popular day for cruise-ship visits.

When the stores are open, Rome is as glittering a shopping centre as you could wish for. All the world's finest clothes designers have shops in the Eternal City. There are galleries of art and antiques, fine fabrics, glassware and ceramics, jewellery and wonderful food and wines. Near the Spanish Steps, Via Borgognona and Via Condotti are the chicest of the chic, while Via del Corso is good for younger and more affordable fashions. Via Veneto is known particularly for luxury leather goods – a wonderful buy.

Lining the fine, vaulted railway station are clothes shops, a book shop with a decent-sized English section (mostly thrillers and romances), and a cookware shop with more Italian cooking gadgets than you could shake a pasta spoon at. Particularly on Sunday, you could do worse than shop in the station itself, but keep in mind that the shops here also observe siesta hours.

Seeing the sights Within easy walking distance of Termini station are both the **Museo Nazionale**

Maps on pages 188 & 200

Noble busts in the Galleria Grassi.

BELOW:
Roman fashion in Via Condotti.

Romano (open Tues–Sun am; fee), which holds many of Rome's important antiquities; and the sumptuous 17th-century Palazzo Barberini, which houses the **Galleria Nazionale de Arte Antica** (open Tues–Sun am; fee), displaying some wonderful paintings by Lippi, El Greco and Caravaggio, among others. Visiting them, then having a leisurely lunch or a drink at any one of the outdoor cafés and restaurants still leaves time to return to the ship.

Alternatively, you could take the metro, which runs from Termini to Colosseo for the Colosseum, Spagna for the Spanish Steps or Barberini for Via Veneto and the Trevi Fountain. A Metrobus card gives inexpensive access to the bus and metro network for a whole day. The metro carriages are adorned with graffiti, and loud and ebullient buskers are apt to leap on, not just with guitars, but often with whole sound systems. It can be a deafening but atmospheric experience.

By the foot of the **Spanish Steps** stands the pink house where John Keats, the romantic English poet, died. **Babington's** (open Wed–Mon), a popular English tea house, is at the other side of the steps. Founded in 1893 by an English woman traveller who despaired of getting a good cup of tea, it is still run by the same family. As befits a palace to the English obsession, excellent speciality teas are served, including a wonderful rose-infused Chinese black tea.

For shoppers, Dior, Gucci, and Moschino cluster among the retail temples nearby. The steps themselves are a magnetic draw for travellers, musicians and street merchants peddling T-shirts, leatherwear and jewellery. Make the climb to the top and you'll be rewarded by a view across the Roman roofline to the Vatican and the seven hills of the city. At the top are upmarket art galleries.

The **Trevi Fountain**, within walking distance of the Spanish Steps, is the most popular coin collector in Europe. The story goes that if you want to return

BELOW: exterior view of the Museo Nazionale Romano.

to Rome, you should stand with your back to the fountain, and toss a coin over your shoulder and into the water. Another legend has it that the offering will assure your return to the sea, a safe bet for cruisers. The fountain was built as the front of the church of **Santi Vincenzo e Anastasio** by sculptor Nicola Salvi between 1732 and 1762.

On Sunday, the most popular flea market in Rome is the **Porta Portese**. It's huge and bustling with stalls full of treasures and trash and Turkish rugs. Do as the Romans do, and keep all your money, wallets, purses and valuables under at least one layer of clothing.

The ruins of the Stadium of Domitian, the scene of Roman chariot races, lie beneath the **Piazza Navona**; popes in medieval times flooded the square to stage sea-battles. Now free from flooding, combat and traffic, the splendid piazza is a great place for lunch or a drink. Eat a thin, crisp Roman pizza, or lunch at one of the fine restaurants. Marvel at Bernini's wonderful **Four Rivers fountain** (1551) and watch people having fun by the water. In the evening, the piazza serves as an open-air gallery for Roman artists.

One of the great remains of the ancient world is the **Colosseum** (open daily, but closes at 3 or 4pm in winter; fee). Formerly clad in marble, at its height it could seat 50,000 for the "bread and circuses" spectacles. It opened in AD80 with a bloody combat between gladiators and wild beasts lasting for weeks, and it is believed that the arena could be flooded for sea battles.

The Vatican In AD324, Emperor Constantine declared Christianity to be the official religion of the Roman Empire, and the first Christian churches were built in the city. But with the empire in decline, Constantine moved the imperial seat

Map on page 200

The Spanish Steps are a popular meeting place.

LEFT:
selling flowers in Piazza di Spagna.
BELOW:
the Trevi fountain.

Visitors admiring some of the vast collection of devotional art in the Vatican Museum.

to Constantinople – formerly Byzantium and now Istanbul, although the papacy remained in Rome. The Holy Roman Empire, as it became, was to prove by far the most enduring phase of Roman influence. The **Vatican City** is a self-contained sovereign state, and with only 400 passport-holders, is one of the world's tiniest nations. For many travellers, this is Rome's most important site. The crowds are usually large, so a visit here could take up most of the day's stay.

Bernini's spectacularly Doric-colonnaded **Piazza San Pietro** is overlooked by the statues of 140 saints. This immense space forms the entrance to **St Peter's** basilica (open daily; fee). St Peter is believed to have been crucified at the Circus of Nero, just to the left of the site. The basilica was built at the order of Emperor Constantine, in AD324. Most of the major Renaissance and baroque artists and architects contributed work to the church.

Some of the greatest devotional art of the Christian world is displayed in the **Musei e Gallerie del Vaticano** (open summer Mon–Fri; winter Mon–Sat am; fee). The vast collections can hardly be sampled in a day, so aim for a few highlights; the Belvedere courtyard and the pope's antique collection in the **Museo Pio-Clementino** and the Raphaels in the **Pinacoteca**, for instance. Alternatively, see the frescoes by Botticelli, Pinturiccino and Ghilrandaio in the **Cappella Sistina** (Sistine Chapel) and, surely the finest fresco the world has to offer, the ceiling by Michaelangelo.

BELOW: The Vatican's Piazza San Pietro, seen from the basilica.

NAPLES

The vast Bay of Naples is dominated by the hazy, cone-shaped mass of Vesuvius, slumbering behind the urban sprawl of the city. Naples (Napoli), along with pretty Sorrento, the glamorous island of Capri, and Amalfi, on the Gulf of

Salerno to the south, are the major ports of call for Pompeii, Herculaneum and the gorgeous, romantic Amalfi Coast.

Even by Italian standards, Naples seems to be a city in a state of permanent organised chaos, with all of its 1½ million-plus inhabitants apparently on the roads at the same time. It has the country's second-busiest port, which is very much the hub of the city, with the most interesting sights within a short radius. There is a €500m-project underway to transform parts of the city, including the port area. The cruise terminal is to be completely refurbished by 2005 and other improvements will include the creation of a pedestrianised promenade and a tourist yacht marina complex.

Currently, though, Naples' appearance on so many cruise itineraries is due to its location rather than its own attractions. Not only are the major archeological sites of Pompeii and Herculaneum just a few miles away, the city is also the gateway to the Amalfi Coast.

Naples is rarely used as a home port. The infrastructure is there but cruise lines prefer to use it as a port of call (always a full-day stay) to enable passengers to choose from a variety of shore excursions.

Arrival and around the dock Cruising into the Bay of Naples is a memorable experience with an impressive entrance into the port which is overlooked by an imposing medieval castle, Sant' Elmo, high on Vemero Hill, and another, the 13th-century Castel Nuovo, right where the ships dock, either side of a large terminal building, the Stazione Maritima.

Reminiscent of a grand, 19th-century railway station, the ship terminal has been partially refurbished, but it still has comparatively few facilities. There is an

Maps on pages 200 & 208

TYPICAL EXCURSIONS, NAPLES

● **Pompeii or Herculaneum** (half-day tour).

● **City tours** (max. three hours).

● Full-day tour combining **Pompeii** with **Sorrento** and **Positano, Capri**, an **Amalfi Coast** drive or a **Mount Vesuvius** hike.

● **Capri** (full-day tour).

BELOW: Vesuvius from Sant Elmo.

information point, just the other side of the security checkpoint, but the building is not air-conditioned and it can seem a long, hot walk up and down a series of steep flights of steps to ground level. There are a handful of rather uninspiring souvenir shops and a couple of newspaper stands where phone cards can be bought for the public telephones by the entrance. Once outside, you are right in the heart of Naples but taxis are plentiful if you want one – there is a permanent line of them outside the terminal – and cheaper than in most other parts of Italy. However, driving (or being driven) in Naples can be a heart-stopping experience.

Although the main city appears to extend to the right of the terminal, the most interesting part is the old quarter, straight ahead past Castel Nuovo and over the Piazza Municipio, or to the left towards the Piazza Plebiscito. Also immediately to the left is Molo Beverello – the dock and ticket station for the ferry and hydrofoil services to Sorrento and Capri.

"Portrait of a Woman" in the Museu Nazionale, Naples.

Shopping   Naples is not as geared for tourism as some of the other Italian cities, and if your ship calls on a Saturday or Sunday, most shops will be shut for most of both days. The cruise lines generally recommend shops in Pompeii, Sorrento or Capri. But there are three good Neopolitan buys: cameo jewellery, Capodimonte porcelain and pizzas. The pizza was invented in the city and the Margherita, originally made for a 19th-century queen to reflect the colours of the Italian flag, remains for many the tastiest memory of the city.

BELOW: no one makes pizzas like the Neopolitans.

Seeing the sights   Although there are short city tours on offer, they devote most of the time to scenic drives outside and above Naples, because the only real way to see what the city has to offer is on foot.

Within a 15-minute walk from the terminal there are three of the city's best-known sights: the **Castel Nuovo**, with an extraordinary Renaissance arch; the **Palazzo Reale** (open daily; fee), with a monumental marble staircase; and the ornate, 18th-century **Teatro San Carlo**, the largest opera house in Italy. A longer walk (or short taxi ride) across the Piazza Municipio and up Via Toledo brings you to a fourth place of interest – the **Museo Archeològico Nazionale** (open daily; fee), which has a huge collection of finds from Pompeii and Herculaneum.

One of the pleasures of Naples, though, is just wandering the old streets. The buzzing of the ubiquitous scooters and the sound of car horns mean it won't be a quiet walk, and you should be very careful about your valuables, but this is the only way to soak up the atmosphere of the narrow streets, festooned with washing and window boxes and the smells of frying fish and garlic.

Further afield   It is possible to make independent visits, by taxi, to the ruins of the two Roman cities, **Pompeii** and **Herculaneum**, buried by the eruption of Mount Vesuvius in AD79. Pompeii can also be reached by train, as can **Sorrento**. Take a taxi 3 km (2 miles) to the Circumvesuviana station – *not* Central station – from where Pompeii is just a 30-minute journey and Sorrento a 1-hour trip.

For **Capri**, the hydrofoil is the only option. The journey time of 45 minutes each way leaves plenty of time to explore the island and there are departures about every half hour. There are also less frequent hydrofoil services to Sorrento, 30 minutes away on the opposite side of the Bay of Naples. Return fares (at 2004 rates) are approximately €24 to Capri and €16 to Sorrento *(see the following text for details of Amalfi, Capri and Sorrento)*.

Map on page 208

AMALFI

Once home to 80,000 people and, in the 9th century, Italy's main trading port, Amalfi, which gives its name to the stretch of craggy Italian coast between Sorrento and Salerno, is now a small, busy tourist town. Even the smaller cruise ships have to anchor off and tender passengers ashore. Ships usually stay a full day but sometimes only a half-day stay is scheduled.

Arrival and around the dock Cruising into the sheltered harbour of Amalfi is one of the most attractive approaches in Mediterranean cruising. With its red-tiled roofs contrasting with the Spanish-style whitewashed houses, the town nestles at the foot of a steeply sloped wooded gorge. Tenders bring you right into the heart of town and, although there is no terminal, the quayside (at Piazza Flavio Gioia) is just across the road from a taxi rank, tourist information centre, telephones, banks and currency exchange bureaux and only 100 metres/yds from the main square, Piazza Duomo.

Shopping Most of the shops are aimed at tourists, which means that they are open all day but that they are not the best places for quality goods. There are some interesting handicrafts, though, and you can't avoid bottles of Limoncello, the locally made liqueur.

Seeing the sights Amalfi is a compact town so a walking tour is easy to do on your own. The main attraction – apart from its many cafés, seafood restaurants, shops and a small beach – is the cathedral, the **Duomo di Sant'Andrea**, with attractive cloisters and crypt, in Piazza Duomo. This dates to the 9th century but has been rebuilt and restored many times. A short walk further inland from the square there is a paper museum (in a former paper mill) and the Limoncello factory. Walk east along the waterfront for 10 minutes from the quayside to reach a former convent, now a hotel (Luna Convento) with a separate restaurant built into a fort overlooking the sea. Another 5–10 minutes' walk brings you to the smaller, less touristy town of **Atrani**. There are buses – the orange-coloured Sita line – to the pretty hill resort of **Ravello** (about 45 minutes) – or a ferry (20 minutes) up the coast to **Positano**, but taxis are the safest option if time is tight; as a guideline, they cost about €50 an hour. **Pompeii** is about 90 minutes' drive away.

SORRENTO

Conveniently located at one end of Italy's Amalfi Coast, Sorrento is a pleasant, atmospheric town with pretty piazzas, lots of shops, cafés and restaurants,

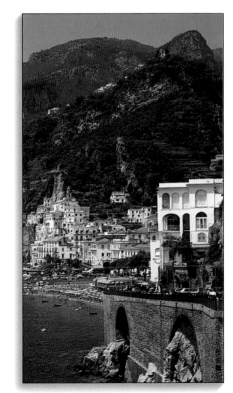

TYPICAL EXCURSIONS, SORRENTO

● **Positano** and **Amalfi** (full-day tour).
● **Naples** (full-day tour).
● **Capri**. Full-day tour (unless your ship's itinerary includes Naples).
● **Pompeii** or **Herculaneum** (half-day tour to either site).

and a few interesting buildings, including a 15th-century cathedral and 14th-century palace. All ships have to anchor off and tender passengers ashore. The usual stay is a full day to allow for the most popular excursions.

Arrival and around the dock The view of Sorrento precariously perched on top of the cliffs makes for a dramatic arrival. Tenders drop you at the foot of those cliffs at Marina Piccola, which has a few shops, a currency exchange and post office. You can walk up the cliffs to the city but, especially in the heat of summer, most prefer to take one of the minibuses which wait under a clump of trees (a 5-minute walk to the right of the tender pier). They depart as they fill up and drop off at the central Piazza Tasso.

Shopping Jewellery stores galore and plenty of designer labels in fancy boutiques makes this an exciting place to shop, but certainly not a cheap one.

Seeing the sights In Sorrento itself, you can visit the **Duomo** (cathedral), the **Palazzo Correale** and an attractive 15th-century **Loggia**, or just enjoy the quiet streets, shops and cafés. There is a tourist information centre just off Piazza di San Antonio, a short walk from Piazza Tasso. Hydrofoil services to Capri and Naples run from the Marina Piccola. There is a taxi rank at Tasso, from where they will run to Pompeii, along the Amalfi Coast, or to Naples. Drivers are not so happy to make short journeys (especially in peak summer periods) so if you want to get a train to Naples, you may need to walk about 15 minutes from Piazza Tasso along Corso Italia to the station at Piazza de Curtis.

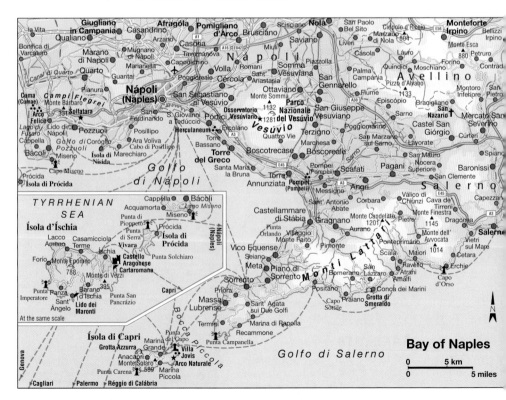

Bay of Naples

CAPRI

Lovely Capri lies at the tip of the Sorrentine Peninsula and is renowned for its dramatic rocky coastline. Capri Town lies between the island's two main peaks, Monte Tiberio and Monte Solaro, while the smaller town of Anacapri lies to the west of Monte Solaro. Ships usually spend a full day here to allow plenty of time for excursions.

Arrival and around the dock Ships tender passengers aboard glossily varnished local motorboats into Capri's Marina Grande, a bustling waterfront lined with shops and restaurants. A couple of minutes' walk away is the funicular which will take you up to the main square, the Piazzetta.

Shopping If you like Italian style, and are prepared to pay rather a lot for it, this is the place to find it. Capri's narrow streets are lined with designer boutiques, jewellery shops, shoe stores and craft studios, many of which have artisans at work on the premises. Look out for the unusual – handmade shoes, hand-woven garments, exquisite lacework and off-beat jewellery items – but be prepared to torture your credit card. Or you could just grab a bottle of the rather refreshing local liqueur, Limoncello.

Seeing the sights Be prepared for steep walking, but Capri's cobbled streets, lined with the bougainvillaea-draped, whitewashed walls of villas and grand hotels, are worth the effort. Your visit could include the **Gardens of Augustus**, a delightful haven from Capri's inevitable crowds, and the **Villa San Michele**, the former residence of Swedish writer, Axel Munthe. Set in a large park, the villa is built on

Map on page 208

TYPICAL EXCURSIONS, CAPRI
● **Blue Grotto and Island Tour** (5 hours). Grotto visit followed by mini-van trip to Anacapri, then the Gardens of Augustus.
● Motorboat cruise to **Faraglioni Rocks** (4 hours) then by road to Anacapri and the Gardens of Augustus.

BELOW: Capri's Marina Grande.

Roman ruins and contains an impressive collection of archaeological artefacts.

Trips to the best-known attraction, the **Grotta Azzurra** (Blue Grotto), with its strange, turquoise light, can be organised at the port (confirm prices in advance). These are not a good idea for the frail – or the very tall – as the transfer to rowing boats can be rocky and the Grotto's entrance is very low. Be prepared for boatmen bawling a cacophonic rendition of *O Sole Mio*. Little **Anacapri** is perfectly lovely and well worth a visit – you can take an open chairlift to the top of Mount Solaro, and enjoy the pretty gardens lining the slopes.

OTHER BAY OF NAPLES PORTS

Within the Bay of Naples, cruise ships also call at **Isola d'Ischia** and its tiny neighbour, **Procida**. Ischia is known for its thermal springs, lush gardens and sandy beaches and is dominated by a volcano, the 788-metre (2,600-ft) Epomeo. Procida is volcanic too, made up of four extinct craters. The only feature of note is an old castle that is now a prison and only very small ships or specialised cruises are likely to visit.

Positano, on the the other hand, oozes glamour, clinging to the steep slope of the Amalfi Peninsula on the southern side of the bay, its steeply ranked pink- and ochre-coloured houses overlooking three islands reputed to be the abode of the mythological sirens. Cafés, restaurants and designer shops are the reason to come here and it's easily accessible from Amalfi or Sorrento by bus as a day trip.

Salerno lies at the east end of the spectacular and hair-raising Amalfi Coast drive and also serves as an access point for Vesuvius and Pompeii. It is a large and busy town with a good beach and a lovely cathedral with beautiful medieval frescoes, and columns that originated in the temple at Paestum.

BELOW: Capri's walls are covered with bougainvillaea. **RIGHT:** idyllic turquoise waters.

LIPARI AND THE AEOLIAN ISLANDS

Located in the southern Tyrrhenian Sea off the northern coast of Sicily, the dazzling Aeolian Islands (Isole Eólie) are increasingly popular with holiday-makers and more and more cruise ships call in here, particularly the smaller vessels. Despite this, the volcanic archipelago, named by the ancient Greeks after Aeolus, the god of the wind, has managed to retain an other-worldly air and sense of isolation. Lipari is the largest and busiest island of the group.

Around the dock Lipari has two harbours separated by a rocky promontory on top of which perches a castle surrounded by 16th-century walls. The town sprawls out behind the castle, spilling into the two bays. Small ships dock at Marina Lunga, to the right of the castle as you approach, while larger vessels tender to the pier.

It is a small and relatively walkable town. One long street, Corso Vittorio Emanuele, runs parallel to the shore. At one end, it's lined with less touristy, neighbourhood shops, selling everything from hardware to vegetables, and towards the second harbour, Marina Corta, there are art galleries, boutiques, dive shops and cafés. Marina Corta has quite a buzz about it, with people milling round the seafront bars and restaurants, and hydrofoils coming and going to and from the other islands in the archipelago.

The climb up to the castle is worthwhile. It's quiet up here, with beautiful views and some pretty, shady courtyards half-hidden inside the old houses. The archaeological park where the castle sits dates to 1700BC. You can see relics from as far back as the Neolithic era in the **Museo Archeològico Éoliano**, housed in several buildings that form part of the complex and is

Maps on pages 188 & 208

BELOW: Lipari's two harbours are separated by a rocky promontory.

Smaller boats can get close to the rugged coastline.

included in most cruise lines' excursions. The cathedral is baroque, but part of the original 12th-century cloister is still visible.

Further afield Some cruise lines offer excursions around the island, visiting sleepy villages, the rugged, wind-blown, northwest coast and a beach or two. In peak season, the beaches are nothing special and extremely crowded. It's a better bet to hire a moped from one of the many operators on the harbourfronts and pick and choose the best spots.

Other islands Reckoned to be the prettiest of the Aeolian islands, **Panarea** is developing a reputation as a jet-set hideaway, with chic boutique hotels and beautiful villas surrounded by lush gardens clinging to the steep slopes. However, there's very little to see once you've wandered round the tiny port of **San Pietro** with its designer shops, whitewashed houses and dazzling purple, yellow and scarlet sub-tropical vegetation. The best way to spend the day is to seek out a decent restaurant with a garden and a view (there are plenty to choose from) and settle down for fresh fish and chilled white wine. Alternatively, rent a boat at the port and explore the island's tiny coves and beaches, which are inaccessible by road. As with any of the Aeolian Islands, the diving and snorkelling are good and the water is deep and crystal clear.

Ponza/Ventotene Cruise ships occasionally visit these tiny specks in the Tyrrhenian Sea, 48 km (30 miles) off the Italian coast, en route from Sicily to Civitavecchia. Frequented by wealthy, yacht-owning Romans, they are also a popular weekend spot for local people and a lazy beach day for cruise-ship

passengers. Both Ponza and Ventotene are sleepy beyond belief, with scuba diving opportunities, beaches, fish restaurants and very little else. Ventotene is perhaps the prettier of the two, with some splendid, crumbling, pastel-coloured mansions around the old port and a pleasant, shaded square at the centre of town. Carry on over the brow of the hill from the square and there are a couple of good tavernas on the beach.

SARDINIA

Sardinia's geographic position prompted D. H. Lawrence to write that the island was "lost between Europe and Africa and belonging to nowhere". Modern travellers who are familiar with Italy will also find striking differences between the island and the mainland, but they will also discover many similarities. The beautiful beaches are some of the cleanest in the Mediterranean, while the expansive interior has opportunities for hiking, rock climbing and caving.

CAGLIARI

Cagliari, the Sardinian capital and chief port, has one of the best harbours in the Mediterranean. It rose to prominence as a Phoenician colony and Roman *castrum*, becoming an important port on the east–west trading route. Cultural domination by successive waves of Pisans, Moors, Aragonese and Spanish has lent the city a faded cosmopolitan air and poignant aspirations to grandeur. Today, this is a quintessentially Mediterranean city, with life lived in the open air, and any transcendental gloom lifted by the prospect of a fish lunch.

Cagliari has long been a favoured port of call for container ships en route from the Far East, as well as being a busy ferry port with connections to Tunisia,

Map on page 188

TYPICAL EXCURSIONS, CAGLIARI
● **Cagliari city tour** (half-day).
● Archeological site at **Nora** (half-day).

BELOW: the extraordinary sight of Stromboli by night.

SAILING PAST STROMBOLI

Stromboli is Europe's most active volcano, spurting steam, gas clouds, pyroclastic bombs and lava from its crater roughly once every 15 minutes. The volcano has several vents at the top of the Sciaria del Fuoco slope. Pyroclastic bombs are emitted from these vents several times an hour, falling mostly in the immediate surrounding area. Lava flows straight down the slope into the sea, usually having no effect on the villages of Stromboli, on one side of the mountain, and Ginostra, on the other.

Naturally, this being an active volcano, things can go awry. In December 2002 there was a massive landslide down the Sciaria del Fuoco slope, causing a *tsunami* (tidal wave) which damaged the island's two villages with waves several metres high and was felt as far away as northern Sicily, some 65 km (40 miles) from Stromboli.

Small cruise ships call here occasionally but most try to sail past at night so that passengers can admire the fireworks and the glowing lava flow sliding down the volcano's vertiginous side and crashing into the sea. Ships cannot drop anchor here because the water is too deep, but it's not uncommon in the peak summer season to see two or three small vessels sailing around the island at night.

Sicily, Naples, Livorno and Genoa. More recently, the city has successfully sought cruise ships as the best means of boosting tourism in the area. Cagliari tends to be favoured by Scandinavian, British and German cruise lines rather than by the Italian-style cruise ships.

Arrival and around the dock The increasing popularity of Cagliari as a cruise port has led to calls for a dedicated cruise terminal in Via Roma, but nothing has yet been finalised. At present, cruise ships moor by various jetties, with a free shuttle service dropping passengers off in the Stazione Marittima on the waterfront. In summer, a tourist train takes visitors on a tour of the town centre – not that it is strictly necessary. Even with few facilities, laid-back Cagliari makes a delightful port of call, particularly as the harbour is right in the heart of town. Arcaded Via Roma, which skirts the port, is the place for shopping and pavement cafés, with any number of narrow streets winding back into the historic centre and the promise of picturesque façades, crumbling churches and fish restaurants. The harbour is best seen during the early evening promenade, the traditional parade of Italian one-upmanship known as the *passeggiata*.

Seeing the sights Rather than embark on a dutiful excursion to see dusty archaeological sites, most visitors would do better to explore Cagliari independently, soaking up its distinctive Mediterranean atmosphere and indulging in people-watching, café-crawling and window-shopping for ceramics. This is also the best place on the island for a fish lunch, a fact that is even more significant given that Sardinia is better known for roast meats than seafood. Only if you are desperate for a sandy beach is it worth stirring from Cagliari itself. If you feel so inclined, then, armed with a picnic, ask any taxi driver to take you to the lido at **Poetto**, set at the beginning of a huge sandy bay, 4 km (2 miles) west of Cagliari, and agree a time for a return pick-up.

With a steep hill overlooking the port, Cagliari has an undeniable down-at-heel charm. Stacked against the hillside are a higgledy-piggledy cluster of terracotta and ochre façades, heavily ornamented with traditional arabesque designs. The sights include the ruins of a Roman amphitheatre and a Roman grid-style street pattern, framed by the bold medieval bastions that loom above the city. Pastel-painted cottages and delicate wrought-iron balconies make the **San Domenico** district the best place to build up an appetite for lunch. From Piazza De Gasperi, on the eastern side of the port, take Via Gramsci northwards; this leads directly to the San Domenico district, close to the Romanesque cathedral.

The energetic can climb up to the Pisan-built **Citadella**, which has sweeping views over the old town, and retains its imposing 11th-century walls. The faint-hearted can get a taxi or the summer tourist train from the port and should ask for Citadella or the scenic Terrazzo Umberto.

Cagliari is a perfect place for aimless ambling and for replacing cruise-line fare with a sizzling seafood lunch

BELOW: Cagliari's Via Roma is the place for shopping.

in the heart of the old town. Just a few streets northwest of the port is Trattoria da Balena, a genuine and unpretentious place for a Sardinian fish grill (Via di San Gilla 123). The Marina district, which extends northwards from the port, is dotted with tiny, family-run seafood restaurants. One such rough-and-ready fisherman's bolthole is Lillicu (Via Sardegna 78). Nearby, and virtually on top of the port, is Dal Corsaro (Viale Regina Margherita 28), a grand restaurant set in a patrician palace and serving the best of Italian cuisine, from fish to succulent roast meats. For a drink or light lunch, the most appealing café in town is Antico Caffe, where little has changed since its opening in 1855 (Piazza della Costituzione 10). If you are fortunate, the superb food in Cagliari will erase any paler memories of the stodgy fare onboard ship.

ALGHERO AND PORTO TORRES

These two ports in northern Sardinian should be thought of as a single entity as far as cruise passengers are concerned. Although set 30 km (18 miles) apart, they have a symbiotic relationship and, even if charming Alghero features in the cruise lines' brochures, charmless Porto Torres may well be the real destination. Nevertheless, similar excursions are on offer from both ports so the only visitors to feel short-changed by anchorage in Porto Torres are independent-minded culture-lovers, looking forward to exploring the ancient city of Alghero. Even so, frequent buses connect the two ports so a trip to Alghero is feasible.

Alghero, the gateway to northwestern Sardinia, is a delightful city in an equally appealing setting. Founded by the Phoenicians, conquered by the Moors, but settled by 14th-century merchant-adventurers from Barcelona and Valencia, it still feels the most Spanish of Sardinian cities. In terms of culture, architecture, language and cuisine, Catalan is the predominant note. For cruise passengers lucky enough to be tendered in to Alghero, the harbour area is as worthwhile as any Mediterranean port of call.

Arrival and around the docks Despite its maritime heritage, **Alghero** has adapted to its modern role as a pleasure port, ideally suited to yachts and smaller craft. The size and depth of the harbour means that most cruise ships need to anchor at sea and tender in; only cruise liners with under 300 passengers are allowed into port, essentially such latter-day sailing ships as the Star Clippers and Windstar vessels. While there are no cruise facilities, Alghero triumphs by having a port in the heart of the historic centre, readily accessible on foot. Moreover, given the current expansion of Porto Torres, there are no plans to transform Alghero, which will remain as it is, an engaging yacht marina which tolerates well-behaved cruise ships.

Porto Torres, 30 km (18 miles) north, is an unprepossessing industrial and commercial port, further marred by the presence of oil refineries, tankers and container ships. As the main port in northern Sardinia, it welcomes the largest cruise liners and despatches ferries to Genoa, Marseille and Corsica. A combined cruise and ferry terminal opened in 2003 but failed to

Map on page 188

BELOW: shrines to the Virgin Mary are seen all over Sardinia.

TYPICAL
EXCURSIONS,
ALGHERO/
PORTO TORRES
● **Grotta di Nettuno**
(Neptune's Grotto) and
the **Capo Caccia**
peninsula (full-day).
● **Nuraghic**
settlements (full-day).

BELOW:
there are good
sandy beaches
near Alghero.

cope with the volume of traffic so is restricted to ferries, with a dedicated cruise terminal due to be fully functioning by 2005. In the meantime, ships with under 1,000 passengers dock in port while the largest cruise liners are forced to tender in. Even so, a number of mainstream companies favour Porto Torres.

Seeing the sights The Aragonese bastion enveloping the port of **Alghero** is still intact, bound on three sides by crenellated fortifications. This ancient quarter is riddled with cobbled alleys, an atmospheric maze dominated by the **Forte de la Magdalena**. After sipping drinks on Piazza Sulis and admiring the battlemented skyline, consider lunch in town. Da Rafel (Via Lido 20) is an authentic fish restaurant with sea views as well as spaghetti and lobster on the menu. Trattoria Maristella (Via Kennedy 9) is an unpretentious trattoria serving grills and the rustic dishes of the Sardinian hinterland. For foodies, Andreini is a gourmet haunt specialising in "new" Sardinian cuisine based on seafood and Mediterranean vegetables (Via Arduino 45).

Porto Torres currently has little to detain cruise passengers, even if it is set in the heart of town and full of cafés and bars, as the industrial gloom casts a pall over the town. Use it simply as a base.

Further afield The most scenic short excursion from Alghero is to **Grotta di Nettuno** (Neptune's Grotto) and the Capo Caccia peninsula, just north of town. If you are not taking the cruise line's excursion, then consider an independent boat trip to the cape and caves. In the harbour area, call in at the tourist office to enquire about current times and prices (Piazza Portaterra 9; tel: 079-979054); alternatively, approach one of the small excursion companies or fishing boats in the harbour. Neptune's Grotto is a series of spectacular, stalactite-encrusted caverns and eerie subterranean lagoons best reached by boat. From here, over 600 steps lead up to the **lighthouse** and the promontory of **Capo Caccia**. The wild beauty of these cliffs appeals to both nature-lovers and bird-watchers, with sightings of peregrine falcons, herring-gulls and rare griffon-vultures.

There are plenty of alternative landscape-and-archaeology based excursions from both Alghero and Porto Torres. Since public transport is not recommended (except for the reliable Porto Torres–Alghero bus service), one option is to hire a taxi to explore the wild coastline of northern Sardinia. For many, Alghero's **Riviera di Corallo** (Coral Riviera) is even lovelier than the over-hyped Costa Smeralda (Emerald Coast; *see Porto Cervo*). The same half-day drive can take in a stretch of the primeval hinterland, which is dotted with olive groves, dwarf palms and the remnants of ancient cork forests. Each taxi driver has his own preferred route, which should be agreed in advance, along with the price, but to allay any fears, ask the port tourist office for a map and advice.

For those interested in archaeology and ancient civilisations, the classic cruise excursion is to the **Nuraghic settlements**. The complexity of the subject makes it a candidate for a specialised tour, not one in the company of an uninformed cab-driver. The

Nuraghic people were a race whose origins and culture are even more mysterious to us than the Etruscans. In their wake, they have left around 7,000 distinctive dwellings scattered around the island. Known as *nuraghi*, these bizarre, conical structures look like a cross between funerary mounds and improvised beehives. Built between 1500 and 400BC, some of these dwellings are clustered west of Alghero, in the Torralba area, others lie further south in the Abbasanta area.

Map
on page
188

PORTO CERVO

Set on the glitziest stretch of Sardinian coastline, **Porto Cervo** is a beguiling tourist trap, with one of the finest marinas in the Mediterranean. As the most chic and cosmopolitan of the Sardinian ports, Porto Cervo has been a celebrity haunt since the days of the Aga Khan in the 1960s. Bewitched by the turquoise seascapes, he spearheaded the commercialisation of the pristine coast north of Olbia, and the legendary Costa Smeralda (Emerald Coast) was born. Porto Cervo remains the miniature capital of the Costa Smeralda and as much a playboy magnet as Monte Carlo.

Arrival and around the dock As the quintessential tourist marina, Porto Cervo is restricted to sleek super-yachts, but cruise ships are discreetly tolerated. A sensible if slightly snobbish decision to control cruise access to the port means that only super-yachts are welcome, although small cruise ships are acceptable if they anchor at sea. Even Bill Gates' yacht was deemed too large, as was the yacht transporting President Bush Sr. The rationale behind this fixation on size is that cruise ships would swamp the tiny port

BELOW: a view of Alghero against the deep blue sea.

Map on page 188

TYPICAL
EXCURSIONS,
OLBIA
● **Porto Cervo** The
glitzy port *(see main
text*; half- or full-day
tour).

BELOW: a watchful
mountain goat
RIGHT: the Stella
Maris church in
Porto Cervo.

and spoil the atmosphere for everyone else, particularly the jet-set at play. A tenuous truce prevails between commercial and private interests: the magnetic appeal of the port ensures that cruise ships of under 500 passengers still tender in to Porto Cervo, but passengers are encouraged to visit in small groups to avoid troubling the natives. Cruise ships with over 500 passengers are obliged to moor in distinctly mundane Olbia.

Seeing the sights Porto Cervo's quaint interpretation of a traditional fishing village is convincingly artless yet faintly surreal. Designer shops sell the latest nautical gear of a kind that looks as chic in the streets of Paris as it does by the harbours of Porto Cervo, Portofino, Capri or St-Tropez. In the morning, the wives of wealthy yacht skippers can be spotted choosing Sardinian cheeses and salami for a perfect picnic. After sunset, bronzed beauties walk by on the arms of wizened Greek shipping magnates. Early evening spells cocktails on the Piazzetta, the tiny square at the heart of this idealised fishing village, before dinner in a private villa or yacht.

Apart from people-watching at chic cafés, visitors can indulge in upmarket shopping for Sardinian crafts, from table linen to hand-woven rugs and straw baskets, filigree or coral jewellery, as well as gnarled wood carvings masquerading as *objets d'art*. Even if there are excursions to archaeological sights in the hinterland *(see page 216)* visitors to Porto Cervo tend to treat it as a destination in itself.

In recent years, the port has acquired a rather louche image as a popular playground for Arab sheiks, although even Porto Cervo drew the line at the antics of Saddam Hussein's murderous sons, who once crashed a speedboat into the port's most prestigious hotel. One visiting sheik caused an uproar by arriving in two yachts, one for himself and one for his armed security team, without revealing his deadly arsenal to the Italian state police. Not that the Italian celebrity circuit has any difficulty being louche on its own terms. The slippery President Silvio Berlusconi has an ostentatious villa in Porto Rotondo, the bay just south of Porto Cervo, that he is vainly trying to turn into an Italian version of Camp David, the US presidential retreat.

OLBIA

Olbia is the gateway to northeastern Sardinia, notably the glitzy Costa Smeralda and Porto Cervo.

Arrival and around the dock The ferry terminal is in the newer Porto Nuovo, while the cruise ships moor in the area of docks known as Isola Bianca, from where a free shuttle bus takes passengers to both the ferry terminal and the town centre, which is also accessible on foot. Up to half a dozen cruise liners call in a week in summer – while Olbia's port also operates ferries to Elba, Livorno and Genoa.

Seeing the sights From the uninspiring port, the classic shore excursion is to **Porto Cervo** *(see page 217)*. Still, if overcome by lassitude in the face of yet more travelling, then consider lunch in Da Gesuino, a well-established Olbia restaurant noted for its seafood specialities (Via Garibaldi 3). ❏

SICILY, MALTA AND TUNISIA

*Only on a cruise could you take in the catacombs of Palermo,
the Great Harbour of Valletta, the slopes of Mount Etna,
and the medina and mosques of Tunis*

Maps on pages 188 & 225

I f your ships calls at any of the Sicilian ports, at Malta's capital, Valletta, or docks for a day in a Tunisian harbour, you will immediately be aware of the historical winds of change that have swept over this central part of the Mediterranean. While Sicily could not be more Italian and Malta bears evidence of almost two centuries of British rule, both show their affinity with North Africa, not so far across the water. Many visitors to Sicily head directly for the slopes of Mount Etna, or to the beautifully preserved Greek temples at Agrigento; in Valletta, the Grand Harbour stirs memories of the Knights of St John; while visitors to Tunisia are captivated by the sounds and scents of the souks.

PALERMO

Palermo's architecture, and Sicily's history, reflect the passing colonisation of the great Mediterranean empires – Carthage, Greece and Rome all made their mark here, as did the marauding Goths and Vandals, until the relative stability of joint Norman and Arab rule from 1072. The Arabs brought lemons and oranges, dates and cane sugar – significant exports to this day. During this golden era, Palermo was one of the wealthiest places in Europe. This is no longer the case, but this remains a warm southern city with a joyful cacophony of colour, scent and sound; grand 18th-century architecture, dogs barking, aromas of citrus fruits and pasta sauces, and that peculiarly Italian traffic noise.

Palermo is usually a full day's stay. A pleasant way to spend it is to tour the sites in town in the morning, then spend the afternoon in the cool hills above, visiting the historic cathedral of Monreale. Organised cruise tours of both Palermo and Monreale are available, but each is easy to navigate independently, and there's enough time in which to do it.

Arrival and around the dock Approaching Sicily, the dry, jagged peaks slope down to Palermo's shoreline. Along the island's pointed ridges, old forts and occasional villas stand among radio masts, but most of the pale buildings are down near the coast.

Ships dock almost in the town itself. At the harbour side, liners are often greeted by an enthusiastic throng, wtih people running alongside, waving handkerchiefs as the ship manoeuvres into place. The customs hall has a cool, light, marble interior with a duty-free shop and a Western Union office offering a good range of international call services, and – a rarity – fast, inexpensive internet access. Downstairs is a Banco Siciliano with an ATM and foreign exchange desk.

The dock is only a 10- or 15-minute undistinguished walk from the Teatro Politeama Garbaldi. Horse carts

PRECEDING PAGES: the Graeco-Roman theatre at Taormina. **LEFT:** Maltese painted boats. **BELOW:** plying for trade in Palermo.

**TYPICAL
EXCURSIONS,
PALERMO**
● **Temples of
Selinunte** and nearby
beach.
● **Historical Palermo**
and Monreale.
● **Cefalù** beach.
● **Mysterious
Palermo** (generally all
are 4-hour or half-day
tours).

decorated with bells and colourful ribbons give romantic rides, but be firm in negotiating the price first. Taxi drivers offer tours of the city, but satisfy yourself that the driver's English is up to it, and be ready to bargain hard.

Shopping The stylish Via di Belmonte is the best place for clothes or jewellery – and it has some good outdoor cafés as well. Palermo is also known for fine ceramics and coral jewellery, delicate embroidery and linens, and for Sicilian wines, which are fast gaining favour abroad. The markets are wonderful, particularly for food. The best is **La Vucciria**, between Corso Vittorio Emanuele and the San Domenico church. **Mercato di Capo** spreads around Via S. Agostino and Via Bandiera, and has the most authentic Sicilian atmosphere.

Seeing the sights The **Teatro Politeama Garibaldi** (open daily) is the older of the city's two opera houses, built in 1875. It is set in the grandly spacious Piazza Politeama, sufficiently far back for the traffic noise to fade. A heroic sculpture over the arched entrance depicts warriors on horses and chariots, holding olive branches aloft. **Teatro Massimo** (tours daily am; fee) on Via Orloggio, built in 1864, is the newer opera house. The majestic entrance has Corinthian columns and grand steps of appropriately operatic proportions.

At the cramped corners of Piazza Vigliena, four small marble fountains depict the seasons, and mark the corners of the traditionally rivalrous quarters of the old city. The junction is known locally as the *teatro del sole* because the sun shines here from dawn till dusk.

Along Corso Vittorio Emanuelle is the **Duomo** (cathedral; open daily). Strikingly proportioned, and set behind formal gardens with cool fountains, the

BELOW:
the striking façade
of the Duomo.

athedral holds some surprises. The curved reddish sandstone battlements esemble a Moorish castle more than a Catholic church. Statues of saints guard he entrance: St Peter, kind and solemn, consulting a large book, and St Paul, olding a stern finger aloft. Whether he is beckoning, warning or simply making a point is hard to tell. Inside, the high knave of the cathedral is Roman classical; square columns and pediments, pale marble vaulting and magnificent rescos of the Ascension over the altar. The side chapels display Arabic influnce, with silver geometric decoration on the domes.

Further along the busy Corso Emanuelle, at Piazza Independenza, the ancient valls of the Norman **Palazzo Royale** (open Mon–Sat; fee) are obscured by the nore recent additions. The palace houses the Parliament of Sicily, and mosaics nd vaulted corridors of the interior give clues to its archaic grandeur. Waternelon stands and quiet, shady gardens stretch in front of the palace. The Cappella Palatina (open Mon–Fri; fee) exhibits gold mosaics from the time of he Crusades, and a fabulous Oriental ceiling.

Across Via di Bastione is the church of **San Giovani della Eremiti** (open Mon–Sat; fee) with lovely Arab domes, seen through the palm and fragrant rrange trees of the garden.

The **Capuchin Catacombs** (Via Cappuccini; open daily; fee) display the unique embalming skills of the Capuchin monks. Bizarre and fascinating, this s not a visit for the faint-hearted. Mummified Palermitans lie in caskets and helves, or stand in nooks along the walls. Congregated by sex, profession and ige, the earthy coils of some 8,000 souls rest in the cold catacombs. Most emarkable is a two-year-old, Rosalia Lombardo, embalmed in 1920. Her golden lair and blue robes seem perfect – her face, even her grey eyes, in eerie repose.

A mummified Palermitan in the Capuchin Catacombs.

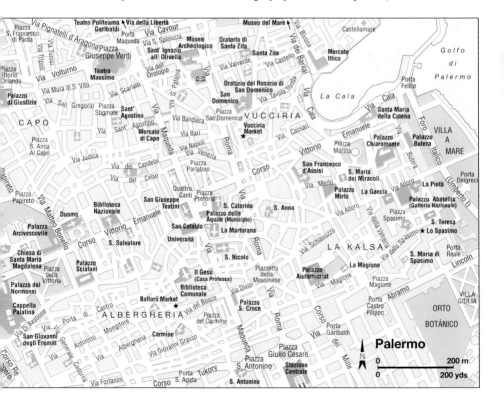

The intricate façade of Monreale Cathedral.

BELOW: Cefalù's old town has its feet in the water.

Further afield A bus from Piazza Independenza to **Monreale** takes about 20 minutes, or it's easy to get a taxi. Buses and taxis run from Monreale's Piazza Vittorio Emanuele for the return journey. This small, airy town in the cooler air of the hills has several shops, bars and pizzerias in which to while away the afternoon.

The **Duomo** has the second-largest gold mosaic in antiquity – the larger one being Sofia in Istanbul. Commenced in 1186, the interior is covered by 6,340 sq metres (62,200sq ft) of intricate Byzantine and Venetian mosaics, illustrating biblical scenes and incorporating 1,200 kg (1.2 metric tons) of gold. As sunlight strikes through the high windows, the gold sparkles and radiates. The cathedral also has a beautiful Romanesque cloister.

The return drive is down tree-lined streets and boulevards, with road-side fruit and vegetable stalls, and the chirruping of cicadas mingling with horns and sirens.

Ships' excursions run to the remains of the ancient temples of **Selinunte** on the west coast, across a promontory, but this is not a journey you would want to undertake independently. The town was all but destroyed in 410BC, but the remains indicate its prosperity and relative sophistication.

Cefalù, a pretty, medieval town with a Norman (Romanesque) cathedral and a sandy beach, clinging to a promontory about 60 km (38 miles) east of Palermo is included on another excursion. You could go alone, but it is really only practical if you hire a car.

Leaving port, the ship sounds a massive horn to signal upcoming manoeuvres. The passage is accompanied by kayaks and catamarans, like flying fish following a whale in the evening sun.

MESSINA

Maps on pages 188 & 225

Set on the Ionian Sea, but with a foothold in both the eastern and western Mediterranean, Messina has long been a key port of call. Rivalled only by Palermo and Catania, Messina is Sicily's cruising hub. However, a fateful earthquake in 1908 flattened the area, with the result that this is Sicily's least impressive coastal city. Even so, with little to detain visitors in the bland centre, the classic shore excursions glitter even more brightly. On offer are Taormina, Sicily's St-Tropez and its most dramatic resort; and an elemental excursion up Mount Etna, which normally obliges thrill-seekers with smouldering volcanic activity. Neither experience should be missed, but if your spirit of adventure is dormant, then consider a stroll to view the Duomo, Messina's over-restored Norman cathedral, followed by a drink on the quayside.

Arrival and around the dock At first sight, the popularity of Messina as a port of call seems disproportionate to its attractions, yet it succeeds, albeit in a uniquely improvised Sicilian way. The lack of a dedicated cruise terminal is mired in regional politics and grandiose plans to build a bridge over the Straits of Messina, a major project scheduled for completion in 2012. In the meantime, the port of Messina is a study in Sicilian chaos, even if the sail into the sweeping harbour suggests vestiges of the city's former grandeur. With excusable artistic licence, one Italian writer likened the city to a "sailing ship, low in the water, ready for a night cruise". The curved, sickle-shaped harbour can be particularly romantic at night, with lights glittering on the waterfront.

If the waterfront seems glassily still, then appearances can be deceptive. Messina is noted for its treacherous waters and mysterious whirlpools that were

BELOW: a ferry in Messina harbour.

TYPICAL EXCURSIONS, MESSINA

● **Mount Etna**. Half-day tour, the last part by four-wheel-drive minibus or cable-car and then on foot to the craters.

● **Taormina**. Half-day tour *(see main text)*.

attributed to the meeting of clashing currents only in the 18th century. This mundane explanation was far from the minds of the ancient Greek sailors who personified Messina's twin demons as Charybdis, the whirlpool, and Scylla, the six-headed monster. Yet watching over the port is the Madonnina, a huge gilded statue of the Madonna, beloved by local sailors.

The Stazione Marittima on the southern tip of the port doubles as a railway station and ferry terminal. Here trains are dismantled and passengers decanted into cavernous ferries which serve the Italian mainland (Genoa, Calabria and Naples) as well as the glitzy island outposts of Capri and Ischia, or the splendid Aeolian Islands *(see page 211)*. The cruise liners do not dock here but anchor off one of several neighbouring jetties where they are met by fleets of tour buses, taxis and a tram which runs straight into the city centre. In summer, a free tourist train meets passengers and sets off on a tour of the city centre.

Seeing the sights The tourist train tour includes the Norman **Duomo**, with an astronomical clock on its campanile, and several Arab-Norman churches that survived the earthquake. But unless you are feeling really lazy, it is an easy stroll into the town centre, which spills over into the port, the quaysides lined with boisterous bars and seafood restaurants.

Further afield While shipping enthusiasts may find it hard to tear themselves away from the sight of entire trains being swallowed up by giant ferries, the majority of cruise passengers will be on the first train or bus to Taormina *(see below for details of the town)*, about 40 km (25 miles) down the coast. Taormina is also offered as a shore excursion, of course. As for trips to Etna, factors such as time constraints, safety, weather conditions and the myriad forms of transport required (from bus to cable-car and four-wheel-drive) make this an option best booked through a cruise company.

Substitute ports of call Messina may be the official port that appears in cruise lines' brochures but the reality is somewhat different. Individual captains may choose to anchor off Giardini-Naxos, which is slightly more convenient for Taormina, the most popular shore excursion. From Giardini-Naxos, a sprawling resort that was the first Greek colony in Sicily, the cruise lines tender in to the shore, a process that often takes as long as the drive down the motorway from Messina to Taormina. Smaller, upmarket cruise lines stipulate Messina in their brochures but may anchor in the port of Milazzo, on the Tyrrenhian coast if excursions to the Aeolian Islands are an option.

TAORMINA

A spectacular location on the slopes of Monte Tauro overlooking the Bay of Giardini, with views west to Mount Etna combined with atmospheric streets and bougainvillea-decked courtyards have made Taormina popular with visitors down the centuries. Ships have to anchor off and tender into the jetty at the opposite end of the Bay of Giardini from Taormina. Cruise ships usually stay a full day.

BELOW: the Graeco-Roman theatre at Taormina.

Arrival and around the dock You can see Taormina on the top of the hill overlooking the port of Giardini-Naxos as you arrive but, if your ship is leaving after dark, the departure is more spectacular as the city walls are illuminated at night. There is a tourist information kiosk at the jetty (although its opening hours are a mystery) and a café opposite. There is a beach around the bay with shops, cafés and bars overlooking it but, although the site of the first Greek colony in Sicily (Naxos, founded 735BC), there is little reason to linger here when Taormina town is so close.

Most ships organise a shuttle bus (either free or for a fee) into Taormina. This now takes a more circuituous route up the hill, via a newish highway. The journey takes 15–20 minutes, about the same as the prettier coast road taken by the taxis which gather at the jetty. They charge about €20 one-way but this covers up to six passengers. All shuttles have to drop passengers off at Level I of an underground car park. You then take the lift to the seventh floor and walk up a small flight of steps to Taormina's Porta Catania (Catania Gate). Taxis also drop off at the gate although some are allowed through into the otherwise largely pedestrianised streets.

Shopping There are some good-quality paintings and prints as well as colourful ceramics and some slightly gaudy jewellery which betrays the region's Greek origins. There are some excellent – and reasonably-priced – cafés and restaurants tucked away in the alleys leading off the main street (Corso Umberto). One word of warning, though: the local police are clamping down on tax-dodging waiters and café-owners so you may be asked to produce receipts after a meal and – in theory – could be fined if you don't have one.

Seeing the sights Cruise passengers on shuttle buses, like those arriving by taxi, arrive at the Porta Catania. Almost immediately inside the gate is the **Duomo**, and 5 minutes' walk further along smart Corso Umberto, where the bars are packed with a well-heeled international clientele, is **Piazza IX Aprile**, with spectacular views over the bay. About 5 minutes' further on, Via Teatro Greco to the right leads almost immediately to the town's most popular attraction – the superbly sited **Graeco-Roman Theatre** (open daily; fee), the third largest in the world.

A tourist office, where train timetables are available, is housed in the Sicilian Museum at the junction with Via Teatre Greco. The station is a short walk away and there are frequent reasonably priced trains to Catania (1 hour away), Messina (70 minutes) and, less frequent, to Siracuse (2 hours 20 minutes).

Behind the tourist office, a steep road leads first to the castle and Sanctuary of the Madonna and then to the picturesque village of **Castelmola** perched 3 km (2 miles) above Taormina. The full walk takes more than 2 hours so most people prefer to take a taxi (around €20 from Taormina itself, €40 from the port).

Further afield It is also possible to organise tours locally which will pick up and drop off at the port. Or you can take a taxi to Mount Etna. Either option

Map on page 188

TYPICAL EXCURSIONS, TAORMINA
● **Mount Etna**. Half-day tour, the last part by a four-wheel-drive minibus or cable-car and then on foot to the craters.
● **Part-island tour.** Half-day, taking in various towns and villages and locations for a couple of the *Godfather* films.

BELOW: on the slopes of Mount Etna.

There is a long tradition of puppet theatre in Sicily.

BELOW: watching the world go by.

should be significantly cheaper than the shore excursion. It is possible to hire cars but the road network and the signage are confusing and, as mentioned before, time and weather constraints must be taken into consideration, so doing this cannot be recommended to first-time visitors.

CATANIA

A sprawling, industrial port town, Catania is plagued with traffic problems and crime. The city's architecture has suffered extensively from a combination over the years of earthquakes, eruptions from Mount Etna and World War II bombing. It does, however, have a certain crumbling charm if you choose to spend the day here rather than using it as a base for excursions. Some cruises start from here, as the city has an international airport.

Arrival and around the dock On a clear day, the huge bulk of Mount Etna smouldering behind the city, sometimes wearing a cap of snow on its summit, is an impressive sight. The main square and centre of interest is just a short walk from the dock.

Seeing the sights Although there is not a great deal to see in Catania, the atmospheric **Piazza del Duomo**, the main square, is pleasant. As you would expect from the piazza's name, it is the site of the 11th-century **Duomo** (cathedral), which was remodelled after a massive earthquake in the 17th century. The centrepiece of the square is the **Fontana dell'Elefante**, made from lava, and there are shops and cafés both in the piazza and in the streets around it. If you are here any day except Sunday, head north up the main boulevard, Via

Etnea, the street where local people take their evening *passeggiata*, and turn right towards Piazza Carlo Alberto to find the colourful produce market (open Mon–Sat am).

Map on page 188

Further afield Most visitors use Catania as a base from which to visit the impressive sites of eastern Sicily – gorgeous, kitsch **Taormina** *(see page 228)*, the fabulous Graco-Roman antiquities of **Siracusa** *(see below)*, and trips up **Mount Etna**. There are trains and buses to the sprawling resort of **Giardini-Naxos** (which, along with Messina, is the port town for hilltop Taormina) but the journey takes 1½–2 hours, which is cutting it fine on a day visit.

The operation of trips to Etna depends on the state of the volcano, which has been particularly active in recent years. Getting there on public transport or by hire car is complicated, as already mentioned, and the hiking trails can take several hours to negotiate, so a guided tour is by far the best option for cruise passengers wishing to get a close view.

TYPICAL
EXCURSIONS,
CATANIA
● **Mount Etna**.
● **Taormina** *(see main text and excursions on previous pages).*

SIRACUSA

Once a powerful Greek city and still packed with archaeological interest, **Siracusa** is a highlight of any visit to Sicily, provided the weather is not too hot. Cruise ships usually spend a whole day here, running excursions to the Neapolis archaeological zone across the city from the port. Alternatively, passengers are free to explore the island of Ortigia, on which the old, and most interesting, part of the city is located. A famous festival of Greek classical drama is held in the Teatro Greco every two years, in May and June, a wonderful experience but one that sailing times make impossible for most cruise passengers.

BELOW: giant drama masks at Siracusa.

Arrival and around the dock

As you approach the wide sweep of the bay, look for the cluster of old houses on the clifftop of Ortigia for orientation. If you're planning to walk anywhere, this is the place to head for. There are several berths for large ships around the bay from where you can walk round to the right and head over the canal bridge and up the hill into the heart of Ortigia.

Seeing the sights

At the foot of the hill, there is a small, 6th century BC archaeological site, the **Tempio di Apollo**, surrounded, incongruously, by busy streets. The main square, Piazza del Duomo, is traffic free and lined with stunning baroque palaces. The **Duomo** (cathedral) stands on the site of an old temple to Athena and is a mixture of Gothic and baroque. Outside are rows of cafés with umbrellas, a good place to rest and refresh. The streets around the square contain a mixture of small designer boutiques and craft shops. Look out for olive oil and products made from citrus fruit, both of which are produced in the area. On the waterfront, the **Fontana Aretusa** is a natural spring next to the sea where the nymph of the same name was turned into a fountain in Greek mythology.

Further afield

The **Neapolis archaeological zone** will take at least half a day, particularly when it's hot. Take a bus or taxi from Piazza Pancali in Ortigia as the walk is uninspiring. The site is located some 2 km (1 mile) inland from the port and is best known for its dazzling white Greek theatre, hewn out of the rock in the 5th century BC. There's also a former quarry, now a garden, the Ear of Dionysius (a strangely shaped grotto) and a Roman amphitheatre.

BELOW: Trapani's harbour is close to the centre of town.

There's a good beach at **Fontane Bianche**, a couple of miles from the city to the south, accessible by bus. Locals head here en masse in summer.

TRAPANI

Trapani is used as a day visit because of its proximity to the medieval hill town of Erice, and the ancient Greek sites of Segesta and Marsala, all popular excursions.

Arrival and around the dock   Trapani is located on a pointed peninsula on Sicily's northwest coast. As you approach, the old town and the old Jewish quarter are directly behind the busy port. Behind the town is the headland of Mount Erice, with the Egedi islands visible in the distance on a clear day. Cruise ships dock right in front of the old town, on the quay next to the ferry terminal.

Seeing the sights   The old town centre has a number of Gothic and baroque buildings. If you just want to relax outside a café, head for Piazza Lucatelli, just behind Piazza Garibaldi, where there are some decent bars and restaurants. Thanks to its historic trading partnership with Tunisia, Trapani specialises in *couscous*, spelt *cuscus* here, which is usually served with a garlicky fish and tomato sauce.

Further afield   Beautiful **Erice**, 750 metres/yds above sea level and packed with historic interest, is about 40 minutes away by bus if you want to make an independent visit. Otherwise, all cruise lines calling at Trapani offer excursions there. Some lines also offer trips to the Graeco-Roman antiquities at **Segesta**, where there is an amazingly well-preserved Doric temple dating from 430BC. Visits to **Marsala**, just down the coast, are popular, too, mainly to taste and buy the famous dessert wine that is produced there.

Map on page 188

TYPICAL
EXCURSIONS,
TRAPANI
● Erice.
● Segesta.
● Marsala.
(see main text).

BELOW: beautiful
Erice sits high
above the sea.

The medieval quarter of Ragusa is built on a hillside.

PORTO EMPEDOCLE

Porto Empedocle, on the southwest coast, is used solely as a gateway to the city of Agrigento and the amazing Valley of the Temples just below it, one of the world's finest examples of ancient Greek architecture.

Around the dock   Ships dock about 2 km (1 mile) from town. You can walk into the centre, but this is a largely industrial town with little of interest.

Further afield   Buses run from Porto Empedocle to **Agrigento**, taking about 20 minutes (a nice old town, even if you just want to wander around and enjoy the shops and cafés). You then have to catch a second bus to take you the remaining 7 km (4 miles) to the classical city in the **Valley of the Temples**. All cruise lines operate excursions to the main monuments: the Tempio di Ercole (Hercules), from the 6th century BC, is the oldest; the beautifully sited Tempio della Concordia, dating from around 430BC, is one of the best preserved in the world; and the ruined Tempio de Giove (Zeus) is the largest Doric temple ever known. Take water, sunglasses and a sun hat as the site is hot and exposed.

Cruise line tours also run to the former Greek colony of Selinunte, two hours' drive away *(see page 226).*

THE REST OF SICILY

BELOW: the Temple of Hercules at Agrigento.

Small cruise ships sometimes call at Sicily's lesser-known ports. **Mazara del Vallo** is used as an alternative port for Erice (although the medieval village is a long drive from the port) or Marsala. Off the northwest coast is the Egadi archipelago, famous for its tuna-fishing festival and used mainly as a beach

stop, with crystal-clear water and small, rocky coves. **Ustica**, an island off the north coast, parallel with the Aeolian archipelago, is again used mainly for a beach day, with ships running tender trips to see the colourful grottoes. The area is a marine reserve, with fabulous diving. **Cefalù** (*see page 226*) is a sleepy little town with old fishermen's houses overhanging the harbour and a maze of medieval streets leading to an impressive Romanesque cathedral in an attractive square. **Ragusa**, in the far south, was badly damaged in the 1693 earthquake and now has two faces – the repaired section, rebuilt in the 18th century, and the original, medieval part. The upper and lower towns are linked by steep steps.

Maps on pages 188 & 236

TYPICAL EXCURSIONS, PORTO EMPEDOCLE
- Agrigento.
- Selinunte.
(see main text).

MALTA (VALLETTA)

Valletta has always displayed an implacable determination to repel invaders, which it matches with its elegant hospitality to visitors. Settlement on the site of the city can be dated back to the Bronze Age, and **Mdina**, the ancient capital, has a similarly long history. The capital city of Malta, Valletta was founded in the 16th century, around the finest natural harbour in the Mediterranean, by the Knights of St John. After the Great Siege by the Turks in 1565, Jean de la Valletta had the town laid out and fortifications added. Francesco Laparelli, the Vatican architect, was responsible for the plan of streets in a regular grid relieved by open squares. French, Italian, Portuguese and Spanish Knights established *auberges* (inns) as residences, and these have been maintained and are open to view. The Knights held dominion over the island until Napoleon invaded and swept them away in 1798. Malta became a part of the British Empire two years later, and remained so until 1964. It finally became a republic in 1974.

Long known as a city built "by gentlemen for gentlemen", Valletta's history is preserved with streets of splendid Renaissance and baroque architecture. The British past is still much in evidence and, while the Maltese now feel strongly about their own national identity, in some ways, the island feels more British than Britain.

BELOW: cruise passengers say goodbye to Valletta.

Arrival and around the dock
Between the cloudless sky and the deep blue Mediterranean are the sheer cliffs and sheltering inlets of the northern Maltese coastline. The shoreline is broken by an impressive divided channel, guarded by Fort Ricasoli to the east and pierced by the bastions of Fort Saint Elmo, the northernmost fortification of Valletta.

The steep honey-coloured walls of Valletta rise behind and around the magnificent sweep of the Grand Harbour. The town makes a pleasing and orderly skyline, punctuated by occasional towers and domes. It's worth making it out on deck to observe the arrival, or choosing a table with a decent view when having breakfast. That's most likely to be forward on the starboard side, but ask a waiter at dinner the night before.

The boat docks at a wide quay, south of the Grand Harbour, set aside for cruise liners. The quay is lined with excursion buses and shuttles, and surrounded by old maritime buildings, many of which are being ren-

ovated or replaced. In the terminal area there are plenty of duty-free shops including those specialising in tobacco, alcohol and perfume. Buying items like these is just as easy on the way back to the ship, and saves lugging them about – especially as incursions into the local shops may add to the walking load.

The town is about 15–20 minutes' walk away from the port, and the walk is hot, dusty and rather steep. Taxis are not expensive, and you should be aware that while officials try to get you to buy tickets before leaving the harbour gates, once beyond the gates there are numerous taxis vying for custom. Water taxis also run from the harbour

Valletta's Armoury Museum is in the President's Palace.

Shopping

Shopping is pleasant, especially as many of the stores are beautifully decorated. Local specialities include lace and embroidery, ceramics and glassware. The street market along Merchant Street, starting at Market Square is particularly good for beach towels and other sunbathing equipment. With two Marks & Spencer stores, shopkeepers all speaking English and bookstores

with a good range of books in English, Valletta is the best place in the Mediterranean to pick up any requisites you may have forgotten to pack. When shopping with cash, it's a good idea to keep a selection of notes handy, as merchants will always give change in local Maltese lira, which are not widely negotiable elsewhere. Euro coins may not be accepted.

Seeing the sights Once you are into town, Valletta is made for walking. There are also taxis, if you want them, and horse-drawn carriages – *karrozzini*. Be sure to negotiate a price before taking a *karrozzini* to avoid any unpleasant surprises. Streets are wide and comfortable, characterised by squat, green palm trees, and distances are short. Handsome, pale stone façades are lined with regular green balconies and shutters. Valletta has many fine churches and museums, spectacular, airy gardens and spacious outdoor cafés.

In Palace Square (Misrah San Gorg), the **Grand Master's Palace** (open summer: Mon–Sat: fee) was built for the founding Knights in 1580, and has artwork and antique trimmings to prove it. The Maltese Parliament is held in the old armoury hall, the separate museum has an interesting collection of armour including a gold-plated set, and the tapestry chamber is where the Knights' Council was formerly convened.

Walk up Old Theatre Street to the **Manoel Theatre** (tours Mon–Fri 10.30am and 11.30am, Sat 11.30am only; fee includes admission to the theatre museum). Founded in 1731, this is where the Knights not only were entertained, but gave performances themselves. Reputedly the second-oldest theatre in use in Europe, the auditorium is finely featured with gilded boxes and an ornate ceiling.

The restored **Basilica of Our Lady of Mount Carmel** (1570) is adjacent to the

Map on page 236

TYPICAL EXCURSIONS, VALLETTA

● **Two Cities**. A tour of Valletta and Mdina by coach and on foot (4 hours).

● **Vittoriosa**. Boat trip across Grand Harbour and a tour of the 16th-century city (4 hours).

● **Jeep safari**. Off-road trip visiting the pretty villages of Birzebbuga and Marsaxlokk (4 hours).

BELOW: the Grand Harbour, Valletta.

Windmills are worth preserving even when they are no longer in use.

Manoel Theatre. The domed basilica was bombed during World War II, when strategic Valletta suffered badly, but it was meticulously reconstructed in the 1950s.

Return to Palace Square and to the right along Republic Street, on St John's Square is **St John's Co-Cathedral** (open Mon–Fri, Sat am only, Sun services only; free). Sir Walter Scott called the spectacular baroque interior, built in 1577, the most striking he had ever seen. Modest dress is required.

In the Auberge de Provence, is the **National Museum of Archaeology** (open daily, am only in summer; fee). The *auberge* itself is sumptuous, and the museum is an interesting bonus, with exhibits from prehistoric temples, including sculptures of fertility goddesses.

At the far (sea) end of Valletta is **Fort St Elmo**, site of the Knights' original fortification, from which they resisted the Great Siege. The **National War Museum** is housed here, and re-enactments and military parades are regular events. The World War II exhibits give clues as to why the whole island of Malta was awarded the George Cross for its bravery and resilience in that conflict. High above town sit the **Upper Barracca Gardens**, which offer a panoramic view of the town and the Grand Harbour.

Further afield

Further afield In the centre of the island lies **Mdina**, Malta's medieval capital, which can actually trace its origins back more than 4,000 years. In medieval times it used to be known as Citta' Notabile, the noble city, and it remains one of the world's finest inhabited medieval walled cities. The oldest Maltese families lived, and still live, among the palazzos and churches of Mdina, making it the seat of power in Malta. The narrow streets and high vantage point (it sits 150 metres/500ft above sea level) made it easy to defend, and also allows it to take the best advantage of the breezes in summer. You enter the old city via a small bridge and a splendid arch. Among many lovely buildings, quite a few of which date from a 17th-century reconstruction after an earthquake, is the **Cathedral**, which has beautiful mosaics and marble tombs.

BELOW: diving trips can be arranged in Malta.

Rabat, Mdina's suburb, can lay claim to the origins of Maltese Christianity, because it was here, in AD60, that St Paul is said to have lived after being shipwrecked in what is now called St Paul's Bay, in the north of the island. There are cruise excursions to Mdina, but it can also be reached by bus from Valletta. Whether you go alone or on a tour, be aware that there is quite a lot of walking involved.

There are cruise excursions to **Vittoriosa**, too, but it is very close to Valletta and can easily be reached by bus, or by taxi. Also known as Birgu, this 16th-century walled city may be worth a visit if you have time. One advantage of the cruise excursion is that it includes a trip across the Grand Harbour on a traditional Maltese *dhajsa* – the brightly coloured boats with "eyes" painted on the prow – but these trips, too, can be negotiated at the harbour.

Boating, jet-skiing and scuba-diving opportunities are included on shore excursions, but these beaches, too, are only a very short distance from Valletta. If you want to go it alone, trips are quite easy to arrange once you are ashore.

TUNIS

Maps
on pages
236 & 239

Widely held to be Africa's most European city, and known as "the Zurich of Africa" for the buzzing concentration of banking activity, modern Tunis is still exuberant with the spirit of trade and commerce of the Phoenicians, who founded the city of Carthage in 1100BC.

Tunis is usually a day's stay for cruise ships, but sometimes it's only a half day. If you haven't been to a North African market (*suuq* or souk), then a visit to Tunis is particularly exciting. Confident and adventurous travellers could make their way around alone, but a reasonable command of French and an air-conditioned taxi or bus are almost prerequisites. The ruins of Carthage are significant antiquities, and the village of Sidi-Bou-Said is pretty, but unless you're highly organised, you'll probably have to choose between visiting Carthage or visiting the medina marketplace

In the summer months Tunisia is likely to be one of the hottest ports of call in a Mediterranean cruise, so flat shoes and loose, light clothing will lend comfort. Although crime is not a huge problem, taking valuables into the crowded souk could be risky. Women are advised to dress modestly.

TYPICAL
EXCURSIONS,
TUNIS
● **Historical and
Cultural Tunis**
(half-day).
● **Carthage and Sidi-
Bou-Said** (full- or
half-day; *see main
text*).
● **The medina**
(half-day).

Arrival and around the dock The liner passes close to the low, rolling terrain, sprinkled with white, low-rise buildings, clumps of trees poking above. It's a surprisingly soft welcome to the coast of Africa. The wide quaysides are punctuated by palms and green shrubs. The port is named **La Goulette**, which means "the mouth" in French, the second language of Tunis.

Down on the quayside, a small expeditionary force of coaches noses into the shade between the sheds familiar air-conditioned coaches alongside smaller,

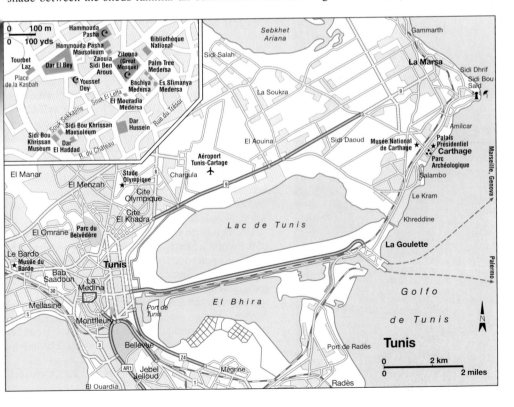

rounded, white shuttle buses with roof-racks. The latter are not air-conditioned, which could make them seem less of a bargain for independent travellers. The prevalence of buses makes a taxi unnecessary, but you should be able to get one if you wish. The terminal is a 20-minute drive from the ancient sites of Carthage, and about 40 minutes from Tunis.

To go ashore, non-Europeans will need to retrieve their passports, retained by the ship, to have them stamped by the port authorities.

Carthage **Carthage** begins almost as soon you leave the port to the north-east, and a 20-minute drive from the port takes you to the remains of the 2nd-century **Colosseum**, used for Roman gladiatorial contests. Surrounded by trees and trinket-sellers, the tiers of seating remain around the circular arena, with a trench through the centre, along which animals and contestants were driven to their fate. Some restoration is visible, but the impression of the Roman "bread and circuses" entertainment is still strong.

Past the French cathedral, and in the shadow of the new mosque, is the site of the 2nd-century **Roman temple**. Sunk about 3 metres (10ft) below the road are lines of red brick pedestals and parts of columns. The broken white Italian marble columns are in fact replicas, the originals, like so much local antiquity, have long since been looted.

Another 10-minute drive gets you to **Sidi-Bou-Said**, a small seaside town overlooking Tunis from the clifftops. Steep cobbled streets are lined with white houses, most with the characteristic blue doors and shutters. The blue panels are frequently decorated with Berber patterns and symbols picked out in ironwork, carvings and black nails. There are attractive cafés in which to sit, sip sweet mint tea from delicate glasses, listen to the birds and enjoy the great views.

BELOW: ruins in Carthage.

Tunis The drive to **Tunis** takes about another 20 minutes or so. The first views of the city are of the large modern complexes by the airport. These give way to residential streets, a playful mixture of columns, balconies and shutters in Arabic and European styles, often with small and highly decorative tiled awnings over windows and doors.

The remains of the **Roman aqueduct** are preserved through the centre of the city. From 5–25 metres (15–75ft) high and divided by the road, the well-preserved arches of pink sandstone were built in the 2nd century to carry a ½-metre (1½ft) channel of water. Now it is occupied by birds and shrubs.

The **Musée du Bardo** houses what is probably one of the world's finest, certainly one of the largest, collections of Roman and Byzantine mosaics. The museum is in a former royal palace just to the west of town, and the building is almost as fascinating as the mosaics themselves. The elegant terrace has Roman marble carvings, including warrior torsos and a large foot, as well as attractive white benches, which can be very comfortable when they are in shade. The building looks out onto a lush, green square.

At the edge of the kasbah (administrative centre) the low, elegant town hall fronts a wide open square.

Leading down to the **medina**, a black and white arched colonnade forms one side of a square lined with low, shady *jujube* trees, pools, benches and fountains.

The medina was the old walled town of Tunis, and is now almost filled by the souk although it is still inhabited. The market heaves and jostles with bewildered tourists and pleasant but insistent merchants, while the brick pathways are worn into a smooth, deep trough by thousands of years of foot traffic. Boys pass around trays with cake and sweet mint tea for sale. It's airless and close inside, and easy to get lost; if you want to wander away from your group, be sure to pre-arrange a meeting point and a time. Euros are accepted everywhere.

The carpet stalls are some of the most beautiful; every inch of wall and floor is covered with intricately woven carpets and rugs in vivid blues and reds, and luxuriant silks. Some carpet-makers demonstrate the arts of weaving, methods that have hardly changed over thousands of years. Perfumiers also demonstrate their craft of distillery. Silver and gold jewellery, mother-of-pearl boxes, incense, carpets and leather are some of the best buys, but perfumes with famous names should be treated with some caution. Don't forget to haggle.

For Europeans and North Americans, Tunis is likely to be the most "foreign" part of a Mediterranean cruise. Watching the land slip into the dusk behind the stern as you depart, remembering the aromas, sounds and sights of north Africa, can be a memorable experience.

BIZERTE

Bizerte has a fascinating history; first occupied 3,000 years ago by Phoenician colonists from Tyre, it then became a Roman colony until the 3rd century BC, when it was taken by the Arabs. When the French took over, in 1881, they

Maps on pages 188 & 239

The Great Mosque in Tunis, framed by an archway in the Palais d'Orient.

BELOW: gate into the medina in Tunis.

TYPICAL
EXCURSIONS,
BIZERTE

● **Beach** and **sports**.
Four-hour tour with
opportunities for
waterskiing, dinghy
sailing, jet skiing,
windsurfing, camel or
horse riding and
tennis.
● **Sidi-Bou-Said** and
Carthage (4 hours).
● **Tunis**, the **medina**
and the **Bardo**
Museum *(see main
text for town visits)*.

dredged canals around Bizerte, widened its harbour and built naval installations. They also endowed the city with broad avenues and boulevards and a pretty, palm tree-lined promenade. During World War II, Bizerte fell briefly into German hands but was liberated in 1943. Bizerte is a port of call in which ships generally spend only half a day, but this allows time for shore excursions.

Arrival and around the dock The outer harbour of the city is linked by canal to two inner harbours, the Bay of Sebra and the Lake of Bizerte. From the entrance to the canal (where the Sport Natique restaurant lies), it is a pleasant walk along the Boulevard Habib Bougatea to the atmospheric old fishing harbour, the Vieux Port. Or you can save time, and your legs, by taking a taxi direct to Place Bouchoucha.

The main thing to remember (for women particularly) before stepping ashore independently is that Tunisia has no public toilets. Hotel facilities are fine, and it is usually possible to use them, but elsewhere be prepared to squat over a crouch hole – and take plenty of loo paper. The port itself is far from grand but there are taxis (negotiate the price in advance or insist the meter is turned on). You can change money into Tunisian dinars at banks.

Shopping In the **medina**, the El Attarine Souk is the best place for wood carvings, basketry and local crafts. For bargains on gold and silver jewellery, make for the Souk El Birka (they are well known; ask for directions).

Seeing the sights It's worth devoting a bit of time, if you can, to Bizerte's attractive old harbour (**Vieux Port**). Lined with craft shops, cafés and restau-

BELOW:
practise your
haggling skills at
stalls in the medina.

Map on page 188

rants, it's a good place to enjoy a coffee, catch your breath and watch the local fishermen adroitly manoevring their brightly painting boats, before you take off for some sightseeing and shopping.

Just behind the Vieux Port lies **Place Bouchoucha**, the lively hub of the old town which is dominated by the spectacular Youssef Day fountain and filled with market stalls. Bouchoucha borders the **medina**, which contains some fine old mosques. The most beautiful – the 17th-century **Grand Mosque** – lies on the Place Bouchoucha itself, opposite the harbour, while the Andalusian-style mosque is slightly to the north. However, the main attraction of a visit to Bizerte's medina is the chance to browse the souks and bazaars, sip sweet mint tea as you haggle for goodies, and soak up the local atmosphere

On the hilltop to the north of the medina is the old Spanish Fortress – not built by the Spanish at all, but by the Turks, in 1750. It's worth the haul uphill for excellent views of the town.

If you fancy lunch ashore, the best restaurants are on the waterfront Rue de la Corniche, where you will find European cuisine as well as local specialities like *kaftaji* (spiced meatballs), *knef* (braised lamb), and *mechoui* (Tunisian-style mixed grill).

Further afield All cruise lines run excursions to the Carthaginian and Roman remains in the ancient town of **Carthage** and to the little coastal town of **Sidi-Bou-Said**, and on a half-day stay in port it would be foolish to attempt to visit them independently. Similarly, it is advisable to take the shore excursion on offer to the medina and Musée du Bardo in **Tunis** *(see pages 240–41 for details of all three towns).* ❑

BELOW:
life moves slowly around Bizerte's old harbour.

VENICE TO ATHENS: THE ADRIATIC AND IONIAN SEAS

Maps on pages 188 & 248

You can see the extraordinary city of Venice, then go via Dubrovnik and other Croatian ports to Greece's Ionian Islands, where you can soak up the culture or just soak up the sun

I n the heady days of the 14th to the 16th century, when the Republic of Venice ruled the waves and the Doge was more feared than the Almighty, the Venetians built great fortresses in Corfu, Crete, the Greek mainland and Dalmatia to resist Ottoman expansion and maintain their mercantile supremacy. Today, traces of this maritime empire can still be seen as you cruise from La Serenissima – the labyrinthine city on the water that alone would make any trip worthwhile. Many cruise lines visit Dubrovnik and other ports on the Adriatic coast of Croatia; others go south to Brindisi, the gateway to Greece. Across the water, rich with history and soaked with sun, the lovely Ionian Islands and the Gulf of Corinth await exploration, before you travel further east, round the tip of the Peloponnese, and dip your toes in the Aegean.

VENICE

An inspiration for writers and artists down the centuries, Venice continues to cast a spell over its many visitors. It's hard to imagine another city more richly deserving of its status as a World Heritage Site. It is, too, just about the perfect cruise call because everything is so immediately accessible. It's seems strange but, for a city that stretches across 118 islands in the Laguna Veneta, it is splendidly walkable. Cars are banned so the maze of narrow cobbled streets and nearly 500 historic bridges at its heart are atmospheric, whether explored in the steamy heat of summer or the misty cool of spring and autumn.

Bustling Piazza San Marco (St Mark's Square) and the ancient Basilica di San Marco, the lavish Palazzo Ducale (Doge's Palace), the imposing Campanile, the shop-lined Rialto Bridge across the Grand Canal – these are the famous icons, but the beauty of Venice is also in the detail, in the exposure to daily life in surroundings seemingly unchanged by the passage of time. Look along from the Bridge of Sighs, built to link the Doge's Palace with the original city prison, and see how Venetians still live and work in buildings that are under increasing siege from the rising water levels.

Napoleon described St Mark's Square as "the finest drawing room in Europe" but it is much more than just a refined stately home, frozen in time; it is a working, living, breathing classical city. For once, the most over-used word in tourism can be accurately applied without fear of contradiction – Venice really *is* unique.

Many lines use Venice as a home port for one or more of their ships; for other lines, it is a port of call

PRECEDING PAGES: a gondola trip is essential on a visit to Venice.
LEFT: golden Santa Maria della Salute.
BELOW: elaborate carnival mask.

Venice

within a cruise. For home-porting or visiting ships alike, though, the usual length of stay is one full day – and it will be a day to remember.

Arrival and around the dock area   Sailing along the Grand Canal into Venice is one of *the* great cruising experiences. The main docking area is beyond St Mark's Square so your ship will sail right past on its way into port.

If you are on one of the larger mega-ships, make sure you are on an upper deck, as this affords a spectacular view across the centre of the city and the outlying lagoon islands. It's like taking a slow-moving hot-air balloon ride.

The main docking area is at the city end of the Ponte della Liberta causeway connecting it to the mainland. The main railway station (Santa Lucia) is just 1 km (⅔ mile) and the airport 16 km (10 miles) from the two cruise passenger terminals. Transfers are usually by road but occasionally water-taxis are used to take passengers between the airport and their ships. All other commercial shipping is diverted to a separate area so these docks are exclusively for passenger ships. Both terminals are twin-level; arriving passengers pass through the ground floor and embarking passengers use the first floor.

The most recently built terminal doubles as a conference centre and has a large restaurant and several shops on the ground floor and a café and shops on the first floor. There are information and TV screens throughout both levels as well as the usual check-in, security controls and baggage conveyor belts. Passengers can check in bags for flights at the cruise terminals so they can spend time in Venice unencumbered by suitcases.

The other terminal has fewer facilities – no shops and just one café on the first floor – but there are more shops and cafés outside in the general dock area.

Some lines will offer a canal shuttle to Piazza San Marco (either free or for a small charge). Alternatively, the *vaporetto* (water bus) station (Tronchetto A and B) is right by the terminals. The fastest route is No. 34. If you plan to make more than four *vaporetto* trips during your stay, it pays to buy a day ticket *(gionaliero)*. While frequent and inexpensive, the *vaporettos* are a slow way to get around because of their many stops. Water-taxis are faster but more expensive while, for the longer journeys across the Grand Canal, gondola ferries *(traghettos)* are the best option.

Your ship may dock at San Basilio, which is a little way away from the main cruise terminals. This has its own *vaporetto* stop for the No. 5 route, a slightly slower service that stops at the San Zaccaria monastery gardens a short walk from St Mark's.

There is another dock (Riva Sette Martiri), which is only used by visiting (not home-porting) cruise ships, as well as by river boats and yachts. It is usually allocated to the few ships that are overnighting in Venice. Their passengers don't miss out on the St Mark's cruise-past, though, as these ships pass it on their turning circle, either when they arrive or when they depart. If your ship docks at Riva Sette Martiri, you can walk to St Mark's via a series of nine bridges and past the famous Hotel Danieli. It takes 10–15 minutes.

Map on page 248

TYPICAL EXCURSIONS, VENICE
- City walking tours (full- and half-day).
- Murano (glassworks), **Burano** (lace), **Torcello** (cathedral). All half-day tours.
- Gondola trips.
- Grand Canal by motor launch (half-day).
- Verona (full- and half-day tours).

BELOW: the house where Tintoretto lived.

St Mark's Basilica is one of the highlights of Venice.

Shopping The shops are a mix of designer boutiques and souvenir stores and, although bargains are few and far between, the Murano glassware, Burano laceware and the ubiquitous carnival masks and marionettes appeal to many visitors, as do the paintings and prints of Venice, both those in the shops and those being created as you watch by artists working by the canals. Look out, too, for the almost Dickensian stationery and cartography workshops which have excellent medieval maps and globes. Some shops observe the traditional siesta, closing from 1–4pm, but most don't – especially during the peak tourist summer months.

Eating The restaurants and cafés around San Marco are expensive, as you would expect. Go a little further afield, across the Grand Canal to the districts of San Polo and Santa Croce to find the typical Venetian inns, called *bacari*, which are less expensive and offer interesting snacks and light meals, good wine and a great atmosphere.

Seeing the sights There is a tourist information centre in Piazza San Marco which can give you information that may help you decide which of the many galleries, museums, palaces and churches to see. It is best not to spread yourself too thinly and try to see too much on a first visit. The unmissable ones are the glorious **Basilica di San Marco** (open daily; fee), the centrepiece of the square; the **Palazzo Ducale** (Doge's Palace; open daily; fee), the seat of Venetian government from the 9th to the 18th century; the **Campanile** (open daily), which you can climb for superb views; and the **Ponte dei Sospiri** (Bridge of Sighs), the most famous bridge in Venice.

BELOW: *palazzos* on the Grand Canal.

Moving away from the square, take a *vaporetto* along the Grand Canal and count off one historic palace after another. The **Palazzo Venier dei Leoni** now houses the **Guggenheim Foundation** (open Wed–Mon; fee) with an excellent collection of modern art; while next to the nearby Accademia Bridge is the **Galleria dell'Accademia** (open daily; fee) the city's favourite gallery, with a superb collection of Venetian art. Or take *vaporetto* No. 52 from Santa Lucia station to the church of **Madonna dell'Orto** (open daily), a masterpiece of Venetian Gothic.

But don't spend all your time on culture. Part of the pleasure of Venice is people-watching from one of the cafés. Having a cappuccino in one of the many places around St Mark's Square is a must – but just the one, as this may well be the most expensive coffee you have ever had. **Caffè Florian** and **Caffè Quadri** are the most prestigious. Prices are more reasonable in cafés away from St Mark's although nearby **Harry's Bar** – Venice has the original Hemingway watering hole – is also pricey.

No visit would be complete without a private gondola ride but you must negotiate hard as the gondoliers will charge as much as they can get away with.

Venice is never quiet but there are certainly fewer people around in the spring, autumn and winter months. This makes for easier sightseeing and shopping but there can also be occasional flooding, with duck-boards out in St Mark's Square.

Although Venice is walkable, the narrow streets are crowded in the summer and the numerous bridges can make it slow-going. In 2003, the Venetian authorities announced a new 10-point code for visitors, designed to reduce crowding, bottlenecks and consequent delays. This included new rules about walking only on the left and not lingering on bridges. It's an overdue initiative but it remains to be seen how effective it proves to be.

Map on page 248

A detail from Tintoretto's "Miracle of St Mark" in the Accademia.

BELOW: the Rialto Bridge.

Exquisite Murano glass makes an even better present or souvenir if you have visited the factory.

Further afield If you want to see the islands of **Murano** or **Burano** as well, allow 30–45 minutes each way from St Mark's. If you have a full day, it is possible to see a fair bit around St Mark's and either Murano or Burano as well, but you must allow ample time to return to the ship. It's probably best to do your own walking tour around St Mark's and then book the ship's half-day excursion to Burano or Murano. There are fee-charging beaches at the Venetian resort of **Lido di Jesolo** – about 45 minutes away – but, especially for first-time visitors, it would be a waste to spend the day there.

Verona, the pink marble city of *Romeo and Juliet*, with a Roman arena, splendid bridges and lovely churches, can be visited independently of excursions offered by cruise lines. There are trains approximately every hour from Santa Lucia, and the journey time is 1 hour 30 minutes.

RAVENNA

Some 140 km (90 miles) south of Venice on the flat coast of Emilia-Romagna, Ravenna was the last enclave of the Roman Empire in the west after the Barbarians overran Rome itself. Built on a series of lagoons like its more illustrious northern rival, it is best known for its superb mosaics – important examples of early Christian art that were bestowed on the city by the remnants of Roman power in the 5th and 6th centuries.

Arrival and around the dock A new cruise and ferry terminal opened in Ravenna in 2004. The air-conditioned terminal is airport-style with all the usual amenites – telephones, exchange, cafe, etc. The port is 5 km (3 miles) from the city centre and railway station. Shuttle-buses are run between port and city.

BELOW:
a ferry sets off from Brindisi for Greece.

Seeing the sights Start with **San Vitale** (open daily; fee), the city's great 6th-century octagonal basilica, famous for the mosaics in its choir and apse. These immediately draw the eye with their marvellous colours and intricate detail. Just north, another set of mosaics may be seen at the **Mausoleo di Galla Placidia**. Through the gate that lies between San Vitale and Galla Placidia are two Renaissance cloisters that now house the **Museo Nazionale** (open daily; fee). A pleasant walk along Via Fanni, Via Barbiani and left on to Via d'Azeglio leads to Ravenna's **duomo**. The 5th-century octagonal baptistry was once a Roman bath house, and contains magnificent Byzantine mosaics.

Map on page 188

TYPICAL EXCURSIONS, RAVENNA
● Ravenna city tour (half day).
● Bologna city tour (full day).

TYPICAL EXCURSIONS, BRINDISI
● Castellana Grotte for the stalagmites and stalactites; and the *trulli* dwellings of **Alberobello** (half-day).

BRINDISI

If you are visiting Puglia (Apulia), in the boot of Southern Italy, most cruise lines call in at **Brindisi**. Slightly off the beaten track, it represents a last taste of Italy before the ship heads east to Greece and Turkey.

Brindisi once played a major role as Rome's main naval base and as Italy's chief trading post for Middle Eastern goods, and a mercantile, cosmopolitan mood lingers on. Even so, this busy commercial port is not ideally suited to cruise ships, as the tangle of oil tankers, merchant ships, passenger ferries and naval craft would imply. It is also well known as the Italian gateway to Greece, which is confirmed by the profusion of passengers who sail away to Pátra and Corfu every summer.

Arrival and around the dock Brindisi is set at the back of a funnel-shaped bay, divided into two antler-like stretches of water, and sheltered by the expanse of the greater port. Only Porto Interno, the innermost harbour, is suitable for yachts and smaller craft. The Stazione Marittima, also sited here, acts as the combined cruise and ferry terminal, and is adequate for basic needs, from bars to travel agencies. Although it is a short, easy walk to the old town centre, taxis are in reasonable supply at the port. Bargaining in advance over a fare to sights beyond the city centre is a worthwhile exercise.

BELOW: *trulli* houses in Alberobello.

Seeing the sights One of the pleasing aspects of Brindisi is that the port is in the heart of the city, essentially occupying a peninsula dotted with such fine monuments as a Swabian castle, Romanesque churches and a baroque cathedral. This former Cretan and Roman colony is readily explored on foot, and the bustling atmosphere on the quaysides is fun as well. They are lined with bars and *trattorie* where you can sample Puglia's local pasta, *orecchiette* (little ears), washed down with strong red and delicate rosé wines.

Further afield A 30-minute coastal train or taxi north leads to **Ostuni**, the "white city", a quaint settlement of Greek origin, which looks more like Santorini than Italy, with whitewashed houses clinging to the hillside. The main shore excursions are to the stalactites and stalagmites of **Castellana Grotte** and to the weird beehive dwellings known as *trulli*, which are clustered around the **Alberobello** area.

An ornamental clock in Split's Old Town.

TYPICAL
EXCURSIONS,
SPLIT
● **Split** (half-day tour).
● **Salona Roman ruins** (half-day tour).

BELOW:
view over Split
from the bell tower.

SPLIT

Situated on the sunny Dalmatian coast of Croatia, **Split** is one of the Adriatic's liveliest and most alluring cities. Arriving here on a cruise ship and catching sight of its old town shimmering in the morning light against a backdrop of sheer limestone mountains creates a memorable first impression.

Arrival and around the dock   There is an existing terminal and five berths for cruise ships, although work is scheduled to start later in 2004 on expanding the terminal and adding a sixth berth. The port is well situated right in the centre of the city, with the centre of the old quarter within 200 metres or 5 minutes' walk. The railway station is even closer (100 metres/yds). There are buses and taxis at the port for longer journeys.

Seeing the sights   The palm-fringed waterfront **Riva** is lined with pavement cafés and cheap restaurants. From here you can head straight into **Diocletian's Palace** through the bronze gate (look out for the entrance to the subterranean museum here, with artefacts from Roman times laid out in the emperor's old living quarters), which used to be right on the water's edge and only accessible by boat. The centre of Split life still focuses upon the palace, built on the waterfront by the Roman emperor Diocletian as a retirement home between AD295 and 305. Over 200 buildings, and around 3,000 residents remain inside the original complex: the old chambers and garrisons have been converted over the centuries into shops, bars, cafés and hotels as well as ordinary homes. **St Domnius Cathedral**, whose lofty bell tower, one of the symbols of the city, was a 13th-century addition. The palace is a UNESCO World Heritage Site.

Further Afield About 5 km (3 miles) inland from Split and accessible by local bus are the ruins of the once thriving Roman town of **Salona** (open dawn–dusk; fee). A number of remains dot the landscape and it is possible to trace the original shape of the city and various structures, such as the amphitheatre that in its heyday played host to a baying 18,000-strong crowd. South from Split the Jadranka Magistrala (Adriatic Highway) takes in some of Europe's loveliest coastal scenery. The **Biokovo Mountains** sweep precipitously up one flank in a massif of karst hulks and forested ravines, while on the other the coastline is punctuated by bays and coves, with the islands of **Brac** and **Hvar** glittering just offshore. The resorts of the **Makarska Riviera** soon appear, tumbling down the hillside from the road towards the pine-fringed Adriatic beaches.

Map on page 188

HVAR

Hvar, the main settlement on the Croatian island of the same name, is visited mainly by smaller ships. Make the most of your time there, as some ships don't stay for very long – a shame, as this traffic-free medieval town is simply lovely.

Arrival and around the dock Cruise passengers tender into Hvar's pretty harbour, which is lined with shops, cafés and hotels. The Palace Hotel, right opposite the harbour, has an internet centre, and if you turn right facing the hotel you'll find the town's huge, marble-paved piazza with more shops and bars. Go left instead and you'll find more shops and cafés and travel agencies selling wine tours, island tours and "Fish Picnic" cruises at affordable prices. In the summer months, a water taxi operates from the harbour to the island's main beaches, and boats can be hired for fishing trips.

Central Dalmatia enjoys the sunniest weather in Croatia, with more than 200 days of sunshine a year. However, beware the "bura", a fierce, cold wind that rips along the coast in the winter and spring months, playing havoc with ferry services.

BELOW: pleasant promenade in Split.

Shopping   There are small boutiques selling fine glassware and maritime knick-knacks like wooden lighthouses, model boats, sailor-shaped soap dishes and so on, making Hvar a good place for buying a few presents for friends and family back home. Credit cards are accepted in most shops but get some kuna if you want to buy jewellery, lacework or lavender products from the little market stalls around the harbour.

Seeing the sights   The main town of Hvar was a naval base for the Venetian fleet from the 12th to the 18th century, and the Venetians have left their mark; the pedestrian-only, marble-paved streets shimmer as though filled with water; a well-preserved walled fortress overlooks the harbour and the town's main square, **Trg Sveti Stjepana** – originally a water-filled inlet which was reclaimed by the inhabitants in the 16th century – is the largest piazza in Dalmatia. In the centre is an ornate well constructed in 1520, and the square is dominated by the **Cathedral of St Stephen** – which has a remarkable Venetian bell tower.

Above the square, just beneath the 13th-century ramparts, are the remains of grand Gothic palaces once occupied by Hvar's aristocracy. The narrow (and unnamed) streets of the town are well worth exploring.

Also worth seeing is the large **arsenal** (its vast arches now occupied by shops) that was built in 1611 to repair, refit and equip war galleons. At its northern end – an area that was once a food store – a theatre was installed in 1612, and this is believed to have been the first theatre in Europe that was open to rich and poor alike, with a pit for the commoners and raised boxes for the gentry.

BELOW: Hvar Island has a pleasant, wooded coastline.

Further afield The island has a lovely coastline and is well-wooded and lush with typical Mediterranean vegetation and lavender fields, dotted with ancient settlements and historical monuments. The simplest way to explore is to hire a car. The small town of **Starigrad** dates from the 2nd century BC and has a beautiful bay, much celebrated by artists and poets down the ages. A highlight here is the Dominican Monastery, which houses a priceless collection of paintings and manuscripts. From here, organised tours usually go on to the village of **Vrisnik** for a cheese and wine tasting (Hvar produces some excellent wines).

If you just want to laze on a beach, you could consider taking a boat from the harbour at Hvar to the **Pakleni Islets**, just a short distance – the pick of the bunch is probably the nearest, **Jerolim**. Alternatively just walk along the coast east of town to reach a series of small coves with pebble beaches.

Map on page 188

KORCULA

The long, thin island of Korčula hangs off the edge of the Pelješac Peninsula. **Korčula Town** is the main attraction, a chocolate-box ensemble of orange-hued roofs and spires. The town plan is straightforward and makes walking around easy – the main thoroughfare runs right through the heart of the old centre and a waterside boulevard circles the peninsula. Only the smaller cruise ships call in at Korčula, docking conveniently right in the centre of town.

Seeing the Sights The town's most striking building is **St Mark's Cathedral**, a triple-naved basilica with an impressive interior containing an *Annunciation* by Tintoretto, who spent time in Korčula as a student. The **Town Museum** (open Mon–Sat; fee) is housed in an impressive 16th-century palace.

TYPICAL EXCURSIONS, KORCULA
● **Island tour** (3–4 hours), including a visit to the resort of Vela Luka.
● **Walking tour** (3–4 hours) of Korčula town.

LEFT: the Dominican Monastery at Starigrad.
BELOW: a rural island scene.

There are several bathing **beaches** around the town – a couple near the Marco Polo Hotel and many more less crowded ones near the town of **Lumbarda** to the south and also at **Blato**, a pleasant village to the west.

DUBROVNIK

George Bernard Shaw described Dubrovnik as '"paradise on earth" and visitors to this supremely beautiful 12th-century walled city will certainly agree. The old town – now largely recovered from the shelling it received during the civil war of 1991 – is crammed with architectural wonders and offers fantastic views of the Adriatic Coast from its high ramparts, while there are more delights just along the coast in the form of lovely countryside, stunning sea views and attractive traditional villages.

Dubrovnik is a popular port of call on Mediterranean itineraries and although it is not a home port, ships spend a full day and sometimes an evening here to allow passengers plenty of time to explore.

Arrival and around the dock While some ships tender passengers into the old harbour in the heart of Dubrovnik's old town, most berth in the main dock at the end of the waterfront marina and provide shuttle buses for the 10-minute drive to the old town's Pile (pronounced *Pee-lay*) Square. If you're feeling active, you could walk to the old centre – it's a pretty route, but uphill. The port is clean, modern and well presented but has little to offer other than an internet café at its entrance (where access is much cheaper than on the ships).

Just to the right as you leave the dock is a pretty harbour filled with well-maintained and colourful boats, some of which offer lunch and dinner cruises.

BELOW: Dubrovnik's old town is right by the beach.

There are also bus stops here with a good network of services for those wishing to explore further afield, and a rank of taxis charging around 25 kuna for hire and around 8 kuna per kilometre.

Just across the road is a tourist office, where helpful English-speaking staff are happy to provide information and bus maps. Bus Nos 1A and 1B go to Pile Square. Around the tourist office there are a few shops and, a little further along, a colourful daily flower and vegetable market.

Shopping Dubrovnik's old town has some excellent shops and art galleries and, although prices are not as low as they were, you can pick up good-quality paintings, pottery and glassware without breaking the bank.

Other good buys are locally made lacework and embroidered cotton goods. But if you want to do some serious shopping, take plenty of cash or travellers' cheques, as some small shops, galleries and stalls don't take plastic.

First to catch your eye will be the shops lining the marble-paved main street, **Placa Stradun**, but have a good look around the city's byways and steep, narrow streets before committing yourself to purchases, as some of the best shops and galleries are hidden away.

Seeing the sights If you're dropped off in **Pile Square**, take a moment to walk to the waterfront balustrade to enjoy the magnificent harbour view before strolling down the ramps into the old city.

The first thing to greet you as you enter via Pile Gate is the imposing **Onofrio's Fountain**, one of Dubrovnik's most famous landmarks, which was constructed in the 1430s as part of an elaborate system of aqueducts and canals

Maps on pages 188 & 259

TYPICAL EXCURSIONS, DUBROVNIK
● **Dubrovnik old town** walking tour (3–4 hours).
● **Best of the Adriatic** (7–8 hours): a drive along the scenic coast, exploring traditional villages and the resort of **Cavtat**.
● **Village Home** tour (3–4 hours); samples local wines in a local village before visiting **Cavtat**.

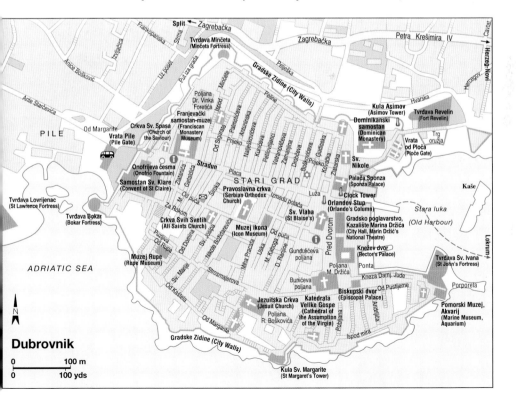

Dubrovnik

0 — 100 m
0 — 100 yds

Visitors and local people in a market in Dubrovnik.

designed to carry water to the city from a well 12 km (8 miles) beyond its walls. Right ahead of you now is Placa Stradun (wear sensible shoes when touring Dubrovnik as the *placa*'s cream marble paving, although spectacular, can be slippery). Immediately to your left, though, is the 14th-century **Franciscan Monastery**, and you should explore here first, as its cloister is exquisite, and was one of the few places to survive the catastrophic earthquake which ravaged Dubrovnik in 1667; the rest of the monastery collapsed and was rebuilt. Of particular interest here is a beautiful statue of the Pietá, carved in 1498, and the world's oldest pharmacy, established in 1391.

Walk to the other end of the *placa* and you'll find the only other building to have survived the 1667 earthquake, the magnificent **Sponza Palace**, which is notable for its elaborate curved portico and Gothic windows. The palace now houses the state archives of Dubrovnik and also contains a small maritime museum and art gallery. Just beyond it, through a stone archway, is the old harbour, while if you head right and cross Puljana Luza, you'll find the gorgeously baroque, 18th-century **Church of St Blaise**, Dubrovnik's patron saint. His remains are in Dubrovnik's **Cathedral of the Assumption of the Virgin**, which lies behind the church. The cathedral also contains a stunning collection of gold and silver medieval reliquaries. Just off Puljana Luza is a paved square where a craft market is held most mornings; good buys are embroidery and lace, flavoured oils and lavender products.

BELOW: coffee break in Placa Stradun.

The 14th-century **Dominican Monastery** (to reach it, go left past the Sponza Palace) houses a collection of religious art and artefacts from the 14th and 15th centuries, and here you will find another lovely cloister, constructed in the 15th century.

If it's your first time in Dubrovnik, do make time (and save some energy) for a walk around the **fortified walls**, which offer panoramic views of the old city. The entrance to the walls is just inside Pile Gate, so you could start or end your tour here. And if that leaves you in need of fortification yourself, you'll find plenty of restaurants tucked away in the alleys of Dubrovnik, as well as lively (if a mite more expensive) outdoor cafés on the main streets.

Local dishes worth a try include *lignje* (fried squid), *pasticada* (stuffed roast beef) and *cevapcici* (spiced meatballs). The local Merlot is excellent and you can round off your meal with a glass of Dubrovnik firewater, Travarica, which is pleasantly flavoured with herbs.

Further afield   Travel agencies on Placa Stradun offer a wide range of day tours – including jeep safaris, Dubrovnik panorama coach tours and even light aircraft flights – at much lower prices than ships' shore excursions – while at the Lokrum Ferry Dock in Dubrovnik's old harbour near the Dominican Monastery you can buy tickets for boat trips to the pretty seaside town of **Cavtat**, a popular haunt for yachties with its lovely seafront promenade and lively cafés – also offered as an excursion. There are also boats to **Korčula** *(see page 257)*, and "fish picnic" cruises around the bay. Just be sure you get back in time to rejoin your ship.

KOTOR

Medieval **Kotor** lies at the head of stunning Kotor Bay – one of the finest natural harbours in the Mediterranean – and at the foot of the 1,770-metre (5,800-ft) sheer wall face of Mount Lovcen, which makes arriving by cruise ship a

Maps on pages 188 & 259

BELOW: you can take a boat trip round the bay with a fish picnic.

memorable experience. Designated a UNESCO World Heritage Site, Kotor is the only port of call on the short coast of Montenegro, which forms part of Serbia and Montenegro (known as Yugoslavia until 2003).

Seeing the sights Kotor is a well-preserved medieval town of winding narrow streets punctuated by leafy squares and brimming with beautiful architecture and encircled by sturdy walls. The town is every bit as charming and dramatic as many of its Croatian counterparts, with impressive palaces and a dozen or so churches dating from the 10th to the 15th century, several containing remnants of frescoes or icons. Highlights include the **Cathedral of St. Tiphun**, constructed in 1166, the **church of St. Lucas**, and numerous palaces including the **Drago Palace** with its Gothic windows dating from the 15th century.

CORFU (KERKYRA)

Corfu (Kérkyra) is one of the largest of the Greek islands and has become a popular holiday destination because of its sunny climate, sandy beaches and relaxed lifestyle. Cruise visitors arrive conveniently close to Corfu town where the old quarter, with its cobblestone streets and alleyways, historic buildings, statues and fountains, is the largest preserved medieval town in Greece that is still fully inhabited and functional. The Venetians, French and British have all had an influence on the architecture and the old (Venetian) fortress jutting out from the coast road is a UNESCO World Heritage Site. Beyond the old town, the island offers many attractive drives through pine woods, a variety of beach resorts and small inland villages where time appears to have stood still.

Cruise lines occasionally home-port ships here – the airport is only a couple of

TYPICAL
EXCURSIONS,
CORFU
● **Corfu's Old Town**
to the 19th-century
Achilleion Palace
(half-day).
● **Beach trip** (usually
half-day) to Dasiá,
Glyfáda or
Paleokastrítsa.
● **Safari trip**
(half-day).
● **Horsedrawn
carriage rides**
through Corfu Old
Town.

BELOW:
a quiet time in
Corfu's old harbour.

miles from the port/Corfu Town – and offer the cruise combined with a stay on the island. But mostly it serves as a port of call, with ships usually staying a full day.

Maps
on pages
188 & 264

Arrival and around the dock There is nothing much to see as you arrive at the island's busy commercial and naval port and it is usually a 5- to 10-minute walk just to get from the ship to the dock entrance where there is a ferry ticket office (ferries go to Igoumenítsa on the Greek mainland) along with some public telephones and a small exchange bureau. There is a free shuttle bus which picks up from the ships to take passengers to the Travel Value duty-free shops halfway between the dock and Corfu's old town but, since Greece joined the EU, genuine duty-free bargains have disappeared. In any case, most ships offer a free (or cheap) shuttle into the old town. This will take you past a market, around the outer edge of town, dropping off across the park from Listón Arcade. If you decide to walk into the old town, it's quicker via the coast road – it's about 1 km (less than a mile) and takes around 15 minutes from the dock gates. But there's not much to see along the way – although you could hire a boat or car from one of the offices along here – so it's probably best to take the shuttle and start your walking when in town.

A Greek island dream – waves lapping on pristine beaches.

Shopping There is a fish, food and clothes market just inside the old town walls at the Venetian gates. Otherwise, the main shopping area is behind Listón Arcade and esplanade. One of the best buys is local olive wood that has been carved into salad bowls, bread boards and even statues. Otherwise, Venetian jewellery, leather and furs, and colourful ceramics are worth a look. A few shops close in the afternoon but most stay open all day.

BELOW: Colonnade of the Muses at the Achilleion Palace.

Orthodox priests in their black gowns and hats are a common sight in the Ionian Islands.

Seeing the sights Corfu old town is compact and easily walkable even if you take taxis (which come right to where the ships dock) or a shuttle bus there and back. The roads are too narrow and the traffic too heavy to make any other kind of transport a better option. Take care though: the streets and alleyways are uneven and full of potholes so it is easy to trip and fall. Watch out, too, for the traffic: often there are no proper pavements and, even where they exist, local drivers are quite willing to use them as a quick way through the traffic.

Road and street signs are usually given in Greek and in transliteration, but may differ a little from the Greek or transliteration used on town maps provided by the ship or locally. The maps are not generally very reliable and it is easy to get lost if you try and follow them closely. However, most local people speak enough English to direct you to where you want to go.

This will probably include the 16th-century **Ágios Spyrídon Church** – its red-domed belfry stands out just behind Listón Arcade; and the 19th-century **Palace of St Michael and St George**, the oldest official building still standing

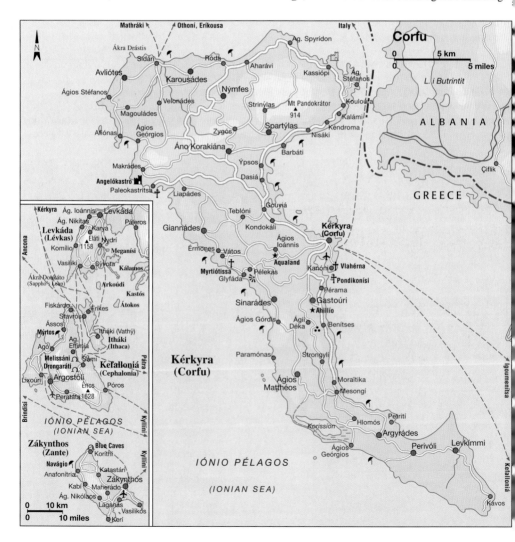

in Greece, on the other side of the esplanade. Its east wing houses the **Museum of Asiatic Art**, which has one of the largest private collections of Asiatic art in the world. The **Archaeological Museum** in Vraïla Street has pieces dating back to Roman times which have been rtrieved from local excavations.

For a drink or lunch, choose one of the cafés along Listón Arcade, which was designed by the French to echo the Parisian Rue de Rivoli, and looks out over the park in front of the Old Fortress – reputedly the largest open square in Greece. There are better – and cheaper – cafés elsewhere in the town but these have the best views. There is a tourist office (EOT) on the corner of Vouleftón and Mandzárou. A smaller, more accessible office can be found on Arseníou – the coast road leading into the old town.

Further afield All the places featured in shore excursions outside the old town are easily accessed, either from the ship or from Corfu Town, by taxi (there are ranks at the old port, the esplanade, G. Theotóki Street and San Rocco Square). If you want to book one for a tour, or have the driver wait to take you back, the hourly charge is about €40 (at 2004 rates).

Paleokastrítsa, which has an ancient Byzantine Monastery as well as fine sandy beaches, is only 24 km (15 miles) from the port and the fare is about €25 each way. Less than 5 km (3 miles) away is **Kanóni**, with glorious views of Mouse Island which – legend has it – was formed when Poseidon turned Odysseus's ship into stone. About 10 km (6 miles) further on, in the village of Gastoúri, is the **Achilleion Palace**. By taxi this trip costs about €20 each way. Buses also operate from San Rocco to places like Gastoúri but, although cheap, they are always crowded and the timetables are not to be relied upon. To visit

Map on page 264

BELOW:
the elegant Listón Arcade conceals a number of cafés.

Dasiá, the public beaches just 12 km (7 miles) away, buses are an option, because they leave San Rocco (and Dasiá) every half-hour.

The vast **Aqualand** waterpark (www.aqualand-corfu.com) with slides, chutes, rafting, lazy river rides, plus shops, bars and restaurants, about 8 km (5 miles) from Corfu town at Ágios Ioánnis, is one of the largest in Greece.

KEFALLONIA (CEPHALONIA)

Kefalloniá (Cephalonia) is the largest of the Ionian islands but has a population of only 30,000 spread throughout its towns and resorts, with relatively few people living in the mountainous interior. Pine-clad Mount Enos, at 1,628 metres (5,340ft), in the south of Kefalloniá, is the highest mountain on the island.

There are some lovely sandy beaches near the west-coast port of Argostóli and also along the south coast but the main towns had to be rebuilt after being badly damaged in an earthquake that hit the island in 1953. So, although Sámi and Argostóli have pretty settings, they are not as attractive as some of the better-preserved towns on other Greek islands. The real bonus of Kefalloniá, however, is that it is far less touristy than many other Greek ports of call and gives visitors a chance to experience the flavour of an authentic Greek island community.

The island of Kefalloniá has six ferry ports, including one for the capital Argostóli, but cruise ships call at only one, **Sámi**, on the eastern side of the island. Although there is an airport near Argostóli, fly-cruises are not an option – this is purely a port of call and ships stay either a half or a full day.

Arrival and around the dock Sámi is set in a pretty harbour overlooked by steep wooded hills and opposite the neighbouring island of Itháki

---

TYPICAL
EXCURSIONS,
KEFALLONIA
● Half-day **island tour** including the caves of Drongaráti and Melissáni and the town of Argostóli *(see main text)*.

BELOW: fishing boats make a brilliant splash of colour in Sámi.

(Ithaca) 2 km (1 mile) away, so it is worth being out on deck as your ship approaches harbour. Some ships dock while other (larger) ones will anchor off and tender passengers in. Either way – as with most Greek island ports – you are deposited right in the heart of town and there is certainly nothing as elaborate as a cruise terminal to pass through on your way there.

Map on page 264

Seeing the sights Because of the slow winding roads in the mountainous interior, journey times are longer than the distances suggest, so bear that in mind if catching buses or taking taxis (hiring a car or scooter is not to be recommended here), especially if the ship's stay is limited to a half-day. There are buses every couple of hours to **Argostóli**, which is only 24 km (15 miles) away but this round-trip is really only feasible if you are in port for the whole day.

There is not much to see in Sámi itself – although it is always pleasant to pause for a drink in one of the harbour-front tavernas and to browse for arts and crafts, ceramics and other souvenirs – but there are a couple of interesting caves to visit in the area. The closest and most interesting are **Drongaráti**, with oddly shaped stalactites and stalagmites; and **Melissáni**, on the road to Agía Evfimía. The sun shining down through a hole in the cave's roof onto an underground lake creates a spectacular lighting effect.

A horse trek sets off through the countryside near Sámi.

ZAKYNTHOS (ZANTE)

One of the main islands of the Ionian group, Zákynthos, or Zante, is famous for its natural springs and wildflowers, which form a dramatic contrast to some of the more barren islands. The beautiful beaches, high cliffs and fragrant banks of

BELOW: the glorious coastline of Zákynthos.

Icon in Zákynthos museum.

TYPICAL EXCURSIONS, KATAKOLO

● **Olympia**, ancient site of the original Olympic Games (half-day tours).

BELOW: mountains shelter tiny villages.

wildflowers have inspired many writers and poets, from Homer to Byron to Dionysios Solomos, who wrote the Greek national anthem.

Around the dock Zákynthos Town, the main port, is a typical Greek scene of dazzling white houses, yacht marinas, fishing boats and tavernas. The whole town was rebuilt after a devastating earthquake in 1953, so there are few old buildings, but the reconstruction has been sympathetically done. Most cruise ships have to tender passengers into the port.

Seeing the sights The focal point away from the port is **Platía Solomoú**, on which you'll find the **Museum of Post-Byzantine Art** (open Tues–Sun; fee). Nearby is the **Museum of Dionysios Solomos**, dedicated to the life and work of the father of modern Greek literature, and to other prominent local people, with many portraits, clothes, furniture, icons and manuscripts to look at. Shop in the town for local wine, honey, jewellery, leather and pottery.

Further afield To appreciate the natural beauty of Zákynthos, you need to hire a bike or scooter, jump on a local bus or, best of all, walk. There are some lovely beaches, particularly the white, sandy stretch of **Navágio** beach (Smugglers' Cove), with dramatic cliffs and a half-submerged shipwreck resting in the sand. However, the beach is only accessible by boat and you need to enquire locally about boat hire or trips. In the **Bay of Laganás**, on the south coast, loggerhead turtles lay their eggs and motorised watersports are not allowed.

Inland, visit the pretty villages of **Maherádo**, with its 14th-century church, and Volímes, which have escaped most tourist development. There are further interesting churches at Mariés and Anafonítria. From the functional east coast port of **Ágios Nikólaos** you can take a boat to the lovely Blue Caves.

KATAKOLO

The small Ionian port of Katákolo, on the Peloponnesian mainland, is used mostly as a base from which to visit ancient Olympia, the sanctuary of Zeus and the location of the first Olympic Games (776BC). It is here that the Olympic torch is lit. The games were held every four years at full moon in August or September, after the harvest, and drew thousands of spectators from all over the ancient world.

Seeing the sights There is not much to see in Katákolo, and almost all visitors head for Olympia, 48 km (30 miles) inland. You'll find a handful of bars and tavernas and shops selling Olympic memorabilia, souvenirs, statues, leather items and jewellery.

Further afield It's best to join a shore excursion to **Olympia**, although there are taxis. The site is set in forests of pine and oak and is still being excavated – it was discovered in 1766 under several metres of mud. It was almost destroyed by forest fires in 1998 but fortunately survived. Today, you can see the Roman baths, the massive gymnasium, where the athletes trained, the **stadium** (open Mon–Sat; fee), the

Temples of Zeus and his wife, Hera, a Roman swimming pool, Roman fountains and the workshop of Phidias, who built a vast gold and ivory statue of Zeus that was considered one of the Seven Wonders of the Ancient World and was housed in the temple of Zeus.

The bronze, marble and terracotta statues in the **Archaeological Museum** (open daily; fee) are absolutely stunning and there's lots of fascinating memorabilia from the ancient games, including weights and discuses. There are more souvenirs in the **Museum of the Olympic Games** in the town, 15 minutes' walk from the ancient site. Most tours allow shopping time in town after a visit.

GYTHIO (GYTHION)

The ancient port of Gýthio, situated on the southern coast of the Peloponnese, was founded by the Phoenecians around 400BC, and for centuries served as the port for Sparta, some 50 km (30 miles) to the north. Nowadays the town is a holiday resort and a deceptively congenial gateway to the austere Máni peninsula. Most cruise passengers calling in at Gýthio take the tour to Sparta and Mystrás.

Seeing the sights The main sights in Gýthio are the **Roman Theatre** and also the **Historical Museum** (open Tues–Sun; fee) on Marathonísi islet (ancient Kranae) tied to the mainland by a causeway. It was here that Paris and Helen legendarily spent their first night together, and so launched a thousand ships. The quay is lined by tiled vernacular houses and pricey fish tavernas; across the Lakonian Gulf the sun rises over **Cape Maléa** and Mount Taýgetos can be glimpsed to the north. Good beaches are easily accessible from town, with the best at **Mavrovoúni** just to the south.

Map on inside back cover

A speedy trip around the coast of Zákynthos.

BELOW: ancient columns still stand tall at Olympia.

Further afield There is not a great deal to see at **Sparta** (Spartí); the ruins are rather thin on the ground, although the museum (open Tues–Sun; fee) is excellent. **Mystrás**, 6 km (4 miles) to the west, is more rewarding. A city of 20,000 under Byzantine rule in medieval times, it remains remarkably complete to this day – a romantically ruined walled town clinging to a conical crag and topped by a castle. It is perfectly possible to reach Spartí by public bus from Gýthio (continue by taxi to Mystrás), although most cruise passengers elect to take a guided tour. To the south of Gýthio is the wild Maní peninsula, the highlight of which is the **Diros Caves** complex (Pýrgos Dhiroú).

KYTHIRA

Several places claim to be the birthplace of Aphrodite, and one of them is Kýthira, a pretty and unspoilt island off the southern tip of the Peloponnese peninsula, towards Crete.

Around the dock There are two ports, one at **Agía Pelagía** in the north and one in the south at **Kapsáli**, which is not far from Hóra, the main town, perched high on a hill overlooking the sea and dominated by a castle. Neither port has many facilities, but cruise lines normally operate shuttles to the towns.

Seeing the sights **Hóra**, with its narrow streets and old mansions, fortified against pirate attack, is an easy and pleasant place to walk around. The **Archaeological Museum** contains an important collection of Minoan vases, Mycenaean pottery and finds from the archaic and classical periods. You can also climb up to the 15th-century Venetian castle.

Map on page 284

Further afield The island is easy to explore independently if you hire a car or motorbike. **Kapsáli** (where you may have disembarked), in the far south, is the main tourist centre, with an attractive harbour and some good beaches.

At **Livádi**, a short drive away, visit the old, frescoed church of Ágios Andréas and the monasteries of of Agía Elésis and Myrtidíon. **Mylopótamos** is one of the most beautiful medieval villages on the island, with a Venetian castle, a monastery and a nearby waterfall. The cave of **Agía Sofía**, which has a frescoed 13th-century shrine, is usually included in ships' tours.

There are plenty of jewellery and handicraft shops in the ports. For additional local colour, venture to **Potamós**, 20 km (12 miles) from Hóra, where the island's main market is located.

NAVPLIO (NAFPLION)

Návplio (Nafplion) was Greece's first capital after the Greek War of Independence (1821–28). Today, this attractive town serves as a base for day trips to the ancient sites at Argos, Nemea, Mycenae, Tiryns, Epidaurus, and Corinth.

Around the dock Návplio is a tender port, and passengers are usually dropped in the busy harbour, close to the walkable town, which has shady parks, stepped side streets and lots of small churches and museums. Don't miss the **mosque** off Platía Sýndagma (Constitution Square) where Greece's first parliament met, or the array of elegant neoclassical civic buildings.

The best shops are on Staïkopoúlou, immediately above Platía Sýndagma, and Vas. Konstantínou, which runs parallel to it. Best buys include jewellery, icons, worry beads, antiques, shadow puppets, Greek wine and honey.

Olympian inscriptions have stood the test of time and weather.

BELOW: it's a steep climb up to Návplio's fortress.

**TYPICAL
EXCURSIONS,
NAVPLIO**
● **Epidaurus**, with the
4th-century theatre.
● **Mycenae** and
Corinth (all full- or
half-day tours).

Návplio has two hilltop fortresses and a miniature castle on an island in the
harbour, exploration of which could easily fill a day. **Akronavplía** fortress was
begun in Byzantine times and finished in the late 17th century, about the same
time that the Venetian **Palamídi** (open daily; fee) was built. There are said to be
999 steps up the rock face, which you can climb to the latter, but it's easier to
take a taxi to both fortresses, especially in hot weather. The views from the top
are breathtaking, with the town spilling away below and the little 15th-century
Boúrtzi Castle squatting on its island in the harbour. The castle can be reached
by a short motorboat trip for a couple of euros.

Further afield Cruise lines offer several different excursions from Návplio.
Epidaurus is famous for the 4th-century **theatre**, which seats 14,000, and is
beautifully preserved. **Mycenae** has some impressive excavations dating back
to 1250BC, while those in **Corinth** include the 6th century BC Temple of Apollo.
And there's the amazing **Corinth Canal**; there's a viewing area here, from
which you can watch ships squeezing through the high-sided, narrow channel.

ITEA

Built on the Gulf of Corinth and surrounded by olive groves, Itéa is a pleasant
little port used as a gateway to Delphi, possibly the most famous and magical
of all the classical sites in Greece.

BELOW:
the Sanctuary of
Athena at Delphi.

Around the dock Cruise ships either tender or dock at the pier near the
town centre. There's not a great deal in the town itself, as everything is geared
towards visiting Delphi and the town is, in any case, relatively modern. If you

don't want to visit the site, you will find pretty tavernas along the waterfront and some decent swimming beaches with shade a short walk away.

Further afield Delphi is 20 minutes away by bus or taxi, on the slopes of craggy **Mount Parnassós**, looking out over the olive groves stretching all the way to the coast. It's a good idea, particularly if you are visiting without a guide, to go first to the **museum** (open daily; fee; combined ticket with Sanctuary of Apollo available), in order to get a better perspective on the region's turbulent history.

Delphi was revered by the ancient Greeks as the sanctuary of Apollo and the home of his oracle, which brought pilgrims from all over the ancient world to seek advice. It was also the site of the Pythian Games, the most famous festival in Greece after the Olympics.

The huge area includes the **Sanctuary and Temples of Apollo** (open daily; fee), the most important site; the ruins of **Hiera Odos** (Sacred Road), the stadium and breathtakingly beautiful theatre, and the **Temple of Athena Pronaia**.

GALAXIDI

A beautifully preserved old fishing port, Galaxídi lies opposite Itéa on the Gulf of Corinth and is used as an alternative port for ships unloading passengers to visit the ancient site of Delphi.

Around the dock Galaxídi is best known for its magnificent **noblemen's houses**, dating to the 18th and 19th centuries, when it was an important port with its own commercial fleet. Most ships tender here and ferry passengers into the

Map on page 284

TYPICAL
EXCURSIONS,
ITEA
● **Delphi**, the ancient site on the slopes of Mount Parnassós (4-hour tours).

BELOW: Galaxídi has a well-preserved fishing port.

Maps on page 284

TYPICAL
EXCURSIONS,
GALAXIDI
● **Delphi**, the ancient
site on the slopes of
Mount Parnassós
(half-day tours).

town, where there are several **museums** (themes include nautical history, archaeology and folk art) and an unusual church, **Ágios Nikólaos**, to visit. The stately old mansions are dotted all over the town. If you don't want to visit Delphi (which involves going by boat to Itéa and then by road), there are several small pebble beaches and some good seafood tavernas.

Further afield To reach **Delphi** you must take a boat across the bay to Itéa, a short, pleasant trip, and then get a bus or taxi to the site, about 20 minutes away. As already mentioned *(see page 273)*, Delphi was revered by the ancient Greeks as the sanctuary of Apollo and became an important place of pilgrimage. The site lives up to its reputation as being among the most magical in Greece, and the sanctuary, the temples, the stadium and the theatre are all quite outstanding.

OTHER PORTS OF CALL

Smaller ships cruising the Aegean en route from Italy to Athens often call at some of the lesser-known ports in the Ionian Sea, usually for a beach day, or for a morning of coffee drinking and shopping. **Párga** is a tiny gem of a town on the west coast of mainland Greece with exquisite Venetian houses in pastel colours set against craggy limestone mountains. There's a castle a short walk above the village with stunning views of the bay and the goods for sale in the village shops are among the most tasteful you'll find in Greece. **Paxí** (Paxós), one of the lesser-known Ionian islands, also has a lot of Venetian influence. **Pýlos**, situated on the south shore of the magnificent natural harbour of Navarino, was the scene of a bloody battle in the Greek War of Independence in 1827, in which 58 Turkish vessels were sunk and remain on the seabed today. **Kalamáta**, meanwhile, is the principal port of Messinia and is famous for its its purple olives, rich olive oil and succulent dates.

BELOW: a boat trip from Ýdra.
RIGHT: the water is inviting.

East of the island of Kýthira, you enter the Aegean Sea. **Monemvasía**, an attractive medieval town with a variety of architectural influences, is built on a rocky cliff in the southeastern corner of the Peloponnese. Things to see here include the ruined fortress, cathedral, ancient fortifications and old, cobbled streets.

Cruise ships occasionally call at the islands of **Aegina** (Égina), **Póros** and **Ýdra** (Hydra), located in the Saronic Gulf close to Athens. These islands, popular with Athenians for a weekend break, will also give you a good taste of island life before or after a cruise, as they're easily accessible from the capital's port, Piraeus, by ferry.

Aegina is mountainous, with vines, olives, figs, almonds and pistachios its principal industries, alongside tourism and sponge fishing. Ýdra, in contrast, is barren and rocky, with donkeys used instead of cars as transport and massive underground cisterns where water was once stored. Póros, a speck off the northeast coast of the Peloponnese, is greener, with a pretty principal town clinging to a hillside, topped by a church bell tower.

Ships also visit **Paleá Epídavros**, the gateway to the ancient sanctuary of Epidauros on the Peloponnese. Today, there's an impressive museum of classical antiquities and a restored Greek theatre which seats 14,000. A festival of Greek drama is held here every summer. ❏

THE AEGEAN

*Whether you like history and archaeology or prefer boat trips
and beaches, the Aegean won't disappoint – and there'll
always be a background of stunning scenery*

Maps
on pages
280 & 284

Athens, the so-called "cradle of democracy", was the centre of the civilised world before the rise of the Roman Empire, and its busy port, Piraeus, is just a short hop from downtown on the efficient metro. The first-time visitor will find that the Greek capital, ancient and modern, has more than enough to offer in terms of sightseeing, culture, hotels, restaurants and nightlife. Athens can also be a jumping-off point for the temples and theatres and other archaeological wonders of nearby Mycenae, Epidauros, Delphi and Cape Sounion. Cruise ships may then head to the Cyclades or the Dodecanese, jewels in the wine-dark Aegean, and most will make a call at Iráklio on the largest island, Crete (Kríti), from where excursions take you to the Minoan palace of Knossos. A few cruises will also head north and northeast to the lesser-known islands of the northern Aegean.

PRECEDING PAGES:
Santoríni view.
LEFT: a dome in
Santorini.
BELOW: the
presidential guard.

ATHENS (PIRAEUS)

Although the decision to stage the Summer Olympics in Athens in 2004 ensured a frenzied clean-up, with tree-planting and landscaping, new buildings and restorations galore, chances are that the city will remain essentially the same chaotic, scruffy, traffic-clogged but entirely compulsive metropolis that has attracted and enthralled visitors for centuries.

Piraeus (Pireás), the port for Athens, is frequently used as a starting point for cruises. At one time, this could only be offered by Greek cruise lines but now all lines are allowed this option. All cruise ships, whether home-porting or visiting, dock alongside rather than anchoring off.

Arrival and around the dock Arriving by ship you may see the imposing Temple of Poseidon perched on Cape Sounion to the southeast; once in the approaches to Piraeus, however, it will be the marine traffic that catches your eye. One of the busiest ports in the Mediterranean, Piraeus receives over 12 million ferry and cruise visitors every year, so ships are coming and going all the time and the port area is frenetic.

There are a variety of cruise berths and terminals – more were added or enlarged for the 2004 Olympics, for which a number of cruise ships were booked to operate as hotels for Olympic visitors. The main terminal has good facilities, with a bank and exchange bureau, a shop or two, phones, a café and tourist information centre, while there are more shops and kiosks among the office buildings along the harbour front (Aktí Miaoúli).

Taxis meet all visiting cruise ships but the traffic in Piraeus and Athens is permanently heavy so, instead of a stop-start, 10-km (6-mile) journey of at least 30

**TYPICAL
EXCURSIONS,
ATHENS**

● **Athens** tour,
including the Acropolis
(full or half day).

● **Classical Greece**
tour to Corinth Canal,
Mycenae and the
amphitheatre at
Epidaurus (full day).

● **Scenic drive** along
the coast to Cape
Sounion (half day).

minutes into central Athens, an excellent option is to take the metro rail service to the main city sights. The station (on Akti Kalamasióti) is set back from the harbour and is a longish walk from the cruise ship dock, so ships usually offer a shuttle service (free or small charge). There is only one metro line from Piraeus so it is difficult to go wrong – the main stations are Omónias (for the second most important square in Athens), Thisío (for the Acropolis) and Monastiráki (for Pláka). Although there are a couple of good museums in Piraeus (archaeological and maritime) and some cafés and restaurants with good views of the swish yachts in harbour, there is no reason to linger here for long when Athens and the Acropolis, not to mention Cape Sounion and the Corinth Canal, are close by.

Shopping Shopping is a mixture of familiar stores in the centre of Athens (particularly the area between Omónia and Sýndagma) selling brand-name goods at reasonable prices, and the more rough and ready stalls and shops, found in abundance in Pláka, stocked with specifically Greek gifts and souvenirs. Leather sandals and bags, carved-wood utensils, highly coloured ceramics and tiles and silver jewellery can be good buys but the quality does vary considerably so choose carefully and barter over the price.

The price of sponges have shot up in recent times so they are no longer a bargain but they remain a genuine memento of Greece, while worry beads can seem a particularly useful purchase when watching your taxi-driver using the pavement to beat the gridlock.

Eating *Mezédes* are a good thing to try in Greece – a selection of small meat, fish and vegetable dishes, including the ubiquitous *dolmádes* (stuffed

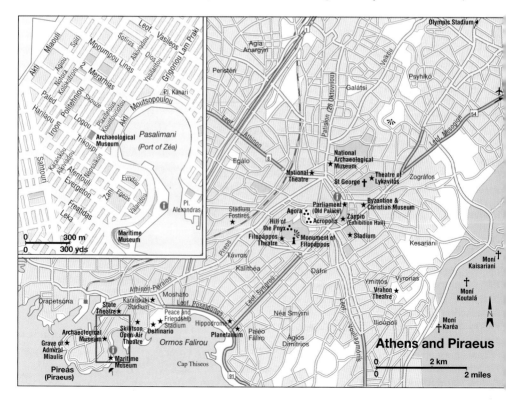

vine leaves). *Mousakás* and Greek salad, washed down with *retsína* or *oúzo*, are other favourites. The ancient **Pláka** area, at the foot of the Acropolis, is a good place to go – it's touristy, of course, given its location, but full of atmosphere. Kolonáki, below Lykavitós hill, is another area with some good, typically Greek, restaurants.

Maps on pages 280 & 282

Seeing the sights The "High City", the **Acropolis** (open daily; fee) is the number-one attraction, of course, with the 4th-century BC **Parthenon**, temple to Athena, the Theatre of Herodus Atticus and the Theatre of Dionysos. The previously traffic-clogged road of Dionysíou Areopagítou around the base of the Acropolis has been pedestrianised. With the Parthenon towering overhead, it quickly established itself as a popular place for the evening *vólta*, or stroll.

The 2nd-century **Hadrian's Arch** is one of several other historic sites nearby. It once marked the point where the classical Greek city ended and the Roman town began. Close by stand the towering columns of the **Temple of Olympian Zeus**. In the other direction, just north of the Acropolis, is the well-preserved, marble Roman Tower of the Winds.

The Temple of Olympian Zeus stands at the south end of the **National Gardens**. At the gardens' far end is **Platía Sýntagma** – Constitution Square – home to the Tomb of the Unknown Soldier and the former royal palace, now the main parliament building, which is guarded by the soldiers whose traditional dress uniform and high-stepping marches have fascinated visitors down the years. Just down from Sýntagma (at Amalías 26) is the new office of the GNTO (Greek National Tourism Organisation).

Greek pottery continues the styles employed by the ancients.

BELOW: the Acropolis and Parthenon.

Fishing boats in Piraeus have remained pretty much unchanged for many years.

Athens really has to be seen in sections; the centre is too large (and usually too crowded) to be walked properly without using some form of transport between the major sights. Taxis are relatively cheap (agree a fare in advance for longer journeys) but it's not always easy to hail one in the street. There are buses, which are cheap but crowded and slow and it can be difficult to work out where they are going. The metro is is the best way to get around, simple to negotiate and fast, and there are stations near the most important sights.

Although not particularly interesting or attractive, **Platía Omónias** (Omónia Square, reached by metro directly from Piraeus) is a good focal point as it stands at the edge of the city's main shopping district and is close to the **National Archaeological Museum** (currently closed for renovation).

If you went directly by metro to Omonia from Piraeus, you could board it again to **Monastiráki**, from which it is about 10–15 minutes' walk along Ermoú – now a pleasant, pedestrianised street, free from the traffic that once clogged it – to Sýntagma, and about the same distance to Pláka and the Acropolis.

From Sýntagma you can walk east along Venizélou Street to reach three excelent museums – the **Goulandris Museum** (open Mon, Wed–Sat; fee) with a collection of beautiful Cycladic idols; the **Benaki Museum** (open Tues–Sun; fee), with two icons attributed to El Greco; and the **Byzantine Museum** (hours as for Benaki), its treasures housed in a Florentine-style mansion.

Further afield Almost next to the tourist office in Sýntagma is the starting point for coach tours to Corinth, Mycenae, Epidauros, Delphi and Cape Sounion. These will be cheaper than the ships' tours but be careful about time: only consider a full-day tour if your ship is leaving Piraeus late in the

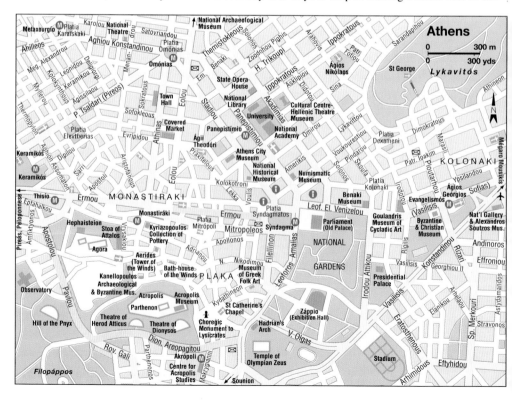

evening. Taking a hydrofoil to the three islands off Piraeus – Aegina, Póros and Ýdra – is not recommended unless as part of an organised tour. **Corinth** (Kórinthos), reached via the narrow Corinth Canal, linking the Peloponnese to the mainland, is the most complete imperial Roman town in Greece. **Mycenae** is an ancient, fortified palace complex. **Epidauros**, near Návplio *(see page 271)* has a magnificent 4th-century BC amphitheatre. Back on the mainland, **Cape Sounion** is about 70 km (42 miles) south of Athens on the tip of the peninsula, where the slender columns of the Doric **Temple of Poseidon** are a landmark for sailors. Also on the mainland, northwest of Athens, is **Delphi**, with the Sanctuary of Apollo and the theatre where the oracle made her pronouncements *(see page 273)*.

Maps on pages 282 & 284

Petros the Pelican on the beach in Mýkonos.

THE CYCLADES

The Cyclades are glorious. There are 56 islands in all, two dozen of them inhabited, but cruise ships usually make for Mýkonos, Páros, Santorini and tiny Delos (Dílos). The atmosphere of each island is very different: Mýkonos is known for it windmills, its nightlife and gay scene; Páros for its white, sugar-cube architecture; volcanic Santoríni for its blue domes and spectacular views; Delos for its huge stock of Graeco-Roman ruins. Náxos and Tínos, two less-often visited islands, both have some exquisite architecture.

MYKONOS

After a turbulent history full of battles, invasions and pirate attacks, the island began a new era in the 1960s when it became the trendiest of all the Greek islands, with the most exciting nightlife. It also became known as the gay capital

BELOW: the Temple of Athena Pronaia, Delphi.

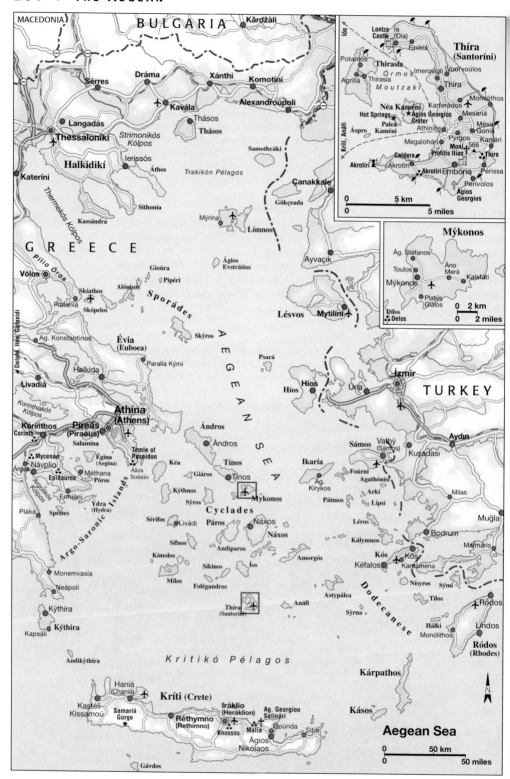

Inset map: **Thíra (Santoríni)**

- Iós
- Lontza Castle
- Ia (Oía)
- Finikía
- Potamós
- Thirasiá
- Órmos Moutzáki
- Agriliá
- Thirasía
- Imerovígli
- Vourvoúlos
- Thíra
- Monólithos
- Néa Kaméni
- Karterádos
- Mesariá
- Gonia
- Hot Springs
- Agios Georgios
- Palea Kaméni
- Athiniós
- Mésa
- Crater
- Áspro
- Pyrgos
- Kamári
- Megalohóri
- 566
- Thíra
- Caldera
- Profítis Ilías
- Périvolos
- Akrotíri
- Akrotíri
- Embório
- Períssa
- Kríti, Anáfi
- Akrotíri
- Périvolos
- Ágios Georgios

0 ___ 5 km
0 ___ 5 miles

Inset map: **Mýkonos**

- Ág. Stéfanos
- Toulos
- Áno Merá
- Mýkonos
- Kalafáti
- Platýs Gialós
- Dílos
- · · Delos

0 ___ 2 km
0 ___ 2 miles

Main map labels:

- MACEDONIA
- BULGARIA
- Kărdžali
- Sérres
- Dráma
- Xánthi
- Komotiní
- Kavála
- Thásos
- Thásos
- Alexandroúpoli
- Langadás
- Strimonikós Kólpos
- Thessaloníki
- Ierissós
- Halkidikí
- Áthos
- Samothráki
- Çanakkale
- Kateríni
- Sithonía
- Gökçeada
- Thermeikós Kólpos
- Kassándra
- Trakikón Pélagos
- Mýrina
- Límnos
- G R E E C E
- Pílio Óros
- Giónra
- Ágios Evstrátios
- Ayvacık
- Vólos
- Pipéri
- Sporádes
- Alónisos
- Skíathos
- Skópelos
- Lésvos
- Mytilíni
- İzmir
- Platániá
- Delphi, Itéa, Galaxídi
- Ag. Konstantinos
- Skýros
- Psará
- Évia (Euboea)
- Paralía Kými
- Híos
- Híos
- Urla
- T U R K E Y
- Halkída
- Livadiá
- A E G E A N   S E A
- Korinthiakós Kólpos
- Kórinthos
- Corinth
- Athína (Athens)
- Salamína
- Ándros
- Sámos
- Vathý (Sámos)
- Kuşadası
- Mycenae
- Pireás (Piraeus)
- Aydın
- Návplio
- Égina (Aegina)
- Temple of Poseidon
- Kéa
- Tínos
- Ikaría
- Foúrni
- Árgos
- Epídauros
- Méthana
- Póros
- Giáros
- Tínos
- Ag. Kírykos
- Agathónisi
- Milas
- Argolikós Kólpos
- Ermióni
- Akra Soúnio
- Mýkonos
- Pátmos
- Arkí
- Pláka
- Ýdra (Hydra)
- Kýthnos
- Sýros
- Lipsí
- Spétses
- C y c l a d e s
- Léros
- Muğla
- Sérifos
- Livádi
- Páros
- Náxos
- Kálymnos
- Bodrum
- Argo-Saronic Islands
- Sífnos
- Náxos
- Marmaris
- Kímolos
- Andíparos
- Amorgós
- Kós
- Kós
- Monemvasía
- Síkinos
- Íos
- Kéfalos
- Kardámena
- Neápoli
- Mílos
- Folégandros
- Nísyros
- Sými
- Kýthira
- Thíra (Santoríni)
- Anáfi
- Astypálea
- Tílos
- Ródos
- Kapsáli
- Kýthira
- Sýrna
- Hálki
- Líndos
- Andikýthira
- K r i t i k ó   P é l a g o s
- Monólithos
- Ródos (Rhodes)
- D o d e c a n e s e
- Kárpathos
- Haniá (Chaniá)
- Kríti (Crete)
- Iráklio (Herákion)
- Ag. Georgíou Selinári
- Kásos
- Kastéli-Kissamoú
- Samariá Gorge
- Réthymno (Rethimno)
- Knossós
- Malía
- Eloúnda
- Sitía
- Ágios Nikólaos
- Gávdos
- **Aegean Sea**

0 ___ 50 km
0 ___ 50 miles

of the Aegean. Some 40 years on, it is still a tourist magnet. The buzzing nightlife remains non-stop, which is why some ships stay late in the evening, and the streets are lined with tantalising – if expensive – shops and restaurants. Outside the town the island does not have too much to offer, apart from some excellent beaches on the south coast, but it is superbly located for a trip (organised or independent) to the neighbouring island of Delos – one of the most important historical and archaeological sites in Greece.

Some ships dock here while others anchor off and use tenders. Mýkonos is always a port of call but the length of stay varies from a half day to a full day with a late-evening departure.

Arrival and around the dock As your ship approaches Mýkonos Town on the west coast, and the stark white houses and line of (now redundant) windmills come into view, this is everyone's dream of a Greek island. Cruise ships dock at Toúrlos to the east of the north-facing harbour. There is a small terminal and a shuttle bus (normally free) to take passengers to the edge of town.

Shopping Don't expect markets or too much in the way of bargain stores – almost every shop is a designer boutique or a jewellery store with high-quality but high-priced pieces. As you wander the streets, though, you will see that there are some places to buy stylish Greek lace, leather and craft goods.

Seeing the sights From the shuttle bus drop-off, it is a short walk along the harbour front to the main square, **Platía M. Mavrogénous**. This is also known as Taxi Square as it is where the cabs congregate. For the town itself, there is no need for transport – its maze of streets and lanes can be confusing but, even allowing for losing your bearings from time to time, it is a compact, easily walkable place to explore. As well as the trendy cafés and restaurants, glitzy shops and boutiques, it also has a surprisingly impressive range of museums – the **Folklore Museum** (open Mon–Sun pm; fee), and the **Archaeological Museum** (open Tues–Sun am; fee) are both interesting, and there are marine and agricultural collections as well.

Further afield There is a good bus service to most parts of the island – buses heading north go from the station near the town beach and the OTE (international telephone office); those heading south go from Ornos Road. From the tender pier in the main town harbour, there are ferries for the sacred island of **Delos** (sometimes these are used by the cruise lines for their excursions, but tours from ships anchored off depart directly from the ship). Be warned: even in good weather, the 8-km (5-mile) journey to Delos can be rough and seem longer than the 40 minutes it takes.

The best beaches are all on the south coast and it is possible to take a *caique* (small boat) directly there from the town harbour or, if time is tight, to take a bus or taxi the 3 km (2 miles) to Platýs Gialós and get a *caique* from that beach to the neighbouring ones of Paradise (nude), Superparadise (gay nude) and Eilá.

Map on page 284

TYPICAL EXCURSIONS, MYKONOS
- **Island tour** (2–3 hours).
- **Delos**, birthplace of Apollo and Artemis (half-day tour).
- **Beach-hopping tour**, by *caique* (6 hours).

BELOW: festival time in Mýkonos.

PAROS

Páros is one of the Cyclades islands that is slightly overshadowed by its more glamorous and dramatic neighbours – Mýkonos and Santoríni. The island is nonetheless very pretty, with attractive villages and plenty of examples of traditional Cyclades "sugar cube" architecture, set against a dazzlingly blue sea.

TYPICAL EXCURSIONS, PAROS

● Island tour, including Náousa, Lévkes and the Valley of the Butterflies (half-day).

Arrival and around the dock First impressions are of a busy, bustling port, with ferries, fishing boats, water taxis and yachts coming and going, and a harbour front lined with bars, cafés and tavernas.

Seeing the sights In summer, Parikía, the capital, bustles with holidaymakers spilling off the ferries and enjoying the busy nightlife after dark. Inland from the waterfront, you'll find a lively market, a good place to shop for local honey, wine and olives. There's also the remains of a Venetian castle and a handsome Byzantine church, the **Ekatondapyliani**, one of the largest in the Greek islands, known as the Church of a Hundred Doors. Legend says that 99 doors have been discovered and when the hundredth is found, Constantinople will be reunited with Greece.

Further afield Take the hourly bus or hire a car and drive to **Náousa** in the north, a resort with good beaches and great windsurfing. Inland, **Lévkes** is a pretty medieval village of narrow streets and well-preserved buildings. Also visit **Petaloúdes**, the Valley of the Butterflies (in reality, tiger moths, at their most dazzling in June) and the Maráthi quarries, from which high-quality white marble has been taken for centuries – it was used for the Venus de Milo statue.

BELOW: Santoríni townscape – the picturesque village of Ía.

SANTORINI

Sitting in the sparkling bay created more than 3,500 years ago by a cataclysmic eruption of the Thera volcano, Santorini was discovered by the Venetians in the 13th century, and named after their patron saint, Irene.

Only 7,000 people live on the island but there are a million visitors a year, most of them arriving by cruise ship and heading first for the capital, Firá, perched on the top of the 300-metre (1,000-ft) cliffs overlooking the bay, which is actually the world's largest caldera (volcanic crater). The most interesting part of the island, however, is further south, at Akrotiri. The ancient city here was destroyed by the Thera eruption, which covered it in a sea of lava; excavations have revealed some of the original buildings still remarkably intact.

Arrival and around the dock When your ship cruises into the bay of Santorini, remember that you are sailing into the huge crater of a still-active volcano. Some claim that it conceals the lost city of Atlantis and this adds an extra frisson to what are already dramatic views of the precipitous rocky cliffs of the island. Sailing out of the bay at sunset is an even more impressive experience. The usual stay in port is a full day but sometimes it is only half a day.

Ships always anchor in the bay and send passengers ashore by tender boats, which dock immediately below the capital, Firá. As soon as you set foot on land, you will be encouraged to pay local hustlers for a ride up a steep and uneven flight of steps to the town on mule-back. This used to be the only alternative to walking, and a pretty uncomfortable one at that, but then a funicular (cable-car network) was built. This is the best option, although it can involve some queuing and the clifftop station is further from the centre of town than the top of the steps. Walking or mule-riding on your way back to the ship can be fun, if you feel up to it.

Apart from a few stalls and a lot of mules, there are few facilities until you reach the town on the clifftop.

Shopping As on Mýkonos, the shops are mainly a mixture of designer-label boutiques, jewellery and souvenir stores. Byzantine-style gold jewellery is a popular buy, as is locally-crafted pottery. Prices are not particularly cheap but there are some unusual styles and pieces available. The jewellery is usually reputable, but always pay by credit card, just in case.

There is a certain amount of flexibility on prices – especially if you buy more than one item at a time – but don't expect haggling to produce huge savings.

Seeing the sights Originally founded in the 18th century, **Firá** was completely rebuilt after another, smaller volcanic eruption in 1956 and, with its striking whitewashed houses, shops and churches, is prettier from a distance than close-up.

The main road in and out is clogged with the usual noisy Greek scooters, taxis and buses, but in the centre there are some interesting cobbled alleyways and a small museum (near the cable-car station) to explore along with the main shopping centre (Gold Street). This runs parallel to the clifftop and is a short walk to the right of the steps and a slightly longer one to the

Map on page 284

TYPICAL EXCURSIONS, SANTORINI

● **Akrotiri**. Half-day tour to the ancient Minoan city.

● **Ía**. Half-day tour to the picturesque village in the north.

● **Paleá Kaméni**. Boat trip to tiny island with hot mud baths.

BELOW: a bell wall in Santorini.

Dolphin mosaics on the floor of the old theatre in Delos.

right of the cable-car station. The views from the some of the cafés down to the bay – and your ship – are worth the trip. The town is completely walkable so there is no need for taxis and buses unless you want to go further afield to the black volcanic-sand beaches or to explore other towns and the countryside.

Further afield   Usually, you will be left to your own devices in Firá, with ships' excursions only arranged for **Akrotiri**, a Minoan town in the south of the island, preserved in volcanic ash; or to the picturesque village of **Ía** (pronounced "ee-ah"), in the north. Ía has a mixture of whitewashed and pastel-coloured houses built into the cliffs, shady squares, art galleries and arty shops, cafés and tavernas. It also has a small maritime museum and there is a steep path down to a couple of black-sand beaches. These are usually half-day tours with stops for cheese and wine-tasting (Santoríni makes its own white wine) but these towns and others such as Pýrgos (overlooked by a medieval monastery) can also be reached easily by taxi, although it helps if you find a driver with good English who can also show you around. Taxis are plentiful and therefore more reliable than buses – always negotiate a fare first, though. If you want to try public transport, the bus station is at the far end of Gold Street but make sure there will be a bus to get you back to the ship in time.

There are also short boat trips – either as a ship's shore excursion or booked individually in Firá – to the tiny island of **Paleá Kaméni**, where visitors can wallow in a hot mud bath.

BELOW: windmill in Parikía, Páros.

In the southeast of the island, the remains of the ancient capital, **Thira**, dating from the 9th century BC, sit on a hill amid fertile plains, but are closed to the public for safety reasons.

OTHER CYCLADES PORTS

Delos (Dílos) is everything that its neighbour, Mýkonos, which is just 11 km (7 miles) away, is not: relatively undeveloped, quiet and spiritual. A few cruise ships stop at this arid, treeless island for visits to the magnificent archaeological sites, which include the **Temples of Apollo and Artemis**. Alternatively, they offer Delos as an excursion from Mýkonos *(see page 283)*. There's also an **ancient theatre**, which once seated 5,500, complete with mosaic floor.

Other Cyclades ports receiving occasional ship's visits include beautiful, mountainous **Amorgós**, with a 13th-century Venetian castle and the amazing monastery of Panagía Hozoviótissa clinging to the side of a sheer cliff. **Ándros** has gorgeous beaches and therapeutic springs, while **Náxos**, the largest of the Cyclades islands, has castles, temples and Byzantine churches to visit. **Sérifos** is great for beaches, walking and practising the art of doing very little. Its port, Livádi, is set in a sheltered bay, and the main town, Hóra, clings to a mountain top. **Sýros**, in comparison, is practically a metropolis, with big hotels, a casino and a working shipyard where wooden *caiques* (small boats) are built. Ermoúpoli, the capital, is regarded as the capital of the whole archipelago, standing on a natural amphitheatre, with old mansions and white houses cascading down to the harbour, which itself is lively with tourist shops and tavernas. Walk around the old quarter, Vapória, its narrow streets lined with neoclassical mansions.

Tínos, meanwhile, has some exquisite Venetian-style architecture, but most Greeks come to worship the icon in the splendid, marble Panagía Evangelístria. Around 1,000 ornate pigeon houses are dotted around the island and many people make a holiday hobby of spotting and photographing them.

Map
on page
284

BELOW: an ancient stone lion at Delos.

CRETE (KRITI)

Crete (Kríti), largest of the Greek Islands and legendary birthplace of Zeus, was home to the powerful Minoan civilisation, which established Europe's first urban culture in the 3rd millennium BC. Its great legacy is still apparent today; Cretans are a race apart from other Greeks with their own dialect, folklore, music, dances and costume – village men still sometimes wear the baggy trousers, boots, sashes and black headbands that are Crete's national dress.

IRAKLIO

Iráklio (Heráklion), the cruise-ship port, has been the capital of Crete since 1971 and is home to almost a third of the island's population.

Arrival and around the dock Ships usually spend enough time in the capital, **Iráklio** (Heráklion) to allow for excursions to Knossos. Taxis are available at the port, or if you fancy walking you can reach the city's main square, Platía Venizelou, by turning right outside the port gates and strolling along the waterfront, then turning left and walking down 25 Avgoústou.

Shopping Arriving in **Platía Venizélou**, you'll be rewarded by the sight of the lovely, 17th-century Morosini Fountain with its famous lion sculptures. You also find yourself at the heart of Iráklio's shopping district, a good area to hunt for local ceramics, lacework and sculptures.

Seeing the sights Before you leave Platía Venizélou, have a look at the 13th-century, Venetian-built basilica, **Ágios Márkos**, which is now an eye-

TYPICAL EXCURSIONS, IRÁKLIO
● **Knossos Palace and Archaeological Museum**. A half-day tour *(see main text)*.
● **Scenic Crete**. A half-day panoramic drive to the resort of Ágios Nikólaos, the Minoan Palace of Malia, the Orthodox monastery of Agíou Georgíou Selinári and Eloúnda Bay.

BELOW:
Iráklio castle wall.
RIGHT:
a simple church.

catching art gallery; a little way north is a beautifully restored 17th-century Venetian *loggia*. Just to the south, a museum housed in the little church of **Agía Ekateríni** (open Mon–Sat am; fee) contains some beautiful icons. High on your list of things to see should be the **Archaeological Museum** (open daily, Sat am only; fee), to the north of the other major square, Platía Elevtherías. Be prepared to spend some time there, as it's one of the best in Greece. The tourist office is almost next door

If you are still intrigued by the remnants of Crete's history, take a look at Iráklio's city walls, which were constructed by the Venetians in the second half of the 15th century. Here you'll find the tomb of Iráklio-born Nikos Kazantzakis, author of *Zorba the Greek*. There's another Italian fortress, the 16th-century **Rocca al Mare**, in the old harbour.

For lunch ashore, you'll find some excellent tavernas along the waterfront and scattered throughout the city. Try *loukoumádes*, delicious local fritters served with syrup. And take home a lasting memory of Cretan cuisine by buying an elaborate Cretan wedding loaf at the food market on Odós 1866. Sprayed with varnish (and insect repellant) they are used as ornaments in Cretan kitchens

Further afield   All cruise lines offer excursions to the Minoan palace of **Knossos**, which, according to legend, was the labyrinth of King Minos, where he imprisoned the minotaur. This huge, mysterious site is stunning – although often very crowded. It lies very close to Iráklio and can be visited independently; agree a fare with a taxi driver before you start. The other places offered as cruise-line excursions – the lovely **Eloúnda Bay**, the Minoan palace at **Malia**, the Greek orthodox monastery of **Agíou Georgíou Selinári**; and the popular and

Map on page 284

A Minoan bull in the Iráklio Archaeological Museum.

BELOW: Ágios Nikólaos – the town, the harbour and the lagoon.

beautifully-sited resort of **Ágios Nikólaos**, are difficult to fit into your limited time on the island if you try to visit them independently. The latter, however, features as a port of call itself *(see below)*.

AGIOS NIKOLAOS

"Ag Nik" has blossomed – or declined – from a fishing village into one of the liveliest resorts in Greece, packed to the gills with sun- and fun-loving holiday-makers throughout the summer. At face value, the port has, however, retained its original charm, the inner lagoon encircled by tavernas and shops.

Bullfighting portrayed on a fresco in the Palace of Knossos, Crete

Arrival and around the dock   On arrival, you see that two islands guard the entrance to the bay, one with little but a lighthouse and the other home to the protected *kri-kri* goat. Ships dock outside the ancient lagoon around which the port sprang up. For centuries, this lagoon was believed to be bottomless but it was connected to the sea in 1867 by a narrow canal and was later found to be 64 metres (208ft) deep.

Seeing the sights   Ágios Nikólaos – often abbreviated to Ag Nik – and once known as the St-Tropez of Crete, is hugely commercial, but very pretty nonetheless, with red-tiled houses and busy tavernas and coffee shops. The best shopping area is up the hill behind the harbour. The town itself has a couple of shingle beaches but local buses run from the bus station south to **Pahiá Ámmos** and **Kaloú Horioú**, which are sandy, and to **Eloúnda**, a busy resort 10 km (6 miles) up the coast. Ferries operate from the harbour across to the island of **Spinalónga**, a former leper colony, the last of its kind in Europe. There's some great snorkelling here and you can see the outlines of roads, columns and old mosaics on the sea bed.

BELOW: the Minoan palace at Knossos.

Further afield   In spring, the high **Lasíthi Plateau** is absolutely stunning, an endless expanse of pear and apple orchards and pink-blossomed almond trees, the pastures dotted with over 7,000 windmills. Most of these are not working but the view is fabulous nonetheless. Millions of butterflies populate the fields in spring and summer. Most tours also call at **Dikteon Cave** where, according to legend, the newborn Zeus was hidden from his murderous father.

Tours also run to **Knossos** to the west, to the brilliantly preserved Minoan palace and labyrinth *(see page 291)*. Some cruise lines also offer trips to the palm grove at **Vaï** in the east, something you don't often find in Greece, and for a beach day.

HANIA

Ancient walls partly conceal a cluster of beautiful Venetian, Minoan and Turkish buildings, with blue and white, onion-domed churches glittering in the sunlight, making **Haniá** (Chaniá) one of the most photogenic ports in the Greek islands. It's used as a day stop for cruises with the option to explore the town or head further afield into Crete's central spine of mountains or along the coast to the Minoan site of Knossos.

Arrival and around the dock You can feel the buzz of this lovely old town, flanked by the White Mountains, as the ship approaches. If you leave at night, stay on deck to admire the bright lights of the harbour tavernas and the old Venetian houses reflected in the still water.

Seeing the sights Haniá is an ancient town with a delightful **Venetian harbour**, exquisite, colourful houses, dramatic fortifications and an old lighthouse. There are many Venetian churches in various states of repair. One of them houses the **Archaeological Museum** (open Tues–Sun; fee) and there are other museums dedicated to naval history and folklore. For shopping, try the streets inland from the harbour; or there's a market next to the public gardens.

Further afield Organised tours always run to Knossos *(see page 291)*, about 100 km (60 miles) or so east along the coast, but you could hire a car and make the trip independently if you wished. Walkers will enjoy the dramatic **Samariá Gorge**, about 42 km (25 miles) away on the south side of the island, although it's a tortuous drive from Haniá. This is an 18-km (11-mile) hike through dramatic rocky scenery, complete with cascading waterfalls and, in spring, abundant wildflowers. The gorge is usually open from May to October and will be both hot and busy in July and August, but it is worth the effort. If your ship does not offer a tour it may be possible to book one locally, or to go by bus from Haniá if you are in port early enough.

Classical stone carvings from the Roman agora, Kós.

THE DODECANESE

The Dodecanese islands have had a chequered history. Ruled by the Ottoman empire for four centuries, taken by the Italians in 1912 and briefly by the Germans in 1943, they became Greece's final territorial acquisition in 1948. The name Dodecanese implies 12 islands, but there are as many as 27 if you count every uninhabited islet. Rhodes, the biggest and most visited island, has a wealth of monuments, built by the Turks and the Knights of St John. Pátmos is famous for its biblical connections, Kós as the site of the Asklepion sanctuary and medical school, and Sámos as birthplace of the goddess Hera.

BELOW: a four-masted cruise ship in Skála harbour.

PATMOS

Pátmos's tiny capital, Skála, is at the end of the huge sweep of an almost-enclosed, circular bay. Cruise lines call here mainly so that passengers can visit the hilltop Monastery of St John the Theologian.

Around the dock Skála has a long quay and deep water, so most ships can dock alongside. The town is close at hand and there are buses from the quay to Hóra and the monastery.

Seeing the sights The little town is a maze of narrow streets and pretty squares, pleasingly untouched by tourism, although you will find some excellent gold and silver jewellery, handwoven fabrics and icons for sale in the rather upmarket shops, and there are a number of atmospheric cafés.

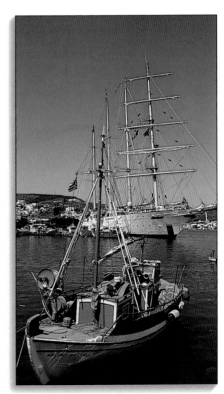

TYPICAL
EXCURSIONS,
PATMOS
● Monastery of St
John the Theologian
and the Holy Cave
(3-hour tour; see
main text).

Further afield The **Monastery of St John the Theologian** in the little town of Hóra is one of the wealthiest in Greece, rich with religious treasures. Looking more like a fortress than a monastery, it was founded in 1088 by Ioannis Christodoulos, a leading figure in the Eastern church. On the way up to the monastery, most tours also visit the **Holy Cave of the Apocalypse**, where St John the Divine wrote the *Book of Revelations*. A sanctuary, encircled by a convent, now protects the cave. This is a trip that is easy to make independently, as it is only a 40-minute walk uphill for the energetic, and a short bus ride from the quay for everyone else.

Kos

Birthplace of Hippocrates, the father of modern medicine, Kós has always been known for the Asklepion, its sanctuary and ancient medical school. Nowadays, it's a popular holiday resort, with beautiful beaches, packed in summer, and a partly wooded interior. There are several resorts, some of them sadly encapsulating the worst of modern package tourism.

Arrival and around the dock Kós Town, where ships dock, is one of the island's best features, with Italian-style architecture blending with the minarets of the significant Turkish quarter. Look for the old castle on the starboard side as you approach. The town centre is not far from the dock.

BELOW: Sými can
be reached by boat
from Rhodes.

Seeing the sights The town is interesting and pleasant enough for exploring. There's a **Roman *agora***, a restored **Roman villa**, and an **18th-century mosque**. There's also an interesting and well-stocked **Archaeological Museum**

(open Tues–Sun; fee), close to the municipal market. Narrow, mainly pedestri-anised, streets are lined with shops and tavernas, as well as cyber cafés and bicycle and moped hire stands. If you're here overnight go ashore in the evening,as there's a lively buzz and the shops are open late.

The **Asklepion** (open Tues–Sun; fee), on an elevated site 4 km (2½ miles) southwest of town, has stunning views of the sea and the Turkish coast. It was a medical school for nearly 1,000 years, although it may not have been founded until shortly after the death of Hippocrates (c.460–370BC), who was born here.

Further afield   There are decent beaches and some good walks in the hills of the south, but the beach resorts are really not worth bothering with. Ferries run every day from the mass-market resorts of Kardámena or Kefalos to vol-canic **Nísyros** *(see page 298)*, or to the Turkish mainland, to **Bodrum** *(see page 311)*, a hugely successful holiday resort. Take a passport and arrive at the ferry one hour before sailing if you want to go to Turkey, but only after ensuring that you will definitely be back in time for your ship's departure.

RHODES

Rhodes (Ródos) is the number-one tourism destination in the Dodecanese, largely because of its magnificent, walled, medieval Old Town – one of the largest in the whole of Europe. It's full of package tourists and the inevitable tat shops and fast-food joints that follow in their wake, but with fine architecture and narrow cobbled streets to explore, and plenty of picturesque, terraced restau-rants dotted about. Ships usually spend more than half a day here to allow for excursions to Líndos.

Maps
on pages
284 & 295

BELOW: Mandráki harbour, Rhodes.

Natural sponges for sale on sparkling white steps.

BELOW: linen for sale at Líndos.
RIGHT: statues at the Sanctuary of Hera, Sámos.

Arrival and around the dock Large ships go into the Commercial Port to the east of the old town, smaller yacht-like vessels and tenders, can get into Mandráki Harbour, which dates back to medieval times. Rhodes is easily walkable and the old town (the only bit worth seeing) is only a 20-minute walk from port. The closest gate to the Commercial Harbour is St Catherine's, while New Gate or Arsenal Gate are closest to Mandráki.

Shopping Tacky shops and fast-food joints have, sadly, spread to Rhodes old town, but ignore the T-shirt shops and look out for little, tucked-away boutiques. Best buys are handmade lace, excellent leather goods, colourful pottery from Líndos and pretty bowls carved from olive wood. Most fun for those who enjoy a bit of local colour, is Sokrátous (Socrates) Street, parallel to the Avenue of the Knights. This has a Turkish bazaar selling rugs, ceramics, jewellery and bric-à-brac and is a great place to go if you enjoy a good haggle. To find a nice place for lunch, just look up – there are some decent traditional restaurants with pretty first-floor terraces where you can eat alfresco.

Seeing the sights Divided into three quarters – the Knights, the Turkish and the Jewish – Rhodes old town charts the island's entire history within its sturdy walls. Enter via St Catherine's Gate and head right to see the magnificent fountain in **Platía Evreon**, which features bronze sea horses.

The Avenue of the Knights, a magnificent medieval thoroughfare which houses the 14th-century **Palace of the Grand Masters** (open daily; fee), could be your next stop. Though partially destroyed by a gunpowder explosion in

1856, it was reconstructed in grand style by the Italians (Mussolini planned to use it as a holiday home). Now a museum, it contains antique furniture, sculptures and mosaics. In this area you'll also find the 14th-century **Hospital of the Knights of St John**, which now houses the archaeological museum (open Tues–Sun; fee). Nearby is the **Museum of Decorative Arts** (open Tues–Sun; fee) – pop in, if time allows, or visit the pink-domed, 16th-century **Mosque of Suleyman** and the **Byzantine Museum**, housed in an 11th-century church.

Beware of the heat as you wander around – it can be intense – take a bottle of water with you and keep in the shade as much as possible.

Further afield If you've seen Rhodes old town before, **Líndos** – 55 km (35 miles) away – is a delight (and you can get a bus there from Rhodes New Town). It has a lovely, horseshoe-shaped sandy beach, higgledy-piggledy whitewashed houses and a fascinating Acropolis.

SAMOS

Sámos is a rugged Aegean island, within swimming distance of the Turkish coast not far from Kusadasi. In Greek mythology, this was the birthplace of the goddess Hera.

Arrival and around the dock and town The capital and port, **Sámos Town** or **Vathý**, is set like an amphitheatre at the end of a deep bay. Good buys include local wine and honey, ceramics and hand-made rugs. In Sámos Town, there are several neoclassical buildings to admire, as well as the excellent archaeological museum.

Maps
on pages
284 & 295

TYPICAL
EXCURSIONS,
RHODES
● **City tour** (3–4 hours) taking in all main sights, part driving, part walking *(see main text).*
● **Líndos.** Picturesque drive and steep walk to Acropolis, plus time for lunch and swimming (4–5 hours).

BELOW: Pythagório's harbour.

TYPICAL EXCURSIONS, SÁMOS

● Some lines run tours to the aqueduct of Evpalínio Órygma and the Sanctuary of Hera (3 hours).

Further afield Sámos has a fascinating past. Hire a moped or take a local bus to see the crumbling remains of **Evpalínio Órygma** (open Tues–Sun am; fee), an underground aqueduct built by Polykratis in the 6th century BC, and considered one of the Seven Wonders of the Ancient World. There's a good **fossil museum** in Mytiliní and the remains of the grand **Sanctuary of Hera** can be seen at Pythagório.

OTHER DODECANESE PORTS

The smaller Dodecanese islands hug the Turkish coast and tend to be visited only by small ships on in-depth Greece cruises. The port of **Mandráki** on **Nísyros**, an island which is actually a dormant volcano, is pleasant to walk around, with a castle and monastery to explore as well as shops and tavernas. Further afield, visit the dramatic monastery at **Paleokastro**. Nearby is **Sými**, either a port of call in its own right or a day trip from the much bigger island of Rhodes (Ródos; 50 minutes by hydrofoil). The harbour town, **Yialós**, is beautiful, with tiers of neoclassical buildings set in a natural amphitheatre around a deep gorge. Horió (Chorio) is the area of town at the top of the hill. Otherwise, there is the famous monastery of Taxiárhis Mihaïl Panormítis and the forested interior is ideal for walking and cycling. Also lying off the coast of Rhodes is the tiny limestone island of **Hálki**. There's not much to see except Ágios Nikólaos church but the port is pretty and the island pleasantly undeveloped. The long, skinny, treeless island of **Kárpathos** lies southwest of Rhodes. Its capital, Pigádia, is a lively little harbour town and there are great walks across the hills, with stunning coastal views.

BELOW: snow-white wall on Lésvos.

THE NORTHERN AEGEAN

Many of the rugged islands in the little-known northern Aegean lie closer to Turkey than Greece. Remote Lésvos is the largest, a fertile, olive-oil producing island; Híos was devasted by an 1811 earthquake but still has medieval features; the dark volcanic soil of Límnos produces some excellent wine; while Samothráki features in Homer's *Iliad*. Back on the mainland, in northern Greece, ships call at Thessaloníki, formerly known as Salonika to English speakers.

HIOS (CHIOS)

Híos, a craggy island in the eastern Aegean, near the Turkish coast, is said to be the birthplace of Homer.

Arrival and around the dock and town

Ships dock or tender at Híos Town (also called Hóra), on the east coast. The harbour is busy, with tavernas, shops and cafés, as is what's left of the old quarter of the citadel after an earthquake destroyed the city in 1881. Buses run to beautiful beaches nearby. For local colour, visit the fruit and vegetable market (Mon–Sat).

Further afield The Byzantine mosaics at **Néa Moní Monastery** are famous, while the exteriors of the houses in the village of **Pyrgí** are decorated with striking black and white geometrical patterns in a style called *xystá*.

LESVOS (LESBOS)

Just 10 km (6 miles) off the Turkish coast, **Lésvos** (Lésbos) is best known for its olive oil, and its rolling hills are dense with olive groves and pine forests. This island has a colourful history and ruins dating back to 3000BC have been found. It is thought to be the birthplace of the poet Sappho and attracts a strong following of gay women in summer. The capital, **Mytilíni** (a name that is sometimes, confusingly, used for the whole island), has beautiful neoclassical mansions, antique shops and a small folk art museum.

Further afield The pretty village of **Mólyvos**, set on a steep hillside overlooked by a castle, has some good art galleries. In **Pétra**, there is a Genoese church built into the rock, while **Ánaxos** close by has secluded coves and deep blue bays. You can also visit the villages of Kástro and Agiássos. Buses run from the port to all these places, and taxis are also a reasonable option.

OTHER NORTHERN PORTS

Vólos, from where Jason and the Argonauts sailed for the Black Sea in search of the Golden Fleece, is on the east coast of the Greek mainland. Ships call here for tours which bring the mythology to life.

    Límnos is a large, volcanic island, green and fertile compared to its neighbours, and famous for its thyme honey and hot springs. There's a strong military influence here – the huge natural harbour near the mouth of the Dardenelles has always given the island strategic importance.

    Neighbouring **Samothráki** (Samothrace), closer still to Turkey, is craggy and mountainous. Homer's *Iliad* claims that Poseidon, god of the sea, surveyed

Map on page 284

BELOW:
the old city walls of Thessaloníki.

Map
on page
284

**TYPICAL
EXCURSIONS,
THESSALONÍKI**

● **City Tour.**
Highlights of the city
including the
Archaeological
Museum, with its
fabulous displays of
ancient gold
(3–4 hours).

BELOW: detail
in Thessaloníki
museum.
RIGHT: freshly-
caught octopus
in Mýkonos.

the battles around Troy from the island's highest point. The Sanctuary of the Great Gods, dating from the 1st century BC, is the main attraction. The statue of the Nike of Samothrace, now housed in the Louvre, was discovered here.

Thásos is a circular island to the north west of Samothráki, the settlement of the same name dating back to the 8th century BC. Nearby **Kavála**, on the mainland, is the site of the ancient city of Philippi, named after the father of Alexander the Great. Kavála was occupied by Turkey for 600 years and there are strong Islamic influences in the architecture.

THESSALONIKI

Thessaloníki (sometimes referred to as Salonika in the West) is the capital of the ancient region of Macedonia and the second most important city in Greece. It is very much a sophisticated town with a distinctive character, excellent restaurants, a decent collection of Roman ruins and fabulous Byzantine churches. Founded in 316BC by Philip II of Macedon, father of Alexander the Great, Thessaloníki became part of the Roman Empire in 168BC. Thessaloníki is a port of call on Aegean, Greece/Turkey and Black Sea itineraries.

Arrival and around the dock   Once predominantly a cargo port, Thessaloníki now attracts ferries and cruise ships after substantial investment in passenger facilities. Its Macedonia passenger terminal, a converted neoclassical building, has seating areas, refreshments, exchange facilities, telephones, a taxi rank and tourist information booths as well as travel agency outlets offering advice on local tours. There are plans to build a second terminal. The port lies a 200-metre/yd walk from the city centre.

Shopping   The women of Thessaloníki have the reputation of being the best-dressed in Greece, so it follows that this is a good place to buy clothes and shoes. **Tsmiskí** is the best street for high quality shops and for fashionable jewellery at affordable prices. Look out, too, for lacework, wooden icons, pottery and rugs. For bargains, head for the reasonably priced shops in the area around **Egnatía**, the main thoroughfare. Both areas are easily walkable from Níkis, the waterfront promenade which stretches from the port to the White Tower, Thessaloníki's most famous landmark.

Seeing the sights   The 15th-century **White Tower** (Lefkós Pyrgos) is the city's symbol. A good place to get an overview of the city's colourful history, is the **Byzantine Museum**, as is **Archaeological Museum**, both of which lie north of the tower, opposite the Exhibition Grounds (both open daily; fee).

After lunch in one of the appetising restaurants you could visit the stunning, 3rd-century **Rotunda of Ágios Geórgios** at the top of Goúnari, built as a Roman mausoleum and converted to a church by Constantine the Great; or take a short taxi ride to **Kástra**, the city's atmospheric Turkish quarter and the only part of 19th-century Thessaloníki to survive the earthquake and fire that devastated the city in 1917.   ❑

EASTERN MEDITERRANEAN

Here you can visit the domes and minarets of Istanbul, the pyramids at Giza, the ancient site of Ephesus, and Black Sea ports where history has been made

Maps on pages 306 & 316

The Eastern Mediterranean is where East meets West, where the everyday seems exotic. It is also an area of great variety and a fusion of several cultures. The city of Istanbul, once Constantinople and the power centre of the sprawling Ottoman Empire, is a glittering delight; and the port of Canakkale draws visitors interested in the memorials and cemeteries of the Gallipoli Peninsula, where so many died in World War I. Further south, Kusadasi is the access port for the ancient city of Ephesus, while Bodrum and Marmaris are busy tourist resorts. Many cruise lines visit Cyprus, a beautiful island despite the troubled division between Greece and Turkey. On the Middle Eastern shores, a stop at Tripoli, in Lebanon, allows you to visit Baalbek, the largest Roman site in existence; while Port Said and ancient Alexandria in Egypt give access to Cairo and the pyramids at Giza. The Red Sea port of Aqaba has one of the world's best-preserved coral reefs, and allows for excursions to "rose-red" Petra; while Black Sea ports of call include sub-tropical Yalta and Odessa, which has a beguiling, mysterious air.

PRECEDING PAGES: Egypt is one of the most exotic of Mediterranean countries. **LEFT:** the *Aurora* comes to Istanbul. **BELOW:** a woman making *pide* bread.

ISTANBUL

Be up on deck as your ship approaches **Istanbul**; its glittering domes and minarets make the skyline of this ancient city one of the world's most memorable sights. Some 3,000 years old, spanning two continents and a crucible of cultures, Istanbul is not really a city to see in a rush, so if your cruise begins or ends here, it's well worth tagging on a few days' stay ashore. However, you can see the main sights on a two-day cruise call so, assuming you have only that much time, these are the experiences and attractions you really shouldn't miss.

Istanbul is a key home port on many Mediterranean itineraries, with numerous cruises operating from there to Athens and back. Even cruises not based in Istanbul usually include an overnight stay so that passengers can make the most of this magnificent city.

Arrival and around the dock Cruise ships dock at Karaköy (at the northern end of the Galata Bridge), which has a substantial international passenger terminal; you'll find bureaux de change, toilets, taxis and phones here, as well as a handy tourist information office, located near the front entrance.

If you've enough time in port to take a boat trip and don't want to do the ship's excursion, you'll find the ferry dock virtually next door. Or head south across Galata Bridge and you can get a tram to the old city from Eminönü Square. Alternatively, catch a bus there from Karaköy Square (you can get directions, check routes and timings at the tourist information office).

The Byzantine Aya Sofya is one of the most spectacular sights in Istanbul.

Ask, too, about travelling by *dolmus* – the minibuses that run along set routes at set fares – and the local ferries, which zip about much quicker than cars (Istanbul traffic can be hellish). Catamarans run from Karaköy, Eminönü and piers along the Bosphorus, serving commuter routes linking the European and Asian sides of Istanbul; they also go up the Bosphorus.

Beware of street touts selling ferry tickets at inflated prices outside the ferry terminal; only buy from the main ticket office. If you decide to travel by taxi, make sure the meter is switched on (it's an offence if not) and, if travelling during the day, check that the meter is showing *gunduz* (daytime rate), rather than *gece* (night-time rate), as night fares are 50 percent higher. A final word of warning – when exploring on foot, never expect cars to stop for you – even on crossings. And watch you don't trip on uneven and cracked paving stones.

Shopping Istanbul is a cornucopia for shopaholics, and despite its huge popularity with tourists you can still get fine carpets and high-quality leather

goods at reasonable prices. Beware of pushy carpet-store owners, though, or you'll spend your entire stay trying to get away from them.

The Beyazit and Aksaray neighbourhoods (near Istanbul University in the old city) are crammed with leather shops, while those in search of a Turkish carpet but reluctant to haggle can shop in peace at a government-run carpet store in the Haseki Hurrem Hamami, which runs between Aya Sofya (also called Haghia Sophia) and the Blue Mosque in the old city *(see below for details)*.

Here prices are fixed and quality assured. In the same area you'll find a handicrafts market selling mosaic panels and plates. Look out, too, for fine silk and chic clothing stores in Beyoglu, north of the Golden Horn and the cruise port. Taksim Square is at the heart of this sophisticated section of the city and a good place from which to start a shopping spree. Istiklai Caddesi is the best street for upmarket clothes shops.

Istanbul's main shopping centre is the Grand Bazaar, the covered market off Sultanahmet Square. This warren of narrow streets contains more than 4,000 shops and stalls, as well as mosques, restaurants, banks and artisans' workshops. Explore the backstreets (and follow local people) to find the best bargains on carpets, rugs, crafts and jewellery – but keep your cash and credit cards safely stowed away from pickpockets.

A mosaic of Christ in the South Gallery of Aya Sofya.

Map on page 306

Eating   The Sultanahmet Square area *(see below)* where you'll do most of your sightseeing, also contains a multitude of restaurants and coffee houses, where, at reasonable prices, exhausted tourists can tuck into local specialities like stuffed cabbage, kebabs, rice *pilav* and *manti* (a Turkish version of ravioli). *Kuzu tandir* (roast lamb) is another good bet.

Seeing the sights   First, get your bearings; the Bosphorus Strait, which links the Black Sea with the Sea of Marmara, cuts straight through Istanbul, dividing the European sector from the Asian sector in the East. Your ship will arrive in European Istanbul, which is further divided by an estuary known as the Golden Horn. The Galata Bridge spans this; north of the bridge and the cruise port is Beyoglu and Taskim Square, while the old city (Eski Istanbul) lies south.

If time is limited, put Eski Istanbul (old Constantinople) at the top of your list, as it contains the Grand Bazaar and the most magnificent mosques, palaces and churches Istanbul has to offer.

Make for Sultanahmet Square; just north of this is the **Topkapi Palace** (Topkapi Sarayi), the Byzantine **Aya Sofya**, the **Blue Mosque** (Sultan Ahmet Camii), the **Archaeological Museum** and the **Hippodrome** (At Meydam) – all within walking distance of each other. Get there early and spend the whole day.

And you can steam away the aches and pains of a hard day's sightseeing at a traditional *hamami* (Turkish bath). There are several of these within walking distance of Sultanahmet Square; easiest to find is the one at 10 Doktor Emin Pasa Sokak, a street off Divan Yolu (the old city's main thoroughfare, which starts right opposite the Hippodrome and runs up past the Grand Bazaar).

BELOW: the grand Bazaar, full of Eastern promise.

TYPICAL
EXCURSIONS,
ISTANBUL
● **Classical Istanbul**
coach tour (5–6 hours)
to the major sights.
Involves lots of
walking.
● **Treasures of
Istanbul** (full-day
tour). Extended version
of the above, with
lunch included.
● **Bosphorus boat
tour** (3 hours)

Divan Yolu is worth exploring in its own right; walking up from the Hippodrome you can see the tombs of the Ottoman sultans and the ruins of the 5th-century Palace of Antiochus.

GEMLIK

Gemlik, a large container port and small town on the rocky southern shore of the Sea of Marmaris, is used as a base from which to visit the inland cities of Iznik and Bursa, although there are beaches nearby. Iznik lies to the east, and Bursa to the west, near the aiport. Most passengers take shore excursions to one or both places. It's more expensive but a lot easier than attempting to go to either independently, and you know you'll get back in time for your sailing.

Further afield Iznik (formerly Nicaea) is a small town with a lovely lakeside setting, ancient city walls and a heritage of ornate tile-making. The ruined Byzantine **Aya Sofya** mosque is well worth a visit, as is the **Yesil Cami** (Green Mosque), with a colourful tiled minaret. **Bursa** is famous for its knives, which are on sale all over the city. If you buy one, don't forget to pack it into your checked-in luggage for the flight home. The city itself has suffered from unsympathetic recent building and is not especially attractive, but there are still many glorious vestiges of its Ottoman past. Chief among them are the 14th-century **Ulucami** (Grand Mosque), the beautiful, 15th-century **Yesil Cami** (Green Mosque), and Sultan Mehmet I's Green Mausoleum – **Yesil Türbe**. The **Muradiye Complex**, comprising a mosque, school and royal tombs, set in lovely gardens, should not be missed. Bursa also has a good bazaar (Çarsi) and an abundance of *hamams* (Turkish baths).

BELOW: yachts in Bodrum marina.

SAILING THE BOSPHORUS

The Dardanelles is a 42-km (28-mile) channel between the long, narrow spit of Gallipoli, which is in Europe, and the coast of Asiatic Turkey. The strait is just 2 km (1 mile) wide in places, giving excellent views of the cliffs of the peninsula on the European side and the city of Çannakkale on the Asian side. South of here are what are thought to be the remains of ancient Troy.

The Dardanelles links the Aegean to the southern side of the Sea of Marmara, while the Bosphorus, 32 km (20 miles) long, leads from the Sea of Marmara to the Black Sea.

As you near Istanbul, you'll see massive fortifications along the waterfront, the minarets of the old city rising in the distance. On the port side, look out for the Topkapi Palace, the bulky dome of Aya Sofya and the Blue Mosque. Further on, the Galata Bridge spans the entrance to the Golden Horn. Leaving the old city behind, there are magnificent palaces on the port side and beautiful old mansions, called *yalis*, on the Asian side.

The Bosphorus is always busy and you'll see a constant stream of ferries zig-zagging across, pleasure boats, fishing smacks, oil tankers and heavily laden freighters. Eventually, the strait widens and the water becomes choppier, as you reach the mouth of the Black Sea.

CANAKKALE

A once-sleepy town at the entrance to the Dardanelles straits, **Canakkale** now receives thousands of visitors who come for the beaches, memorials and cemeteries of the Gallipoli Peninsula, a poignant reminder of the events here which cost 500,000 soldiers their lives in World War I.

If you stay in town, it's a 10-minute walk from the dock to the centre. The **Archaeological Museum** (open daily; fee) with artefacts from Troy, is a short taxi ride away. There are fish restaurants, bars and cyber cafés along the seafront promenade where you can sit and watch the busy traffic on the water.

Further afield   However, most people go straight to **Gallipoli** (Gelibolu) where you can visit **Anzac Cove**, where Australian and New Zealand troops are buried, the Military Museum, and the Turkish Memorial. Trips also operate to **Troy**, where you can see a replica of the Wooden Horse and remains of the ancient city walls, and imagine the great battles that took place there in 1200BC.

Maps on pages 306 & 316

Th Odeion at Troy – stones with many tales to tell.

KUSADASI

Kusadasi may not be the traditional fishing village of yesteryear, but despite the march of commercialism there are still pockets of old-world Turkey, notably in the narrow streets of the Kaleici quarter, the oldest part of town, and good beaches nearby. Kusadasi's proximity to the ancient city of Ephesus means it attracts ships for full-day stays to allow for excursions.

Arrival and around the dock   The joy of a Kusadasi call is that your ship will anchor very close to the action; the cruise terminal is built on an arm

BELOW: the sweeping bay of Edremeit.

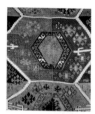

Traditional Turkish carpets are designed in intricate patterns.

reaching out into the bay. You can stock up on cash at a bureau de change, and the dock gates lead straight onto the shop- and restaurant-lined waterfront. Just cross the road and you're in the town, which is easily explored on foot. Or, if you fancy stretching your legs first, go right at the seafront and you'll see **Güvercin Adasi** (Pigeon Island), which is topped by a small stone fort. You stroll across a causeway to get there and can enjoy a pleasant woodland walk up to the hilltop, where an open-air café offers snacks or lunch with a view.

The seafront, lined with traditional restaurants, is a good place for lunch; the seafood is freshly caught and meat grills are good and cheap. Stick to thoroughly cooked food and bottled water if you're prone to tummy bugs

Shopping

You can shop big-time in Kusadasi. Turkish rugs, leather goods, copper trays, traditional Turkish tea services and intricate silver and gold jewellery are still good buys but be careful in the main bazaar, as stallholders inflate prices when ships are in port. The best bet is to offer a third of the trader's price and haggle, hard, from there. Unless you have the patience of a saint, don't respond to the blandishments of carpet storekeepers inviting you into their shops – you'll be there all day. The best buy for foodies is fragrant Turkish honey; *cam bali* (pronounced chahm bah-li) is pine scented and *portakal* is made from orange blossom.

Seeing the sights

For **Kaleici**, old Kusadasi, head north along the main street (Barbaros Hayrettin Caddesi); from the top, it's easy to get directions to the bazaar and Kaleici neighbourhood. Beware of the marble-topped pavements as you wander around, they can get slippery when wet. You could while away

BELOW:
Trajan's Fountain at Ephesus.

a few hours very pleasantly at a *hamami*, a traditional Turkish bath house. These are more modern (and expensive) than they used to be but still worth trying.

Further afield Ephesus is offered as an excursion by all the cruise ships and it really must be seen; it's the best-preserved ancient city in the eastern Mediterranean. Highlights are the Temple of Hadrian, the harbour bath and the theatre. **Dilek National Park**, 30 km (18 miles) south of Kusadasi, is a lovely spot that is also offered as a shore trip. Alternatively, you could just be lazy and enjoy a day at the beach. **Kadinlar Denizi** is a pretty spot about 3 km (2 miles) south of Kusadasi – you can take a minibus or taxi from the port.

BODRUM

Bodrum, which is built on the ruins of ancient Halicarnassus and is the birth-place of the historian Herodotus, combines fascinating history and scenic beauty with some of tourism's worst excesses. It's undeniably pretty but hugely crowded at the peak of summer, and villa developments are beginning to scar the pine-clad hills behind the town. The approach to the lovely harbour, however, is stunning, with the crusader castle of St Peter dominating a small promontory and polished wooden *gulets* (sailing boats) gliding in and out of the port.

Around the dock and town Cruise passengers are tendered in from their ships but, once in, all Bodrum's attractions are within easy walking distance. The tomb of the former ruler, Mausolus, is considered one of the Seven Wonders of the Ancient World and gave rise to the word mausoleum. Only the foundations

Map on page 316

TYPICAL
**EXCURSIONS,
KUSADASI**
● **Ephesus** (4 hours or full day).
● **Religious and Antique Kusadasi** (6–7 hours).
● **Dilek National Park** (3–4 hours). Pretty beaches and country walks.

BELOW: enjoying the maritime lifestyle.

Ripe and juicy mel-
ons are hard to resist.

remain. The castle of St Peter, now the **Museum of Underwater Archaeology**, houses some interesting treasures, including the hull of a Byzantine ship. Behind the town, there's a 4th-century BC amphitheatre that once seated 13,000 people.

The curved harbour is lined with open-air restaurants facing beautiful old *gulets* (sailing boats) whose owners noisily encourage passers-by to take day trips to surrounding beaches and coves. Behind the restaurants, extending towards the castle, are narrow streets packed with shops, nightclubs and rooftop bars. Natural sponges, Turkish *kelims* (rugs), some good gold and silver jewellery and a lot of fakes are the main things on offer and there are markets on Tuesday (textiles) and Friday (food and souvenirs). By night, these streets are packed with revellers and clubbers, but the harbourside restaurants are a pleasant way to spend an evening ashore and the quieter rooftop bars are romantic. Bodrum has no beaches to speak of; you need to take a *dolmus* (shared taxi) further along the peninsula for sunbathing, swimming and snorkelling.

Further afield Most people spend the day in Bodrum but the surrounding villages are pleasant for a day trip, particularly **Gumusluk**, which has excellent fish restaurants. The *dolmus* taxis are cheap and efficient but make sure you leave plenty of time to get back to the port.

M ARMARIS

Marmaris is one of the most popular holiday resorts in Turkey, and has consequently suffered from over-development. It is, nonetheless, a scenic setting, on a vast bay ringed with mountains and pine forests, the water often brilliant with the white sails of thousands of yachts that congregate here in summer.

BELOW:
looking over
Marmaris and bay.

Map on page 316

Around the dock and town   Cruise ships either tender or dock at the ferry terminal, from which a small square leads to the narrow streets and bazaar of the old town. This has spread out around a small citadel, dating from 3000BC and subsequently rebuilt by Alexander the Great and Suleyman the Magnificent. Here, you'll find the usual souvenirs – *kelims*, fabrics, leather jackets, hold-alls and handbags, herbs and spices, brassware and onyx chess sets.

If you have a whole day, take a boat trip to **Turunc**, a pretty fishing village, or Paradise Island, where the rocks in the Blue Cave reflect the colour bouncing off the water. **Cleopatra's Island**, a 12-km (8-mile) minibus ride and a short boat trip from the town (bookable through a local operator at the port), is famous for its clear water and powdery sand.

Further afield   Cruise ships and local entrepreneurs offer excursions to the Datca Peninsula, to **Knidos**, one of the most fabled sites of antiquity, where a shrine to Aphrodite is now in ruins. The site is under excavation but you can see the Greek theatre, Byzantine basilicas and a Corinthian temple. To the west is the Dalyan River delta, with beautiful beaches, where you can spot turtles. **Kaunos** is famous for the ancient Lycian tombs cut into the cliff face. The best way to see them is by boat. Around the port, owners of *gulets* (wooden fishing boats) advertise these trips, or you could book a shore excursion.

TYPICAL EXCURSIONS, MARMARIS
● **Datca Peninsula** to the ancient site at **Knidos**, the Dalyan River delta and the Lycian tombs at **Kaunos** (full- or half-day tour).

ANTALYA

A major holiday resort on the Turkish Mediterranean coast, **Antalya** is set on a pretty crescent bay, surrounded by the purple Taurus Mountains, rocky coves and dramatic cliffs.

BELOW: Antalya's old city walls are still standing.

Around the dock and town The ferry port, where most cruise ships dock, is a short taxi ride away from the lovely old part of town, Kaleici. Recently renovated, its narrow streets, ancient walls and old wooden houses are delightful. Mingling with the sights is the usual collection of shops, bars and restaurants. It's easy enough to climb up from the harbour to the **Kalepapisi** (Castle Gate), where a Selcuk tower is built into the Byzantine walls. You can also visit the triple-arched Hadrian's Gate, the Kesik Minare (Broken Minaret), all that remains of a 13th-century mosque, and the **Archaeological Museum** (open Tues–Sun; fee), one of Turkey's best.

The modern part of the city has wide, palm-lined promenades and a tram, which runs along the seafront and encircles Kaleici.

Further afield There are sandy beaches and scenic waterfalls at Duden and Kursunlu. Excursions also run to the antiquities at Aspendos, Perge and Side.

ALANYA

Alanya is a pleasant coastal town, its old centre set on a promontory that slices the city centre in two. You can see the crumbling castle walls here as you approach the harbour.

Around the dock and town The remains of the **Tersane**, an ancient shipyard, are close to the harbour. It's not difficult to hike from here up to the **castle**, with 13th-century walls, barracks, cisterns and a miniature Byzantine basilica. The small archaeology museum is also worth a look. There are some good shops, bars and restaurants in the old town and around the fine harbour.

TYPICAL
EXCURSIONS,
ANTALYA
● To the ancient sites
at **Aspendos**, **Perge**
and **Side** (3–4 hours).

BELOW:
bright woven
slippers for sale.

Further afield   Take a short boat trip to **Damlatas Magarasi** (Cave of Dripping Stones) and the pretty beaches around the town, or join a shore excursion to the ancient sites of **Perge** and **Aspendos**.

Map on page 316

MINOR PORTS IN SOUTHERN TURKEY

Turkey's southern Mediterranean coast is characterised by pine-clad mountains, rocky coves, sandy beaches and clear, unpolluted water. Several small cruise ships call at the resort towns along the coast. **Fethiye** is one of the larger settlements, a busy market town built over the site of the ancient Lycian city of Telmessos. The old theatre and Lycian rock tombs are still visible and several sites of historic interest are within easy reach.

Kalkan is a sleepy, very pretty, whitewashed town tumbling over a hillside to a small harbour, from which boats take visitors to deserted rocky coves around the headland. The excavations of **Patara**, once the principal port of Lycia, are nearby.

Just off the coast lies **Kastellórizo**, a tiny island that actually belongs to Greece, and is used as a beach stop by some cruise lines.

Kekova Island, further along the coast, is famous for the sunken Byzantine city, **Batik Sehir**, which you can see clearly under the water. **Phaselis**, south of Antalya, is set around three bays against a backdrop of woodland and the sometimes snow-capped peak of **Mount Solyrurius**. The area is rich in history, featuring the remains of the longest Roman aqueduct in the ancient world, Hadrian's marble road and a theatre dating back to the 2nd century AD.

Tasucu is a small and somewhat uninteresting port on the southern coast of Turkey between Antalya and Mersin. Ferries depart from here for Northern

Mosaics in Antalya's excellent Archaeological Museum.

BELOW: the Bay of Goçek, undisturbed by ships.

TYPICAL EXCURSIONS, LARNACA

● **Amathus, Kolossi Castle, Kourion**, the **Sanctuary of Apollo** and **Páfos** (half- or full-day tours).

● **Nicosia** (Lefkosia)

● **Hill villages**, including **Lefkara**, the lace-making centre (half-day tour).

● **Salt Lake** to see flamingos and other migrating birds; **Hala Sultan Tekke** mosque and **Cape Kiti** (half-day).

BELOW: the Agía Phaneromeni chapel, Larnaca.

Cyprus. There are attractions in the vicinity, though. High in the Toros Mountains is the lonely Hellenistic ruin of **Uzuncaburc** where you will find a Roman theatre, a monumental gateway, a nymphaeum, the Temple of Zeus Olbios and the Temple of Tyche. To the east there is the sea castle at Kizkalesi, and from Narlikuyu you can go into the hills for the impressive limestone caverns of Cennet ve Cehennen (Caves of Heaven and Hell).

CYPRUS

The third-largest island in the Mediterranean, Cyprus became an independent republic in 1960, but, following the 1974 Turkish invasion became divided between the Turkish north and Greek south. The Greek section (roughly two-thirds of the island) dominates the tourist scene, with the popular resorts of Agía Napa – famous for its non-stop nightlife – and Páfos in the southwest.

Much of the island remains unspoilt by hotel or resort developments, with plenty of rugged coastline and mountain scenery (skiing is a winter option) left to explore and enjoy. There are nearly 200 km (120 miles) of hiking trails, and a variety of archaeological sites, particularly in and around Páfos, one of several UNESCO World Cultural Heritage sites on the island. Both can be reached from the cruise ports of Larnaca and Limassol; although Páfos is a long way west (70 km/43 miles from Limassol), fast roads make the journey easy.

LARNACA

Although situated just 8 km (5 miles) from the island's main airport, Larnaca is not quite as well located for touring Cyprus as is Limassol, which is why many ships visiting Cyprus – and those home-porting there – use the latter. Páfos and

the other west-coast sights are nearly 2 hours' drive away from Larnaca, but both Nicosia and the best-known holiday resort, Agía Napa, are less than an hour away. Built near the the site of the 13th-century city of Kition, Larnaca has a number of places of historical interest including the Byzantine Ágios Lazarus church, the final burial place of Lazarus.

Map on page 316

Arrival and around the dock

There is an attractive, palm tree-lined promenade and a neighbouring marina to view as your ship docks in Larnaca harbour. At the port is a small passenger terminal with the basic facilities (bank, duty-free shop, roof-top restaurant, telephones). As with Limassol, there are plans for a new, much larger and more sophisticated terminal, but this is part of a major public/private redevelopment of the entire harbour front, aimed at attracting many more cruise ships. As the finance has yet to be raised for this, work may not start, let alone be completed, before the end of the decade.

Cruise visitors arriving in Larnaca have a major advantage over those docking in Limassol – the town centre is just across the road from the terminal and the main shopping area and museums are just a short walk, straight ahead. Even so, as from summer 2004, a shuttle bus will operate to and around town.

Making lace by hand in Lefkara.

Shopping

Look out for the laceware made by the villagers of Lefkara. The best selection is in the village itself (a regular tour stop), but their handiwork is sold across the island. Otherwise, there are the standard Greek-style souvenirs (leather belts and bags, ceramics, etc.) but, among more international items, there are few bargains now that the Cypriot pound is linked to the euro.

BELOW: the Salt Lake, where flamingos can occasionally be seen.

In charge of a glass-bottomed boat in Agía Napa.

Seeing the sights The promenade along the harbour makes a pleasant walk, past the snazzy marina. There is a mixture of hotels, shops, restaurants and tavernas along the front and the beach is good – better than that at Limassol – with shallow water making it safe for children to swim. Worth a longer walk or short taxi ride (to the west of the harbour front) are the cliff-top 17th-century **fort and medieval museum**, and the nearby **Ágioss Lazarus** church.

In the town, the **Archaelogical Museum** (open Mon–Fri; fee) and the remarkable collection of prehistoric and medieval artefacts in the private **Pierides Museum** (open Mon–Sat; fee) are both worth seeing.

Further afield Places included on shore excursions, such as the **Salt Lake**, **Cape Kiti** and **Lefkara** aren't far and can be visited independently if you hire a car. The bus service from here isn't very good, but there are shared taxi services linking Limassol, Larnaca, Páfos and Nicosia.

LIMASSOL

Limassol is the second-largest town in Cyprus and the centre of the local wine industry. It is also the main cruise port and, partly because of the influx of cruise visitors, has become a major resort in its own right.

One of the busiest cruise ports in the eastern Mediterranean, Limassol is both a home port – primarily for Cyprus cruise lines operating short cruises to Egypt, Lebanon, Syria and the Greek islands, but also for international lines (there are airports within an hour's drive at both Larnaca and Páfos) – and a popular port of call. Ships always dock rather than anchor off and almost always stay a full day, although departures are normally early rather than late evening.

BELOW:
the beach at Cape Greco, Agía Napa.

Arrival and around the dock There is nothing too memorable about sailing into this busy cargo/passsenger port, although the Troodos Mountains do form an attractive backdrop to the town. Because of the many short cruises operated, there are often half a dozen or more ships docked at a time.

A new passenger terminal is being built (due to open in 2006) when the passenger and cargo operations at the port will be completely separated. The new terminal will be three times the size of the existing one, which has fairly basic facilities: a bank, telephones, a duty-free shop and a café outside.

There is also a Cyprus Tourism Organisation (CTO) office, from which you can pick up maps, brochures and other information about local attractions. Most usefully, it has local and island bus timetables and a list of companies offering shared taxi services. There are private taxis at the port and the local authority also operates a (usually free) shuttle bus into the centre of Limassol (about 3 km/2 miles from the port) for cruise visitors.

From the port, it is a short walk across a roundabout to the junction with the main road into town (to the right) but it is a 20–30-minute and not very interesting hike before you reach the old port, which is the start of Limassol proper.

Shopping Cyprus joined the European Union in 2004 and the Cypriot pound has been pegged to the euro – it is expected to join the single currency in 2007 – pushing its value, and local prices, upwards. In any case, there are few essential purchases for visitors. Leather goods remain fairly cheap but the quality is variable so the best bet is probably the well-crafted laceware produced by the villagers of Lefkara which is sold across the island. Ceramics made at some of the other hill villages can also make interesting purchases.

Map on page 316

Cyprus remains mostly warm and sunny throughout the year, with flowers in bloom in all seasons

BELOW: trinkets to tempt tourists at Platres.

Seeing the sights

The centre of Limassol is walkable, either along the coast road which has a manicured promenade overlooking its man-made beach, or through the main shopping area (Agíou Andreou Street) which runs parallel to the coast road and is partly pedestrianised.

Just across from the old port (over the roundabout at the junction with the coast road) is the **Crusader Castle** (open daily; fee), where Richard the Lionheart married Berengaria and which later belonged to the Knights of St John of Jerusalem, then to the Turks. It now houses the excellent **Medieval Museum**. Close by is the Turkish quarter, with its twin mosques and a Turkish bathhouse.

Off to the right, the colourful market is fun. Going north, you can visit the **Agía Trias** (Holy Trinity) church and end up in the Municipal Gardens, where there is an open-air theatre and a rather sad little zoo.

The public transport system is fairly limited throughout the island but it is worth noting that the No. 30 bus links the new port with the old one and the rest of Limassol, and the No. 6 links the old port with other parts of Limassol (but doesn't go to the new port).

Further afield

Situated about halfway along the south coast of Cyprus, Limassol is an ideal base for exploring the island, as none of the main towns or attractions are more than 60–90 minutes' drive away. There are hourly buses on weekdays from the marketplace in Limassol to the capital, Nicosia (Lefkosia) but services are less frequent at weekends and so are best avoided – as are the patchy bus services to Larnaca and to the hill resort of Platres.

A better bet are the shared taxis which link Limassol, Larnaca, Páfos and Nicosia. They run every half-hour (hourly at weekends) and usually will pick up and drop off anywhere within those towns, but you do have to ring to book (the CTO office has a list of numbers). Fares are very reasonable; ordinary taxis are more expensive but still good value.

The island roads have improved a lot over the past 10 years, with new motorways and dual-carriageways between the major towns. This makes hiring a car a good option. Driving is on the left and signposting is comprehensive – the only thing to note is the increasing use of Greek versions of place-names (e.g. Páfos for Páfos, Lemesos for Limassol and, potentially most confusing, Lefkosia for Nicosia.

About 12 km (7 miles) to the east of the town centre is the archaeological site of the ancient city kingdom of **Amathous**. The recently excavated site (excavations didn't begin until the 1980s) includes an early Christian basilica, and the ruins of a sanctuary to Aphrodite, the latter on Acropolis Hill, above the road. You can catch a No. 6 or No. 30 bus, or take a taxi, or drive if you've hired a car.

Páfos, which is always a shore excursion, can easily be visited independently, by shared taxi or hire car. The 95-hectare (235-acre) site of the ancient city, **Nea Páfos** (open daily; fee), a UNESCO World Heritage Site, has some extraordinary mosaics in its excavated houses. The modern, lower town and resort of **Kato Páfos** has a pretty harbour and good fish restaurants.

The beaches in and around Limassol are not

particularly attractive, being shingly or pebbly, although the surrounding streets are kept clean and tidy and there is some attractive landscaping. Easily the best is Lady's Mile, a sandy beach about 5 km (3 miles) west of the town.

Map on page 316

TARTOUS/LATAKIA (SYRIA)

Bordered by Lebanon, Iraq, Jordan and Turkey, Syria is located at the geographical heart of the Middle East's political hot-spots and is considered by many cruise lines as either not mainstream enough or just too risky. But it is a beautiful country, with a warm Mediterranean climate and historical sites such as Palmyra, and the stunning medieval castle of Crac des Chevaliers high on many people's lists of things they simply must see.

Arrival and around the dock Ships dock at either Tartous or Latakia, both busy fishing and commercial ports. Both the cruise berths are around 10 minutes' drive from the respective city centres.

Almost all passengers choosing to cruise to Syria book excursions to the historical sites, most of them a couple of hours' drive away, so independent exploration isn't easy. Latakia has decent beaches, and cruise lines will often make arrangements with a local hotel for guests to use the facilities. Both towns have a souk for souvenir shopping; take local currency or US dollars and haggle for carpets, silverware and spices.

Further afield There are several excursions to choose between, none of which is easy to arrange independently. They include the Hellenistic and Roman settlement of **Apamea**, the resort of **Latakia**, and **Saladin's Castle**, one of the

TYPICAL EXCURSIONS, TARTOUS/LATAKIA

● **Aleppo** and the **Crac des Chevaliers**.
● **Palmyra**, to see Roman ruins.
● **Saladin's Castle**, (half-day tours; see main text).

BELOW: minarets and fishing boats are a beguiling mixture.

greatest crusader castles ever built, surrounded by deep ravines. **Aleppo** has a spectacular moated citadel; the 12th-century **Crac des Chevaliers**, built by the crusaders and inhabited by the Knights of St John, is spectacular; and there are vast Roman ruins in the desert city of **Palmyra**.

TRIPOLI (LEBANON)

Tripoli is a thriving, busy city in which 45 buildings, many dating back to the 14th century, have been registered as historical sites. The city is divided into two parts: the modern area and El-Mina, the port area and site of the ancient city.

Arrival and around the dock and town Tripoli is built on a rocky promontory on the Mediterranean coast. You may see a string of offshore islands as you approach, the largest of which is a nature reserve for green turtles and seabirds. The old city is dominated by a massive crusader citadel.

While Tripoli's **El-Mina** district has a great deal to offer, tour groups are often escorted by armed guards, and cruise lines will often caution against independent sightseeing. Visitors should take stock of the security situation at the time. If it is considered safe to walk around, there are mosques, souks, *hammams* (public baths) and churches to visit, as well as the citadel. The city centre is about 10 minutes' drive from the dock.

Further afield Nothing is far away in Lebanon. The three top cruise-ship excursions are the following. **Byblos**, one of the oldest continuously inhabited cities in the world and formerly one of the four principal towns of Phoenicia, which is a half-day trip. **Beit ed Dîne**, a village set amid vines, olive trees, fruit orchards and cypress groves is another short trip. Here, a Lebanese folk museum is housed in a magnificent oriental palace, designed by Italian architects in the early 19th century. The most popular excursion, however, is a full-day trip to **Baalbek**, the largest and best-preserved Roman architectural site in existence, with a huge and fascinating temple complex.

BELOW: a splendid Port Said mosque.

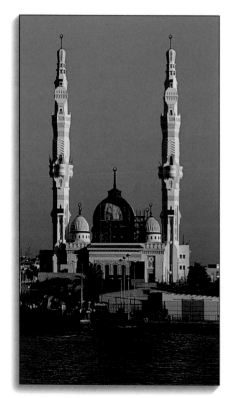

BEIRUT

Ships sometimes call at Beirut, including the mini-cruises which operate from Cyprus. The dock is some 25 minutes' drive from the centre, where there are incredible archaeological excavations and an impressive museum. The city is being rebuilt after 16 devastating years of civil war, although many visitors have a certain ghoulish fascination with the terrible damage that was done, and the Green Line no-man's land which runs through the city centre. Take advice from your cruise line on security; it may not be safe to wander round alone.

PORT SAID (EGYPT)

By Egyptian standards, the city of **Port Said** is in its infancy, not founded until 1859 when work began on the Suez Canal. Many parts of the city are even younger, having been rebuilt following bombing raids during the Suez Crisis in 1956 and Egypt's wars with Israel in the 1960s and 1970s. Despite its relative modernity, Port Said is a city full of atmosphere; once notorious for hashish dens and dealers in pornographic postcards, the city has retained a certain disreputable charm, mainly thanks to the wooden-balconied, late 19th-century houses which make some neighbourhoods reminiscent of old New Orleans.

While not a major tourist destination in its own right, Port Said is a free port and offers some of the best shopping in Egypt. It also has uncrowded beaches, some decent restaurants, museums and pretty public gardens, so it's worth a wander ashore if you've already seen Cairo (or can't face the long haul). The other advantage is that there are fewer street-hustlers than in Cairo or the towns along the Nile, largely because foreign visitors, other than cruise passengers, are rare.

Port Said (together with Alexandria) is the main gateway for ocean-cruise passengers wishing to visit **Cairo** and the pyramids at **Giza**. It is rarely a home port, most ships using it only as a port of call but spending at least a full day there to cater for excursions.

Arrival and around the dock Cruising into Port Said, you get the chance to see one of the world's most dramatic sights – the line of vessels waiting to enter the Suez Canal, which is narrower than you might imagine. Before you head ashore, have a good look around Port Said's cruise terminal (opened in 2003), which has money-changing facilities, a tourist information desk (useful for guidelines on how much to pay for taxis, and the exact opening times of museums) and an Oriental Bazaar.

Shopping You'll find more shops a short walk away in Gomohhoria Street and at the Noras Beach Shopping Arcade, which lies 2 km (1 mile) from the pier.

Map on page 316

Snake charming is fascinating, whether it appeals or appals.

BELOW: looking down his nose at the Daran camel market.

Good buys include Egyptian cotton goods, jewellery (particularly *cartouches* – gold blocks inscribed with your name in hieroglyphs), woodwork, leather goods, carpets, copper and brassware and every type of exotic spice you can imagine. The local currency is the Egyptian pound.

Seeing the sights A taxi ride away and worth a visit is the **National Museum** (open daily; fee) on Juillet Street, opposite the statue of Ferdinand de Lesseps. While not as well-endowed as Cairo's Museum of Antiquities, it has exhibits from every period of Egyptian history. There is also a **Military Museum** (open Sat–Thur am; fee) with exhibits on ancient Egyptian warfare and displays of armoury from more recent conflicts with Israel (including – rather alarmingly – unexploded bombs). On a more peaceful note, the city has a **Museum of Modern Art** (open daily; fee) in Shohada Square. If you prefer a quiet day on the beach, grab a taxi and head for **Ismailia**, which lies mid-way between Port Said and Suez, on the western shore of Lake Timsah. It's known as the City of Gardens for its verdant scenery and fine orchards, and has some excellent lakeside beaches. If that's too far, take a free ferry across to **Port Fouad** on the eastern side of the Canal; this is Port Said's quiet residential area, and has many lovely parks in which to stretch your legs and enjoy the peace.

But perhaps one of the greatest pleasures Port Said has to offer is a simple stroll along its seafront with the local people, who are relatively unspoiled by tourism and still dress in traditional garb; here you can watch fishermen go about their business as they have for many years, and there is even a ladies' beach where women bathe fully clothed.

ALEXANDRIA

Alexandria, built in 331BC on the orders of Alexander the Great, was a port long before that; originally called Rhatokis, it was used by the pharoahs as far back as the 9th century BC.

But it was as Alexandria that it made its name as one of the most important cities of the ancient world, home to one of its Seven Wonders – the Lighthouse – and one of the world's greatest libraries, containing more than half a million books and manuscripts. Some of that ancient grandeur is still to be found. The Graeco-Roman Museum has exhibits dating from the 3rd century BC while Pompey's Pillar, soaring more than 27 metres (80 ft) high and made of rose-pink granite, was erected in AD297 and is perhaps Alexandria's best-known Roman monument.

Alexandria is a popular base for eastern Mediterranean cruise itineraries, offering access to Cairo and the pyramids at Giza but also well worth exploring in its own right.

Arrival and around the dock The modern port of Alexandria is well equipped to handle cruise visitors; it has four passenger quays and its main terminal has exchange booths, shops, tourist information, telephones and toilets. A second passenger terminal is due to be completed by the end of 2004. Taxis are available at the port but always negotiate a rate in advance. From the docks it's a short walk to the corniche. There are numerous banks or you can change cash at the waterfront hotels, but credit cards are widely accepted.

Shopping Alexandria's main souk is just one block inland from the seafront. Be prepared to devote some time to this, as it's a fabulously atmospheric one-

Map on page 316

TYPICAL
EXCURSIONS,
ALEXANDRIA
● **Cairo**. Full-day tour similar to those offered from Port Said.
● **Alexandria**. Half-day coach tour of the city.

LEFT: lots of junk for sale in Alexandria.
BELOW: a man and his *felucca*.

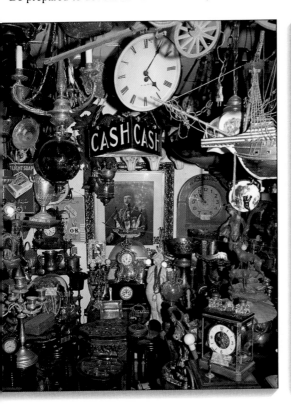

The Apis bull at Alexandria's Graeco-Roman Museum, dating from the reign of the Roman emperor Hadrian.

stop-shop for everything from spices and elaborately patterned rugs to intricate jewellery and beautifully-worked brass and copperware.

Seeing the sights   There are fascinating Roman remains to be seen at the 2nd-century BC **Kom ash-Shuqafah catacombs** (open daily; fee) which hold three tiers of burial chambers. Alexandria also has Egypt's only Roman amphitheatre, which was excavated in the 1960s and has glittering white marble terraces. Now there are hopes of excavating something even more remarkable – Cleopatra's palace – from the seabed off Alexandria's coast; vast columns and statues have already been recovered. The excavations at **Kom al-Dikkah** and the **Graeco-Roman Museum** (both open daily; fee) are on most visitors' sightseeing list. A visit to the **Royal Jewellery Museum** is interesting too, not just for its display of glittering contents, but because it is housed in the former palace of a princess, and is one of the most beautiful buildings in the country. Alexandria also has a **Museum of Fine Arts** and a **Hydrobiological Museum**, where you can discover the marine life of the Mediterranean and the Nile Delta.

But there's more to Alexandria than ancient ruins; stretching along a strip of land with the Mediterranean on one side and Lake Mareotis on the other, the city's sandy beaches combine with a pleasant climate to make it a thriving year-round seaside resort.

Many of the best beaches are accessible from the corniche, the broad boulevard bordering Alexandria's waterfront, which is lined with imposing, grand 19th-century hotels – a good choice for lunch with a view of the bay.

Kofta (ground meatballs), *mulukhia* (green soup), *hamam mahshi* (stuffed

Map on page 316

pigeon) and *baba ghannoug* (tahini and aubergine) are good choices, as is the fresh seafood. For a special treat, you could visit the elegant Cecil Hotel, where Winston Churchill stayed.

If you'd like to combine sightseeing with a beach stop and an excellent lunch, take a taxi to **Abu Qir** – site of famous battles between Nelson and Napoleon in the 1790s. (Alexandrian taxis are orange and black and can be flagged down anywhere.) This area is rich in Greek and Roman monuments but it also has a good beach where local fishermen supply the catch of the day to seafood restaurants along the waterfront.

Also worth a taxi ride (or else a long stroll along the Corniche) is the medieval **Qaytbay Fort**; this was built on the site of the ancient lighthouse (the famous **Pharos**) and contains some relics from the original building. Anyone who enjoys gardens shouldn't miss a trip to the **Al-Montazah Palace**, which is surrounded by magnificent grounds, beaches and woodland. There is a hotel in the gardens where you can enjoy a pleasant lunch. Even more atmospheric are the multi-level, fountain-filled **Shallalat Gardens**, a gorgeous pocket of old Arabia in downtown Alexandria. If animals are more your thing, the **Antoniadis Zoo** is the second-largest in Egypt and has a lovely Botanical Garden.

INTO THE RED SEA

A handful of Mediterranean cruise operators sail down the Suez Canal to enter the sub-tropical Red Sea, the long thin strip of pristine waters wedged between Africa and the Arabian peninsula that runs for around 2,000 km (1,250 miles) to reach the Indian Ocean. The narrow sliver that is the Gulf of Aqaba at the

BELOW: vivid underwater life.

**TYPICAL
EXCURSIONS,
AQABA**

● **Petra**. Long full-day
tour to the desert city.
Extensive walking is
involved.

● **Transport-only**
packages to Petra,
offered by some lines.

● **Jeep safaris**
around the Wadi Rum,
a spectacular desert
region (4 hours).

landlocked end of the sea, is bordered to the east by Jordan and to the west by the Sinai Peninsula, while the southernmost point of Israel reaches down from the north. The Red Sea itself is a divers' paradise, and the year-round heat and sun has encouraged a string of resorts to develop on the long Egyptian coast as well as the much shorter Israeli and Jordanian sections.

AQABA

Aqaba has clean, sandy beaches, warm waters and one of the world's best-preserved coral reefs containing 140 species of coral, many unique to the region. As well as good diving and snorkelling, there are facilities for parasailing, water skiing, windsurfing, fishing and other watersports. The only cruise port in Jordan, it is used as a gateway to the ancient site of Petra.

Arrival and around the dock   Aqaba has a modern port terminal with exchange facilities, tourist information and taxis. It lies about 3 km (1½ miles) to the east of central Aqaba, where some of the best beaches and shops are found. Near the ferry terminal, adjacent to the port, is an aquarium. Travellers heading for the beach are strongly advised to dress modestly – women should wear one-piece bathing suits and both sexes should cover up on the way there.

Shopping   The best souvenirs are handmade Bedouin rugs and tapestries brought in by local tribes, or elaborately-worked brass or copper coffee sets. Glass ornaments containing multi-coloured sand from Petra worked into intricate patterns are also popular buys.

BELOW:
the restored
Mameluk Fort,
Aqaba.

Seeing the sights The square-built **Mameluk Fort** – a crusaders' castle – is currently Aqaba city's prime historic site but excavations of a medieval Islamic quarter are well underway in the city centre and an ancient gate and city wall, towers, a mosque, courtyards and baths have already been unearthed.

Map on page 316

Further afield Petra, which Victorian poet Dean Burgon called "the rose-red city, half as old as time" was carved by the Nabataeans from the soft desert rock, and lost in the sands for nearly two millennia until it was discovered in the 1800s and excavated in the 1950s.

It used to be possible to enter Petra – via the *siq*, a narrow fissure between the cliffs – on horseback or by horse-drawn cart, but horses are now banned from entering and can carry you only from the coach park to the entrance. This means a lot of hot, dusty walking but it's worth it. The massive, exquisite façade of **al-Khazneh** (the treasury), Petra's most famous monument, is the first sight to greet you as you emerge from the *siq*. Beyond the treasury lie huge temples, elaborate tombs lining the Street of Façades and a gigantic, 3,000-seat Roman theatre. Petra is a magical, unforgettable place, and an absolutely essential thing to see on any cruise calling at Aqaba.

INTO THE BLACK SEA

Encircled by Turkey, Bulgaria, Romania, Ukraine, Russia and Georgia, the Black Sea ports are incredibly diverse in terms of both scenery and architecture. A cruise here is really for the culture lover and historian. Highlights include the battlefields of Crimea, the lovely coastal resort of Yalta, a performance at the opera in Odessa, and the old wooden houses of Nessebur in

BELOW: a casino by the Black Sea.

A Nessebur woman welcomes visitors.

BELOW: an Orthodox church in Odessa.

Bulgaria. There are opportunities to lie on the beach, but most passengers are attracted by the sightseeing.

The Black Sea is also rich in wildlife, and birdwatchers should be able to spot a huge variety of seabirds and wading fowl in the many deltas and estuaries. There are superb botanical gardens at Sochi and Batumi and beautiful mountain scenery near Trabzon. Conditions may be primitive compared with other regions, but prices reflect this and the shopping, particularly for art, is great.

NESSEBUR

The fishing village of **Nessebur**, a UNESCO World Heritage Site, is best known for the attractive wooden fishermen's houses lining its winding, cobbled streets. The town was founded in 510BC and still has some four dozen churches dating from this period. Nearby is the family resort of Sunny Beach, which is a popular excursion for a taste of beach life, Bulgarian style. Cruise lines do not usually offer excursions further afield – the town itself is the main attraction.

Around the dock and town Ships dock 5–10 minutes' walk from the old town. There are usually guided tours on offer but you can just as easily explore independently; the town is not very big and can be seen in 2 hours. The new **Museum of Art and History** is worth a visit, but the main attractions are the many churches (there were 40), built between the 11th and 14th centuries, including the oldest one, **St John the Baptist**, and the ruined **St John Aliturgetos**, overlooking the sea.

In the shops, look out for leather goods, jewellery, religious icons and handcrafted musical instruments. Eating out is good here and it's excellent value. Try aubergines stuffed with meat, and cheese-filled pastries, washed down with local wine: crisp whites and strong, heavy reds.

ODESSA

Situated on the northwestern shore of the Black Sea, Odessa has a strong French influence. The Odessa Opera House, with its Italian baroque façade, is prized throughout the former Soviet Union. Some cruises spend an evening in port so guests can attend a performance here.

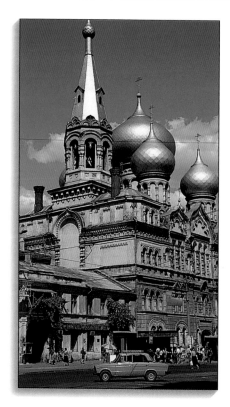

Around the dock and town Ships dock a 10-minute walk from the famous **Potemkin Steps**, built in 1841. You can walk around independently, rather than take a town tour but whichever you do, remember that there are a lot of steps to negotiate. Art is the best buy here – ceramics, paintings and jewellery, either from galleries or directly from street artists.

You can visit the fabulous 19th-century Opera House, its ceiling decorated with images from Shakespeare's plays, and the **Uspensky Cathedral** (also known as the Dormition or Assumption) with five impressive blue and white domes. Other sights in town are **Pushkin's statue** (he was exiled here), the **Vorontsov Palace** on the waterfront, and the **Archaeological Museum**, with exhibits from the Black Sea area and Egypt.

Further afield Half an hour's drive away is one of the entrances to the cat-acombs, a network of over 1,000 km (725 miles) of tunnels under the city that were used by smugglers, revolutionaries and, most notably, World War II partisans. At the village of **Nerubayskye**, you can see the catacombs that sheltered partisans and still bear witness to their occupation. If you are on a tour, a visit is usually included to the small Resistance Museum.

Cruise lines also run tours to the **Uspensky Monastery**, 40 minutes away, or you can go by tram. There is an **icon museum** nearby, as well as the summer residence of the Patriarch of Moscow and All Russia.

Map on page 316

YALTA

Sub-tropical Yalta is a fashionable harbour town, where the former Russian nobility built summer palaces. On the approach to the port, which is surrounded by wooded hills and vineyards, look out for the dramatic Swallows' Nest, a turreted tower perched high on a hill.

Arrival and around the dock The town centre is 5–10 minutes' walk from the dock. The centre of everyday life is around the mouth of the little Bystraya River, although visitors flock to the shops and restaurants on the seafront promenade, stretching west from the Bystraya. Things to see include **Levadia Palace**, summer residence of Tsar Nicholas II and the scene of the famous conference between Churchill, Stalin and Roosevelt in 1945, when the post-war map of Europe was decided; **Massandra Palace**; and the **Chekhov residence**, built by the writer in 1898 and now a museum. Also worth seeing are the Nikitski Botanical Gardens and Crimean Parks and Palaces.

TYPICAL EXCURSIONS, YALTA
● **Levadia Palace** (3-hour tour).
● **Summer House** (half-day tour).
● **Alushta Nature Reserve** (3-hour tour).

BELOW: sunset over the Black Sea.

Further afield Most cruise lines offer excursions to the summer house of Alexander III, which later became Stalin's *dacha* (summer house) and is located 2½ hours from the port. There's usually an opportunity to taste the famous Massandra wine while you're here.

Alternatively, 3-hour visits are arranged to **Levadia Palace** (*see previous page*). There's also a nature reserve at **Alushta** in the Crimean Mountains, a short drive from the port, home to some 2,600 species of wild plants as well as an abundance of birdlife.

SEVASTOPOL

Sevastopol was once home of the Russian Black Sea fleet and the gateway to the battlefields of the Crimea, so visits are often dedicated to exploring the heritage of the Crimean War (1853–56).

Around the dock and town In town, visit the **Panorama**, a huge circular tableau depicting the defence of the city during the Crimean War, and the **Maritime Museum**, which traces the history of the Black Sea fleet. There's good shopping, with plenty of street stalls and open-air galleries (you can pay in US dollars but not sterling) and a wide choice of amazingly reasonable places to eat (well, reasonable if you drink the excellent local wine; expensive otherwise). The indoor flower market near the Hotel Ukraine is worth seeing; a lot of people buy flowers here to place at the war memorials.

Further afield **Balaclava**, scene of the Charge of the Light Brigade, is only half an hour's drive and there will be plenty of taxi drivers offering tours.

TYPICAL
EXCURSIONS,
SEVASTOPOL

● **Balaclava**. Scene of the Charge of the Light Brigade during the Crimean War (half-day tour).

● **Chersonesos**. The ancient Greek city (half-day tour).
(See main text for both sites.)

BELOW: sunbathing at Arcadia Beach on the Black Sea.

There's a viewpoint on Sapoune Heights that overlooks the battlefield. You can also see the North Valley, where Russian guns were positioned, and the port, which was the main British supply base.

The ancient Greek city of **Chersonesos**, situated on a headland by the sea, is worth a visit as a well-preserved example of an ancient countryside settlement, with many of the stone houses and allotments still in existence, their foundations dating back to the 4th century BC.

BATUMI

The industrial town of Batumi, on the Georgian coast, is uninspiring; the main reason to come here is to see the amazing **Botanical Garden**, considered to be the second-largest in the world, with a collection of more than 5,000 species of plants. Cruise lines tend to manufacture entertainment away from the gardens, with folklore shows and wine tasting. Beach visits are also arranged.

Further afield   Some 20 minutes away by coach is **Gonio**, dating back to the 2nd century BC, when it played an important role as a strategic point on the crossroads from the West to the Caucasus. There's a fortress and an interesting museum, with some 1,000 exhibits, including gold and silver handicrafts dating to the 5th century BC. This is a cruise-ship excursion run from the port.

SOCHI

The summer resort of **Sochi** lies at the foot of the Caucasus and was a favourite of the Russian élite, thanks to its many mineral springs. You'll see citrus and tea plantations around the port, which is 10 minutes by coach from the town centre

Map on page 316

TYPICAL
EXCURSIONS,
BATUMI
● **Gonio**. Ancient
fortress and museum
(3-hour tour).

LEFT:
the port at Sochi.
BELOW: warm hats,
warm hearts.

TYPICAL
EXCURSIONS,
SOCHI
● **Dagomys** tea
plantation and folklore
show (4-hour tour).

(visa restrictions mean you are not allowed to walk back to the ship, so most cruise lines operate shuttles).

Around the dock and town In the town itself, there are colourful flea markets on Ulitsa Mokovskaya, open-air handicraft stalls in Riviera Park on Kurortny Prospect and plenty of atmospheric cafés.

Things to see include the State Winter Theatre and Matsesta Sanatorium. The 12 hecatres (30 acres) of the Botanical Gardens are stunning, with thousands of citrus trees as well as cypresses, palms and magnolias.

Further afield An hour away by coach, you can visit **Dagomys**, which is home to the most northerly tea plantation in Europe, and taste the tea while a folklore show, usually organised as part of a shore excursion by the cruise lines, takes place.

OTHER BLACK SEA PORTS

Cruise ships on in-depth voyages around the Black Sea may call at the lesser-known ports of Varna (Bulgaria), Constanta (Romania) Trabzon and Sinop (both in Turkey).

Varna just north of Nessebur *(see page 330)* is best known for its ethno-graphic and archaeological museums and its 2nd-century Roman baths. Near the archaeological museum is an amazing petrified forest of 300 limestone pillars up to 10 metres (30 ft) high. There is also an impressive cathedral. The best shops and restaurants are to be found around the big square in front of the opera house and theatre.

BELOW:
the lovely Aya
Sofya at Trabzon.

Constanta is the principal resort on the Romanian "riviera", with a pleasant Mediterranean climate and a profusion of mud baths and therapeutic mineral lakes. The old town is quite attractive, with an excellent archaeological museum containing 3rd-century Roman mosaics and the Orthodox Cathedral of St Peter and Paul with beautiful frescoes. Just an hour away are the ruins of 7th-century **Histria**, Romania's most ancient city. Alternatively, several cruise lines offer private boat cruises on the **Danube delta**, two hours from Constanta – one of the best-preserved wilderness areas in Europe, sheltering a wide variety of wildlife.

Trabzon (ancient Trapezus) is a medieval city on Turkey's northeast coast. The town and harbour themselves are not very attractive, and are not much geared to tourism, but there are numerous Byzantine landmarks, including the church of the Virgin of the Golden Head (now the Ortahisar Mosque) and the church of St Eugenius (Yeni Cuma Mosque). The most important Ottoman monument in the city is the Gulbahar Hatun Mosque. Alone on a cliff overlooking the Black Sea, Agía Sofya (Church of the Holy Wisdom), completed in 1263, is home to some outstanding frescoes. Most tours also include a visit to Atatürk's villa. For shoppers, there's a good bazaar to the north of the main square.

An hour away and 1,370 metres (4,500ft) above sea level is the ruin of **Sumela Monastery**, seemingly embedded into 305-metre (1,000-ft) high cliffs and one of the most important Byzantine monasteries of its time.

Sinop, once an important port, lies on the southern coast of the Black Sea in northern Turkey, surrounded by high, forested mountains. You can still see the ruin of the huge citadel and walls. The main attractions are the **Alaeddin Cami Mosque**, built in 1214; and the lovely coastal scenery around Hamsilos Bay outside the town. ❑

Map on page 316

BELOW: local festivals celebrate the coming of summer.

INSIGHT GUIDES
Travel Tips

CONTENTS

Getting Acquainted

The Mediterranean

Area: the Mediterranean is an intercontinental sea situated between Europe to the north, Africa to the south and Asia to the east. Its total surface area, including the Sea of Marmara but excluding the Black Sea, is some 970,000 sq. miles (2,512,000 sq. km).

There are only three narrow entrances to the Mediterranean: the Strait of Gibraltar to the west; the Dardanelles, the Sea of Marmara, and the Strait of the Bosporus to the north east; and the Suez Canal to the southeast. The Mediterranean's greatest recorded depth is in the Ionian Basin, south of Greece at 5,120 metres (16,800 ft) below sea level.

Many rivers flow into the Mediterranean but only a few, including the Ebro, the Rhone, the Po and the Nile, have created large deltas. Away from these, the coastline is mainly rocky and often mountainous (particularly in France, Italy, Greece and Turkey), with other areas characterised by long, sandy beaches, including Morocco, Tunisia, parts of Italy and parts of Spain. Typical vegetation is pine, olive, cork, cypress, holm oak and citrus trees.

Many coastlines are peppered with small islands, including Greece, Croatia and Sicily, while there are several much larger islands, including Mallorca, Corsica, Sardinia, Sicily, Crete, Cyprus and Rhodes. There are numerous active volcanoes in the region, among them Stromboli and Etna in Sicily. Mild (and sometimes stronger) earthquakes are common in the south and east.

Language: some 13 languages are spoken around the Mediterranean, including Spanish (Castilian), Catalan, French, Italian, Serbo-Croat, Slovene, Albanian, Greek, Turkish, Armenian, Kurdish, Hebrew and Arabic. Cruises venturing into the Black Sea will encounter Bulgarian, Russian, Ukranian and Romanian. English is understood in the principal tourist centres but less so on small islands and in more remote areas.

Time Zone: most of Europe is on GMT +1 in winter and GMT +2 in summer, with clocks changing in October and March. The far west of the continent (Portugal, Morocco and the UK) are on GMT in winter and GMT +1 in summer. Cyprus, Greece, Turkey, the Black Sea countries and the Levant are on GMT +2 in winter, GMT +3 in summer.

Currency: countries in the eurozone include Austria, Belgium, Finland, France, Germany, Greece, Ireland, Italy, Luxembourg, Netherlands, Portugal and Spain. Other countries have their own currency, although euros are widely accepted in tourist resorts in countries bordering the eurozone and places like the markets of Morocco. Sterling and US dollars are not generally accepted and if they are, you will be stung by the exchange rate.

Electricity: the voltage on cruise ships is either 110 or 220, depending on where the ship was built and at which nationality it is aimed. Some ships have dual voltage. Take an international adaptor, or buy one on board.

Climate

Most of the Mediterranean falls into the eponymous climate category: hot, dry summers and mild, wetter winters. North Africa and the Levant are hotter, with drier winters. October to March are the wettest months throughout the region. In summer, expect temperatures of 30–35˚C (86–95˚F), dropping to 10–18˚C (50–64˚F) in winter. There are numerous winds specific to the region, including the fierce *mistral* in France; the hot southerly *sirocco* in the central Mediterranean, which precedes rain; and the cooling *meltemi* in Greece.

Culture and Etiquette

The Mediterranean region encompasses many different religions and cultures, from Greek Orthodox to Muslim to Latin, and from lively, broad-minded party islands where anything goes, to sleepy villages where old-fashioned values are observed.

Etiquette Dos and Don'ts

Some basic rules apply everywhere.
• Do not enter a church, cathedral, monastery or mosque in inappropriate clothing. Both men and women should cover shoulders and legs. Shoes should be removed before entering a mosque.
• Do not wear skimpy beachwear away from the beach. Scantily clad women are likely to be hassled if they walk around a Moroccan souk in shorts and a cropped top.
• Having said this, topless sunbathing is considered de rigeur in many parts of the Med, including Spain, France, Italy, Greece and the resort areas of Turkey.
• Avoid use of the left hand for eating or touching other people in Muslim countries.
• Ask someone's permission before photographing them.
• Learn a few basics in the local language.
• Tipping etiquette varies from one country to another but is generally more relaxed than in the USA.
• In markets, expect to barter for anything from fruit to a carpet.
• Be aware of your body language. Certain gestures have different meanings in Mediterranean countries and may be considered obscene, such as the OK signal.
• Remember that in most Mediterranean countries, the family is dominant. Religion is another big influence.
• Things may happen at a slower pace under the burning Mediterranean sun. Adjust to local time by taking a siesta in the heat of the day and taking an early evening stroll, if the port stop permits.
• In many Latin and Arab countries, people can be excitable. A lot of shouting and arm-waving does not necessarily mean someone is angry.
• Do dress stylishly to look the part in countries like France, Spain and Italy. Shell suits, T-shirts with slogans and string vests are not appropriate for an evening in Portofino or St-Tropez.

Business Hours and Holidays

These vary enormously. Christian countries (Spain, France, Italy, Croatia, Slovenia, Greece and Cyprus) celebrate Christmas and Easter (although Greek Orthodox Easter falls on different dates from Protestant/Catholic Easter). Muslim countries (mainly Bosnia, Turkey, Syria, Egypt, Libya, Tunisia and Morocco) observe the month of Ramadan (usually well outside the cruise season) and other Muslim holidays, for which dates vary. Business hours around the Mediterranean vary, but generally shops open 9am–1pm then 4–7 or 8pm, so don't plan shopping trips for an afternoon port stop. However, places that cater to tourists are increasingly staying open throughout the day. In principal resorts, shops will stay open fairly late in the evening and may open on Sunday. See individual countries for more details on hours and holidays.

Planning the Trip

Choosing a Cruise

Picking the right ship and itinerary is critical to the success of a cruise holiday. Don't assume all ships are the same, or all itineraries. A cruise might, for example, include several days at sea, or a port a day, with sailing only at night. Some ships overnight in certain ports for the nightlife, or for extended shore excursions. Others cram two ports into one day.

TYPES OF CRUISE

Just about any type of cruise is on offer in the Mediterranean. The mega-ships of Princess Cruises and Royal Caribbean offer the whole big-ship experience – Broadway shows, different dining options, lots of deck sports and a high proportion of balcony cabins. SeaDream Yacht Club and Seabourn are at the other end of the scale, providing a setting similar to a large, very luxurious, private yacht.

Star Clippers, Sea Cloud, Peter Deilmann's Lili Marleen and Windstar

Hot Tips for Cruisers

● If the "alternative dining" restaurants are full, turn up on spec, or have a quiet word with the maître d', who may be more flexible than the reservations clerk.
● If something is not visible in the dining room – marmalade, or HP sauce, for example – just ask for it. It may magically appear.
● If you're cruising in a family group, consider taking a two-bedroomed suite instead of two cabins.
● Look carefully at exactly what you get in a higher-grade cabin. Often, it's an almost identical cabin on a different deck.
● On a busy cruise, book spa treatments the minute you get on board. Days at sea and captain's dinner night always go first.
● Check to see if your cabin has a dvd or CD player, so you can bring your own music.

Cruises are the ones to choose for the romance of a sailing ship, whether it's a square rigger or a fully automated gin palace.

For the cost-conscious, Thomson, Airtours, Island Cruises and Ocean Village provide great cruise-and-stay offers and seven-night itineraries out of Mallorca.

Meanwhile, Costa Cruises, MSC and Festival have big, modern ships and a more international flavour than the British or US-run vessels. Ships belonging to P&O and Fred Olsen, on the other hand, will carry mainly Brits.

Cruising with Children

Some ships are more suitable than others for families. Generally speaking, the larger and newer the ship, the better the facilities. P&O (except *Adonia*, which is adults-only), Princess, NCL and Royal Caribbean are all excellent, with superb playrooms for all ages from tots to teenagers, and creative activity programmes. Cunard's QM2 and QE2 have nurseries staffed by Norland nannies. Celebrity and Holland America Line offer good childcare in peak season, while Ocean Village has the best facilities of the budget cruise lines. Costa and MSC's big new ships are also family-oriented, although the child carers may be Italian and the other children of varying nationalities.

It used to be the case that parents could not go ashore and leave their offspring in the children's club, but this has changed, with some ships providing day-long care. Exhausted parents of babies and toddlers should consider a ship with a night nursery, so they can dine alone while their children are cared for. But don't just plan to dump children in a playroom – one of the joys of cruising is that you can make short forays into interesting ports as a family and retire to the ship when it gets too hot.

Disabled Travellers

Cruising is an ideal form of travel for disabled people. All new ships are built with cabins suitable for wheelchair users, as well as lifts able to take wheelchairs and ramps at the doors, both on the ship and leading out to the deck. Lift buttons and signs are usually in Braille and some theatres are adapted with headphones for the hard of hearing. The key to success is to book early, as the wheelchair-adapted cabins go fast, and go over the arrangements for airport transfers and boarding the ship very thoroughly with your travel agent. Note that if the sea is choppy, the crew may not be able to get wheelchair users onto the ship's

tenders, for safety reasons, so choose a cruise with as few tender ports as possible (these are indicated in the brochure).

CABINS

The choice is between an inside cabin, outside cabin, balcony cabin or suite. Specific cabins can be pre-booked on all ships, although some cruise lines charge for this.

Booking an inside cabin, particularly on a lower deck, is the cheapest way to cruise. Balcony cabins are more and more commonplace and offer the luxury of private sunbathing. Some ships (such as Royal Caribbean's Radiance Class vessels) have extra-deep balconies at the aft end, which are better still.

When booking, bear in mind the direction in which the ship is travelling; from Genoa to Barcelona, for example, the views will all be on the starboard side. Anyone worried about seasickness should opt for a cabin on a lower deck, near the more stable centre of the ship. Ironically, the suites are always at the top and will get the roughest ride in choppy seas. They do, however, often come with butler service, dining privileges and red-carpet treatment.

CRUISE LINES

Airtours Sun Cruises, UK: Holiday House, Sandbrook Park, Sandbrook Way, Rochdale, Lancs OL11 1SA, tel: 0870 900 8639; www.airtours.co.uk.
Costa Cruises, US: World Trade Center, 80 SW Eighth Street, 27th Floor, Miami, FL 33130-3097, tel: 800-447 6877/305-358 7325. UK: 5 Gainsford Street, London SE1 2NE, tel: 020 7940 4499; www.costacruises.co.uk. Italian-run subsidiary of Carnival Corporation. Fleet of mixed-age including some large modern ships ideally suited to Mediterranean cruising. Passengers are of mixed nationalities (including many Italians) and are of all ages.
Crystal Cruises, US: 2049 Century Park East, Suite 1400, Los Angeles, CA 90067, tel: 800-804 1500. UK: Quadrant House, 80–82 Regent Street, London W1B 5JB, tel: 020 7287 9040; www.crystalcruises.com. Large, elegant ships sailing the world (Europe in summer) and offering a luxurious experience in a big-ship setting.
Cunard Line, US: 6100 Blue Lagoon Drive, Suite 400, Miami, FL 33126, tel: 800-728 6273. UK: Mountbatten House, Grosvenor Square, Southampton SO15 2BF, tel: 02380

716605; www.cunard.co.uk. Subsidiary of Carnival Corporation, with a fleet including the famous QE2 and the new *Queen Mary 2 (QM2)*. QM2 carries an international mix of passengers, particularly on its regular transatlantic runs. Cunard operates cruises from the UK and fly-cruises in the Mediterranean.

Fred Olsen Cruise Lines, Fred Olsen House, White House Road, Ipswich, Suffolk IP1 5LL, tel: 01473 742424; www.fredolsencruises.co.uk. Three ships appealing to a mainly British market. Comfortable rather than the height of luxury and with a very loyal following.

Hebridean Island Cruises, UK: Griffin House, Broughton Hall, Skipton, North Yorkshire BD23 3AN, tel: 01756 704704; email: reservations@hebridean.co.uk; www.hebridean.co.uk. Very small, deluxe ships sailing imaginative itineraries in Scotland and all over the Mediterranean.

Holland America Line, US: 300 Eliot Avenue West, Seattle, WA 98119, tel: 206-281 3535. UK: 77–79 Great Eastern Street, London EC2A 3HU, tel: 020 7940 4466; www.hollandamerica.com. Subsidiary of Carnival Corporation. Large fleet of elegant ships appealing mainly to US citizens in the older age bracket. Some wonderfully adventurous itineraries in Europe.

Island Cruises, UK: Olivier House, 18 Marine Parade, Brighton, East Sussex BN2 1TL, tel: 08707 500414; www.islandcruises.com. Large, informal ship sailing seven-night itineraries out of Palma, Mallorca.

Louis Cruise Line, 54-58 Evangoros Avenue, PO Box 1306, Nicosia, Cyprus; UK tel.0207 383 2882; www.louiscruises.com. Budget cruise line operating two- and three-night short breaks from Cyprus.

Mediterranean Shipping Cruises, US: 420 Fifth Avenue, New York, NY 10018, tel: 212-764 4800; www.msccruisesusa.com. UK: Walmar House, 296 Regent Street, London W1B 3AW, tel: 020 7637 2525; www.msccruises.co.uk. Italian-owned cruise line. Lively, value-for-money ships appealing to all ages and nationalities.

Norwegian Cruise Line, US: 7665 Corporate Center Drive, Miami, FL 33126, tel: 305-358 6670. UK: 1 Derry Street, London W8 5NN, tel: 0845 6588030; www.uk.ncl.com. Large, pioneer of Freestyle Cruising, with all ships offering an informal setting and a wide choice of dining options. Appeals mainly to US nationals, with a good mix of ages, including families.

Ocean Village, UK: Richmond House, Terminus Terrace, Southampton SO14 3PN, tel: 0845 4567888; www.oceanvillageholidays.co.uk. Modern, funky ship aimed at younger cruisers, sailing seven-night itineraries out of Palma. Subsidiary of P&O Cruises.

Orient Lines, UK: 1 Derry Street, Kensington, London W8 5NN, tel. 0845 658 8050; www.orientlines.com; US: 7665 Corporate Center Drive, Miami, FL 33126, tel: 0800 333-7300. Cultural cruises aimed at an international market on the popular and elegant Marco Polo.

P&O Cruises, US: c/o Princess Cruises, 24305 Town Center Drive, Santa Clarita, CA 91355-4999, tel: 800-252 0158 (California only); 800-421 0522, 213 553 1770. UK: Richmond House, Terminus Terrace, Southampton SO14 3PN, tel: 08453 555333; www.pocruises.com. British sister company of Princess Cruises. Large, modern ships appealing to a mainly British market. Particularly suited to families.

Princess Cruises, US: 10100 Santa Monica Blvd, 1800, Los Angeles, CA 90067. UK: Richmond House, Terminus Terrace, Southampton SO14 3PN, tel: 08453 555800; www.princesscruises.com. US arm of P&O. Large, luxurious, modern ships with broad appeal across all ages.

Royal Caribbean International/ Celebrity Cruises, US: 1050 Caribbean Way, Miami, FL 33132, tel: 800-327 6700; 305-539 6000. UK: Royal Caribbean House, Addlestone Road, Weybridge, Surrey KT15 2UE, tel: 0800 0182020 (Royal Caribbean); www.royalcaribbean.com; or 0800 0182525 (Celebrity); www.celebritycruises.com. Sister cruise lines, of which Celebrity is the more upmarket. Both operate a large, luxurious, modern fleet. RCI in

particular appeals to families and has some very well-equipped new ships sailing in Europe in the summer.

Royal Olympia Cruises, www.royal-olympic-cruises.com; US: One Rockefeller Plaza, New York, NY 10020. Good-value cruises from Piraeus, but at time of going to press the future of the company was uncertain.

Seabourn Cruise Line, US: 6100 Blue Lagoon Drive, Suite 400, Miami, FL 33126, tel: 305-463 3000. UK: Mountbatten House, Grosvenor Square, Southampton SO15 2BF, tel: 0800 0523841; www.seabourn.com. Elegant yacht-ships cruising small, chic Mediterranean islands and ports. All-inclusive and very upmarket.

SeaDream Yacht Club, US: 2601 South Bayshore Drive, Penthouse 1B, Coconut Grove, Florida 33133, tel: 800-707 4911 or 305-631 6100; email: info@seadreamyachtclub.com. European office: Smalvollveien 65, Post Office Box 50, Bryn N-0611 Oslo, Norway tel: 47 23 28 96 60; email: info-europe@seadreamyachtclub.com. 100-passenger luxury motor yachts; sophisticated but casual.

Seven Seas Cruises, US: Radisson Seven Seas Cruises, 600 Corporate Drive, Suite 410 Fort Lauderdale, Florida 33334, tel: 800-477 7500, www.rssc.com. UK: Suites 3 and 4, Canute Chambers, Canute Road, Southampton SO14 3AB, tel: 02380 682280; www.rssc.co.uk.

Silversea Cruises, US: 110 East Broward Blvd, Fort Lauderdale, FL 33301, tel: 800-722 9955. UK: 77/79 Great Eastern Street, London EC2A 3HU, tel: 0870 3337030; www.silversea.com. The ultimate in luxury; four elegant, all-inclusive ships with international appeal.

Star Clippers, US: 4101 Salzedo Avenue, Coral Gables, FL 33146, tel: 305-442 1611. UK: c/o Fred Olsen, Fred Olsen House, White House Road, Ipswich, Suffolk IP1 5LL, tel: 01473 292229; www.starclippers.com. Romantic sailing cruises on elegant clipper ships. International appeal.

Swan Hellenic, UK: Richmond House, Terminus Terrace, Southampton SO14 3PN, tel: 08453 555111 or 02380 531990; email: reservations@swanhellenic.com; www.swanhellenic.com. USA/Canada: 631 Commack Road, Suite 1A, Commack NY 11725, tel: 877-800 SWAN (toll-free) or 631-858 1263; email: swanhellenic@kainyc.com. Cultural cruises on board the smart, new *Minerva II*, which roams the world and spends summer in Europe.

Thomson Cruises, UK: Thomson Holidays, Greater London House, Hampstead Road, London, NW1 7SD tel: 0870 5502562; www.thomson.co.uk.

Taxes

The cost of port taxes will usually be included in the cruise fare, as will airport taxes.

Many European countries charge a version of Value Added Tax (VAT) This sales tax is usually included in the price (unlike some US states, where the tax is added as you pay). In some countries, like Spain, there are different levels of tax. Anyone living outside the EU is entitled to a tax refund on items bought in the EU; claim this at any port or airport where there is a Global Refund office (listed on www.globalrefund.com).

Seven-night cruise-and-stay holidays in the Mediterranean on a fleet of three popular and well-equipped ships.
Voyages of Discovery, UK: Lynnem House, 1 Victoria Way, Burgess Hill, West Sussex, RH15 9NF, tel: 01444 462140; www.voyagesofdiscovery.com. Affordable cultural cruising aimed at the British market.
Windstar Cruises, US: 300 Elliott Avenue West, Seattle, WA 98119, tel: 206-281 3535. UK: Carnival House, 5 Gainsford Street, London SE1 2NE, tel: 020 7940 4488; www.windstarcruises.com. Luxurious large yachts, which travel partly under sail and have a very glamorous appeal. Popular with honeymooners.

Booking from the US

Some European cruise holidays are sold as fly-cruises but it is also possible to buy "cruise only" and make separate flight arrangements. The main European gateways for cruise passengers are Barcelona, Rome, London, Lisbon, Athens and Istanbul. Book a cruise through an agent accredited by the Cruise Line International Association (CLIA), www.cruising.org.

Booking Agents in the US

Cruise Holidays has stores all over the USA and Canada, tel: 800-866 7245; www.cruiseholidays.com.
Cruise Planners has stores in Florida and California, tel: 866-418 5672; www.cruiseplannersforyou.com.
Liberty Travel has over 200 stores all over the East Coast, tel: 1-888-271 1584; www.libertytravel.com.
Cruise Store USA, tel: 800-462 6832; www.cruisestoreUSA.com.
Cruise.com claims to be the world's largest seller of cruises on the internet, tel: 888-333 3116; www.cruise.com.

Booking from the UK

There is a vast choice of Medittteranean cruises for people from the United Kingdom, some aimed directly at the UK market and packaged as fly-cruises and some operating from UK ports. Look for an agent which is affiliated to PSARA, the Passenger Shipping Association Retail Agent Scheme, www.psa-psara.org.

Booking Agents in the UK

Mundy Cruising, Quadrant House, 80–82 Regent Street, W1R 6JB, tel: 020 7734 4404; www.mundycruising.co.uk.
The Cruise People, 88 York Street, W1H 1DP, tel: 020 7723 2450; www.cruisepeople.co.uk.

Marion Owen Travel, 23 Portland Street, Hull, HU2 8JX, tel: 01482 212525
Cumbria Cruise Club, Andrews Court, Andrews Way, Barrow-in-Furness, LA14 2UD, tel: 0800 540540
Premier Travel, 10 Rose Crescent, Cambridge, CB2 3LL, tel: 01223 500007
Cruise Direct, 4 Buckingham Parade, The Broadway, Stanmore, HA7 4EB, tel: 020 8385 9000
Cruise Control, Units 9 & 10, Stanton Gate, 49 Mawney Road, Romford, RM7 7HL, tel: 0870 7000 4444; www.cruisecontrolcruises.co.uk.

Booking from Australia New Zealand

Most European cruises are sold with the air fare included. Both Australia and New Zealand have a good choice of specialist cruise agents; choose one that is a member of the International Cruise Council of Australasia, www.cruising.org.au.

Booking Agents in Aus/NZ

Harvey World Travel, Highpoint, Victoria, tel: 03 9317 4677; email: highpoint@harveyworld.com.au; also at 27 Belgrave Street, Manly, NSW, tel: 02 9976 2822; email: cruising.manly@harveyworld.com.au; www.ecruising.com.au; Suite 202, Level 2, 80 Clarence Street, Sydney NSW 2000, tel: 02 9249 6060
Worldwide Cruise Centre (in Brisbane, Gold Coast and Melbourne), tel: 1 300 889 777 (Brisbane), 1300 137 445 (Gold Coast), 1300 889 240 (Melbourne); www.cruisecentre.com.au.
Harvey World Travel, 63 Clyde Street, Browns Bay Auckland 1330, tel: 09 478 7118; www.harveyworld.co.nz.

When to Go

The Mediterranean/European cruise season starts in April and extends until early November. July and August are peak season and ports can be both hot and crowded. May/June and September are ideal for cooler weather and fewer crowds.

Very few ships operate year-round in the Mediterranean specifically; Costa, MSC, Thomson, Airtours Sun Cruises, Fred Olsen and P&O have ships in Europe year-round but they tend to spend the winter season in the Canary Islands.

What to Take

Study the itinerary carefully; it will tell you how many "formal" nights to expect. For these, the dress code is

black tie. "Informal" means cocktail dresses (lounge suit for men) and "casual" means smart resort clothes. Be aware that cruise lines which may have formal nights in, say, South America may drop this policy in the hot Mediterranean summer.

Also bring swimwear, walking shoes (for excursions), deck shoes, gym kit if you plan to work out, lots of sunblock, a sun hat, spare film/memory flash cards for your camera (expensive on board), binoculars, small umbrella, walking pole/collapsible shooting stick if you're less mobile; a day pack; seasickness remedies; and any regular medication you need, which the ship's doctor should NOT be expected to supply.

What NOT to Take

Masses of books – get them from the ship's library; a ghetto blaster; duty-free drink (it will be confiscated and stored for you on some cruises); unnecessary sharp objects or things that look like weapons (these may be confiscated).

Money and Costs

Theoretically, you don't have to spend any money once you've boarded your ship, although inevitably you will unless you are going to limit yourself to the bare essentials. You should budget for drinks and personal extras on board, shore excursions and spending money when in port. You can save money by eating a big breakfast, missing lunch ashore and feasting on afternoon tea back on board. You can also save by organising your own shore excursions, with a bit of careful planning.

Money Matters – What to Bring

Payment of your on-board account for all personal extras and excursions is best done by credit card (although you can pay cash if you lodge a deposit when you board). For shore visits, bring charge or credit cards for large purchases and a supply of euros (for Austria, Belgium, Finland, France, Germany, Greece, Ireland, Italy, Luxembourg, Netherlands, Portugal and Spain). Cashing travellers cheques is a pain when you are on a shore excursion or have limited time in port, although they are a secure way to keep your money. For countries outside the eurozone, you can change money on the ship (at a premium) or look for an ATM ashore. Most modern cruise terminals have one.

What is Included in the Price

All food; all entertainment; use of the gym and sports facilities (but not always all of them); transfers from the port (usually); port taxes; room service (sometimes); shuttle buses into town (sometimes); flights (usually); use of the ship's self-service laundry (usually); use of the ship's library; the captain's cocktail party (if there is one).

What is NOT included in the price

Alcoholic drinks (except on Silversea, Seabourn, SeaDream Yacht Club, Seven Seas Cruises and Hebridean Island Cruises); tips (unless stated); travel insurance; spa treatments; shore excursions (except on Hebridean Island Cruises and Swan Hellenic); medical care; internet access and telephone calls from the satellite phone. Some cruise lines also charge extra for the following: bridge visits; use of some sports equipment on board; "premium" exercise classes like yoga; mineral water in cabins; room service; tea and coffee; and shuttle buses. Most charge extra for dining in the "alternative" restaurants.

Passports and Visas

On a cruise, you give up your passport on boarding the ship and only collect it on the last day. Usually, cruise lines will obtain group visas for all passengers where appropriate and permits are handed out if people want to go ashore. Some countries require individuals to apply for visas, in which case the cruise line/travel agent will advise *(see also individual country listings in this section)*. Sometimes, cruise lines will not be able to obtain group visas for holders of certain passports, in which case it is the responsibility of the passenger to get their own visa before departure.

Getting Married

Because of legal issues, few ships' captains will conduct an actual wedding (although the captains of *Golden, Grand* and *Star Princess* are allowed to). But anybody bringing along a vicar, priest or rabbi can get married on a ship, either in port or at sea. Many cruise lines, including Holland America Line, Princess and P&O, have wedding packages and wedding co-ordinators and some vessels have wedding chapels.

An alternative is to marry ashore and honeymoon on a ship; or to marry and have a reception on the ship in port, and then sail off into the sunset on honeymoon. Many cruise lines also offer "renewal of vows" packages, which are increasingly popular.

Life on Board

Food and Drink

That you can eat round the clock on a cruise is no exaggeration, so eat in moderation to avoid being winched off as freight. Unless there is a "speciality" restaurant on board, all the food on a cruise is included in the price. Silversea, Seabourn, Hebridean Island, Radisson and SeaDream Yacht Club all include drinks as well (just the wine on Radisson).

Restaurants

All ships have a main dining room and many have speciality restaurants (Italian, Japanese, Mexican and Mediterranean being just some examples) where a small premium is usually charged for a different menu and more exclusive surroundings. Book these early, as reservations go quickly.

Some ships offer from two to four different dinner sittings in the dining room, while others have "open seating", meaning you eat when you like and sit where you like. All ships also offer a casual dining option, which is popular in the Mediterranean in summer if it permits dining alfresco on deck. Don't miss the themed buffets, which are often spectacular. Vegetarians, vegans and any other dietary requirements are usually well catered for. If in doubt, check with the cruise line.

Bars

Ships' bars can be fun, elegant and atmospheric, ranging from sophisticated martini bars and club-like cigar rooms to Irish theme pubs. Champagne bars are currently in vogue; the QM2 has one, as do some of the Royal Caribbean ships. All drinks bought in the bar can be signed for. Be aware that many ships will add an automatic "gratuity" of 15 percent.

Cafés

Most modern ships have cappuccino and espresso machines and the queues at the speciality coffee shops are testament to the fact that cruise-ship tea and coffee are generally awful. Many ships combine a coffee shop with internet terminals. More traditionally minded passengers may prefer afternoon tea, which on many ships is offered with white-glove

service, dainty cakes and sandwiches with the crusts cut off.

Room Service

Room service is usually included in the cost of the cruise, although some lower-budget cruise lines either charge for it or do not offer it. Service will range from the decadence of a five-star ship, where passengers can order filet migon and caviar in the middle of the night if they wish, to a more basic menu. Many ships, particularly those catering to British people, now have tea- and coffee-making facilities in the cabins.

Facilities

Ship designers are constantly pushing the limits of entertainment at sea. Modern ships may offer anything from ice skating to mini golf and a climbing wall up the funnel. Also expect basketball courts, nightclubs with rotating dance floors and, most recently, a planetarium (on QM2). On the other hand, a small ship may simply have one elegant bar and a library.

Banks

See Money and Costs previous page

Casinos

See box on page 343.

Gyms and Exercise Rooms

Most ships have a gym with modern equipment – sometimes more impressive than on-shore facilities. Most also run exercise classes. A premium is usually charged for popular classes such as yoga and pilates. Large ships usually have a jogging track on deck.

Spas

Spas at sea are now winning awards over land-based retreats. Many ships' spas are run by Steiner (which includes the Mandara brand), with a couple of exceptions, among them QM2's Canyon Ranch and the Judith Jackson concessions on Radisson Seven Seas' ships. Anything from hot-rock massage to massage for couples and "chakra balancing" is offered – at a price. Rates are adjusted to match the demographics of the passengers, so expect to pay a premium on an upmarket ship.

Cinema, TV and Video

All ships offer in-cabin TV, usually showing satellite channels, movies and the ship's own channels, be it shopping talks or televised lectures. Many ships have a cinema, too, showing first-run movies. Some also have video and DVD libraries, which are free to use.

Library

The ship's library is a great invention, providing a quiet retreat and an endless source of free reading material, from novels to atlases and guidebooks. Ships attracting an international audience may have books in German, French, Spanish and Italian as well as English.

Newspapers and Magazines

Most ships carry a selection of magazines in the library. "Newspapers" are provided by satellite link, condensed, printed out and delivered directly to cabins. This tradition continues, despite the fact that the internet and satellite TV make it much easier for passengers to keep up to date with world events.

Board Games and Video Games

Cruise ships usually carry a selection of board games; a tradition is to have a large jigsaw puzzle on display for general amusement. Many vessels have dedicated card rooms offering bridge sessions and tuition.

Telephone, Fax and Internet

Telephoning from a ship's satellite system is expensive. It is much cheaper to make calls from a land line in port, or even from a mobile phone with a roaming agreement – when the ship is at sea are usually out of range of mobile/cellphone transmitters. See individual country listings starting on page 345 for international codes. Internet access is offered on practically all ships, at varying prices, either per minute or per kilobyte. Cruise passengers are advised to set up a webmail account before leaving home. It is cheaper and more reliable than sending and receiving emails via the ship's system.

Swimming Pools and Hot Tubs

All ships offer at least one salt-water pool and a hot tub on deck; some have three or four pools, multiple hot tubs and water slides. Several vessels have a retractable roof over a second pool for cooler weather. The pool will be emptied when seas are rough.

Other Deck Facilities

Paddle tennis (using a slightly smaller tennis court than is usual) is hugely popular at sea. A paddle tennis court will usually double up as a volleyball/basketball court. Most ships offer deck quoits and shuffleboard, the traditional cruising games. Also look out for golf-driving nets and putting greens, jogging tracks, climbing walls and table tennis.

Watersports

Smaller ships may have a retractable watersports platform which is lowered for swimming, windsurfing, banana boat rides, water skiing and dinghy sailing. All the equipment is carried on board and is usually free of charge. Large ships may have arrangements with local hotels in the Mediterranean for the use of watersports equipment. Several vessels also carry a dive boat and their own scuba equipment.

EVENTS ON BOARD

Art Auctions

Don't expect to find any Grand Masters in the ship's art auction. While the auction itself may be fun, a lot of the art is tacky. Serious buyers should research galleries in the different ports of call instead.

Live Music

Ships nowadays offer everything from concert pianists to scantily clad female string quartets. Some have great tribute bands (Madonna, or the Beatles, for example), talented jazz musicians and excellent orchestras. Cruise ships today play a significant role in keeping music live.

"Las Vegas" Shows

Big "production" shows can be spellbinding at sea, with new ships having technical facilities superior to those of a London theatre. Big-name musicals, futuristic circus shows (including trapeze acts) and opera have all been staged on ships.

Talks and Lectures

Many ships carry guest lecturers who will speak on topics related to the cruising area, from marine biology to Moorish architecture. The lectures are free and are often broadcast on the ship's TV channel.

Religious Services

Interdenominational services are held on most cruise ships, conducted either by the captain or staff captain, or an on-board chaplain. Special Jewish charters will usually have a rabbi on board and some offer kosher food.

You can attend services in churches or mosques in port if you are dressed appropriately. Many Greek Orthodox churches and services are particularly beautiful, for example. Women and non-Muslim men will not expect to attend a service in a mosque. The local tourist board will have details of services in the area. Research these on-line before departure if possible.

Excursions

Shore excursions represent a major cost on any cruise, and an important source of income for the cruise line (apart from Swan Hellenic and Hebridean Island Cruises, which include shore excursions in their fares). Passengers are encouraged to book in advance, which can be done on-line with some cruise lines. Popular excursions do sell out, but don't feel pressurised to book everything before boarding the ship; a couple of days off may be welcome on an intensive Mediterranean itinerary.

A shore excursion will provide an overview of a new place, or greater detail on a specific site, like Pompeii, or Ephesus. It may be an opportunity to try a new sport, like kayaking or mountain biking, in a group. If you want to linger in a gallery, or dedicate the day to shopping or a long lunch, go it alone. Shore tours do have free time built in, but not much.

Going it Alone

There are numerous ways to get around in the Med, from walking to cycling, hiring a powerboat, car, taxi or moped for the day, taking ferry, local bus or train. Remember to bring a driving licence and photo ID for hiring any vehicle; note also that driving is on the right and drivers are often fairly aggressive.

Research the destination thoroughly before you arrive and take a good map. Always check that train, bus and ferry times coincide with the ship's arrival and departure (for

Casinos

Most modern cruise ships have a casino. On some, it is the hub of activity while on others it is tucked away discreetly. Some cruise lines, like Crystal, ply gamblers with free drinks and the casinos are lively late into the night.

The daytime gambling lessons offered by cruise lines are fun and very helpful; usually, ships' casinos are friendly and un-stuffy compared to those ashore, although they are governed by the same rules and etiquette. Just remember to set yourself a budget and to know when to quit.

Ships' casinos are closed when the ship is in port, but there are some fine casinos ashore around the Mediterranean for serious players, in places like Monaco, Cannes, Marbella and Palma. Take a passport to get in and dress appropriately.

example, the hydrofoil from Sorrento to Capri). Make reservations for particularly special lunch venues and check that important museums and galleries are open; many close for one day a week and most close for a couple of hours at lunchtime. Plan shopping trips to avoid the heat of the day and early-afternoon shop closures.

Joining forces with other passengers and hiring a minibus or a large taxi is often cost-effective, but establish the fare first.

Remember that it is your responsibility to get back to the ship on time and if you miss it, to catch up with it at the next port.

Health

Health Hazards

All cruise ships have a doctor and nurse on board (the exception being cargo ships or private yachts carrying fewer than 12 people, which are not required to have a doctor). Facilities vary from ship to ship but a doctor should be able to treat most ailments, including heart attacks and appendicitis. Seriously ill passengers may be stabilised until the ship arrives in port, or airlifted off. There will always be a fee for consulting the ship's doctor, although many ships hand out sea-sickness tablets free of charge. Passengers should, however, bring their own supplies of any medication they use, as the ship's doctor will not be able to provide it.

Norovirus (a common gastro-intestinal virus) occurs on cruise ships, as it does in hospitals and hotels. It can spread quickly. If you have diarrhoea, vomiting and fever, report to the ship's doctor immediately. Avoid the virus by using the antiseptic hand wipes that are handed out on board and by washing hands scrupulously.

There are few health risks in the Mediterranean, although a typhoid vaccination is recommended for some North African countries. Excesses of sun or alcohol, or contaminated water, are the most likely causes of illness. Wasp and jellyfish stings can be treated with over-the-counter remedies.

Sun Protection

It's all too easy to relax by the pool, lulled into a false sense of security by a cooling sea breeze. But the Mediterranean sun is very strong and the reflection of the sea can increase its intensity.

Bring a high-factor sunscreen and wear it whenever you go out. For starters, expose yourself for only brief periods, preferably in the morning or late afternoon when the sun's rays are less intense. As your tan builds, you can increase your sunning time and decrease your protection factor – though you will still need some sort of protection. Bring a brimmed hat, especially if you plan to do any extended hiking, walking, or playing in the midday sun.

Drinking Water

If you are prone to stomach upsets, it is best to avoid drinking tap water, although it is generally clean and perfectly safe. Bottled water is available everywhere.

Drinking water on cruise ships is heavily chlorinated and while safe, does not taste good to most people and also explains why cruise-ship tea and coffee can be so strange tasting. All ships provide bottled water, although many charge for it.

Insects

Mosquitoes are generally only a nuisance in port in the evening. To combat them, pack a plentiful supply of insect repellent. Wasps are common in July and August. Small scorpions may be encountered in rural areas, but they are pretty rare.

For a detailed description of every aspect of the cruising experience, plus money-saving tips and exhaustive reviews of more than 250 cruise ships, we recommend the *Berlitz Guide to Ocean Cruising and Cruise Ships* by Douglas Ward, published annually.

Tipping on Board

Tips are not usually included in the fare but do check; on Silversea, Hebridean Island Cruises, Airtours Sun Cruises and SeaDream Yacht Club, they are included. Elsewhere, it is expected that passengers tip their waiter, cabin steward and sundry others (who may not have played any role in serving you at all). A 15 percent "gratuity" is often added to all drinks purchases, particularly on ships for US passengers.

Tips may be added automatically to your on-board account. Some cruise lines place envelopes in the cabins on the final evening. There is no obligation to pay using either method if you are not happy with the service, although it helps all concerned if you take any complaints up with the hotel manager on board. Some people take a view that the staff are not paid very much and depend on tips; others prefer to reward only those who have helped them personally. Others still are of the opinion that they should

Diving

The Mediterranean cannot be compared to, say, the Caribbean or South Pacific when it comes to marine life. Some of the best scuba diving, though, is off the islands of Malta and Gozo (where the water is very deep and clear); the Aeolian Islands off Sicily; certain Greek islands, including Turkey's Turquoise Coast. A few cruises continue to the Red Sea, which offers spectacular diving.

Both BSAC and PADI qualifications are recognised by European dive schools. Some cruise lines offer basic training courses on board and some, including Star Clippers and SeaDream Yacht Club, carry their own diving equipment.

not be responsible for paying the crew's wages.

In addition to a tip, the biggest favour you can do for a ship's employee is to write a grateful letter to their manager.

Etiquette

If you are unhappy with your dining companions, ask the maître d' discreetly if you can be moved; plenty of people do, but you stand a much better chance if you do it on the first night.

If someone is hogging a sunlounger with unclaimed belongings, move them and claim the lounger for yourself, provided you are prepared to accept the same treatment.

Don't be shocked if fellow passengers ask how much you paid for your cruise. In today's competitive market, many people consider it a sport to shop around. You don't have to answer the question, of course.

If you are invited to dine with the captain, consider it an honour and reply immediately. Observe the dress code for the evening.

Most ships nowadays are non-smoking in public areas other than the cigar bar. This must be observed. If you hate smoking and the person in the next-door cabin puffs smoke over your balcony, there is not much you can do other than ask to be moved.

Bridge visits can sometimes be arranged. Ask politely and then wait for a note to be sent to your cabin. Some ships no longer allow bridge visits for security reasons.

Do not expect to befriend the crew and be invited to the crew bar. This is their private space – and they don't get much of it.

Practical Information by Country

The following pages contain essential travel information for each country covered in the guide, arranged in the same west to east order used in the Places section.

Notes: Airport information and lists of recommended hotels have only been included for "homeports" – those ports where cruises typically start or finish (i.e. where this information is of use to the traveller).

Portugal (inc. Madeira)

Fact File

Area 92,072 sq. km (33,549 sq. miles) including Madeira and the Azores.
Population 10.3 million.
Language Portuguese.
Religion predominantly Roman Catholic.
Time zone mainland Portugal and Madeira are on GMT (summer time GMT +1); the Azores are 1 hour behind the rest of Portugal.
Currency the euro (€).
Weights and measures metric.
Electricity 220 volts, two-pin plug.
International dialling code 351.

Getting Around

To/from Lisbon Airport

Lisbon airport is only 6 km (4 miles) from the city centre, a 15-minute drive (allow twice as long at rush hour). There is a helpful tourist information office in the main terminal. Taxis will take you to the city centre. All have meters and lists of charges for out-of-town journeys. Drivers are entitled to charge an excess for luggage over 30 kg (66 lb). Bus 91, the AeroBus airport shuttle, runs from the yellow bus stop outside the terminal every 20 minutes and takes about 20 minutes (7am–9pm) to the centre of

town, and can be quicker than a taxi when traffic is heavy. Tickets allow you a free day's travel on the city's trams and buses (though not the metro subway). The AeroBus shuttle also picks up passengers at selected hotels throughout Lisbon. If you are spending extra time in Lisbon, check with the tourist information office to see if your hotel is one of those designated for pick-ups.

By Hire Car

To rent a car in Portugal most agencies require you to be at least 21 years old and to have had a valid drivers' licence for a minimum of one year. An international licence is not necessary.

Drive on the right, giving priority to traffic on your left. Do not park within 18 metres (60 ft) of a road junction, 15 metres (50 ft) of a bus stop or within 3 metres (10 ft) of a tram or bus stop. Park facing the same direction as the moving traffic on your side of the road. Seatbelts are compulsory in both front and rear seats and children under 12 must travel in the back. Offences for this

EU Customs, Health and Currency

CUSTOMS REGULATIONS

The European Union states covered in this guide are Portugal, Spain, France, Italy, Malta, Greece and Cyprus (Malta and Cyprus joined the EU in May 2004). For all other countries, see individual listings.

In theory, there are no customs barriers for alcoholic drinks and tobacco when travelling between EU countries. However, there are still recommended allowances, which are shown below.

The following quantities can be exceeded, provided proof is shown that the goods bought are for personal consumption (for example, a family wedding) and not for resale.

Customs allowances for each person over 18 years of age are:
• 10 litres of spirits or liqueurs over 22 percent vol.
• 20 litres of fortified wine
• 90 litres of wine (of which no more than 60 litres may be sparkling wine)
• 200 cigars, or 400 cigarillos or 3,200 cigarettes or 1 kg tobacco
• 110 litres of beer
Non EU-visitors can bring in €7,600 in currency. Vistors over 17 years of age from a non-EU country (note that this applies to Andorra, which is outside the EU) are entitled to import the following articles duty-free: 200 cigarettes or 100 small cigars 250g of tobacco, 1 litre of spirits and 2 litres of wine, and 50g of perfume.

United States citizens should check duty-free allowances with the US Customs Department before departure, and on their return must complete the CBP Declaration Form 6059B.

Canadian travellers returning home must declare all goods acquired abroad. It is important to keep original receipts for possible

inspection. Personal exemptions available to Canadian residents returning from a trip abroad are $750-worth of duty-free goods, excluding alcohol and tobacco.

Upon returning to Australia, citizens can bring in 250 cigarettes or 250g of loose tobacco; and 1.125ml of alcohol.

EU HEALTH COVERAGE

Emergency treatment is given free, but this covers only immediate treatment. EU residents (including UK and Irish nationals) will be able to get some further free treatment, but must carry a form E111 to obtain it. E111 forms must be validated before you leave your home country. This can be carried out at any main post office.

It is always advisable to take out health/accident insurance to cover you for a health emergency while on a trip. Insurance will reimburse the cost of treatment or repatriation should the need arise.

THE EUROZONE

Most EU countries have used the euro (€) as their national currency since January 2002 (the exceptions are the UK, Sweden, Denmark, and new members including Malta and Cyprus). There are coins of 1, 2, 5, 10, 20 and 50 cents, plus 1 and 2 €, as well as notes of 5, 10, 20, 50, 100, 200 and 500 € (the latter two denominations rarely seen). Bills are unvarying throughout "euroland", but each of the member countries mints its own coins – which are again valid everywhere. The eurozone has made the tedious (and expensive) currency conversions of the typical Mediterranean cruise largely a thing of the past. On the negative side, the single currency has resulted in slightly higher prices in most places.

and other regulations are subject to heavy on-the-spot cash fines.

The *Yellow Pages* are full of car rental firms; look under *Automóveis Aluguer com e sem Condutor* (cars to hire, with or without driver).

Lisbon
Avis: Airport, tel: 21 843 5550; Gare do Oriente (main station), tel: 21 895 3915.
Europcar: Airport, tel: 21 353 5115; Gare do Oriente, tel: 21 894 6071.
Hertz: Airport, tel: 21 843 8660.
Porto
Avis: Airport, tel: 22 943 6900; Estacão Nacional, tel: 22 539 0274.
Europcar: Airport, tel: 22 948 2452; Estacão Nacional, tel: 22 941 0092.
Hertz: Airport, tel: 22 943 7690.
Algarve (Faro)
Avis: Airport, tel: 289 810 120.
Europcar: Airport, tel: 289 818 726; Av. de la República, tel: 289 823 778.
Hertz: Airport, tel: 289 818 248.
Madeira
Atlas: Av. do Infante 29, tel: 223 100.
Avis: Airport, tel: 524 392; Largo António Nobre 164, tel: 764 546.
Bravacar: Caminho do Amparo 2, tel: 764 400
Europcar: Airport, tel: 524 633
Hertz: Airport, tel: 523 040

By Taxi

In all Portugal's cities, taxis are plentiful and cheap. The great majority of them are cream-coloured, while older ones are black with green roofs. In the city, they charge a standard, metered fare, with no additions for extra passengers (they carry up to four people). Outside city limits, the driver may use the meter or charge a flat rate per kilometre, and is entitled to charge for the return fare (even if you don't take it). You should tip taxi drivers about 10 percent.

In Madeira, standard tariffs have been established for the main tourist destinations (e.g. Monte, the Botanical Gardens); these prices also include waiting times. Each taxi driver carries an official list, which should be consulted if misunderstandings arise. Tariffs for other destinations are at least partially negotiable.

Lisbon Public Transport

The metro is useful for travel in the central zone of Lisbon. The system is easy to use and very cheap. Lisbon has an extensive system of buses and trams *(eléctricos)*. Pre-World War I trams ply the smaller, steeper streets where buses are unable to navigate. Some of them are quite beautiful, inside and out; they are slower and cheaper than the buses and are a good way to see the city. The **Lisboa**

Public Holidays

1 January New Year's Day
February Shrove Tuesday
March/April Good Friday
25 April Anniversary of the Revolution (1974)
1 May Labour Day
10 June Portugal and Camões Day
May/June Corpus Christi
15 August Day of the Assumption
5 October Republic Day
1 November All Saints' Day
1 December Restoration of Independence
8 December Day of the Immaculate Conception
25 December Christmas Day

Card, on sale at tourist offices and elsewhere, give free travel and free or discounted museum entrance fees for 1–3 days.

Tickets and Passes

It is worth considering buying a 3-day or 7-day tourist pass, which gives unlimited access to public transport. If you have no pass, you pay a flat rate when you board, which works out more expensive. Less expensive are the prepaid *modulos* that you can buy in packs of 20 from kiosks. Don't board the bus without paying – if you are caught, the fine is steep.

Information kiosks scattered all over the city provide information and sell tickets and passes. Two of the most convenient kiosks are in Praça da Figueira, near the Rossio Station, and near Eduardo VII Park.

Madeira Public Transport

Bus services on Madeira are excellent, clean and inexpensive, though they are designed for the needs of commuters and so do not always run at times that are convenient for visitors. All buses depart from stands strung out along Avenida do Mar, stretching from the São Lourenço palace at the eastern end to the Monte cable-car station in the Zona Velha. This is the best place to catch buses because there are ticket booths with helpful staff right next to the bus stops. Some bus services pass through the hotel zone, however, so if you are spending an extra day or two here it is worth checking with your hotel concierge whether there is a bus stop nearby.

You must buy a ticket in advance if getting on at Avenida do Mar, but you can buy a ticket from the driver if you board elsewhere. Note that tickets bought on the bus are more expensive than those bought in advance from kiosks.

Entry Requirements and Customs

Entrance requirements are the same as for other European Union countries – *see box on page 345*. However, Madeira has separate duty-free status from Portugal and the rest of the EU. Thus, despite the demise of duty-free throughout the rest of the EU, the allowances for duty-free goods are (per person aged over 17): 1 litre of spirits or 2 litres of table wine and 2 litres of sparkling or fortified wine; 75g of perfume; 200 cigarettes, 100 cigarillos, 50 cigars or 250g of tobacco.

Money Matters

The euro (€) is the unit of currency (*see box on page 345*). While you may want to buy a small amount of euros before you leave home, you'll get a better exchange rate if you wait until you are in Portugal. Once you have bought euros, however, it may be costly to re-exchange them for foreign currency. The best policy is to change money as you require it.

The easiest way to obtain euros is to use your credit card (or debit card) in one of the numerous ATMs (Automatic Teller Machines), usually called *Multibanco*. Otherwise, money is best changed at banks, rather than at hotels or travel agencies; this works out cheaper than the commission paid on travellers' cheques.

Major credit cards can be used in most hotels, restaurants and shops, but check in advance to avoid embarrassment. Country restaurants and *pensãos* may only accept cash.

Tipping

A tip of 10 percent is sufficient in restaurants and for taxi drivers. Barbers and hairdressers expect to receive the same.

Opening Times

Most **shops** in Portugal (and Madeira) open for business Monday–Friday 9am–1pm, and 3–7pm. Most open Saturday 9am–1pm, and are closed Sunday and holidays. Some malls and supermarkets are open on Sunday and all day during the week. **Banks** open Monday–Friday 8.30am–3pm and are closed Saturday, Sunday and holidays. **Museums** usually open 10am–12.30pm and 2–5pm, and are generally closed on Monday.

Telecommunications

All **phones** are equipped for international calls and accept coins, phone cards or credit cards, the latter being by far the easiest way to make an international call.

A phone card can be bought at kiosks and many shops. Instructions for using the phone are written in Portuguese and English. You can also make calls (international and local) from post offices. Go to the window for a cabin assignment and pay when the call is finished. PT Comunicacãos is the national communication company. In Lisbon there is an office with phone booths and computers for using the **internet** at 68 Restauradores, open 8am–11pm. In Porto there is one at 61 Praça da Liberdade.

In Lisbon there is a phone office in the Rossio railway station, open daily 9am–11pm; in Porto, there is one in Praça da Liberdade (same hours). Many village stores and bars in Portugal have metered telephones. Phone first, pay later, but be prepared to pay more than the rate for call box or post office calls. As elsewhere, calls made from hotels are higher still.

For US phone credit card holders, the major access numbers are:
AT&T: tel: 800 800 128.
MCI: tel: 800 800 123.
Sprint: tel: 800 800 187.

Emergency Numbers

Fire, Ambulance and Police: 112
Lost property: Lisbon tel: 21 853 5403; Funchal tel: 208 200.

Mobile Phones

Mobile phones with reciprocal GSM network arrangements will function throughout most of the country. Alternatively, the three national cellular networks (Telecel, TSM and Optimus) have short-term rental facilities at the main airports.

Security and Crime

Portugal has a well-deserved reputation for non-violence. It remains one of the few developed countries where you can both feel and be safe when walking almost anywhere at any time of day or night. This is changing in one or two of the larger cities, though, and petty theft is becoming a problem in some of the more run-down areas of Lisbon and Porto, and close to some of the larger shopping centres. Foreign-registered cars or cars obviously rented may be targets for thieves if left unattended in out-of-the-way locations.

Lisbon Hotels

Avenida Palace
Rua 1º de Dezembro
Tel: 213 460 151
Fax: 213 422 884
A grand 19th-century building, smack in the old town centre, between the Rossio and Praça dos Restauradores. €€€€

Meridien Park Atlantic Hotel
Rua Castilho 149
Tel: 213 818 700
Fax: 213 890 500
Elegant. Overlooking the park. €€€€

Pálacio Belmonte
Páteo Dom Fradique
Tel: 218 862 582
Fax: 218 862 592
A place for a special treat: beautiful bedrooms and enormous suites have been created in this 15th-century palace beneath the castle. The black marble pool is divine. €€€€

Pensão York House
Rua Janelas Verdes 32
Tel: 213 962 435
Fax: 213 972 793
In a class by itself, with comfort and charm combined. In an interesting neighbourhood, about 15 minutes by bus from the Rossio. Reserve well in advance. The annexe is down the street at number 47. €€€€

Albergaria Senhora do Monte
Calçada do Monte 39
Tel: 218 866 002
Fax: 218 877 783
Beautiful views overlooking São Jorge castle, Alfama and down to the Tejo River. €€€€

As Janelas Verdes
Rua de las Janales Verdes 37
Tel: 233 968 143
Fax: 213 968 144
Next to the Museum of Ancient Art, this noble mansion belonged to an 18th-century writer. Beautifully furnished, some rooms with river views. €€€

Hotel Botânico
Rue da Mãe d'Agua 16–20
Tel: 213 420 392
Fax: 213 420 125
Between the Bairro Alto and the Avenida da Liberdade; pleasant and comfortable. €€€

Solar do Castelo
Rua das Cozinhas 2, Castelo
Tel: 218 870 909
Fax: 218 870 907
In an 18th-century mansion inside the castle walls, with a contemporary makeover, this is a romantic place to stay. €€€€

VIP Eden Aparthotel
Praça dos Restauradores 24
Tel: 213 216 600
Fax: 213 216 666
The central Art Deco Eden Theatre

Hotel Prices

Price categories are based on the cost of a double room for one night in high season.
€€€€ = above €200
€€€ = €120–200
€€ = €60–120
€ = up to €60

has been beautifully converted into a hotel with one-bedroom and studio apartments. A wonderful rooftop pool with views over the city. €€€

Fluorescente Residencial
Rua das Portas de Santo Antão 99
Tel: 213 426 609
Fax: 213 427 733
Tiled hallways and bright, clean rooms, some with full-length baths. Very centrally located in a street of restaurants, near Praça dos Restauradores. €€

Residencial Alegria
Praça da Alegria, 12
Tel: 213 220 670
Fax: 213 478 070
A small family-run hotel just off Avenida do Liberdade. €€

Residencial Dom João
Rua José Estêvão, 43
Tel: 213 144 171
Fax: 213 524 569
In a quiet residential neighbourhood, slightly off the beaten track, but only a 15-minute walk to the central Praça Marquês de Pombal. €€

Roma Residencial
Travessa da Glória 22-A
Tel/Fax: 213 524 569
Has many of the amenities of a hotel, including private bath and TV in every room. In the heart of Baixa. €

Morocco

Area 710,850 sq. km (274,461 sq. miles), including the Western Sahara.
Population 29 million.
Language Arabic, Berber and French
Religion Muslim, with a tiny percentage of Jews and Christians.
Time zone GMT throughout the year.
Currency dirham (dh).
Weights & measures metric.
Electricity 220V/50Hz AC is standard, but older installations of 110V can still be found; check before plugging in. Sockets and plugs are of the continental European type, with two round pins.
International dialling code 212.

Getting Around

By Hire Car

The major international hire companies are all represented in Morocco and it is possible to make arrangements to pick up a vehicle at any of the airports. In cities there are always local companies who will undercut the rates of the major companies. Drivers must be over 21, and be fully insured against claims by third parties. The insurance is automatically included on hiring a car. Your own national licence is valid, but it does no harm to carry an international driving permit as well (it has French and Arabic translations), available from motoring organisations. Major roads are well surfaced, minor ones good with lapses (some treacherous potholes) and mountain roads often not as bad as you'll have been led to expect.

Agadir
Europcar: tel: (048) 84 02 03.
Hertz: tel: (048) 84 09 39.

Casablanca
Avis: tel: (022) 29 11 35.
Hertz: tel: (022) 29 44 03.

Tangier
Avis: tel: (039) 93 30 31.
Budget: tel: (039) 93 79 94.
Europcar: tel: (039) 94 19 38.
Hertz: tel: (039) 93 33 22.

Public Holidays

Secular holidays
1 January New Year's Day
11 January Independence Manifesto Day
1 May Labour Day
30 July Feast of the Throne
14 August Reunification Day
20 August King's and People's Revolution Day
6 November Anniversary of the Green March
18 November Independence Day

Religious holidays (these fall on different dates each year)
A'd es-Seghir, "Little Feast", the end of the month of Ramadan
A'd el-Kebir "Great Feast", commemorating the sacrifice of Abraham
Moharem Muslim New Year
Mouloud Birthday of the Prophet Mohammed
Ramadan occupies the four weeks preceding A'd es-Seghir.

By Taxi

Petits taxis are small cars that operate as city taxis for short trips within town. They seat a maximum of three passengers. They can be hailed in the street or picked up at a rank, and in the larger cities can be ordered by telephone. They have meters, but as the drivers sometimes forget to switch these on for foreigners you should negotiate the fare before getting in. Fares are increased by 50 percent after dark, but are still cheap by European standards.

Grands taxis are a faster and slightly more comfortable alternative to the bus for shorter journeys between towns. They are usually large Mercedes Benz that shuttle back and forth along a set route; in most cases six passengers are squeezed in. There are no fixed departure times; the taxi departs when all the seats are full. To find a place, you simply turn up at the "terminal" (the tourist office or your cruise-ship staff will tell you where this is; it is often next to the main bus station) and ask the drivers. Fares are per person for a full car; ask other passengers (or check onboard) what the standard fare is if you fear being overcharged. The cost should work out only slightly more than the bus fare.

Entry Requirements

Citizens of the UK, Republic of Ireland, US, Canada, Australia and New Zealand need only a full passport. Visas are not required for stays of less than 90 days. (Visa regulations

change from time to time, however, and should be confirmed through your travel agent or cruise line.)

Customs Regulations

When arriving in Morocco and upon leaving, restrictions for citizens of most countries are 200 cigarettes per person and one or two litres of wine. You can take as much foreign currency as you like into or out of the country, but amounts in excess of the equivalent of 15,000 dirhams must be declared on entry. It is illegal to import or export Moroccan dirhams.

Money Matters

The unit of currency is the dirham (dh), which is divided into 100 centimes. Centimes are occasionally referred to as francs. The exchange rate is controlled by the government, so there's no point shopping for the best rate – they're all the same. Recent exchange rates have hovered around 15Dh to £1 or 10Dh to $1/€1.

Banks and Currency Exchange

The easiest banks to deal with are the Bank Al-Maghrib, the BMCE and the Société Générale Marocaine de Banques. As the exchange process can entail queuing twice (first to obtain the paperwork and then to pick up the cash), changing money can prove to be a time-consuming business. In the more popular tourist resorts such as Tangier, Marrakesh and Agadir there are faster exchange booths that open independently of the banks; they're often open 8am–8pm, including weekends.

Travellers' Cheques

These are generally accepted at the banks listed above, though smaller

Tipping

It is customary to offer a tip *(pourboire)* for services rendered. A couple of dirhams is the norm for café waiters, porters, parking attendants, petrol station attendants, and the attendants at monuments and museums *(gardiens)*, and you should give restaurant waiters 5dh on top of any service charge. Porters at airports and ferry terminals usually charge per piece of luggage. If a taxi driver uses his meter, it is customary to tip around 10–15 percent of the fare; if you agree on a price beforehand, nothing extra will be expected.

branches may refuse to cash them.
You will need your passport and
occasionally the purchase receipts
too; a small commission is charged
on each cheque. Exchange offices at
airports and ferry terminals are
notorious for being closed or "out of
money". However, you can exchange
cash easily in most hotels and in
some tourist shops.

Credit Cards

Major credit and charge cards are
accepted in the more upmarket hotels
(three-star and above) and restaurants
in the larger cities, by tourist shops, car-
rental firms and larger petrol stations.

ATM Machines

There are an inceasing number of
ATMs in all the main towns. BMCE
banks have internationally connected
ATM machines at Place des Nations
Unies in Casablanca, and on Rue Bab
Agnaou, near Djemaa el Fna in
Marrakesh – look for the Cirrus-NYCE
logo. The rate of exchange is better
than for cash or travellers' cheques.

Opening Times

Banks open Monday–Friday
8.30–11.30am (2pm in summer) and
3–4.30pm.
Currency exchange desks usually
open 8am–8pm daily in popular
resorts like Tangier, Agadir and
Marrakesh.
Museums open 8.30am–12.30pm
and 2.30–6pm; often closed Tuesday.
Post offices open Monday–Friday
8.30am–noon and 2.30–6.30pm.
Shops open Monday–Saturday
8.30am–noon and 2.30–6.30pm.

Telecommunications

Domestic and international telephone
calls can be made from public
telephones in the main post office, or
from phone boxes on the street
(cabines), which take 1 and 5Dh coins
or phone cards, available from post
offices and some grocery stores.
Telephone boutiques (rooms with pay
phones) are found all over the place.
　To make an international call, dial
00 and wait for a second tone, then
dial the number. To make a reverse-
charge (collect) call, dial 12 for the
operator, and ask to be connected to
an operator in your home country.

Security and Crime

Morocco is a safe country, and
although many tourists may feel
uncomfortable about being
approached by *faux* guides and
hustlers, this problem has lessened

Emergency Numbers

Police: 19
Ambulance: 15
Fire: 15

since police began to clamp down.
Most Moroccans, especially
shopkeepers, are extremely helpful in
giving directions
　As in most countries, pickpockets
are the most serious problem;
travellers should keep wallets and
identification in deep, securely
fastened pockets or money-belts. Do
not leave valuables in your hotel room
or a parked car.
　Foreign women travelling in
Morocco are sometimes subject to
harassment from local men. A woman
accompanied by a man is less likely to
attract unwanted attention but is not
immune. Having said all this, the
majority of Moroccans are courteous
and friendly, and will show you
genuine hospitality.
　The way you dress is all-important;
shorts and a halter top, for example,
are not a good idea (this does not
apply to resorts like Agadir, where
beachwear is the norm, nor to
downtown Casablanca and Rabat).
The best strategy is to dress modestly
in trousers or below-the-knee skirt and
a loose-fitting top with sleeves.

Spain (inc. Canary Isles)

Fact File

Area 504,880 sq. km (194,885 sq.
miles).
Population 41 million.
Language Spanish (Castilian), plus
Catalan, Basque and Galician.
Religion predominantly Roman
Catholic.
Time zone GMT +1 hour (summer), +2
hours (winter), except for Canary
Islands which are on GMT in winter and
GMT +1 hour in summer.
Currency the euro (€).
Weights and measures metric.
Electricity 220 volts.
International dialling code 34.

Getting Around

To/from Barcelona Airport

Barcelona airport, El Prat (tel: 93-298
3838), 12 km (7 miles) south of the
city, is easily accessible by train or
bus. A smooth, efficient bus service,
the Aerobús, runs every 15 minutes
between the airport and Plaça de
Catalunya, and vice versa, stopping at
Sants station and other strategic
places en route. It takes about 35
minutes. There are also trains to
Sants and Plaça de Catalunya every
30 minutes, and the journey takes
about 20 minutes.

To/from Palma Airport

Palma de Mallorca's massive Son
Sant Joan Airport is 11 km (7 miles)
from the city centre. Taxis and regular
buses link the airport with Palma, a
15- to 20-minute trip. Official taxi
fares to all parts of the island are
posted by the airport exit doors. A bus
service operates to Plaça de Espanya
(near Palma's railway and bus
stations) every 15 minutes from
6am–9pm, then every 30 minutes
until 1am.

By Hire Car

Foreign motorists in Spain must have
either an international driving licence
or a valid licence from their country of
origin. Third-party insurance is
included in the price of a hire car but

Public Holidays

There are so many holidays, what with national and local fiestas, that it is said there is no one week in the whole year when all of Spain is working.
National holidays:
1 January New Year's Day
6 January Epiphany
March/April Good Friday
1 May Labour Day
15 August Assumption
12 October Columbus Day or *Día de la Hispanidad*
1 November All Saints' Day
6 December Constitution Day
8 December Immaculate Conception
25 December Christmas Day.

Each town is also entitled to two local holidays in honour of its patron saint.

it may be worth paying a little extra for "all risks" insurance so you are not liable for any dents or scratches.

Spain has greatly expanded its motorway network since the mid-1990s. **Tolls** are payable on some motorways *(autopistas)*, which have rest areas, bars and service stations. Other motorways *(autovías)* are toll-free. Roadside telephones are placed at convenient intervals for assistance in case of emergency or breakdown.

The **speed limit** is 120 kph (75 mph) on motorways, 100 kph (60 mph) on all other roads and 60 kph (35 mph) going through cities and towns.

Seatbelts must be worn by the driver and all passengers. Your hire car should be equipped with a spare set of headlight and rear-light bulbs or you could face a penalty fine.
A few useful care hire agency phone numbers are:

Alicante
Avis: Airport, tel: 965 682 779.
Europcar: Airport, tel: 965 682 770.
Barcelona
Avis: Airport, tel: 932 983 600; World Trade Center, Moll De Barcelona, tel: 932 302 028.
Europcar: Airport, tel: 932 983 300; Gran Via de les Corts Catalanes 680, tel: 933 020 543; Estación de Sants, tel: 934 914 822.
Hertz: Airport, tel: 932 983 638.
Cádiz
Avis: Puerto De Santa María, tel: 956 861 021.
Europcar: Estación RENFE (railway station), Plaza de Sevilla, tel: 956 280 507.

Málaga
Avis: Airport, tel: 952 048 483/952 224 949.
Hertz: Airport, tel: 952 233 086.
Europcar: Airport, tel: 952 048 518.
Palma de Mallorca
Avis: Puerto de Palma, Terminal 2, tel: 971 730 735; Paseo Marítimo 16, tel: 971 286 233.
Hertz: Airport, tel: 971 789 670.
Canary Islands
Tenerife (central no): **CICAR** (Canary Islands Car), tel: 928 822 900.
Gran Canaria: **Avis**: Airport, tel: 928 579 578.
Europcar: tel: 928 574 244.
Hertz: tel: 928 579 577.

By Taxi

There are prominently marked taxi ranks in city centres and fares are very reasonable – there are usually fixed prices displayed on a board at the main taxi ranks, giving the fares to the most popular destinations. If in doubt about the fare, ask the driver before you set off. Taxis display a green light in the front windscreen indicating "libre" when available. A 10 percent tip is usual, though in no way required or expected.

Barcelona Public Transport

Barcelona has an excellent **metro** system. Trains run from 5–12am during the week and until 2am at weekends and holidays. A multi-trip ticket *(tarjeta multi-viaje T-10)* allows you 10 journeys and is much cheaper than buying single tickets.

Barcelona's **bus** timetable is not easy to understand, but once you have got used to the system, it will save a number of long trips on foot from the metro stations – and it's fun to cross the city overground, at least outside rush hour.

Bus No. 100 is a tourist service, from Easter to January. Two bus routes (Ruta Nord and Ruta Sud) start at Plaça de Catalunya and make a two-hour trip via the main sights. You can interrupt your journey at any point.

Tipping

Service is not usually included in bars and restaurants, so it is customary to leave the spare change in the dish at a bar. In a restaurant, 10 percent of the bill is appropriate, unless you're charged for service in which case the bill will be marked *servicio incluído*.

A €0.20 tip is fine for an average taxi ride, or for a hairdresser; and public toilet attendants expect around €0.10–0.20 per person.

Entry Requirements and Customs

As for other EU countries – *see box on page 345*.

Money Matters

The Spanish currency is the euro (€) (*see box on page 345*). ATMs are easily found and are the most convenient way of accessing cash. Best rates for travellers' cheques and foreign currency are obtained at banks but you can also change money in cities at currency exchange shops, *casas de cambio*, hotels (where the rates are lower), major department stores and shops frequented by tourists.

Opening Times

Bank hours vary slightly from one bank to another. Most are open Monday–Friday 8.30am–2.30pm, and some are open Saturday until 1pm, though not usually between June and September. All are closed on Sunday and holidays and some on Thursday afternoon

Shops are open Monday–Friday 9.30 or 10am–1.30 or 2pm and then reopen again in the afternoon from 4.30 or 5 until 8pm, or a little later in summer. Many close on Saturday afternoon in summer and all day Sunday. However, major department stores and large supermarkets and many shops in tourist areas and city centres are open without interruption six days a week, 10am–9pm, and frequently on Sunday. *Panaderías* (bakeries) are open every morning, including Sunday.

Telecommunications

All telephone numbers in Spain begin with their respective regional code which must be dialled for both local and international calls. Coin- and card- operated telephone booths are plentiful. Wait for the tone, deposit a coin and dial the number. It is possible to place a **long-distance call** by depositing several coins at once. Most bars have coin-operated or meter phones available for public use. You can also purchase phone cards of various values at any tobacconist.

For **overseas calls**, it's probably better to go to privately run telephone outlets where you can talk first and pay later and not worry about having enough coins. (Although it is convenient to ring from a hotel room you will be charged much more than you would on a public phone – at least

Emergency Numbers

National police: 091
Local police: 092
Medical emergencies: 061
Fire brigade: 085

16 percent VAT will be added to the cost of your calls.)

To make a direct overseas call, dial 00 and then the country and city code without the initial 0. It is cheaper to call before 8am and after 10pm.

There are no additional discounts at weekends. Retevision, an alternative company to Telefónica, has started functioning in Spain. If the hotel is registered with them, you need to dial 050 00 plus the country and city codes to call abroad.

Security and Crime

Spain's crime rate has caught up with that of other European countries. Be on your guard against purse-snatchers and pickpockets in markets and other crowded places. The rules are the ones you should follow anywhere. Don't leave valuables unattended, don't take them to the beach or leave them visible in a car. Make use of hotel safe-boxes where possible. Don't carry large sums of money or wear expensive jewellery, and keep hold of your camera. Be especially careful when getting money from automatic cash machines.

Barcelona Hotels

It is advisable to book well in advance, especially during peak periods. Increasingly popular is the idea of B&B or apartment renting. A well-respected agency is BCN Rooms, tel: 93-226 5467, fax: 93-226 2269; www.bcnrooms.com
Hotels are listed alphabtically in order of price category.

Comtes de Barcelona
Passeig de Gràcia 75
Tel: 934 674 780
Fax: 934 674785
Top-of-the-range hotel in a converted *Modernista* mansion in the elegant Eixample quarter. €€€€

AC Front Marítim
Passeig de Gràcia i Fària 69
Tel: 933 034 440
Fax: 933 034 441.
One of the new wave of hotels near Diagonal Mar, HQ of Forum 2004. Ask for a room with a sea view. €€€.

Colón
Avinguda Catedral 7
Tel: 933 011 404
Fax: 933 172 915
In the Gothic quarter, a comfortable

classic, though the cathedral bells may keep you awake. Front rooms have a view. €€€

Banys Orientals
Argenteria 37
Tel: 932 688 460
Fax: 932 688 461
Very good value for such a stylish new hotel in the vicinity of Santa María del Mar. €€

Cuatro Naciones
La Rambla 40
Tel: 933 173 624
Fax: 933 026 985
Long-established hotel right at the heart of things. Good value, although somewhat noisy at night. €€

Hotel España
Sant Pau 9 and 11,
Tel: 933 181 758
Fax: 933 171 134
Though the bedrooms are plain, the public rooms have outstanding *Modernista* work by Domènech i Montaner. Just off La Rambla. €€

Hotel Gran Via
Gran Via de les Corts
Catalanes 642
Tel: 933 181 900
Fax: 933 189 997
Very good location near Passeig de Gràcia, with a brocaded, Regency feel and a charming, individual personality. €€

There are lots of inexpensive *pensiones* and hotels on the roads leading off both sides of the Rambla, and they are generally more seedy towards the port. Near Plaça de Catalunya at the top there are 1- and 3-star hotels on Carrer de Santa Anna, including the **Cortes**, tel: 933 179 112, fax: 934 126 608; and the **Nouvel**, tel: 933 018 274, fax: 933 018 370. Further down off to the right on Carrer del Carme, there are several, including the **Carmen**, tel: 933 171 076; **Aneto**, tel: 933 019 989, fax: 933 019 862; and **Selecta**, tel: 933 014 484. The **Peninsula** on Sant Pau is good value, with a delightful inner courtyard, tel: 933 023 138. The **Sant Agustí**, Plaça Sant Agustí 3, tel: 933 181 658, fax: 933 172 928, is pleasantly situated in a quiet square behind the market; on the opposite side of La Rambla overlooking two attractive squares is the very popular (book early) **Hotel Jardí**, Plaça Josep Oriol 1, tel: 933 015 900.

Palma Hotels

Palacio Ca Sa Galesa
Miramar 8
Tel: 971 715 400
Fax: 971 721 579
In a grand 17th-century palace, this tiny

hotel has an indoor pool, Jacuzzi and sauna. Wheelchair access. €€€€
Sa Font
Carrer Apuntadores 38
Tel: 971 712 277
Fax: 971 712 618
Designer chic in a 16th-century building. Business-meeting facilities. €€€€
Saratoga
Passeig de Mallorca, 6
Tel: 971 727 240
Great location close to the heart of the city, with spacious rooms and comprehensive facilities. €€€€
Convent de la Missió
Carrer de la Missió 7
Tel: 971 227 347
New in 2003, this stylish hotel, in a converted 17th-century convent in the old quarter, has light, airy rooms, roof terrace, sauna and an excellent restaurant. €€€
Costa Azul
Passeig Marítim, 7
Tel: 971 731 940
An old favourite with families and business travellers over the years. Right on the harbour front. €€€
San Lorenzo
San Lorenzo, 14
Tel: 971 728 200
Fax: 971 711 901
In a 17th-century house in a lively section of town. Just six rooms, all individually decorated. Small swimming pool. Book well in advance. €€€
Almudaina
Avinguda Jaume III 9
Tel: 971 727 340
Fax: 971 722 599
Comfortable and moderately priced, with obliging staff, this central hotel is on Palma's foremost shopping street. Rooms on upper floors have magnificent views over the city. €€
Hotel Born
Carrer Sant Jaume, 3
Tel: 971 712 942
Fax: 971 718 618
In a restored 16th-century palace, in the heart of the city, with a beautiful courtyard under Romanesque arches. Very good value for money. Reserve well in advance. €€
Apuntadores
Carrer Apuntadors 8
Tel: 971 713 491
Cheerful, English-owned hostel with downstairs café in the busy restaurant quarter. Shared bathrooms. €

Hotel Prices

For a standard double room
€€€€ = Over €180
€€€ = €120–180
€€ = €60–120
€ = Under €60

Hotel Prices (Spain)

For a standard double room
€€€€ = Over €180
€€€ = €120–180
€€ = €60–120
€ = Under €60

Outside Palma

Hotel Formentor
Playa de Formentor
Tel: 971 899 100
Fax: 971 865 155
Overlooking the beach, this peaceful, traditional hotel is family run and exclusive. Surrounded by pine trees and gardens. €€€€

L'Hermitage
Carretera de Alaró a Bunyola
Tel: 971 180 303
In a converted 17th-century mansion a few kilometers east of the village of Orient, this fine hotel is set at the foot of the mountains in a beautiful valley. Excellent restaurant and marvellous exotic gardens. Closed Dec–Jan. €€€€

Bon Sol
Passeig de Illetes, 30, Illetes
Tel: 971 402 111
Fax: 971 402 559
Beautiful location surrounded by a subtropical garden, this well-run hotel is handy for Palma yet supremely relaxing. €€€€

Es Molí
Carretera Valldemossa, Deià
Tel: 971 639 000
Fax: 971 639 333
Traditional luxury hotel, in a manor house surrounded by lush vegetation and with a spring-fed pool. €€€€

Mar i Vent
Carrer Major, 49, Banyalbufar
Tel: 971 618 000
Fax: 971 618 201
Attractive hotel with sea views and a rooftop swimming pool. Closed Dec–Jan. €€€

S'Hotel d'es Puig
Es Puig 4
Deià
Tel: 971 639 409
Fax: 971 639 210
Tucked away on the stone streets of Deià, this delightful little hotel has airy rooms, a serve-yourself bar, a small pool and a relaxed and friendly atmosphere. €€

Brismar
Almirante Riera Alemany 6
Port d'Andratx
Tel: 971 671 600
Fax: 971 671 183
This comfortable and simple seafront hotel is a bargain given the coveted location. Ask for a room with a harbour view, although these are the noisiest. Has a good family-style restaurant. Wheelchair access. €€

France (inc. Corsica)

Fact File

Area 543,965 sq. km (210,026 sq. miles).
Population around 60 million.
Language French, but regional languages still exist. In Corsica, around a quarter of the population regard themselves as fluent in Corsican – a language closer to Italian than French.
Time zone GMT +1 (GMT +2 in summer). Note that France uses the 24-hour clock.
Currency euro (€).
Electricity generally 220/230 volts, but still 110 in a few areas. Visitors from the US will need a transformer for shavers, hairdryers and other equipment; visitors from the UK just need an adaptor plug.
Weights & measures France uses metric for all weights and measures, although old-fashioned terms such as livre (about 1lb or 500g) are still used by some shopkeepers.
International dialling code 33. The area code for Corsica is 495 (from elsewhere in France: 0495).

Getting Around

To/from Nice Airport

Nice-Côte d'Azur Airport is 7 km (4 miles) from the city centre. Bus services connect the airport with Nice city centre and with other main towns along the Mediterranean coast. A taxi to central Nice takes 15–20 minutes and is expensive (typically €30 or more).

By Hire Car

Hiring a car is an expensive business in France, partly because of the high tax rate of 33 percent on luxury items. Weekly rates are often better than daily hire and it can be cheaper to arrange before leaving for France. Major car hire companies are listed below:
Ada Central: tel: 01 55 46 19 99
Avis: tel: 01 55 38 68 60
Budget: tel: 08 00 10 00 01
Europcar: tel: 08 03 35 23 52
Hertz: tel: 01 39 38 38 38
Rent-a-Ca: tel: 08 36 69 46 95

Corsica

ACL Rent-a-Car: tel: 04 95 51 34 45,
Avis: tel: 04 95 23 56 90
Budget: tel: 04 95 35 05 04,
Europcar: tel: 04 95 30 09 50
Hertz: tel: 04 95 23 57 04

Roads to and around the main Riviera resorts get completely choked up during July and August. Many of the "D" roads that lead up into the mountains are narrow and winding and they too become clogged during the summer. In most towns parking meters have generally been replaced by horodateurs, pay-and-display machines, which either take coins or cards (available from tobacconists). If you are using the east–west autoroutes for short journeys along the French Riviera, try to keep a supply of small change to hand for the motorway tolls.

Drivers who exceed speed limits or drive negligently can be stopped by the police and given heavy on-the-spot fines. At autoroute toll booths the time is printed on the ticket so speed can be checked. In certain circumstances, vehicles can even be confiscated. Nearly all busy sections of road have radar checks. The blood alcohol limit for drivers is 70mg of alcohol per 100ml.

Despite the fact that major roads in **Corsica** are relatively new and well maintained, most of the island's roads are narrow and have an abundance of sharp bends. Potholes are no rare occurrence either and you should be aware that honking before driving into a blind curve is mandatory. It is quite possible that the road you're on suddenly becomes blocked by a herd of cows or pigs. When organising a longer journey, plan on a maximum average speed of about 40 kph (25 mph). Petrol stations can only be found in larger towns.

By Taxi

In addition to those in the main towns there are also taxis in many smaller places. For passengers wanting to hire

Public Holidays

1 January New Year's Day
March/April Easter Monday
Ascension Day (forty days after Easter)
1 May May Day/Labour Day
8 May Victory in Europe Day 1945
Pentecost (seventh Monday after Easter)
14 July Bastille Day
15 August Assumption of the Virgin Mary
1 November All Saints' Day
11 November Armistice Day
25 December Christmas Day

Emergency Numbers

Police: 17
Ambulance: 15
Fire *(sapeurs-pompiers)*: 18

a taxi for a longer journey or excursion, it's best to agree on the price with the driver beforehand. Rates increase after 8pm and at weekends.

Public Transport

Public transport on the **mainland** is fairly efficient and avoids the problem of finding a parking space. **Train** fares vary according to whether you travel on a peak "white" day or a cheaper, less-busy "blue" day. Stations have leaflets showing the calendar of blue and white days. All tickets purchased at French stations have to be put through the orange machines at the stations to validate them before boarding the train. These are marked "compostez votre billet".

With the exception of those operating along a few major traffic routes, **bus** connections in **Corsica** are not particularly good. For the most part there are several buses a day which travel along the major roads between the larger settlements of Ajaccio, Bastia, Porto-Vecchio and Corte. Buses destined for smaller towns and the more remote valleys run just once a day or even less.

Running across the mountains from Ajaccio to Basita via Corte, with a branch line veering northwest to Calvi, Corsica's **narrow-gauge railway** – le Chemin de Fer Corse (or CFC) – provides a dependable all-weather link between the island's main towns.

Entry Requirements and Customs

As for other EU countries – *see box on page 345*.

Money Matters

The French currency is the euro (€) *(see box on page 345)*. Credit cards are widely accepted though sometimes American Express is not. French bank cards use a PIN number but you should also be able to sign the receipt. Credit and bank cards can be used at ATMS to withdraw money and instructions will be available in English.

Opening Times

Shops normally open Monday–Saturday 8am–noon and 2–7pm. *Boulangeries* (bakeries) open at 7am even on Sunday. Supermarkets and hypermarkets open 9am–9pm, except Monday when they often start at noon or 1pm. Generally, there are no strict regulations for opening hours and shops (and banks) in country areas open for shorter periods than town branches and nearly always close for the midday meal between noon and 2pm or even 3pm. During the summer season, however, shops stay open until fairly late.

Banks open Monday–Friday 9am–noon and 2–5pm; they are closed Saturday, Sunday and sometimes Monday.

Chemists open 8am–12.30pm and 3–7pm. A sign in the chemist's window will indicate the nearest *pharmacie de nuit* (late-night chemist).

Museums: national museums close on Tuesday, while municipal museums are closed on Monday. There are no fixed opening times for smaller museums. Ask at the local Syndicat d'Initiative or Office du Tourisme.

Post offices (PTT – Postes et Télécommunications, Télédiffusion) open Monday–Friday 9am–7pm (in rural areas Monday–Friday 8am–noon and 2–5pm) and on Saturday until noon.

Tipping

You do not usually need to add service to a restaurant bill in France. A charge of 10 percent is added automatically as part of the bill. (To be sure, check that it says *Service compris* on the menu, or ask ("*Est-ce que le service est compris?*") Taxi fares also include service, but drivers mind a bit extra.

Telecommunications

Card-operated telephones are now common throughout France, and the old coin-operated machines are a threatened species. Post offices or bar-tabacs sell *télécartes* for either 50 or 120 units. The cheap tariff for long-distance calls applies weekdays 7.30pm–8am, Saturday 1.30pm–Monday 8am and on public holidays.

To make an international call, lift the receiver, insert the money (if necessary), dial 00, wait for the tone to change, then dial the country code followed by the area code (omitting any initial 0) and the number.

Security and Crime

Sensible precautions regarding personal possessions are all that should be necessary. Be aware of pickpockets in cities (especially in the market at Nice), and don't flash money about.

Drivers should follow the rules of the road and always drive sensibly. Heavy on-the-spot fines are given for traffic offences such as speeding, and drivers can be stopped and breathalysed during spot checks. Police are fairly visible on the main roads of France during the summer months.

Nice/Monaco Hotels

Négresco
37 Promenade des Anglais, Nice
Tel: 04 93 16 64 00
Fax: 04 93 88 35 68
Nice's most glorious hotel with its great pink dome dominating the Promenade des Anglais. It offers every luxury and impeccable service. €€€€

La Pérouse
11 Quai Rauba-Capeu, Nice
Tel: 04 93 62 34 63
Fax: 04 93 62 59 41
Great view of Baie des Anges with terrace, swimming pool and garden restaurant. €€€

Hotel Windsor
11 Rue Dalpozzo, Nice
Tel: 04 93 88 59 35
Fax: 04 93 88 94 57
Very reasonably priced, funky hotel, with every room decorated by a different artist. Charming small garden and pool. €€

Hôtel Hermitage
Square Beaumarchais, Monte Carlo
Tel: (00 377) 92 16 40 00
Fax: (00 377) 92 16 38 52
Beautiful Edwardian architecture, spacious comfortable rooms. Swimming-pool and fitness centre. €€€€

Hôtel de Paris
Place du Casino, Monte Carlo
Tel: (00 377) 92 16 30 00
Fax: (00 377) 92 16 38 49
The most prestigious of Monte Carlo's luxury hotels. Indoor swimming-pool and fabulous restaurant. €€€€

Abela Hotel
23 Avenue des Papalins, Fontvieille, Monte Carlo
Tel: (00 377) 92 05 90 00
Fax: (00 377) 92 05 91 67
A little way out of the centre, a comfortable modern hotel overlooking the new harbour. €€

Hotel Prices (France)

For a standard double room
€€€€ = above €250
€€€ = €125–250
€€ = €75–125
€ = under €75

Italy

Area 301,164 sq. km (116,280 sq. miles).
Population approx. 57 million.
Language Italian.
Religion predominantly Roman Catholic.
Time zone GMT +1 hour, +2 hours in summer.
Currency euro (€).
Weights & measures metric.
Electricity 220 volts – two-pin plug.
International dialling code 39.

Getting Around

To/from Rome Airports

Rome's **Leonardo da Vinci Airport** (Fiumicino) is 35 km (22 miles) southwest of central Rome. There is a direct hourly train service (until about 10pm) to Stazione Termini, the capital's main railway station. Tickets cost around €8 (2003 rate), journey time is 30 minutes.

Roma Ciampino Airport is 15 km (10 miles) southeast of Rome. Easyjet, the British low-cost airline, is one of many firms who fly to Ciampino. The shuttle bus to Via Marsala, close to Stazione Termini, costs €8 (2003 rate) and takes around 30 minutes. Another bus (called Cotral) runs roughly every 30 minutes from the airport to the Anagnina metro station at the end of Linea A. From there, it's 30 minutes to Stazione Termini and the centre of town (trains leave every 5–10 minutes). Bear in mind that buses stop running at 11pm, so late arrivals will need a taxi. Taxis typically cost around €40 (2003 rate) – although the official price is closer to €25 so try to negotiate beforehand.

To/from Venice Airport

Venice's **Marco Polo Airport** is at Tessera on the mainland 9 km (5½ miles) north of Venice. To reach Venice there is a public bus to Piazzale Roma (30 minutes), taxis (20–25 minutes), or the hourly Alilaguna waterbus, which crosses the lagoon to Piazza San Marco via the Lido and takes about 75 minutes,

depending on your stop. The waterbus is quicker between 11.30am and 3.30pm and it costs about €10 (2003 rates). The luxury option is to take a private water-taxi; these cost about €80 and are identifiable by their black-on-yellow numbers. Taxis have the right to negotiate prices with passengers

Treviso Airport is an alternative for travellers to Venice or the Lakes. A reliable coach service runs to Venice.

To/from Genoa Airport

Genoa's C. Colombo Airport (GOA) is 11 km (7 miles) from the city. The Volabus departs every 30 minutes to and from the city centre, including Brignole and Principe railway stations, from 5.30am–10.15pm. Journey time is approximately 25 minutes and the fare is €3 (2003 rate).

Taxis are available 24 hours a day from outside the terminal. Taxi drivers are obliged to switch the meter on before the start of the journey.

By Hire Car

Hiring a car is expensive – the best rates are usually found by booking directly with an international rental company and paying for your car before you leave home, or as part of a "fly-drive" deal. Check that the quoted rate includes collision damage waiver, unlimited mileage and tax, as these can greatly increase the cost. You must be over 21 to rent a car, and you will need to have held a full, valid driver's licence (EU model for EU citizens) for at least 12 months; this must be shown at the time of collection. You must also show your passport and a major credit card, as cash deposits are prohibitively large. N.B. there are still many petrol stations in Italy that do not accept credit cards.

Genoa
Avis: Airport, tel: 01 0650 7280.
Europcar: Airport, tel: 01 0650 4881; Via Casaregis 42/1, tel: 01 0595 5428.
Hertz: Airport, tel: 01 0651 2422.
Livorno
Avis: Calata Carrara Stazione Marittima, tel: 05-86880090.
Europcar: Piazzale XI de Maggio 6, tel: 05 8621 9973.
Rome
Avis: Leonardo da Vinci (Fiumicino) Airport, tel: 06 6501 1531; Via XVI Settembre 6/8, Civitavecchia, tel: 07 6650 0336; railway station, tel: 06 481 4373.
Europcar: Leonardo da Vinci (Fiumicino) Airport, tel: 06 6501 0879.
Hertz: Leonardo da Vinci (Fiumicino) Airport, tel: 06 6501 1553.

Public Transport Tickets

Buy tickets for buses and trams in advance at tobacco shops, newsstands or bars. There are Metrò ticket machines at underground stations.

Bus and metro tickets must be validated with a time stamp from the machines at the entrance to the metro and at the rear of buses. The system is complicated: if you have a multi-use ticket, use the space provided on the ticket for multiple validation stamps each time you board, making sure that the last (third) space is stamped within 75 minutes of the first. A standard single-use ticket (*biglietto a tempo*) is valid for a journey of up to 75 minutes. A one-day ticket (the *Metrebus*, also known as a *biglietto integrato giornaliero*) allows you to use all modes of transport excluding the airport bus and the so-called tourist bus (Line 110); it expires at midnight on the day purchased. Weekly and monthly passes are also available.

Naples
Avis: Airport, tel: 08 1780 5790; Stazione Centrale, tel: 08 128 4041.
Europcar: Airport, tel: 08 1780 5643; Corso Colombo 33, tel: 08 1530 1447.
Hertz: Airport, tel: 08 1780 2971.
Sardinia
Europcar: Cagliari Airport, tel: 07 024 0126.
Hertz: Cagliari Airport, tel: 07 024 0037.
Sicily
Europcar: Palermo Airport, tel: 09 159 1688; Stazione Marittima, tel: 09 2259 5024.
Hertz: Palermo Airport, tel: 09 121 3112.
Venice
Avis: Airport, tel: 04 1541 5030; Piazzale Roma 496/G, tel: 04 1523 7377.
Europcar: Airport, tel: 04 1541 5654; Piazzale Roma, 496/H, tel: 04 1523 8616.

By Taxi

Taxis can be picked up at a taxi rank or ordered by telephone. Extra charges for luggage and for trips at night, on public holidays and to airports are posted inside every cab. It is normal practice to round up the fare.

A yellow or white official taxi with a meter from one of the airports can be a good alternative to public transport; but do ask what the fare is likely to be before you set off. Unofficial taxis can charge extortionate fares and may even be dangerous.

Public Transport (City)

In addition to **bus** (autobus) services, some big cities operate trams/streetcars (tram in Italian). Rome, Milan and Naples have underground/subway (metropolitana, abbreviated **metrò**) systems.

The latest transport novelty in a few Italian city centres is the **"Motobeep"**, an egg-shaped capsule on wheels that is a cross between a covered scooter and a tiny car. (The passenger sits in a covered seat behind the driver, who acts as a tour guide.) Motobeeps are proving popular in Palermo and Rome and are due to be introduced in Naples.

AMT (Azienda Mobilità e Trasporti) runs an efficient bus service in **Genoa** that links the stations, the airport and all the major sites. You can buy a public transport travelcard, which is cheaper than individual tickets.

Tickets for **Rome's buses** and subways (**metrò**) can be purchased in books of 10; one-day, three-day, and weekly tickets are sold at the ATAC (Rome's transport authority) booth in Piazza dei Cinquecento, in front of the Stazione Termini, the central railway station. Board **buses** at the rear and punch your ticket in the orange or yellow machine.

The **metrò** system (Metropolitana) has two lines, A and B, which meet at Stazione Termini, the main city railway station, and run between 5.30am and 11.30pm. A third line is under construction.

Transport in **Naples** has improved dramatically in terms of efficiency and reliability.

Buses run to most places in the city and they are the only public transport along the waterfront. However, they are generally very crowded during rush hours. Owing to congested traffic, taxis are not much faster than buses, although they are far more expensive.

Naples' main **metrò** line, the Metropolitana FS, covers most of the city and suburbs. It connects Piazza Garibaldi with Piazza Cavour, Monte Santo, Mergellina, Campi Flegrei and Bagnoli.

Two good local **railways** for tourists include Circumvesuviana, which goes from Piazza Garibaldi to Pompeii, Herculaneum and Sorrento, and the Circumflegri, which leaves from Piazza Montesanto for Cuma.

Venice's water buses (vaporetto, and the smaller and faster motoscafo) ply the Grand Canal and shuttle between islands. Tickets can be bought from bars, kiosks and at most stops. Apart from ordinary single tickets (buy one and get it validated when boarding or you'll have to pay a surcharge), there are passes valid for 24 hours. Venice has several water-taxi stations. Although theoretically the rates are fixed, they tend to vary according to distance; clarify destination when purchasing ticket. This also applies to trips by gondola.

Entry Requirements and Customs

As for other EU countries – see box on page 345.

Money Matters

The euro (€) has been Italian currency since 2002 (see box on page 345). Italy is a society that prefers cash to credit cards, except for large purchases, or, for instance, hotel bills. In the case of petrol stations, more modest restaurants and smaller shops, it is usual to pay in cash. Check beforehand if there is any doubt. Most shopkeepers and restaurateurs will not change money, so it is best to change a limited amount at the airport when you arrive, especially if it is the weekend, when banks are closed. Try to avoid changing money in hotels, where the commission tends to be higher than in banks.

Travellers' cheques are still recommended in Italy, as they can be replaced if stolen or lost. Note, however, that commission will be charged for changing them.

Banks generally open Monday–Friday 8.30am–1.30pm and for one hour in the afternoon (usually between 3pm and 4pm). Unfortunately, most banks are notoriously inefficient, and currency conversion can easily turn into a tedious saga, so use cashpoints (ATMs) where possible. You can also change money at airports and main railway stations. You will find current exchange rates are published in the press and posted in banks.

Cash Machines & Credit Cards

As mentioned above, it is simplest to get cash from cashpoint machines (ATMS), which are widely available. Most Switch cards work in Italian machines, with your normal PIN number, as do credit cards, though you may sometimes have to look for particular "Bancomats" (cashpoint machines) that take your card. In cities, many restaurants, hotels and shops will take major credit cards (Visa, American Express, MasterCard and Carte Blanche), but in rural areas, especially, you may be able to pay only in cash.

Opening Times

Shops open 9am–12.30pm and 3.30 or 4–7.30 or 8pm. In areas serving tourists, hours are generally longer than these, for instance in Taormina, Venice and popular towns in Tuscany, many shops remain open on Sunday, while elsewhere almost everything is closed on that day. Shops often also close on Monday (sometimes in the morning only) and some shut on Saturday.

Telecommunications

In Italy it is always necessary to include the area code when dialing a number, even if you are calling from within that area. Another oddity is that you must always include the initial 0 in the area code when calling Italy from abroad.

Public phones are found in bars and shops displaying a yellow dialling symbol. In addition to coins and phone tokens (gettoni) most accept pre-paid phonecards (schede telefoniche), available from tobacconists and many bars. Beware of exorbitant hotel charges for direct calls and service charges for toll-free calls on their phone lines.

To make an international call from Italy, dial 00, followed by the country code. Then dial the number, omitting the initial 0, if there is one. The SIP telephone offices on Piazza San Silvestro and the main station are open 24 hours.

Public Holidays

1 January New Year's Day
March/April Good Friday, Easter Monday
25 April Liberation Day
1 May Labour Day
15 August Assumption of the Blessed Virgin Mary
1 November All Saints' Day
8 December Immaculate Conception
25/26 December Christmas

In addition to these national holidays, almost all cities have a holiday to celebrate their own patron saint, for example St Mark, 25 April (Venice); St John the Baptist, 24 June (Turin, Genoa and Florence); Sts Peter & Paul, 29 June (Rome); St Rosalia, 15 July (Palermo); St Gennaro, 19 September (Naples); St Petronius, 4 October (Bologna); St Ambrose, 7 December (Milan).

Emergency Numbers

Police: 112/113
Fire : 115
Ambulance: 118
Breakdown service: 116

Security and Crime

The main problem for tourists is petty crime – pick-pocketing, bag-snatching and theft from cars; it is wise to have insurance coverage against this and to take basic, sensible precautions against theft. Always lock your car and never leave luggage, cameras or other valuables inside. This applies particularly in major cities, and in the south. If walking, especially at night, in the tiny alleys of the historic city centres of Bari, Genoa or Palermo, for example, try to blend in and avoid wearing flashy jewellery that may attract attention.

If you are the victim of a crime (or suffer a loss) and wish to claim against your insurance, it is essential to make a report at the nearest police station and get documentation to support your claim. If you need a policeman, dial 113 (112 for the Carabinieri, a national police force).

Recommended Hotels

GENOA

Bristol Palace
Via XX Settembre 35
Tel: 01 059 2541
Fax: 01 056 1756
Traditionally Genoa's grandest hotel, the Bristol Palace is on the city's most elegant shopping street, close to Old Genoa. The modest entrance belies its history and though rooms vary greatly in quality, some have appealing features, such as old marble bathrooms, while others have Jacuzzis. There is a small bar, and the bright and stylish dining room is decorated in Louis XVI style.
€€€–€€€€
Jolly Plaza
Via Martin Piaggio 11
Tel: 01 083161
Fax: 01 0839 1850
Freephone: 167 017 703
This small but distinguished *palazzo* has been transformed into a four-star hotel. Bedrooms vary in style but all of them are well-equipped and many have Jacuzzis. The restaurant is in the adjoining Villeta di Negro. €€€
Savoia Majestic
Via Arsenale di Terra 5
Tel: 01 026 1641
Fax: 01 026 1883
Freephone: 167 877 077

This four-star hotel occupies an imposing 19th-century palace by Porta Principe train station, a short walk from the historic district. Many rooms are wood-panelled, floors are marble, and some bedrooms are furnished with antiques. €€€

ROME

Aldrovandi Palace Hotel
Via Ulisse Aldrovandi 15
Tel: 06 322 3993
Fax: 06 322 1435
This imposing 18th-century palace, overlooking the Villa Borghese gardens, is in the prestigious Parioli district. A former college, it is now one of Rome's leading hotels and its suites are among the most expensive in the city. Décor is sumptuous rather than stylish – a mood that is reflected in both the facilities and service. The hotel's many amenities include a business centre, several restaurants, private parking, a fitness centre, gardens, and, exceptionally for Rome, an outdoor swimming pool. €€€€
D'Inghilterra
Via Bocca di Leone 14
Tel: 06 69 981
Fax: 06 992 2243
Old-fashioned it may be, but this hotel, in the main shopping area close to Trinita dei Monti, is arguably the most atmospheric of the grand hotels and is certainly the most redolent of times past. Bedrooms are mostly spacious and elegant, with marble bathrooms. In the public areas, frescoes, antiques, chandeliers and antiquarian prints add to the elegant atmosphere. The roof garden is one of the loveliest in the city. €€€€
Westin Excelsior
Via Vittorio Veneto 125
Tel: 06 47081
Fax: 06 482 6205
This grand hotel has been a meeting place for celebrities and society figures since the 1950s. To many, this hotel is quite simply synonymous with Roman *dolce vita*, even if some of this indefinable quality has otherwise moved on from the Via Vittorio Veneto. €€€€
Fontana
Piazza di Trevi 96
Tel: 06 678 6113
Fax: 06 679 0024
Set in a restored 13th-century monastery by the Trevi Fountain, the main attraction at this small three-star hotel is its beautiful rooftop bar. €€€
Forum
Via Tor dei Conti 25
Tel: 06 679 2446
Fax: 06 678 6479
This is a lovely hotel in the Roman

Forum area, with a view of the ancient city, including the Forum, from its roof garden. 82 rooms. €€€
Hotel Celio
Via Santi Quattro 35/C
Tel: 06 7049 5333
Fax: 06 709 6377
This boutique hotel is just a stone's throw from both the Colosseum and the Forum. It occupies an attractive *palazzo* that has been completely and sensitively restored, including its fine mosaics. The atmosphere is elegant and the bedrooms achieve a particularly high standard of comfort.
€€€
Gregoriana
Via Gregoriana 18
Tel: 06 679 4269
Fax: 06 678 4258
Close to the Spanish Steps, in a central location, this former 17th-century monastery is now a three-star hotel with a quiet, cosy atmosphere. Especially admirable is the art deco interior, with room letters designed by the celebrated 1930s' fashion illustrator Erté. Although there is no restaurant, the hotel does have a pleasant terrace where breakfast is served. €€–€€€
Margutta
Via Laurina 34
Tel: 06 322 3674
Fax: 06 320 0395
Near Piazza del Popolo, this little hotel occupies an 18th-century *palazzo*. Rooms are simple, with dark furniture and iron bedsteads; bathrooms are tiny and there is no restaurant, but atmosphere and value are compensation enough. €€
Select
Via V Bachelet 6
Tel: 06 445 6383
Fax: 06 444 1086
Though it's close to the station and the main ministries, this friendly little hotel has the feel of a secluded villa, and its inner courtyard and tiny garden are ideal places to sip a cool drink on a hot day. Ground-floor rooms

Tipping

A service charge of approximately 15 percent is added to hotel and restaurant bills. If hotel prices are quoted as all inclusive (*tutto compreso*), the service charge is included, but not necessarily the IVA (VAT/sales tax); ask if you're not sure. In addition to the restaurant bill's service charge, it is customary to give the waiter something extra. Bellboys, doormen, bartenders and service-station attendants all expect a tip of a euro or two, depending on the situation.

lack privacy but open onto the courtyard. The owner is president of the *Logis d'Italia* association, which promotes authenticity, unpretentiousness, a friendly welcome and good value for money. Not surprisingly, this lovely hotel meets those criteria. €€

VENICE

Cipriani
Isola della Giudecca 10
Tel: 04 1520 7744
Fax: 04 1520 3930
The Cipriani is the most glamorous of Venetian hotels and the destination for travellers on the famed Orient Express. Lavish bedrooms are furnished with Fortuny fabrics, and amenities include one of the only private swimming pools in Venice. There are gardens, tennis courts, a yacht harbour, piano bar and a water-launch service, which whisks guests in a couple of minutes to San Marco. €€€€

Gritti Palace
Campo Santa Maria del Giglio 2467
San Marco
Tel: 04 179 4611
Fax: 04 1520 0942
The 15th-century Gritti, decorated with Murano-glass chandeliers and 16th-century damask furnishings, is the most legendary Venetian hotel and has a price tag to match. It is renowned for its formal luxury, fabulous setting on the Grand Canal and discreet, attentive service. Distinguished cuisine can be enjoyed on the canalside terrace. €€€€

Luna Baglioni
Calle Langa dell'Ascensione
San Marco 1243
Tel: 04 1528 9840
Fax: 04 1528 7160
The Luna is the oldest hotel in Venice, dating to 1118, when it was founded as a Knights Templar lodge for pilgrims travelling to Jerusalem. Countless restorations and refurbishments mean that the hotel does not really look its age, and the decor is currently in traditional Venetian style: a riot of Murano glass, inlaid marble, swagged curtains and frescoes. There is an 18th-century ballroom with original ceiling frescoes. The hotel has an impressive restaurant and the grandest breakfast room in Venice. €€€€

Metropole
Riva degli Schiavoni 4149,
Castello
Tel: 04 1520 5044
Fax: 04 1522 3679
This popular patrician residence is decorated in fine 19th-century style

and is dotted with well-chosen antiques. There are excellent views over courtyards and the lagoon and the hotel is noted for its attentive service. It is a little tricky to find, so request directions or, better still, take a private gondola to the hotel jetty. €€€€

Hotel Prices

For a standard double room
€€€€ = above €250
€€€ = €125–250
€€ = €75–125
€ = under €75

Accademia Villa Marevege
Fondamenta Bollani
Dorsoduro 1058-1060
Tel: 04 1521 0188
Fax: 04 1523 9152
Set in the Dorsoduro district at the Grand Canal end of Rio San Trovaso within easy walking distance of the Accademia gallery, this remodelled Gothic palace maintains its charm, with delightful gardens front and back. The building was remodelled in the 17th century and was once the Russian consulate. Reserve months in advance. €€–€€€

San Cassiano Ca' Favretto
Calle della Rosa, Santa Croce 2232
Tel: 04 152 41768
Fax: 04 172 1033
One of the few hotels actually on the Grand Canal, the three-star San Cassiano is a converted 14th-century *palazzo*. About half the rooms have canalside views looking across to the Ca' d'Oro, one of the city's loveliest Gothic palaces, but, as everywhere in Venice, these rooms vary dramatically in size and quality. Given that the stairs are steep and there is no lift, less agile visitors are advised to stick to rooms on the ground floor. The hotel has its own jetty, so you can arrive in style in a gondola. €€–€€€

Malta

Fact File

Area: *Malta:* 320 sq. km (124 sq. miles). *Gozo:* 67 sq. km (26 sq. miles). *Comino:* 2.5 sq. km (1 sq. mile).
Population: 375,000.
Language: Maltese and English.
Religion: Roman Catholic.
Time zone: GMT +1 hour. GMT +2 in summer.
Currency: Maltese Lira (Lm).
Weights and measures: metric.
Electricity: 220/240-volt and 110 for shavers. Visitors from the UK may use their normal three-pin plug items. Visitors from elsewhere will need an adaptor.
International dialling code: 356.

Getting Around

By Hire Car
In August, a small car will cost around Lm80 per week (2003 rates). Collision damage waiver is expensive (around Lm6 per day) but is probably worth it. Always check with your credit card or domestic insurance provider as you may be insured through your existing policies.

All the major car-hire companies – Hertz, Avis and Europcar – have offices on the island; however, some are run as franchises rather than as main branches. Some have desks at the airport, and it is possible to pick up a car immediately upon your arrival if you are flying to Malta and joining your ship here. A number of the larger hire companies offer more competitive rates if you reserve the car from home. Contact details:
Avis tel: 2122 5986; fax: 2123 5754.
Hertz tel: 2131 4636; fax: 2133 3153.
Europcar tel: 2138 8516; fax: 2137 3673.

By Taxi
The white taxis are fitted with meters

Emergency Numbers

Police: 191
Ambulance: 196
Fire: 199

and should charge government-controlled rates displayed in the cab. If a driver is reluctant to use his meter, agree on a price before starting your journey. Many car-hire companies such as Percins (tel: 2144 2530) and Wembleys (tel: 2137 4141) have chauffeur-driven Mercedes that are no more expensive than taxis and can be pre-booked. They are available for all-day hire, too, for sightseeing.

Public Transport
The local **bus** service on Malta is comprehensive, reliable and cheap. Services start from a central hub just outside City Gate in Valletta.

Horse-drawn Buggies (Karrozin)
These offer tours rather than journeys. Official fares are rarely enforced and a fare should be agreed before you start your journey. You will find them in Valletta, Mdina and Sliema.

Entry Requirements and Customs

Malta became part of the European Union (EU) in May 2004 and shares entrance and customs regulations with the rest of the Union. *See box on page 345 for details.*

Money Matters

Despite EU membership (as of 2004), the official currency – at least for the time being – remains the Maltese lira, abbreviated to Lm and often called pounds by older local people (this goes back to the use of the British pound on the island before independence in 1964). Each lira is divided into 100 cents.
A large number of banks have

Public Holidays

1 January New Year's Day
10 February St Paul's Shipwreck Day
19 March St Joseph's Day
31 March Freedom Day
March/April Good Friday and Easter Monday
1 May Labour Day
7 June Commemoration of 7 June 1919 – Sette Guigno
29 June St Peter and St Paul's Day
15 August Assumption of the Virgin Mary
8 September Victory Day
21 September Independence Day
8 December Immaculate Conception
13 December Republic Day
25 December Christmas Day

Tipping

Tipping for good service is expected. Some restaurants will include a service charge in the final bill but most will expect you to add 10–12 percent. The following guidelines apply for other services: taxi driver: no tip; chauffeur Lm1; porters 15c per piece of luggage; maids 30–40c per day; hairdressers Lm1.

ATMs which accept international debit and credit cards – look for the familiar symbols on the machine. Some machines will impose an extra charge on withdrawals from foreign bank accounts. Credit cards are widely accepted throughout the islands in hotels, shops and restaurants.

Opening Times

Opening hours, as in many Mediterranean countries, can be complicated. Winter hours are longer than those in summer when the heat becomes oppressive in the afternoon. Generally, longer working days begin on 1 October and end on 16 June. If you have any important business to attend to, do it in the morning. All commercial activity stops at lunchtime whatever time of year it is; even major churches are closed so that the Maltese can observe the tradition of a substantial midday meal and afternoon siesta.
Shops open Monday–Friday 9am–1pm and 4.30–7pm, Saturday 9am–1pm. Many shops in tourist areas do not close for lunch and are open longer hours, especially in summer. Only newsagents can open legally on Sunday.
Banks' opening hours vary, but generally they are Monday–Friday 8am–12.45pm, Saturday 8–11.30am, plus Friday 2.30–4pm. Main branches open Monday–Friday 4–7pm.
Museums are generally open Monday–Saturday 8.15am–5pm, Sunday 7.45am–2pm.

Telecommunications

Phone calls, including international calls, can be made from call boxes and kiosks using coins and credit cards, although older boxes may accept only coins. Phone cards of various denominations can be bought from newsagents, post offices and supermarkets.
When making an international call, dial 00 before the country code. Most hotels will offer direct-dial long-

distance and international phone facilities, but these can be expensive. Maltacom has a 24-hour office offering telephone, fax, and email facilities at Mercury House, St George's Road, Paceville.

Security and Crime

Malta is relatively crime-free, but petty crime such as handbag snatching is on the increase in tourist areas. Keep valuables in the hotel safe if you are staying on for extra days in Malta. Otherwise, don't bring valuables off the ship, don't carry large amounts of cash, look after your camera and don't leave valuables unattended on beaches or visible in a vehicle. Walk only on well-lit streets at night. If you do become a victim of crime, you should report this to the police immediately. In order to claim on your insurance for loss or theft you must do this within 24 hours.

Tunisia

Fact File

Area 162,155 sq. km
(63,000 sq. miles).
Population: 9.4 million.
Language Arabic, but French also
widely spoken.
Religion predominantly Sunni Muslim.
There are small communities of Jews
in Tunis, Jerba and a few other towns.
Time zone GMT +1 hour all year round
(no daylight savings time).
Currency Tunisian dinar, divided into
1,000 millimes.
Weights and measures metric.
Electricity most of the country's
supply is 220 volts, but some places
have a 110-volt supply. Sockets and
plugs are the continental variety, with
two round pins.
International dialling code 216.

Getting Around

By Hire Car

Car hire in Tunisia isn't cheap,
especially in high season, and it can
be difficult finding a firm with cars left
to hire. It is cheaper and easier to
book in advance from home through
one of the larger car-hire firms. Out-of-
season prices are lower. There are
many firms to choose from but prices
do not vary a great deal.

When you pick up your car, it is
important to check its general state of
repair – make sure it has a spare
wheel and jack. Also, examine the
insurance and be clear about any
exclusions. Don't assume oil and
water have been checked.

Most firms (not just international
companies) have offices in both Tunis
and Monastir airports.

Tunis

Europcar: Avenue de la Liberté,
tel: 71-794 432.
Carthago: Avenue Habib Bourguiba 3,
tel: 71-349 168.
Hertz: Central Agency, Charguia 11,
tel: 71-702 099, Airport,
tel: 71-754 000.
Traffic joining a road from the right
has priority, unless signs or markings
indicate otherwise. Most importantly,
this means that cars already on a

roundabout (traffic circle) must give
way to those joining it (i.e, the
opposite of what happens in most
other countries). One local quirk you
should be prepared for is that drivers
making a left turn on a two-lane road
often cross to the wrong side of the
road before turning. This can be rather
disconcerting if you are travelling in
the opposite direction.

Outside the cities, the main routes
are generally good, with long, straight
stretches and little traffic. Minor roads
are often wide enough for one vehicle
only, and you will have to move onto
the gravel shoulder to pass oncoming
traffic. Look out for pedestrians,
donkey carts and mopeds, especially
near towns, where the former two
often wander across the road without
any apparent concern for their own
safety. They also make driving after
dark particularly hazardous.

By Taxi

Taxis can be hailed in the street, or
picked up at a rank. Meters are used,
and rates are low by European
standards. All taxis levy a 50 percent
surcharge for night travel (usually
April–September 10pm–6am,
October–March 9pm–7am), when you
will probably have to negotiate a price,
especially from the airport.

The *louage* is similar to the
Moroccan grand taxi. This is a large
estate car seating six passengers,
which shuttles back and forth along a
set route. There are no fixed
departure times; the taxi departs as
soon as all the seats are full. To find a

Public Holidays

State Holidays
1 January: New Year's Day
20 March: Independence Day
21 March: Youth Day
9 April: Martyrs' Day
1 May: Labour Day
25 July: Republic Day
13 August: Women's Day

Religious Holidays
These change annually – falling 11
days earlier each year (12 days in a
leap year).
Dates for the years 2004 and
2005, respectively, are:
Start of the month of Ramadan
From 13 October, from 2 October.
Aid el Seghir (end of Ramadan) 12
November, 1 November.
**Aid el Kebir (feast of Abraham's
sacrifice)** 31 January, 19 January.
**Ras el Am Hejri (Muslim New
Year)** 21 February, 10 February.
Mouled (the Prophet's birthday) 1
May, 20 April.

seat, you simply turn up at the
"terminal", usually a piece of waste
ground on the edge of the town centre
(the tourist office, your cruise ship
staff or hotel will tell you where –
there's usually a different location for
different destinations), and ask the
drivers. Fares are per person for a full
car; ask other passengers (or your
hotel receptionist or cruise-ship staff)
what the standard fare is.

Tunis Metro

Tunis's light-rail network is the metro.
The most useful line is Line 4, linking
Place Barcelone in the centre (via Line
2, change at République) with the
Bardo Museum. The metro is linked
(via Tunis Marine station at the foot of
Avenue Habib Bourguiba) with another
railway, the TGM (Tunis–Goulette–
Marsa), which runs every 15 minutes
during the day to Carthage, Sidi Bou
Saïd and La Marsa.

Entry Requirements

Citizens of the EU, USA and Canada
need only a passport and return
ticket; the passport must be valid for
a minimum of three months after the
date you arrive. If you are coming by
air, you will have to fill in an
immigration form before your flight
lands: hand it to the immigration
officer, with your passport, on arrival.
If you are on a port-of-call stop your
cruise line may have arranged it in
advance – check with the line before
you go. The officer will stamp both
copies and return one to you: keep
this with you at all times, as it serves
as your identity card when in Tunisia.

Citizens of Australia and New
Zealand must have a visa to enter
Tunisia. Visas must be applied for at
least three weeks before the date of
travel, at any Tunisian Embassy. Visa
regulations change from time to time,
and should be checked with your
travel agent or cruise line before you
leave home.

Customs Regulations

People over 18 years of age are
allowed to take the following goods
duty-free into Tunisia: 400 cigarettes
or 50 cigars or 500g of tobacco; 2
litres of wine and 1 litre of spirits; 250
ml of perfume or 1 litre of toilet water.

You can take as much foreign
currency as you like into or out of the

country, but anything more than the equivalent of 500 dinars must be declared on entry. The amount of dinars you can reconvert on departure must not exceed 30 percent of the total of all your exchange receipts, up to a maximum of 100 dinars, so keep all currency exchange receipts. It is illegal to import or export dinars.

Money Matters

The unit of currency is the Tunisian dinar (D), divided into 1,000 millimes (M). The exchange rate is controlled by the government, so there's no point shopping around for the best rate – they're all the same.

Changing money in a bank can be a time-consuming business; the most efficient service is usually the STB (Société Tunisianne de Banque). Most hotels, three-star and above, exchange money as well.

Travellers' cheques (chèques de voyages) are accepted by most banks and hotels, though smaller establishments may refuse to cash them and will direct you elsewhere; Thomas Cook and American Express are the most widely accepted. You will need your passport, and occasionally the purchase receipts too; no commission is charged. You can exchange cash easily in hotels and tourist shops.

Major credit and charge cards are accepted in the more expensive hotels (three-star and up) and restaurants in the larger cities, and by tourist shops and car-hire firms. If you are unsure whether an establishment will accept your card, ask first. Visa and Access/MasterCard can also be used in large branches of banks to obtain cash advances, though this can take time.

Opening Times

Shops generally open 8am–12.30pm and 2.30–6pm; some close for short periods on Friday, the Muslim holy day **Banks** normally open Monday–Thursday 8am–noon and 2–4.30pm, Friday 8am–noon and 1–4.30pm in winter; during Ramadan hours are 8am–2.30pm; and in July and August 7–11.30am only.
Currency exchange offices open daily 8am–8pm in popular resorts. Airport exchange desks are open 24 hours, but may close between flight arrivals.
Post offices generally open Monday–Friday 8am–noon and 2–6pm, Sat 8am–noon in winter; Monday–Saturday 8am–1pm in summer. During Ramadan hours are Monday–Saturday 8am–3pm. Main post offices are open longer for the

Tipping

It is customary to offer a tip for services rendered: 100 millimes is usual for café waiters, porters, petrol-pump attendants and guardians at monuments and museums; restaurant waiters expect 10–15 percent or 500M per person on top of any service charge. If a taxi driver uses his meter, then tip 10–15 percent of the fare; if you agree a price beforehand, nothing extra will be expected.

sale of stamps and sending telegrams. In Tunis, Sfax, Houmt Souk and Sousse, these services are available 24 hours a day.
Museums generally open Tuesday–Sunday 9am–noon and 2–5pm.
Archaeological sites generally open daily 8.30am–5.30pm; sometimes longer in summer.

Telecommunications

It is possible to make direct international calls from public phones, called "taxiphones" in all towns. You can also phone at a post office via an operator who will tell you how much you owe after you have finished. To dial abroad, first dial 00, then the country code. In Tunis, calls can be made from the Centre d'Exploitation des Telecommunications, 29 Rue Gamal Abdelnasser, 24 hours a day.

Security and Crime

Although Tunisia has a relatively low crime rate, you should take precautions to avoid trouble: don't carry valuables, don't flaunt wealth, keep an eye on handbags in restaurants and cafés, always lock car doors and use the safe deposit box if you are staying in a hotel.

Croatia

Fact File

Area the mainland is approximately 56,500 sq. km (21,800 sq. miles).
Population 4,800,000.
Language Croatian.
Religion largely Roman Catholic.
Time Zone GMT +1 hour, +2 hours March to October.
Currency kuna (1 kuna = 100 lipa).
Weights and measures metric.
Electricity 220V, 50Hz, two-pin round pronged plugs.
International dialling code 385.

Getting Around

By Hire Car

It is fairly expensive to hire a car in Croatia. For international car-hire firms, it generally works out cheaper to hire before you arrivie in Croatia, but you may manage to get a good deal on the spot from a local company.

Drivers must be at least 21 years old and have held a full driving licence for two years; they also need a valid passport or national identity card. Hire periods are for a minimum of 24 hours. Prices include unlimited mileage, third-party insurance, collision damage waiver, theft waiver and local taxes. A credit card imprint is required as a surety when hiring a car. Always check the insurance carefully to be clear about any excess charges that may be applied in case of an accident.

Public Holidays

1 January New Year's Day
6 January Three Kings' Day
March/April Good Friday and Easter Monday
1 May Labour Day
May/June Corpus Christi
22 June Anti-Fascist Struggle Day
25 June Croatian National Day
5 August Victory Day/National Thanksgiving
15 August Feast of the Assumption
8 October Independence Day
1 November All Saints' Day
25/26 December Christmas

Major car-hire companies have offices throughout Croatia. Bookings are best made through a central reservations number.
Budget tel: 01 4805688
Avis tel: 01 4836006
National tel: 021 399043
Sixt tel: 01 6219900

By Taxi

Metered taxis that can be found at ranks, hailed on the street or pre-booked by telephone offer poor value. A fixed-tariff list is displayed in many taxis, but it can be difficult to work out at what rate the meter is running. The starting fare is around 28kn, with each additional kilometre costing 6kn.

Public Transport

Croatia has an extensive local and national **bus** network. Tickets for local services should be bought from the driver or at a tobacco kiosk. Services generally operate Monday to Sunday 4am–11pm.

Rail travel is slow, with few direct connections between major towns and cities, and most Croatians do not travel by train. Tickets are cheap and can be purchased from railway stations or the onboard conductor.

Jadrolinija is the main car and passenger **ferry** operator in Croatia, with numerous routes along the Dalmatian coast and between the mainland and the islands. Tickets must be purchased from the ticket office near the ferry dock prior to departure. In the summer months it is advisable to buy vehicle tickets well in advance to minimise the risk of waiting in lengthy traffic queues to board a ferry. Foot passengers can usually purchase tickets just before departure.

Entry Requirements

Every visitor needs a valid passport, but for stays of less than 90 days many Europeans (including all EU citizens) and those from the USA, Canada, Australia and New Zealand do not need a visa to enter Croatia. South Africans require a 90-day visa to enter Croatia and should seek advice from any Croatian Embassy.

Customs Regulations

Visitors can bring personal possessions, 2 litres of wine, 1 litre of spirits, 60 millilitres of perfume and 200 cigarettes or 50 cigars or 250g of tobacco into Croatia duty free. Foreign currency can also be taken freely into the country. The transportation of kuna is restricted to 2,000 kuna per person.

Expensive goods such as cameras and laptop computers should be reported to customs officials upon arrival to prevent difficulties when trying to take them out of the country.

Money Matters

The national currency is the kuna (abbreviated kn), divided into 100 lipa (lp). Although the euro is not an official currency in Croatia, prices are frequently quoted in both kuna and euros.

Normal banking hours are Monday–Friday 7am–3pm and Saturday 8am–2pm. Currency can also be obtained in exchange offices, hotels and at any post office counter.

Cashpoints (ATMs) are readily available and debit or Credit cards carrying the Maestro, MasterCard, Visa, Cirrus and Plus symbols can be used to obtain cash. You will rarely find ATMs in villages.

Credit cards are not accepted everywhere, even among the most expensive shops, hotels and restaurants, so always check in advance.

Euro or US dollar travellers' cheques can be exchanged at any bank and many exchange offices for a commission of up to 2 percent. You must take your passport.

Tipping

Hotel and restaurant bills usually include tax and service, but it is customary to round up your bill to the nearest 10kn and to leave an extra tip for exceptional service. Taxi drivers often round up the fare or overcharge tourists, so an additional tip is not needed.

Opening Times

Shops and **department stores** open Monday–Friday 8am–7pm and Saturday 8am–2pm. In the resorts shops often open Monday–Friday 8am–1pm, close for the afternoon and open 5–11pm.

Some larger towns have a 24-hour pharmacy and some have 24-hour grocery shops.

Banks are open Monday–Friday 7am–3pm and Saturday 8am–2pm.
Café-bars open Monday–Sunday 7am–midnight and most restaurants open from midday to midnight.
Museum opening times vary, but are generally Monday–Friday 9am–1pm or later. Some are open until 8pm in the summer. They are often closed on Monday.

Many Croatian towns and resorts have a fresh food **market** and a general market. These are open Monday–Saturday 8am–2pm. Markets selling souvenirs often have extended opening hours.

Office hours are generally Monday–Friday 8am–4pm.

Emergency Numbers

Police: 92
Fire Brigade: 93
Ambulance: 94

Telecommunications

Most public telephones only accept phone cards (telekarta), which can be bought from tobacco kiosks or post offices. Direct-dial international and domestic calls can also be made from larger post offices, where you pay at the end of the call. Local, national and international calls can be made from most hotel telephones, but at a very high call rate.

Security and Crime

Crime rates in Croatia are lower than in most European countries and crimes against tourists is rare. Simple precautions such as not leaving valuables in vehicles, carrying personal belongings securely and avoiding walking alone in dark areas at night minimise the risk. It is advisable to photocopy the identification pages of your passport, so that if it is lost or stolen the consulate will be able to issue a replacement quickly.

The Croatian government was quick to remove land mines at the end of the war and most areas are completely safe.

Greece

Fact File

Area 131,950 sq. km (50,950 sq. miles), including around 25,050 sq. km (9,670 sq. miles) of islands.
Population almost 11 million. Greater Athens and Piraeus have a population of over 4 million. Thessaloníki, the second-largest city and port, has nearly 1 million residents.
Language Modern Greek.
Religion predominantly Greek Orthodox Christian, with small minorities of Muslims, Catholics, evangelical sects and Jews.
Time Zone GMT +2 hours; +3 hours in summer.
Currency the euro (€).
Weights and measures metric.
Electricity 220V, round two-pin plugs.
International dialling code 30.

Getting Around

To/From Athens Airport

Eleftherios Venizelos Airport is around 30 km (18 miles) from central Athens. There are various connecting services into the city and on to Piraeus. As of July 2004, a light-rail line should whisk you from the airport to Stavrós station, the new terminus of the metro network. Tickets to town are valid on all Athens public transport for 24 hours. Other possibilities include taking the E94 express bus (every

Public Transport Tickets

The best strategy for visitors using the Athens metro is to buy a day pass, which includes one journey to or from the airport; the ISAP line M1 and lines M2/M3 have separate pricing structures, with M1 tickets not valid on M2/M3, and if you're caught by the ubiquitous plainclothes inspectors with the wrong ticket, or no ticket, you get a spot fine of 20 times the standard fare.

Bus tickets, also valid on trolley buses, are sold individually or in books of 10 from specific news kiosks and special booths at bus and metro stations.

15–30 minutes from 6am–midnight) from outside arrivals to metro station Ethnikí Ámyna and then continuing by metro. Alternatively, take the E95 express bus all the way to central Sýndagma Square (every 25–35 minutes), or the E96 express bus to Pireás port (every 20–40 minutes).

A taxi from the airport into Athens will cost €12–20 (2003 rates) depending on time of day/night and your final destination, but including airport supplement and per-bag fee. Traffic congestion has improved since the opening of the Attikí Odhós or ring highway around northern Athens, but the journey time can still be over an hour.

By Hire Car

Hiring a car in Greece is not as cheap as you might hope, owing to high insurance premiums and import duties – more than Spain, a bit less than France is a good estimate. Prices vary according to the type of car, season and length of rental and should include CDW (collision damage waiver) and VAT at 18 percent. Payment can, and often must, be made with a major credit card. A full home-country driving licence (for EU residents) or an International Driving Permit (for all others, including US citizens) is essential – you won't be able to hire a car without this. Drivers must be at least 21 years old, sometimes 25.

You can book a car in advance through major international chains such as Avis, Budget or Hertz.
Avis: Athens office: Amalías 48, tel: 210 322 4951; Airport: tel: 210 353 0578.
Budget: Athens office: Syngroú 8, tel: 210 921 4771; Airport: tel: 210 353 0353.
Hertz: Athens office: Syngroú 12, tel: 210 922 0102; Airport: tel: 210 353 4900.

There are also many reputable, smaller chains, some particular to Greece, that offer a comparable service at lower rates. In Athens, most are on, or just off, Syngroú Avenue in the district known as Makrighiánni.
Antena: Syngroú 52, tel: 210 922 4000.
Autorent: Syngroú 11, tel: 210 923 2514.
Just Syngroú 43, tel: 210 923 9104.
Kosmos: Syngroú 9, tel: 210 923 4695.
Reliable: Syngroú 3, tel: 210 924 9000.

By Taxi

Taxis are cheap, but finding one can be difficult at certain times of the day

Public Holidays

1 January New Year's Day
6 January Epiphany
February/March First day of Lent
25 March Annunciation
March/April Good Friday; Orthodox Easter (Monday)
1 May Labour Day
May/June Pentecost (50 days after Easter)
15 August Feast of the Assumption
28 October "Ohi" Day
25/26 December Christmas

in Athens – probably worst before the early afternoon meal. However, in recent years various radio taxi services have started up in Athens and most other larger towns. They can pick you up within a short time (usually) of your call to a central booking number. Hotels will call a taxi for you that will pick you up at the reception.

When you hail a taxi, try to get in before stating your destination. The drivers are very picky and often won't let you in unless you're going in their direction. Make sure the taxi meter is on "1" when you start out, and not on "2" – that's the double fare, which is only permitted from midnight to 5am, or outside designated city limits. Once inside, you may find yourself with company. Don't be alarmed. It is traditional practice for drivers to pick up two, three, even four individual riders, provided they're going roughly in the same direction. In these cases, make a note of the meter count when you get in. You should pay the difference in meter reading between embarking and alighting, plus the €0.74 minimum.

There are extra charges for each piece of luggage in the boot, for leaving or entering an airport or seaport, plus bonuses around Christmas and Easter.

Some drivers will quote you the correct price, but many others will try to rip you off, especially if it seems you're a novice. These rules apply more to Athens than to the islands, although it's still necessary to be assertive on Crete and Rhodes.

Athens Public Transport

The Athens **metro** system opened in January 2000, halving travel times around the city and making a visible reduction in surface traffic. The stations themselves are spacious and clean, with advertising placards kept to a minimum.

With an influx of modern, air-conditioned rolling stock, travelling by the Athens blue-and-white buses is much less an ordeal than it used to be. They are still usually overcrowded, and the routes are a mystery even to long-time residents. However, prices are very reasonable. Most bus services run until just before midnight. Trolley buses are marginally faster and more frequent, and serve points of tourist interest. No. 1 links the centre of the city with the railway stations, No. 5 passes the archaeological museum, and No. 7 does a triangular circuit of the central districts.

Entry Requirements and Customs

As for other EU countries – *see box on page 345*.

Money Matters

The Greek currency is the euro (€) – evró in Greek (*see box on page 345*). Though it's safer to carry most of your currency in travellers' cheques, it is also worth carrying a limited sum in US dollars or pounds sterling. On those occasions when you can't find a place to cash cheques, there will usually be a shop or post office able to convert those currencies into euro. Exchange rates go up or down daily. To find out the current rate of exchange, check illuminated displays in bank windows, or the newspapers; you can read the tables even in Greek.

Credit/Debit Cards

Many of the more expensive hotels, restaurants and shops accept major credit cards, as does Olympic Airways and the larger ferry companies or travel agents. The average pension or tavérna does not, however, so be sure to enquire, if that is how you intend to pay. You will find that most brands of card are accepted by the numerous cashpoint machines (ATMs). However, use debit rather than credit cards in ATMS, as credit cards tend to have ruinous surcharges, often amounting

Tipping

Service is included in restaurant and bar bills although it is customary to leave any small change on the table. Taxi drivers expect a 10 percent tip. Unless service is included (check, as many hotels add 12 percent to the price of the room), hotel chambermaids should be left a tip of around €1 per day. Porters and doormen should be tipped up to €1.50, depending on services provided. Attendants in toilets should be left around €0.30.

Emergency Numbers

Police 100
Ambulance 161
Fire 199
Tourist police 171 (Athens only; outside of Athens, ring 210 171)

to over 4 percent of the transaction value. This caveat aside, you will find that this is the most convenient and least expensive way of getting funds, and many of the machines operate around the clock.

Opening Times

Banks are open Monday to Thursday 8am–2.30pm, until 2pm on Friday.

Shop hours are complicated and vary according to the type of business and the day of the week. The main thing to remember is that most open at 8.30am or 9am and close on Monday, Wednesday and Saturday at 2.30pm. On Tuesday, Thursday and Friday most businesses close at 2pm and reopen in the afternoon from 5–8.30pm (winter), 5.30 or 6–9pm (summer).

You'll soon learn that schedules are very flexible in Greece (both in business and personal affairs). To avoid disappointment, allow ample time when shopping and doing any kind of transaction.

Telecommunications

The Telecommunications Company of Greece (OTE, known as oh-tay) controls domestic and international communications. Most public telephones accept cards for both international and domestic calls rather than coins. Purchase cards at OTE offices in 100-unit, 500-unit or 1,000-unit capacities. Kiosks and newsstands also sell the smaller unit cards. OTE offices have call booths where you can make international calls and pay when you have finished. The main OTE office in Athens is at Stadíou 15, tel: 210 331 2926; open Monday–Friday 7am–midnight, Saturday–Sunday and holidays 8am–midnight. The OTE office at Patission 85 is open 24 hours a day.

Most hotels have direct-dial international lines, but add a huge surcharge to the cost of your call. Avoid this by using a pre-pay international card with an access number.

Security and Crime

Greece is still one of the safest countries in Europe; violent crime remains relatively rare. Sadly,

however, petty theft does occur, and locked cars and front doors in the countryside are now the norm. Because of security considerations post-September 11, it is unwise to leave luggage unattended anywhere except perhaps in a hotel lobby, under the gaze of the desk staff. Belongings left behind in a café will still usually be put aside for you to collect.

Athens Hotels

Athens Hilton
Vas. Sofías 46
Tel: 210 728 1000
Fax: 210 728 1111
The new-look Hilton, open after a major refit, is extremely plush and very expensive. Silent lifts whisk you up to dimly lit but chic corridors where you sink into plush carpets – and that's all before you get to the rooms. Two good restaurants, including the rooftop Galaxy which has stupendous views. €€€
Grande Bretagne
Sýntagma Square
Tel: 210 333 0000
Fax: 210 332 8034
Almost as expensive as the Hilton and just as plush in its own special way, the Grande Bretagne is the doyen of Athenian hotels. Also just emerged from a refit, this historic building oozes class, from its luxurious rooms, to its beautiful spa, to its highly recommended restaurant. €€€

Price Categories

Prices are per night for a double room during the high season.
€€€ = Expensive over €100
€€ = Moderate €50–100
€ = Inexpensive under €50

St George Lycabettus
Kleoménous 2, Kolonáki
Tel: 210 729 0711
Fax: 210 729 0439
In a pre-Olympic fit of enthusiasm, this hotel too has undergone renovation and now styles itself a "boutique hotel". The external (more expensive) rooms have some of the best views in the city. The cool, comfortable rooms and suites are elegant and subdued, and the rooftop swimming pool is a delight. There are also two good restaurants, one funky, the other more restrained but with a superb view over the Acropolis. €€€
NJV Athens Plaza
Sýntagma Square
Tel: 210 33 52 400
Fax: 210 32 35 856
Modern, swish, and just a bit corporate, the Plaza does, however,

kit out its rooms with fabrics by Ralph
Lauren and Versace and tries hard to
pander to your every whim. The lobby
café is a good retreat from the heat or
cold. €€–€€€

Acropolis View

Webster 10 and Robértou Gáli
Tel: 210 921 7303
The Acropolis view of the name is
from only a few rooms, but also the
roof terrace. The rooms themselves
are small but clean and well cared for,
and the hotel has had the inevitable
pre-Olympic makeover. The location is
excellent and the metro is close-by. €

Attalos

Athinás 29
Tel: 210 321 2801–3
Fax: 210 324 3124
Fairly standard but comfortable rooms
in a hotel close to Monastiráki Square
(noisy during the day but quietens
down at night). The staff are attentive
and friendly, and there is a fine view of
the city and Acropolis from the roof
terrace. They will also store luggage
for free. €

Aphrodite

Einárdou 12 and M. Vóda 65
Tel: 210 881 0589/881 6574
Clean, unpretentious and friendly, this
small hotel is a good deal. Slightly off
the beaten track but midway between
Viktoria and Stathmos Lárisas metro
stations. There is a pleasant
basement bar and an excellent deal
on the inter-island pass. They also
offer free luggage storage. €

Turkey

Fact File

Area 780,000 sq. km (300,000
sq. miles).
Population 67.8 million; Istanbul 10
million; Ankara 4 million.
Language Turkish.
Religion officially 99 percent of Turks
are Sunni Muslim, and 1 percent are
Orthodox, Catholic or Protestant
Christians and Jews.
Time GMT +2 hours; GMT +3 hours in
summer.
Currency Turkish lira (TL).
Weights and measures metric.
Electricity 220 volts AC. Two-pronged
round plug.
International dialling code 90.

Getting Around

To/From Istanbul Airport

There is an efficient bus service from
Atatürk Airport (25 km/15 miles
southwest of Istanbul) to the city
centre, operating every 30 minutes
between 6am and 11pm, and
continuing at longer intervals through
the night. This makes one stop (at
which you should alight for
connections to the old-city districts of
Sultanahmet and Eminönü) before
terminating in the centre of the new
city at Taksim Square.

The city's metro system is being
extended to reach the airport, though
the opening date of the airport line
has not been announced. A taxi ride
from the airport to Sultanahmet or
Taksim takes about 45 minutes and
costs around €12–15 (2003 rates).
You can also make the trip by dolmus,
a less expensive, shared taxi *(see
below)*.

By Hire Car

Drivers from the US, Canada, UK,
Australia, New Zealand and South
Africa require only a valid licence from
their home countries (an international
driver's permit is no longer required).
Many major companies (Avis, Budget,
and Hertz) have outlets in Turkey and
provide very competitive rates,
especially for rentals of a week or
more. Cars with automatic

transmission and air-conditioning are
much more expensive.

You'll find any number of car-hire
agencies in all the major resorts,
though you should expect to pay more
per day than you would on a weekly
basis. Try to avoid any agency that
charges per kilometre, as rates can
climb rapidly, and also be wary of
some local agencies that demand you
turn over your passport for the
duration of the rental.

While most companies provide
basic insurance that covers damage to
the vehicle you are driving, collision
damage waiver (CDW), which covers
damage to other vehicles, is usually
not included — you should definitely
pay the extra fee for this coverage, as
accidents are not uncommon in Turkey.

Istanbul

Avis: Airport, tel: 0212 662 0852;
Taksim (at the Hilton Hotel),
tel: 0212 246 5256.
Budget: Airport, tel: 0212 663 0858;
central Istanbul, tel: 0212 253 9200.
Europcar: Airport, tel: 0212 663
0807; central Istanbul, tel: 0212 233
7101.
Hertz: Airport, tel: 0212 663 0807;
central Istanbul, tel: 0212 233 7101.

By Taxi and Dolmus

A fleet of yellow taxis also serves
most larger towns. It is often
unnecessary to look for one; they will
find you, signalling by slowing to a
crawl alongside you or hooting. You
should check the meter is switched on
(one red light on the meter for day
rate and two for evening) – it almost
invariably will be, but it is worth
checking. Whatever you're quoted, it
will probably be a lot less than you
would pay in many other places.
However there are drivers who try to
multiply the fare by driving round in
circles or simply saying that the meter
is broken; try and check roughly how
much it should be before getting in.

An economical method of travelling
around a city or to a neighbouring
town is by *dolmus* (literally "full",
sharing the same root as the Turkish
word for the country's stuffed
vegetables). A kind of shared taxi,
usually a minibus, the *dolmus* travels
along a fixed route for a fixed fare,
paid to the driver. At the start of the
route, it may not set off until it is full,
which can entail a wait. After that,
passengers can get on and off
whenever they want.

Emergency Numbers

Police: 155
Ambulance: 112
Fire: 110

Istanbul Public Transport

Istanbul has an efficient, if limited, **metro system**, running from Taksim Square, in front of the Marmara Hotel, to the shopping and business districts of Gayrettepe and Levent 4 and down to the Tünel. There is a **tram** beginning at the Eminönü ferry docks, passing through the main tourist centres before branching off to the intercity bus garages and out to the airport.

A "nostalgic" tram runs up Istiklal Caddeşi between Tünel and Taksim every 20 minutes, while the tiny "tünel" underground saves commuters the steep walk up the hill from the Karaköy ferry docks. For metro and tram information, tel: 0212 568 9970.

City buses, run by the municipality, have the letters IETT on the side. They are red and white with a blue stripe on the side and follow fixed routes. There are also similar but older-looking orange and cream full-sized private buses (*Özel Halk Ötöbüsü*). These are, in fact, retired municipality buses, and on them you pay the driver's attendant who sits just inside at the front, ready to take your money. The fare is the same as on the public buses.

There are also **private minibuses**, usually white or pale blue, which are faster. On these you pay a fare to the driver or his assistant.

Entry Requirements

Visa regulations change frequently, so check the latest situation with your travel agent or cruise line. At the time of going to press, citizens of the following countries required visas, which can be obtained at the point of entry into Turkey (not in advance from consulates): UK (£10), Canada (US$40), Australia (US$20) and Ireland (€10). You must pay in hard currency at the border before immigration. Photographs are not required. You will be issued with a multiple-entry tourist visa valid for three months.

US citizens may buy a three-month visa (US$100) either at the point of entry or from a Turkish consulate in advance of travel.

Provided that they have a valid passport, nationals of many countries (including New Zealand) do not need a visa for visits of up to three months.

Customs Regulations

You are allowed to bring into the country up to 200 cigarettes (400 if bought in a Turkish duty-free shop), 50 cigars, 200g pipe tobacco (500g if bought in Turkey), 75 cl alcohol, 5 litres wine or spirits, 1kg chocolate and 1.5kg coffee.

Bus Tickets

Buy bus tickets in advance either from one of the many ticket booths or from shops, kiosks and street sellers near bus stops. *Tam bilet* means full fare, i.e. a normal adult ticket. Drop your ticket into a small box as you board the bus (at the front). Some longer urban journeys require more than one ticket. On the orange and cream private buses you simply pay the driver's attendant who sits inside at the front.

A new system has been introduced, using the *Akbil* or "intelligent ticket", which uses an electronic token on to which fares can be loaded. You buy a certain number of journeys, and put your token into the special machine at the front of the bus, where the fare is deducted. The token can easily be recharged. Look for the *Akbil* sign at ticket booths.

Money Matters

The unit of currency in Turkey is the lira, usually abbreviated as TL. Banks are generally open Monday–Friday 8.30am–noon and 1.30–5pm; very occasionally, a bank in a major resort will open on Saturday morning as well. Major banks in cities and at least one bank in most towns have currency exchanges. Post offices also usually have currency-exchange windows, and many local travel agencies, especially those in popular tourist areas, exchange money.

Travellers' cheques and credit cards are widely accepted, though most establishments give an unfavourable exchange rate on travellers' cheques; you are better off cashing them at a currency exchange and paying in cash. Visa and MasterCard are the most widely accepted credit cards; many establishments do not take American Express cards.

ATMS are easily found even in smaller Turkish towns and resorts these days. However, malfunctioning communications systems with central banks often render ATMS outside of major cities useless, so plan accordingly.

Opening Times

Shops open 9.30am–7pm (as late as midnight during the summer season in some resorts).
Banks open Monday–Friday 8.30am–noon and 1.30–5pm.
Tourist offices open Monday–Friday

8.30am–12.30pm and 1.30–5.30pm and sometimes at weekends as well.
Archaeological sites open daily 8am–6pm (with many variations).
Museums open Tuesday–Sunday 9.30am–5.30pm (with many variations).
Restaurants open noon–2.30 or 3pm for lunch, 7 or 7.30–10 or 10.30pm for dinner (those that have music and offer drinks will sometimes remain open into the small hours).

Telecommunications

Public phone kiosks in Turkey are usually blue. They are located all over cities and towns, and take tokens or phone cards, available at post offices and newsstands. Phone cards come in 30-, 60- and 100-unit denominations. Calls are very inexpensive in Turkey – only a few cents for a local call. To use public phones, pick up the receiver, insert the token or the phone card, and dial the number you wish to reach when the light on the phone goes off, indicating you have credit in the machine.

When dialling from city to city in Turkey, you must precede the number with a zero and the city code (for instance, when calling European Istanbul from elsewhere in Turkey, dial 0212); however, you do not dial a city code when calling within that city (for example, drop the 0212 when calling from a number in European Istanbul to another number in European Istanbul).

To call internationally, you must first dial 00, then the country code, then the city or area code, then the number.

Most hotels apply large surcharges to long-distance calls. One way around this is to use a telephone calling card and charge all calls to that. Your calling card company can supply the access code you need to reach its system; simply dial the code, and an English-speaking operator will come on to assist you or you can follow a

Public Holidays

1 January New Year's Day
23 April National Sovereignty and Children's Day (folk dancing)
19 May Atatürk's Commemoration and Youth and Sports Day
30 August Victory Day
29 October Republic Day
10 November Anniversary of Atatürk's death

In addition to these state holidays, there are numerous religious festivals and holidays.

Tipping

It is customary to tip a small amount to anyone who does you a service: the hotel cleaner, porter, the doorman who gets you a taxi and so on. Even in cinemas you give something to the person who shows you to your seat.

The only difficulty is arming yourself with plenty of small notes. For some inexplicable reason, change (bozuk para) is always in short supply. At the time of writing, anything between 500,000 and 2,000,000TL (approx. 20–70 pence/US30 cents–$1 would be in order.

In restaurants, round up the bill by 10–15 percent; if service has been included, leave 5 percent on the table in cash for the waiter.

Taxis are the exception: you don't tip taxi drivers and they do not expect it, though you can round the fare up to the nearest suitable figure as change can be a problem.

series of English-language prompts. You can also buy a pre-paid international phone card at some newsstands; you will be instructed, in English, to dial a toll-free access number, enter your PIN (which is printed on the card) and then to dial the number you wish to reach; the rates you pay when using these cards are often quite low.

For directory assistance in Turkey, dial 118.

Security and Crime

Turkey is relatively safe, and even in Istanbul crime is rarely more serious than pick-pocketing or purse-snatching; be especially careful in crowded markets. This said, you should be aware of some heists that are increasingly being perpetrated against tourists. These include a scam in which Istanbul cab drivers take your money, substitute it with lower denomination bills, and flash them at you insisting that you have underpaid; to avoid this situation, take note of the money you are handing the driver and call for the police immediately if an argument ensues. Far more serious is someone (usually a man), who will offer assistance with directions, only to lure you to an accomplice who may attempt to mug you. There have also been several instances in which seemingly friendly strangers have slipped drugs into tourists' drinks and stolen away with money and valuables while the victims slept off

the effects. However, we must emphasise that these are rare occurrences.

Two of the most serious offences tourists themselves might commit are possession of illicit drugs or antiquities; both incursions are punishable by stiff prison sentences and are not to be taken lightly.

Istanbul Hotels

Ceylan inter-Continental
Taksim
Tel: 0212 231 2121
Fax: 0212 231 2180
In the city centre, this luxurious hotel commands superb views of the Bosphorous and city skyline. Restaurants include Turkish, French and Californian, and there are bars and deluxe banqueting and convention rooms, sports facilities and so on. €€€€

Conrad International Istanbul
Barbaros Bulvarı, Beşiktaş.
Tel: 0212 227 3000
Fax: 0212 259 6667
A huge hotel with excellent Italian and Turkish restaurants, a French patisserie, and live jazz in the bar every night. The health club has indoor and outdoor swimming pools and there is a 24-hour business centre. Convenient location with wonderful views of the Bosphorus and Yıldız Imperial Gardens. €€€€

Divan
Cumhuriyet Caddesi, Elmadağ.
Tel: 0212 231 4100
Fax: 0212 248 8527
A relatively small, first-rate hotel with 169 rooms and 11 suites. The Divan has one of the most distinguished restaurants in Istanbul, serving Ottoman and international dishes, as well as a popular café for quick meals. A few rooms have private terraces. €€€€

Merit Antique
Ordu Caddesi 226, Laleli
Tel: 0212 513 9300
Fax: 0212 512 6390/513 9340
This lovingly restored early 20th-century apartment complex in the heart of the old city is now an attractive hotel with 275 rooms. Superb Chinese, Turkish and Kosher restaurants, patisserie, wine bar and health club. €€€€

Four Seasons
Tevkifhane Sokak 1, Sultanahmet
Tel: 0212 638 8200
Fax: 0212 638 8210
There are views of Aya Sofya and the Blue Mosque from this neoclassical building, with 54 rooms and 11 suites, as well as top-notch service, splendid decor (complete with Ottoman antiques), and all modern

conveniences. The restaurant offers top-quality Turkish and Continental cuisine. €€€€

Pera Palas
Meşrutiyet Caddesi 198/100, Tepebaşı
Tel: 0212 251 4560
Fax: 0212 251 4089
The historic "Orient Express" hotel retains its 100-year-old aura of spy intrigue as well as its original decor. €€€€

Anemon Galata
Büyükhendek Caddesi 11, Kuledibi Beyoğlu
Tel: 0212 293 2343
Fax: 0212 292 2340
Delightfully restored old hotel with 23 rooms and 7 suites, in a perfect position right beside the Galata Tower. The rooftop bar and restaurant has one of the finest views in the city, over the Bosphorus and Golden Horn. €€€

Ayasofya Pansiyonlar
Soğukçeşme Sokak, Sultanahmet
Tel: 0212 513 3660
Fax: 0212 513 3669
Great location on a charming cobbled lane lined with restored wooden houses directly behind Aya Sofya. The hotel is furnished with period furniture and has 57 rooms, 4 suites, 3 restaurants (one in a Byzantine cistern), café, bars, Turkish bath and even a research library on old Istanbul. €€€

Price Categories

Prices are per night for a double room during the high season. Please note that euro symbols are used for consistency only (Turkey does not use the euro). Check current conversion rates when you travel.
€€€€ = above €150
€€€ = €70–150
€ = €50–70
€ = below €50

Yeşil Ev
Kabasakal Caddesi 5, Sultanahmet
Tel: 0212 517 6785
Fax: 0212 517 6780
A restored wooden mansion, previously the home of an Ottoman pasha, located between Aya Sofya and the Blue Mosque. 18 rooms and 1 suite with period decor, intimate walled rear garden with conservatory and good restaurant. Book well in advance. €€€

Empress Zoë
Akbıyık Cad, Adliya Sokak 10, Sultanahmet
Tel: 0212 518 2504
Fax: 0212 518 5699
Owner Ann Nevins from the US has

turned this small hotel (16 rooms, 3 suites) near Topkapı Palace into something unique, complete with Byzantine wall paintings and a garden that incorporates the ruins of a 15th-century Turkish bath. €

Hotel Fehmi Bey
Üçler Sokak 15, Sultanahmet
Tel: 0212 638 9083/85
Fax: 0212 518 1264
This 18-room restored townhouse has friendly hosts, slick decor, a sauna and a spectacular sea view from its rooftop terrace. €

Hotel Kybele
Yerebatan Caddesi 35, Sultanahmet
Tel: 0212 511 7766/67
Fax: 0212 513 4393
A treasure house of Ottoman antiques with a lobby lit by over 1,000 antique lamps; 16 rooms, restaurant, phone, etc. and delightful courtyard. English, Japanese and other languages spoken. €

Hotel Nomade
Divanyolu, Ticarethane Sokak 15, Sultanahmet
Tel: 0212 511 1296
Fax: 0212 513 2404
Run by French-educated twin sisters, this homely 15-room hotel will appeal to well-travelled internationalists, intellectuals and solo females. It has a rooftop terrace, and its own bistro (Rumeli Cafe) across the street.

Cyprus

Fact File

Area 9,251 sq. km (3,572 sq. miles), with the south under the control of the internationally recognised Republic of Cyprus, and north under Turkish military occupation.
Population of the estimated 833,000 people living on the island, approximately 616,000 are Greek Cypriots, 210,000 are Turkish Cypriots, 7,000 Armenians, Maronites and several Latin (Western Christian) minorities.
Languages Greek (southern Cyprus) and Turkish (north).
Religion Greek Orthodox and Muslim.
Time zone GMT +2 hours, +3 hours in summer.
Currency Cyprus pound (CY£), divided into 100 cents. Turkish lira is used in the north.
Weights & measures metric.
Electricity 240 volts; flat three-pin plugs. Some hotel rooms have a 110-volt outlet for electric shavers.
International dialling code Republic of Cyprus: 357, **North Cyprus**: 392.

Getting Around

By Hire Car
Distances in Cyprus are relatively large and, as many sights are spread out beyond the reach of public transport, it is worth hiring a car. Budget, Thrifty, Hertz, Avis and Eurodollar all have offices in the major cities, and representatives at Larnaka and Pafos airports and at the main resorts. Rates are cheap, although Collision Damage Waiver (CDW) insurance is extra, as is cover for damage to tyres or windscreen. In summer, air conditioning is essential. Cypriot firms generally charge slightly less than international agencies and provide equally good cars and service. Note that the rate always includes unlimited mileage.
Reserve a car in advance – especially for the high season. To hire a car, you must have a valid national driver's licence (held for at least three years) or an International Driving Permit. Depending on the company, the minimum age is 21 to 25. Drivers

under 25 pay an insurance premium. A deposit is usually required, payable by credit card.
Driving conditions are generally good in Cyprus, with well-surfaced, well-marked roads and fast motorways running along the south coast, linking Limassol, Larnaka and Pafos, and heading inland to Nicosia.

By Taxi
Vehicles are metered and rates are low, making private taxis a favourite form of transport. Many visitors, daunted by the difficult road conditions, travel around the island exclusively by taxi.

Entry Requirements

Entry regulations for the **Republic of Cyprus** is the same as for other EU countries (it became a member in May 2004) – *see box on page 345*. For **Northern Cyprus** *see Turkey, page 366*.
Currently the only way to visit both the southern and the northern part of the island during the same holiday is to arrive in the former and take a day's excursion into the north.

Customs Regulations

The **Republic of Cyprus** shares customs regulations with the rest of the EU. *See page 345 for details.* In **Northern Cyprus**, you can bring in/take out 1.5 litres of wine; 1.5 litres of spirits; 400 cigarettes or 100 cigars or 500g tobacco; 100ml perfume; 100ml eau de toilette.

Money Matters

Despite EU membership, the unit of currency in the **Republic of Cyprus** remains the Cyprus pound (CY£), called the *lira* in Greek. The pound is divided into 100 cents. It is usually more advantageous to exchange money at a bank or bureau de change in Cyprus than in your own country. In the **north** the Turkish lira – the same money in circulation in Turkey – is the official currency.

Emergency Numbers

Republic
Police: 112
Ambulance: 112
Fire: 112
Night pharmacies: 112

North
Police: 155
Ambulance: 112
Fire: 199
(Operators in both sectors usually speak good English.)

Exchange Facilities

Republic In addition to banks, most hotel receptions will exchange cash and travellers' cheques. Most banks have automated cash dispensers (ATMs) which you can use for withdrawing cash using cash cards, credit cards and cards linked to the Plus and Cirrus networks. As a rule, banks are open Monday to Friday 8.30am–12.30pm, and also from 3.15–4.45pm on Mondays from September to June. In tourist centres, however, banks frequently stay open from 3.30–5.30pm (October–April) and 4–6pm (May–September) *except* Monday. Some are open on Saturday morning.

North You are best off taking one of the main international currencies, such as dollars or pounds sterling, as exchanging money can be less straightforward than in the south. Banks operate only limited hours (generally 8.30am–noon), but there are money exchange houses in all the major centres. These are open longer hours (Monday–Friday 8am–6pm, with a lunch break, and Saturday morning), offer a fast, reliable service and do not charge commission.

Opening Times

Republic of Cyprus

Shops open Monday, Tuesday, Thursday, Friday 8.30am–6pm, till 7.30pm in summer; Wednesday and Saturday 8.30am–2pm. Most shops close for an afternoon siesta from approximtely 1–4pm in summer.
Business/office hours open Monday–Friday 8am–1pm, 3–6pm in winter, 8am–1pm, 4–7pm in summer.

North Cyprus

Shops open Monday–Saturday 8am–6pm.
Offices open Monday–Saturday 8am–1pm and 4–6 or 7pm.
   Although banks, shops and businesses are closed on public holidays, in resort and coastal areas shops and certain services may remain open.

Telecommunications

To call the UK from Cyprus, dial 0044 plus the area code, then the number. To call the US, dial 001, then the area code, then the number. For directory enquiries in Cyprus dial 192.
Public telephones can be used for local and international calls. All have instructions in English. A phone card, available in C£3-, C£5- and C£10- denominations, is the easiest way to make international calls. In most hotels, you can dial long distance from your room, but charges are high. Standard rates and other information is available from long-distance operators, all of whom speak good English (tel: 194).
Area codes do not exist. Instead, there are 8-digit numbers. In Nicosia they start with 22; Agia Napa 23; Larnaka 24; Limassol 25; Pafos 26.

Security and Crime

There is still so little crime on Cyprus that the few robberies which do take place make headlines. The island's only violence generally occurs in drunken brawls in Agia Napa (and an occasional fatal shooting or car-bombing linked to organised crime). Cypriots are normally very honest, but there are always exceptions, so take the usual precautions of locking your hire car and depositing money and jewellery in the hotel safe, or taking as little as possible with you when you go ashore.

Public Holidays

Republic of Cyprus

1 January New Year's Day
6 January Epiphany
Feb/March First day of Lent
25 March Greek Independence Day
March/April Good Friday, Easter Monday
1 April Greek Cypriot National Day
1 May Labour Day
May/June Pentecost
15 August Assumption
1 October Cyprus Independence Day
28 October Greek National Day, *Ochi* ("No") Day
25/26 December Christmas

North Cyprus

1 January New Year's Day
23 April National Sovereignty and Children's Day
1 May Labour Day
19 May Young People's and Sports Day
20 July Peace and Freedom Day (the anniversary of the invasion of the northern part of the island)
1 August Communal Resistance Day
30 August Victory Day (Turkish victory over the Greeks in 1922)
29 October Turkish National Day
15 November Anniversary of the proclamation of the "Turkish Republic of Northern Cyprus"

In addition, Northern Cyprus observes Islamic festivals such as Ramadan and Islamic New Year, whose dates vary according to the Muslim calendar.

Other Destinations

Bulgaria

Fact File

Area 110,910 sq. km (43,000 sq. miles).
Capital Sofia.
Population 7.7 million.
Language Bulgarian.
Religion Bulgarian Orthodox with a substantial Muslim minority.
Time zone GMT +2 hours.
Currency the Lev.
International dialing code 359.

ENTRY REQUIREMENTS

Western nationals do not require visas for short stays; only passports are required.

CUSTOMS REGULATIONS

Duty-free allowances for visitors are: 1 litre of spirits, 2 litres of wine, 200 cigarettes or 50 cigars. To avoid complications upon departure, declare anything of value, including jewellery and cameras, when entering the country.

MONEY MATTERS

Private exchange offices offer better rates than banks. Credit cards are not widely accepted, except in the top hotels and resorts. ATMs are common only in the capital and in the coastal resorts. Travellers' cheques are rarely accepted and a high commission is payable.

OPENING TIMES

Shops mostly open Monday–Friday 9am–7pm, with speciality stores open from 10am–6pm; most shops also open 9am–1pm on Saturday.
Banks are open Monday–Friday 8–11.30am and 2–6pm. Some open Saturday 8.30–11.30am.

However, opening times for shops and banks can be unpredictable; your cruise line may be able to give guidance on specific places.

PUBLIC HOLIDAYS

1 January New Year's Day; **3 March** National Day (Day of Liberation); **March/April** (dates variable) Orthodox Easter Sunday and Monday; **1 May** Labour Day; **6 May** St George's Day (Day of Bulgarian Army); **24 May** St Cyril and Methodius Day (Day of Culture and Literacy); **6 September** Unification of Bulgaria Day; **22 September** Independence Day; **1 November** Day of the Spiritual Leaders of Bulgaria; **25–26 December** Christmas.

SECURITY AND CRIME

Don't carry all your cash in one place, and avoid displaying large sums of money. Behave sensibly and be aware that street crime in the cities of Eastern Europe is generally as rife as it is in any big city in the world.

Crime against foreigners has increased in recent years.

It's a good idea to deposit any valuables in the safe if you are staying in a hotel, or to take as little as possible with you when you go ashore. Pickpockets are on the increase in Eastern Europe. Keep valuables out of sight and hang onto your bags.

Emergency Telephone Numbers
Police: 166
Ambulance: 150
Directory enquiries: 144
Operator: 121
International operator: 0123

Romania

Fact File
Area 237,500 sq. km (91,700 sq. miles).
Capital Bucharest.
Population 22.4 million.
Language Romanian; minorities speak Hungarian and German.
Religion Romanian Orthodox with substantial Catholic and Muslim minorities.
Time zone GMT +1 hour.
Currency the Leu.
International dailling code 40.

ENTRY REQUIREMENTS

EU and US citizens do not require visas; other nationalities do.

CUSTOMS REGULATIONS

Duty-free allowances for visitors are: 1 litre of spirits, 2 litres of wine, 200 cigarettes or 50 cigars. Romanian customs officials may be strict at the best of times in regards to antiquities and medicines.

MONEY MATTERS

The best deals for currency exchange are at bureaux de change, though official tourist offices also exchange currency. Very high rates are charged for cashing travellers' cheques, if they are accepted at all. ATMs do exist but they are often out of service. Credit cards are becoming more accepted at more expensive establishments.

OPENING TIMES

Shops mostly open Monday–Friday 9am–7pm, and Saturday 9am–1pm, with speciality stores open 10am–6pm.
Banks are open Monday–Friday 9am–4pm.

Opening times can be unpredictable; your cruise line may be able to give guidance.

PUBLIC HOLIDAYS

1 January New Year's Day; **March/April** (dates variable) Easter Monday (Romanian Orthodox); **1 May** Labour Day; **1 December** Day of National Unity; **25–26 December** Christmas.

SECURITY AND CRIME

Street crime is generally as rife as it is in any big city in the world and crime against foreigners has increased in recent years. Take the usual precautions: don't carry all your cash in one place and avoid displaying large sums of money.

It's a good idea to deposit any valuables in the safe if you are staying in a hotel, or take as little as possible with you when you go ashore.

Emergency Telephone Numbers
Police: 955
Ambulance: 961
Fire: 981
International Operator: 971
Operator: 991

Ukraine

Fact File
Area 603,700 sq. km (233,100 sq. miles).
Population: 48.4 million.
Language: Ukrainian is the official language; Russian is widely spoken.
Religion Orthodox with substantial Roman and Greek Catholic and Protestant minorities.
Capital: Kiev (pop 2.6 million).
Time zone: GMT + 2 hours
Currency: hryvna
International dialling codes: 380

ENTRY REQUIREMENTS

A valid passport and visa are required. Visas are obtained from Ukrainian embassies or consulates worldwide. Travellers from countries where there is a Ukrainian embassy or consulate cannot obtain visas on arrival, so make sure you have the proper visa before you get here. A tour/cruise company voucher is required to obtain a visa, unless you are a citizen of the EU, US, Canada, Japan, Switzerland, Slovakia or Turkey.

CUSTOMS REGULATIONS

You are exempt from customs formalities if you are carrying less than US$1,000 (or equivalent) and less than US$250 worth of jewellery and valuables. Otherwise you have to fill in a declaration form.

MONEY MATTERS

Ukraine has a cash economy, but travellers' cheques and credit cards are gaining wider acceptance in larger cities. Use of credit cards is limited to the more expensive hotels, tourist restaurants, international airlines and select stores. Changing US dollars or any other currency is legal only at banks, currency exchange desks at hotels, and at licensed exchange booths.

OPENING TIMES

Shops are usually open Monday–Saturday 10am–8pm. More and more businesses work the whole day, foregoing closure at lunch time, but some do close for an hour, either between 1–2pm or 2–3pm. Don't be shocked if service is not courteous; sales personnel are slowly being taught that the customer is most important.

Banks usually open Monday–Friday 9am–5pm but sometimes close from 1–2pm or 2–3pm.

PUBLIC HOLIDAYS

1 January New Year's Day; **7 January** Russian Orthodox Christmas Day; **23 February** Defenders of the Motherland Day; **8 March** International Women's Day; **April** (movable date) Easter; **1–2 May** Labour Day/Spring Holiday; **9 May** Victory Day; **12 June** Russian Independence Day; **7 November** Great October Socialist Revolution Anniversary; **12 December** Constitution Day.

SECURITY AND CRIME

Don't carry all your cash in one place, and avoid displaying large sums of money. Behave sensibly and be aware that street crime is generally as rife as it is in any big city in the world.

It's a good idea to deposit any valuables in the hotel safe, if you are staying in a hotel, or to take as little as possible with you on a shore visit. Beware of pickpockets in crowded places. Keep valuables out of sight and hang onto your bags.

Emergency Telephone Numbers
Police: 02
Ambulance: 03
Fire: 01

Georgia
Fact File
Area 69,700 sq. km (26,910 sq. miles).
Capital T'bilisi.
Population 5.1 million.
Language Georgian (71 percent); Russian, Armenian, Azeri.
Religion Georgian Orthodox.
Time zone GMT +4 hours; +5 hours in summer.
Currency the Lari.
International dialling code 995.

ENTRY REQUIREMENTS

Visitors need a passport that is valid for 6 months after leaving Georgia. Visas are required, but travellers on cruises should submit all documentation (completed application form, a recent passport-size photo with the name of the applicant clearly written on the reverse, valid passport) to the operator making the travel arrangements. Application forms are available from the Georgian embassy in your home country.

CUSTOMS REGULATIONS

Works of art and antiques can not be exported. There are few restrictions on items that can be brought into the country, except the usual ones on firearms, drugs, pornography, etc.

MONEY MATTERS

There are no ATMs but no doubt there will be soon. Credit cards are accepted in some hotels. Travellers' cheques are not accepted. US dollars are the most widely acceptable foreign currency.

OPENING TIMES

Shops are usually open Monday–Friday 9am–6pm and Saturday morning.
Banks are usually open Monday–Friday 9.30am–5.30pm.

PUBLIC HOLIDAYS

1 January New Year's Day; **7 January** Orthodox Christmas Day; **19 January** Epiphany; **April** (moveable date) Orthodox Easter Monday; **26 May** Independence Day; **28 August** Assumption of the Virgin (Mariamoba); **23 November** St George's Day (Giorgoba)

SECURITY AND CRIME

Be vigilant against street crime. Do not carry large amounts of cash and avoid displaying the money you are carrying. Keep all valuables out of sight, behave sensibly and beware of pickpockets in crowded places. Foreign women may attract a certain amount of attention in the street.

Emergency Telephone Numbers
Police: 02
Ambulance: 03
Fire: 01

Syria
Fact File
Area approximately 185,000 sq. km (71,500 sq. miles).
Capital Damascus.
Population 17 million.
Language Arabic. French and some English are also spoken by the better educated.
Religion Islam, plus Orthodox and Roman Catholic and Jewish minorities.
Time zone GMT +2 hours.
Currency Syrian lire (sl).
International dialling code 963.

ENTRY REQUIREMENTS

A valid passport and entry visa are required for all visitors.

CUSTOMS REGULATIONS

You can bring US$5,000, one carton of cigarettes and 1 litre of alcohol into Syria without declaring them. You can leave with up to $2,000 and up to sl2000 ($40) without declaration.

MONEY MATTERS

The Syrian Commercial Bank is the only bank operating in Syria and here you can change money at the official rate. Neither the Syrian Bank nor hotels will provide cash on credit cards.

OPENING TIMES

Shops usually open 9am–8pm, but their closing day varies according to the owner's religious affiliation. Muslim-owned shops are closed on Friday, except for a few establishments catering for Westerners. Jewish shops are closed on Saturday. Gold shops owned by Armenians are shut on Sunday.
Banks open Saturday–Thursday 9am–2.30pm.
Museums, historic sites and many tourist attractions are closed on Wednesday.
Business offices open Saturday–Thursday 9am–2.30pm and 6–8pm.

PUBLIC HOLIDAYS

1 January New Year's Day; **8 March** Revolution Day; **March/April** Catholic Easter and Orthodox Easter (moveable dates); **17 April** National Day; **1 May** May Day; **6 May** Martyrs' Day; **1 August** Army Day; **6 October** Liberation War of October Day; **16 November** Correctionist Movement Day; **25 December** Christmas Day.

Muslim holidays are governed by the Hegira calendar and move forward by 11 days every year (12 in a leap year): Eid Al-Fitr, end of Ramadan, the Islamic month of fasting; Eid Al-Adha, Feast of the Sacrifice; Al-Hijira, New Year's Day; Mouloud, Birthday of the Prophet.

SECURITY AND CRIME

The Syrian government prides itself on maintaining calm and security. There is great embarrassment when it fails to provide security for its citizens and visitors, so police and security personnel are prevalent and highly visible in the streets.

The biggest problem that visitors face is petty theft. Take care with valuables, cameras and important papers. Foreign passports sell for a lot of money on the black market and are susceptible to theft.

Lebanon

Fact File

Area 10,500 sq. km (4,050 sq. miles).
Capital Beirut.
Population just under 4 million.
Language Arabic, but English and French fluently and widely spoken.
Religion Sunni, Shia, Druze plus Orthodox and Greek Catholic and other minorities.
Time zone GMT +2 hours; +3 hours in summer.
Currency Lebanese lira (known as Lebanese pounds) and US dollar.
International dialling code 961.

ENTRY REQUIREMENTS

Visitors from most Western countries, including Europe, the US, Australasia and Japan, can obtain a visa on arrival at Beirut Airport (if flying in to join a cruise) or from the Lebanese embassy in their own country. Warning: if you have a passport with Israeli entry stamps, you will not be allowed into Lebanon.

CUSTOMS REGULATIONS

Customs procedures on arrival and departure are very relaxed, and Western travellers are rarely checked. Tourists are allowed to bring in two bottles of alcohol, 500g of tobacco or 400 cigarettes, or 20 cigars), as well as 100 ml of perfume.

There is no restriction on bringing into the country, or exporting, any amount of local or foreign currency, and Beirut is a regional centre for changing money. Importing or exporting pornography or narcotics is illegal. On departure, exporting antiquities, defined as items more than 300 years old, is prohibited.

MONEY MATTERS

Many transactions are conducted in US dollars. This means you don't have to buy Lebanese currency on arrival.

However, should you wish to do so, all areas have bureaux de change as well as dozens of banks. Shops, hotels and restaurants frequently give a confusing mixture of Lebanese currency and dollars in change, but it is possible to insist on one currency or the other.

There are plenty of ATMs (cash machines), but some only accept only their bank's own cards.

OPENING TIMES

Shops are open Monday–Saturday 8am–7pm. Some open for only half a day on Saturday and a few close at 6pm on weekdays.
Banks mostly open Monday–Friday 8am–2.30pm, Saturday 8am–noon.

PUBLIC HOLIDAYS

With 18 official religions, Lebanon seems to have more public holidays than anywhere in the world, celebrating various Muslim and Christian festivals as well as national holidays.
1 January New Year's Day; **9 February** Maron Day; **March/April** Easter. Both the Orthodox and Catholic Easters are celebrated, one week apart (moveable dates for both); **1 May** Labour Day; **6 May** Martyrs' Day; **1 November** All Saints' Day; **22 November** Independence Day; **25 December** Christmas Day.

Muslim holidays are governed by the Hegira calendar and move forward by 11 days every year (12 in a leap year). Eid Al-Fitr, end of Ramadan, the Islamic month of fasting; Eid Al-Adha, Feast of the Sacrifice; Al-Hijira, New Year's Day; Mouloud, Birthday of the Prophet.

Ashoura, a Shia Islamic holiday is celebrated on the tenth day of the first month of the Muslim calendar.

SECURITY AND CRIME

Personal crimes, such as muggings and pickpocketing, are virtually unknown in Lebanon, and the country's wartime reputation is very much out of date. Foreigners can walk the streets at any time, day or night, and be much safer than in any Western city. The biggest danger for tourists is traffic, because of the appalling driving habits of most Lebanese.

All tourist areas are safe to visit, though the British and US embassies still suggest that visitors visiting Baalbek and Tyre

travel only as part of organised groups.

There is no overall regular police force in Lebanon, and therefore don't be surprised to see young soldiers patrolling the streets. Identification documents should be carried at all times, but keep them, and large amounts of money, out of sight and hang onto your bags.

Emergency Telephone Numbers
General emergencies (fire, theft, and accident): 112
Police: 160
Medical emergencies: Red Cross 140
Fire: 175

Egypt

Fact File

Area 1,002,000 sq. km (626,000 sq. miles).
Capital Cairo.
Population over 66 million.
Language Arabic (official). English and French are widely understood by educated people.
Time zone GMT +2 hours.
Currency Egyptian pound = 100 piastres.
International dialling code 2.

ENTRY REQUIREMENTS

All travellers entering Egypt must have a passport valid for at least 6 months and a valid visa. For most visitors, including EU and US nationals, it is easiest and cheapest to get a tourist visa at the point of arrival. They can be obtained from Cairo International Airport, Sharm al-Shaykh and Alexandria Port among other points of entry.

CUSTOMS REGULATIONS

Visitors are permitted to enter Egypt with 250g of tobacco, or 50 cigars, one litre of alcohol, and personal effects. Duty-free purchases of liquor (3 bottles per person) may be made at ports of entry or at the tax-free shops in Cairo. If you have any expensive electronic equipment you may be required to declare it on arrival so that authorities can check that it is with you when you leave (and has not been sold).

MONEY MATTERS

Credit cards are used in most major hotels, but not always in shops. It is advisable to bring some travellers' cheques.

OPENING TIMES

Shops keep hours according to demand, but most open Saturday–Thursday 9am–6pm, sometimes with a lunchtime closure. In central Cairo, many shops, including those owned by Muslims and Jews, are closed on Sunday. The Khan al-Khalili bazaar is open daily 10am–7 or 8pm (later in summer and during Ramadan).
Banks are open Sunday–Thursday 8.30am–1.30pm.

PUBLIC HOLIDAYS

1 January New Year's Day; **25 April** Liberation of Sinai Day; **1 May** Labour Day; **23 July** Anniversary of the 1952 Revolution; **6 October** Armed Forces Day. In addition, there are Islamic and Coptic holidays spread throughout the year.

SECURITY AND CRIME

In recent years Egypt has been troubled by radical Islamic terrorists. A heavy military response from the government, designed to protect tourists and deter further terrorist activities, seemed to have calmed the situation at the time of writing. Common caution is advised at all times. Social restrictions on women in Egypt can make foreign women seem particularly enticing to young Egyptian men. The number of petty thefts have increased, although you are still more likely to have a lost wallet returned intact in Egypt than in most Western countries. If you do experience problems, you should report immediately to the nearest tourist police post or police station. Lost or stolen passports must be reported to the police immediately. New passports can be issued in a matter of hours at the consular office of your embassy in Egypt but you'll require a copy of the police report verifying the loss.

Emergency Telephone Numbers
Police: 122
Ambulance: 123
Fire: 180

Jordan

Fact File

Area 9,411 sq. km (55,900 sq. miles) excluding the West Bank which comprises 5,440 sq. km (2,100 sq. miles).
Population around 5 million.
Language Standard Arabic.

Religion Islam with Christian, Shishani and Circassian minorities.
Currency Jordanian Dinar (JD) divided into 1,000 fils or 100 piastres (or 'irsh).
Time zone GMT +2 hours, +3 hours in summer.
International dialling code 962.

ENTRY REQUIREMENTS

All visitors require an entry visa which is free of charge for some nationals and expensive for others. The price you pay usually depends on the amount your country charges for Jordanians to enter your country. Check with your cruise line, who will probably arrange visas for passengers making group visits.

CUSTOMS REGULATIONS

Personal effects such as cameras, clothes, typewriters, computers and digital equipment are exempt from duty, but if you are bringing in taxable goods such as a laptop computer, ask the customs officials to enter details in your passport to avoid paying tax. Upon exit you will be asked to show that your goods were tax exempted. Visitors are also allowed to bring in up to 200 cigarettes, 200 grams (7 oz) of tobacco, 1 litre of spirits and 2 litres of wine.

MONEY MATTERS

You can change foreign cash or travellers' cheques in any bank in Jordan; only for travellers' cheques will you be charged a commission (this varies from bank to bank) Credit cards are acceptable in major hotels, restaurants and shops; the most widely accepted being American Express, Visa, Diners Club and MasterCard (in this order). You can also use your cards to draw cash (up to 500JDs only) at any bank linked with your credit card network at no extra charge. Automatic cash machines outside banks in Amman are generally limited to Jordanian bank account holders.

OPENING TIMES

Shops open Sunday–Thursday 9am–6.30 or 7pm in winter, 9am–8 or 9pm in summer. Most shops close in the afternoon for about two hours any time between 1pm and 4pm. Amman's downtown souk remains open on Friday. During Ramadan most open 9am–1pm and after the break of fast most will reopen until 9 or 10pm.
Post offices open Sunday–Thursday 8am–5pm in winter, 7am–7pm in summer. During Ramadan 8am–3 or 4pm.
Banks open Sunday–Thursday 8.30am–3pm; during Ramadan 9am–1 or 2pm.
Museums generally open Sunday–Thursday 8am–5pm.

PUBLIC HOLIDAYS

1 January, Christian New Year; **31 January** King Abdullah's Birthday; **March/April** Greek Orthodox, Roman Catholic and Protestant Easter (moveable dates); **25 May** Independence Day; **9 June** King Abdullah's Ascension to the throne; **10 June** Army Day; **14 November** King Hussein's birthday; **25 December** Christmas Day.

Muslim holidays follow the lunar calendar, moving back each year by 11 days (12 days in leap year). The main ones are Ayd Al Fitr: the feast that marks the end of Ramadan; Ayd Al Adha: the feast of sacrifice, which falls at the end of the month of the pilgrimage to Mecca (Hajj); Muslim New Year; Mawoulid An-Nabawi: the Prophet Mohammed's Birthday; Ayd Al Isra wa Al Miraj.

SECURITY AND CRIME

Jordan is a relatively safe country to travel in but obvious precautions should be taken; keep your money in the safe if you are staying in a hotel, don't take valuables with you when on a shore excursion, and keep an eye on your belongings in public places. It is common wisdom that women travelling alone should stick to places where other people are present and should avoid isolating themselves. The whole region, however, is affected by the fighting between Israelis and Palestinians. Travellers should be aware of the risks, be vigilant and keep alert to news reports.

Emergency Telephone Numbers
Police 192
Ambulance 193
Fire 193

Further Reading

Complete Guide to Ocean Cruising & Cruise Ships by Douglas Ward, Berlitz (2003). The industry's bible, it contains detailed, candid reviews of 254 ships, plus impeccable advice.

Porthole, a US-based cruising/lifestyle magazine featuring ships and advice. *Cruise Traveller* magazine, advice aimed mainly at the UK market.

General Reading

Portugal
The Portuguese: The Land and Its People by Marion Kaplan. Penguin, 1992. Revealing, readable and entertaining.
A Small Death in Lisbon by Robert Wilson. HarperCollins, 1999. An excellent read as a novel and description of life in Portugal.
Portuguese Voyages 1498–1663: Tales from the Great Age of Discovery, edited by Charles David Ley. Weidenfeld & Nicholson, 2000. Contemporary accounts of the great sea voyages.
Southern Spain
As I Walked Out One Midsummer Morning by Laurie Lee. Penguin, 1983. Romantic young man's vision of pre-Civil War Spain. Also by Lee *A Rose for Winter*. Penguin, 1983. Lee's post-war return to Andalusia.
South from Granada by Gerald Brenan. Cambridge University Press, 1988. Classic account of life in a remote village near Granada.
Tales of the Alhambra by Washington Irving. Granada: Miguel Sánchez. Legends and colourful view of Granada in the early 19th century.
Barcelona
Barcelona by Robert Hughes. Harvill Press, 2001. Describes the city's development in relation to the rest of Catalonia, Spain and Europe. Good on Gaudí and modernism.
Barcelona: A Guide to Recent Architecture by Suzanna Strum, Ellipsis London Ltd, 2001. A look at some of the city's stunning buildings.
Malta
Malta: A Guide to the Fortifications by Quentin Hughes. Said International,

1993. Reprint of a classic guide to Malta's forts and bastions.
5,000 years of Architecture in Malta by Leonard Mahoney. Valletta Publishing, 1996. A Maltese architect takes a learned look at the architecture that makes the islands so distinctive. Finely illustrated.
Siege: Malta 1940–1943 by Ernle Bradford. Penguin, 1987. Malta's second great test of wartime fortitude written with the immediacy of a novel.
France
France Today by J.E. Flower (ed). Methuen, 1997. Essays on contemporary France.
When the Riviera was Ours by Patrick Howarth. Century Hutchinson. The development of the Riviera as a tourist resort.
Tender is the Night by F. Scott Fitzgerald, Penguin.
Perfume by Patrick Süskind, 1985. Well-written best-seller set in the perfumed world of Grasse.
Italy
A Room with a View by E.M. Forster, Penguin.
The Architecture of the Italian Renaissance by Peter Murray. Thames and Hudson.
Rome: Biography of a City by Christopher Hibbert. Penguin.
The Italians by Luigi Barzini. Hamish Hamilton.
Naples '44 by Norman Lewis. Fascinating account of the author's experiences in Naples between 1943 and 44.
Greece
A Concise History of Greece, by Richard Clogg. Clear and lively account of Greece from Byzantine times to 2000, with helpful maps and well-captioned artwork. The best single-volume summary; be sure to get the second edition, 2002.
Captain Corelli's Mandolin by Louis de Bernières. Secker & Warburg/Minerva. Heart-rending tragicomedy set on occupied Kefalloniá during World War II which acquired cult status in the 1990s.
Prospero's Cell and *Reflections on a Marine Venus* by Lawrence Durrell Faber and Faber/Penguin. Corfu in the 1930s and Rhodes in 1945–47, now looking rather old-fashioned, alcohol-fogged and patronising of the "natives", but still entertaining.
A Taste of the Aegean by Andy Harris with photographs by Terry Harris Pavilion Books. Two Greek-resident brothers take you on a gastronomic tour, with recipes.
Lebanon
The Hills of Adonis by Colin Thubron. An account of Thubron's travels and adventures through Lebanon prior to the civil war.

Insight titles cover the world, with more than 400 books in three series. **Insight Guides** profile a destination and its culture in depth. **Insight Compact Guides** are encyclopaedias in miniature, ideal for on-the-spot use. **Insight Pocket Guides** provide personal recommendations from an expert and include a full-size fold-out map. In addition, Insight **Flexi Maps** and **Travel Maps** cover the world.

Insight Guides to Europe include *Continental Europe*, plus 70 further titles ranging from Iceland to Greece.

Other Insight Guides to cruising are *Caribbean Cruises* and *North American and Alaskan Cruises*.

We do our best to ensure the information in our books is as accurate and up-to-date as possible. The books are updated on a regular basis, using local contacts, who painstakingly add, amend and correct as required. However, some mistakes and omissions are inevitable and we are ultimately reliant on our readers to put us in the picture.

We would welcome your feed-back on any details related to your experiences using the book "on the road". Maybe we recommended a hotel that you liked (or another that you didn't), as well as interesting new attractions, or facts and figures you have found out about the country itself. The more details you can give us (particularly with regard to addresses, e-mails and telephone numbers), the better.

We will acknowledge all contributions, and we'll offer an Insight Guide to the best letters received.

Please write to us at:
Insight Guides
APA Publications
PO Box 7910
London SE1 1WE
Or send e-mail to:
insight@apaguide.co.uk

ART & PHOTO CREDITS

Patricia Aithie/ffotograff 121
akg-images London 24
Alvey & Towers 48/49, 58, 66, 67, 80
Jon Arnold/Alamy 100
Pam Barrett 156T, 157, 158
Liz Barry/ffotograff 124
M. Barlow/Art Directors/Trip 330, 332
Tom Le Bas 177
R. Belbin/Art Directors/Trip 2/3, 118, 129
Pete Bennett/Apa front flap & back cover bottom, 4B, 178, 179,180L/R, 180T, 181, 182, 270, 279, 281, 281T, 282T, 283, 288T, 289, 293T, 293, 296R, 297, 298, 301, 308
Bettmann/Corbis 33
E. Boleman-Herring/Apa 263, 264T
Nick Bonetti/Apa 12, 266, 267, 269T
The Bridgeman Art Library 19
The British Library/HIP/TopFoto 23
Marcus Brooke 98/99, 163, 183, 216, 220/221, 224, 234, 334
Chris Catton/Survival Anglia 333L
Chris Coe/Apa 112
Comstock Images/Alamy 88
Costa Crociere 4/5
Cunard back flap top, spine, 3B, 10/11, 59, 61, 74, 78, 94/95
M. Cristofori/Marka 206
Jerry Dennis/Apa back cover right, 128L/R, 131T, 131, 134, 135, 137, 138
Nevio Doz 217
Andrew Eames 27
Annabel Elston/Apa 150T
Fotomas/TopFoto 25
Guglielmo Galvin/Apa 110, 198, 294, 295, 296T, 296L
G. Galvin & G. Taylor/Apa 195, 196T
Glyn Genin 73, 90, 91
Glyn Genin/Apa 42, 70, 155, 211, 212T, 212L/R, 223, 225T, 226T, 226, 227, 228, 229, 230T, 230, 231, 232, 233, 234T, 236T, 238T, 238, 249, 250T, 250, 251, 251T, 252T, 291T, 292,292T, 330T
F. Good/Art Directors/Trip 275
Frances Gransden/Apa 197T, 202, 203T, 203L/R, 204T, 204
Ronald Grant Archive 46, 47
Jeff Greenberg/Art Directors/Trip 56, 82, 235

Albano Guatti 302/303
Semsi Guner 335
Tony Halliday/Apa 306T, 307
Robert Harding Picture Library 219
J. Highet/Art Directors/Trip 120
Bryan Hemphill 81, 108L/R
Mary Ann Hemphill 127, 147, 247
E. Boleman-Herring/Apa 263
John Heseltine 253
The Image Works/TopFoto 65, 213
W. Jacobs/Trip 214
Britta Jaschinski/Apa 153, 154, 155T, 159T
Axel Krause/Apa 39, 322, 324R, 325R, 326
Bob Krist back cover left, 222, 237, 244/245, 246
Martini Collection 26
Mike Merchant/Apa 144, 145T, 145
Anna Mockford/Apa 267T, 268T
MSC Lirica 79
Museo Nazzionale 206T
NCL 62, 63, 75
Negre 17
Gary John Norman/Apa 113, 114T, 115, 116, 240
Christine Osborne Pictures 45, 122, 122T, 123, 125, 160/161, 162, 321, 327, 328
Carl Pendle/ffotograff 276/277
Tony Perrottet 252, 315
P&O Cruises 14/15, 60, 71, 304
Pressnet/TopFoto 93
Princess 6/7, 83, 100
Sarah Louise Ramsey/Apa 36/37, 323T, 323, 324L, 325L, 326T
Mark Read/Apa front flap top, 104, 106, 106T, 117, 117T, 130, 143, 147T, 148, 148T, 149, 189, 190,

Cartographic Editor **Zoë Goodwin**
Production **Linton Donaldson**
Design Consultant
Klaus Geisler
Picture Research **Hilary Genin**

191T, 192, 193T, 193, 194, 254, 257R
C. Rennie/Art Directors/Trip 329
RPS/HIP/TopFoto 31
Mick Rock/Cephas 105
Franco Stephano Ruiu 218
David Sanger/Alamy 8/9
Alessandra Santarelli/Apa 201T
SeaDream 54, 76, 77, 85
Silversea 51, 52, 53L/R
Robin Smith/Trip 196
Jeroen Snijders/Apa 142, 150
Stin/Firsov 333R
Nick Tapsell/ffotograff 305
George Taylor/Apa 316, 317T, 317, 318T, 318, 319T, 319, 320, 331
Thomas Cook 28
C. Toms/Art Directors/Trip 102
TopFoto 21, 22, 32, 34, 35, 64, 86, 87
A. Tovey/Art Directors/Trip 132/133
A. Turney/Art Directors/Trip 191
Th-foto Werbung/Art Directors/Trip back flap bottom, 5BR, 186, 187
UPPA Ltd/TopFoto 89
V&A Picture Library 1, 30
Bill Wassman/Apa 103, 109, 139, 151T, 151, 152, 158T, 159, 164, 165, 166T, 166, 168T, 168, 169, 170, 171, 172T, 172, 174, 175T, 175, 176T, 176, 199, 201, 282T
David Whelan 50, 55, 57, 92
Marcus Wilson Smith/Apa 41L, 68, 69, 96/97, 309T, 309, 310, 311, 312T, 312, 314
Windstar Cruises 184/185
Katy Winn/Corbis 84
Phil Wood/Apa 4BL, 38, 40, 43, 108T, 120T, 205, 207, 209, 210L/R, 307T, 310T, 313, 315T
Chris Wormald/Art Directors/Trip 126
Gregory Wrona 215
Gregory Wrona/Apa 41R, 44, 72, 114, 140, 140T, 141, 241, 241T, 242, 243, 254T, 255, 256, 257L, 258, 260T, 260, 261, 262, 263T, 265, 268, 269, 271T, 271, 272, 273, 274, 278, 285, 286, 287, 288, 290L/R, 291, 299, 300

Map Production Laura Morris
© 2004 Apa Publications GmbH & Co. Verlag
KG Singapore Branch, Singapore

Index

Abbreviations for these countries are used (following placenames):
Bulgaria (B)
Croatia (Cro)
Cyprus (Cyp)
Egypt (E)
France (F)
Greece (G)
Lebanon (L)
Malta (M)
Morocco (Mor)
Portugal (P)
Serbia & Montenegro (SM)
Spain (S)
Syria (Syr)
Tunisia (Tun)
Turkey (T)
Ukraine (U)

Insight Guides Website
www.insightguides.com

*Don't travel the
planet alone.
Keep in step with
Insight Guides'
walking eye,
just a click away*

INSIGHT GUIDES

The classic series that puts you in the picture

👁 INSIGHT GUIDES

The world's largest collection of visual travel guides & maps